HORSE RACING IN BRITAIN

HORSE RACING IN BRITAIN

Barry Campbell

'If I were to begin life again I would go to the turf to get friends. They seem to me to be the only people who really hold together. I don't know why; it may be that each knows something that might hang the other, but the effect is delightful and most peculiar.'
Harriet, Lady Ashburton

LONDON
MICHAEL JOSEPH

First published in Great Britain by
Michael Joseph Limited
52 Bedford Square, London W.C.1
1977

ISBN 0 7181 1427 2

Filmset and printed in Great Britain by
BAS Printers Limited, Wallop, Hampshire

Contents

List of Illustrations

Acknowledgements

I should like to thank the following organisations for their kind assistance in supplying both help and information in connection with this book:—

The Bookmakers' Protection Association
The Horserace Betting Levy Board
The Horserace Totalisator Board
The Injured Jockeys' Fund
The International Racing Bureau
The Jockey Club
The Joe Coral Group
The National Association of Bookmakers
Racecourse Technical Services Ltd.
The Racing Information Bureau
The Sporting Life
Tattersalls
Tattersalls' Committee
Weatherbys Ltd.

I should also like to thank the following individuals for their help and advice:—

Mr Henry Alper
Miss Alice Bennett
Mr David Brimacombe
Mrs Janet Campbell
Mr Alan Dymott
Mr Anthony Fairbairn
Mr O. W. Fletcher
Miss Louise Gold
Mr William J. Guard
Mr R. Hammond

Miss Dorothy Laird
Mr J. Long
Lord Oaksey
Mr Pat Reekie
Mr P. Twite
Mr Mike Waterman
Mr Simon Weatherby
Mr John White
Mr S. Woodman

Foreword

Some years ago, whilst on holiday in France, I tried, unsuccessfully, to obtain a book which would give me some insight into the French method of betting and racing. On returning to England, I searched for an English equivalent, again without success for, although there were many excellent racing annuals, histories and memoirs available, I was unable to find a book which would provide the newcomer or, indeed, the overseas visitor with a basic introduction to the sport. I have tried to fill this gap by providing a book which contains something of the basic history, method and practice of racing in Britain.

Introduction

by

Anthony Fairbairn of the Racing Information Bureau

Horse racing in Britain . . . a sport, an entertainment, an industry. It's part of our national heritage; the splendour of Royal Ascot with its pageantry and spectacle, the thrill of steeplechasing which warms the cold, damp days of winter.

Horse racing in Britain . . . it's glorious Goodwood on a balmy summer's day, the vast expanse of open heath at Newmarket, the hurly burly of Derby Day at Epsom, the traditional festivals of Ayr, York, Chester and Cheltenham.

Horse racing in Britain . . . it's the historic world of yellowing sporting prints, the sophisticated world of camera patrol films and video replays. It's the raffish playground of intrepid gamblers, the subject of a multitude of 10p accumulators which one day might just pay off the mortgage. . . .

Horse racing in Britain is all of these things and many more. So much so that to the newcomer it can be shrouded in a mystique all of its own.

And yet horse racing in Britain lives on the support it can attract from the racegoer, the punter. It is dependant upon a constant stream of newcomers to the sport. For them Barry Campbell's book will prove invaluable. It is entertaining because racing is meant to be fun. It is instructive because the newcomer must learn to find his way through the complexities of the sport.

It is an ideal companion for the racegoer because it offers advice and guidance without once giving the reader an absolute cert in the 3.30.

CHAPTER ONE

Flat Racing

'The Derby is lost, the Derby is won;
The race of all races is come and is gone.'

(verses on William Crockford)

SOMETHING OF THE HISTORY AND DEVELOPMENT OF THE SPORT OF KINGS

The British have always been a nation of horse lovers, and Britain has produced skilled horsemen from the earliest times. In 55 B.C., when the Roman legions invaded these islands, they were particularly impressed with the horsemanship of those Britons who fought against them. Julius Caesar wrote: 'Thus in action they perform the part both of nimble horsemen and stable infantry. And by continual exercise and use they have arrived at that expertness, that in the most steep and difficult places they can stop their horses upon a full stretch, turn which way they please, run along the pole, rest on the harness, and throw themselves back into their chariots with incredible dexterity.'

Although the development of horse racing, as we know it today, did not really start until the seventeenth century, there are recorded instances of race meetings having taken place well before that time. It is thought that the first horse races in Britain took place at Netherby, Yorkshire, in A.D. 210, and that they were organised by Roman soldiers. The first recorded organised race meeting in Britain took place during the reign of Henry II at Smithfield, in 1174, outside the gates of London during a horse fair.

The first racing trophy to be competed for was a wooden ball, decorated with flowers, which was presented by the organisers of the Chester Fair in 1512 – the first instance of a municipal race meeting.

Incidentally, it is from Chester that we get the tradition of the 1st, 2nd and 3rd prizes: in 1609, three silver cups were presented to the horses finishing in that order. One legend has it that the Sheriff of Chester agreed to present a cup but was disappointed with the silversmith's finished article. Accordingly, the sheriff asked for it to be made again, and then yet again, ending up with three silver cups of varied quality.

Henry VIII was keenly interested in racing and he imported numbers of foreign mares and stallions for breeding purposes. However, it was not until the seventeenth and eighteenth centuries that thoroughbred breeding began in earnest.

Henry's daughter, Elizabeth I, retained her father's studs at Eltham and Greenwich, and also founded another at Tutbury in Staffordshire. Queen Elizabeth is known to have attended race meetings at various places, and at Croydon a special stand was built for her party – at a cost of 34 shillings.

During the Roman occupation of Britain, Queen Boadicea and her people, the Iceni, are thought to have lived in the vicinity of Newmarket Heath. It is interesting to note that the coins used by the tribe at this time carried the effigy of a horse on one side. And it is Newmarket, the headquarters of racing, which provides us with an interesting study of the further development of the sport. In 1605, James I discovered the little village of Newmarket and spent much of his time there hunting, riding and hawking – so much so that in 1621 the House of Commons petitioned the King to turn his gracious attention to affairs of state.

Horseracing at that time had become fashionable amongst the nobles of Scotland (there had been racing in Scotland since 1504) and it is thought that James I's Scottish nobles encouraged him to establish the sport at Newmarket and elsewhere.

The unfortunate Charles I came to the throne in 1625. Shortly after this, regular Spring and Autumn race meetings were established at Newmarket, and a Gold Cup was first run for in 1634. Charles, like his predecessor, spent much of his time at Newmarket with his court.

Following Charles's execution, and during the period of Cromwell's Commonwealth, there was little racing – in fact, all racing was banned in 1654. The Royal Stud was sacked, and many gentlemen's horses were requisitioned for the use of the State. Cromwell, it seems, was not averse to racing (indeed he kept a stud of his own) but the Puritans would not allow anything as entertaining as racing to continue, and did not wish to encourage large gatherings of the populace in those troubled times.

It was not until the restoration of Charles II, therefore, that racing really began to develop. Charles II was a keen horseman, often riding in races himself. He became the recognised arbiter in all matters relating to racing disputes. In 1664 he instituted the Newmarket Town Plate, framing the rules himself – 'Articles ordered by His Majestie to be observed by all persons that put in horses to ride for the Plate, the new round heat at Newmarket set out on the first day of October, 1664, in the 16th year of our Sovereign Lord King Charles II, which Plate is to be rid for yearly, the second Thursday in October for ever.' And, happily, the Newmarket Town Plate is still competed for today. Charles II is also commemorated at Newmarket by the Rowley Mile, which was named after his favourite hack – 'Old Rowley'.

During the reign of James II there was not much progress made in the development of racing but his successor, William III, took a great interest in the sport. He raced his own horses in matches and founded a Royal Stud at Hampton Court.

William III's horses were trained by Tregonwell Frampton, who was to become known as 'the Father of the Turf'. Queen Anne carried on the racing traditions of Newmarket and, with her consort, Prince George of Denmark, kept a string of racehorses which were often run, either in the Queen's own name or in that of Tregonwell Frampton. Queen Anne proved to be a great benefactress to racing, and it was mainly due to her that Royal Ascot was founded. And, in the nice way that racing honours its heroes and benefactors, the opening race of the Ascot Meeting is called the Queen Anne Stakes.

By the time that Queen Anne died in 1714, there were many long-established race meetings being held regularly at Chester, Doncaster, York, Ascot, Richmond in Yorkshire, and in many other places, at which a variety of plates, cups and other prizes were raced for. In addition to these fairly well-organised meetings (Doncaster had a stand built as early as 1614) horse races of all sorts and conditions were being held at places all over the country. Sharp practices abounded – each meeting seeming to have its own rules and no official records being kept.

However, in 1740, Parliament introduced an Act 'to restrain and to prevent the excessive increase of horse racing'. Such were the terms of the Act, though, that little, if any, notice was taken of it. What was needed at that time was not so much external legislation but rather some form of control within the sport itself. This came about early in the 1750s, with the founding of the Jockey Club. Later, Mr James Weatherby became Secretary of the Club, and the control and development of racing was properly under way.

THE CLASSICS

The second half of the eighteenth century saw the introduction of the first of the 'Classic' races – the supreme test for three-year-old thoroughbred racehorses. Before the advent of these races, the three-year-olds had seldom raced. Races were usually for horses of six years old and above and were over much greater distances than would be permitted today – often as great as six or eight miles. Again, races were often run in 'heats', and for a horse to run in four one-mile 'heats' at the same meeting was quite usual.

Then, in 1776, a group of racing enthusiasts, including Lord Rockingham and Colonel Anthony St. Leger, agreed to subscribe to a new sweepstake for three-year-old colts and fillies, to be run over a distance of two miles (this was reduced to 1 mile 6 furlongs in 1816), with one 'heat' only to be run. This race was first run at Doncaster, where it was won by Lord Rockingham's filly, Alabaculia. In the following year, the race was run again, with an increased number of entries and, in 1778, at the suggestion of Lord Rockingham, the race was named the St. Leger Stakes.

Also in 1778, Edward Smith Stanley, the 12th Earl of Derby, took over the lease of 'The Oaks', a house near Epsom which belonged to his uncle, General Burgoyne (who, incidentally, commanded the British Forces during the American War of Independence). At a dinner party held at 'The Oaks', Lord Derby and his friends planned a sweepstake for three-year-old fillies, to be run over a distance of $1\frac{1}{2}$ miles. This race was first run in 1779, when it was won by Lord Derby's horse, Bridget. Since that time, the race has been known as The Oaks.

At a party following the first running of the Oaks, a further sweepstake was proposed – this time for three-year-old colts and fillies, over a distance of one mile (altered to 1 mile 4 furlongs in 1784). It is recorded that Lord Derby and Sir Charles Bunbury tossed a coin to decide whether the race should be called the Derby or the Bunbury. Sir Charles lost the toss, but won the first race with his horse, Diomed.

The remaining Classic races were introduced at much later dates. The Two Thousand Guineas Stakes, for three-year-old colts and fillies, was first run in 1809, while the One Thousand Guineas Stakes, for three-year-old fillies, was first run in 1814. Both of these races are run over the Rowley Mile course at Newmarket.

During the reigns of George I and George II racing continued to flourish, although the amount of royal patronage at that time seems to have been negligible. However, George II's second son, the Duke of Cumberland (known as the Butcher of Culloden) was the first Royal member of the Jockey Club. He was to have an important and lasting influence on British racing. It was the Duke of Cumberland who bred the great horse Eclipse and also Herod. It is through three horses – Eclipse, Herod and Match'em – that the descent of every thoroughbred horse in the world can be traced.

THE THOROUGHBRED RACEHORSE

All thoroughbred racehorses are descended in direct male line from one or other of three foreign steeds (out of some hundreds which were imported into England between the years 1689 and 1730). The three horses were known as the Godolphin Arabian, the Byerley Turk and the Darley Arabian. Dennis Craig, in his excellent book, *Horse Racing*, has defined the thoroughbred as 'the result of many years of progressive development from an original blend of the high qualities of the Arabian horse crossed with the sterling attributes of the mixed English breed at one particular and important stage of its evolution'. *

THE GODOLPHIN ARABIAN: This horse, which was foaled in 1724, was a present from the Emperor of Morocco to King Louis XV of France. The story is told that the horse was stolen from the royal stables and that it was discovered in the year 1729 by a Mr. Coke, who saw it pulling a water cart in Paris. Mr Coke purchased the horse for the sum of £3. Eventually, the horse became the property of the Earl of Godolphin who kept him as a private stallion at his stud in Cambridgeshire. The horse died in 1753, it is said of remorse following the death of his favourite companion – a cat named Grimalkin. The Godolphin Arabian's son, Old Cade, sired Match'em in 1748. This horse became the leading stallion in the north of England, siring some 354 winning horses.

THE BYERLEY TURK: The horse was acquired by a Captain (later Colonel) Byerley when he was fighting against the Turks at Buda in Hungary in 1688. Later, in 1690, Colonel Byerley used the horse as a charger at the Battle of the Boyne in Ireland, when he was in command of the 6th Dragoon Guards. The Byerley Turk was the great great grandsire of Herod, which was bred by the Duke of Cumberland in 1758. Herod's progeny won over £200,000 in prize money.

THE DARLEY ARABIAN: The Darley Arabian was foaled in 1700. He was bought for a Mr Darley by his brother, who was a merchant in Aleppo. The horse was the great great grandsire of the unbeaten Eclipse, who was foaled in 1764 (the year of the great eclipse of the sun). Incidentally, one of the Darley Arabian's sons – Bulle Rock – was the first thoroughbred horse to go to America. Eclipse sired some 344 winners before he died in 1789.

Only three lines have lasted to the present day, in direct male-tail descent from the Godolphin Arabian, the Byerley Turk and the Darley Arabian. These are known as the Eclipse, Match'em and Herod sire lines.

★   ★   ★

* From *Horse Racing* by Dennis Craig, published by J. A. Allen & Co. Ltd.

King George III and Queen Charlotte were not themselves particularly interested in racing, but their son, the Prince of Wales (later George IV) was a great racing enthusiast. In 1788 he became the first member of the Royal Family to win a Derby, with his colt Sir Thomas which he had bought for 2,000 guineas.

Prinny, as the Prince was known, raced on a lavish scale and his stable expenses were in the region of £30,000 a year. So extravagant did he become that, in 1786, Parliament had to bail him out by paying his debts and increasing his income. Between the years 1800 and 1807 he won over a hundred races.

However, prior to this, in 1791, a curious incident had occurred which was to terminate his association with the Turf for some years. This was known as the Escape affair (see Jockey Club chapter) when, as a result of an enquiry into the running of one of the Prince's horses – Escape – the Prince was warned by the Jockey Club that if he continued to employ Sam Chifney as his jockey no gentleman would race against him. The Prince, furious at this, withdrew his patronage of racing, and it was not until 1828, when the Prince (who by then had succeeded to the throne as George IV) gave a dinner to the Jockey Club, that the breach was healed.

During the latter half of the eighteenth century, attempts were being made by the Jockey Club to introduce some order and discipline into racing. This was to prove a slow process, however, as the Turf was in a state of chaos at that time. Such rules as did exist were continually being broken, and all kinds of crooked dealing went on. Matches were fixed, horses were poisoned, racecourse crowds were often riotous, and owners and trainers were up to all manner of tricks. But slowly the Jockey Club was beginning to make itself felt and its attitude towards the Prince of Wales over the Escape affair must have greatly increased its prestige in matters of discipline.

In 1766 Richard Tattersall opened his famous horse sales at Hyde Park, and he also provided a room as a London base for the Jockey Club. In 1780 he opened a subscription room for the laying and settling of bets. Later, in 1843, when the Jockey Club declined to arbitrate any further in betting disputes, Tattersalls' Committee was set up. Ever since then it has been the recognised arbiter in all matters relating to betting disputes.

In 1791 Mr James Weatherby published his first Stud Book, and thereafter Weatherbys continued to provide a complete record of all thoroughbred racehorses.

In 1830, following the death of George IV, William IV, who was known as the 'sailor King', ascended the throne. William had been a member of the Jockey Club for some years. Although he was mildly interested in racing, he does not seem to have possessed a great knowledge of the sport. As an example of his vague knowledge of racing, the following story is told. When the King was asked by his trainer, William Edwards, which of the royal horses should run at the Goodwood meeting in 1830, he replied: 'Take the whole fleet.' This was done and the royal horses, perhaps by sheer weight of entry, finished first, second and third in the Goodwood Cup.

During his reign, William IV did much to improve the Royal Stud at Hampton Court and also added to the number of Kings' Plates. In 1832 he presented the Jockey Club with a hoof of Eclipse, which was set in a gold plate. This was to be competed for as a challenge trophy but, alas, it was only run for on one occasion, when Lord Chesterfield won it with his horse, Priam.

William IV is alleged to have lost interest in racing after being struck in the eye by a ginger-nut biscuit thrown by a member of the crowd at the Ascot meeting of 1832.

By the middle of the nineteenth century there were more racecourses and racehorses in training than ever before. The Jockey Club's influence continued to spread, both inside and outside Newmarket, and Rules were formulated which slowly began to impose some sort of order on the sport.

The first half of the nineteenth century had seen the rise of the 'legs' (bookmakers) many of whom, such as William Crockford and John Gully, were sharks of the first order. At that time all kinds of tricks were resorted to, to ensure that well-fancied and therefore heavily backed horses did not win. Indeed, many a favourite was lucky to get to the starting post.

The outstanding Turf administrator of the time was Lord George Bentinck, who assumed the mantle of Sir Charles Bunbury as overall controller of the Turf in the 1840s.

Bentinck was succeeded as the leading figure in racing by the famous Admiral Rous (see Jockey Club chapter). During the 1840s there emerged on the racing scene the new breed of bookmakers, who offered odds on a number of runners, very much in the modern manner and who were, by and large, quite honest.

Soon after Queen Victoria's accession to the throne, in 1837, she decided to dispense with the Royal Stud at Hampton Court. Later, however, the stud was revived and a number of winners were bred there – including Imperieuse, winner of the One Thousand Guineas and the St Leger; Briar Root, One Thousand Guineas winner; and Sainfoin, a Derby winner. Queen Victoria, who was reputed to be a good judge of a horse, attended a number of race meetings early in her reign, but following the death of Prince Albert in 1861 she took no further interest in racing.

In 1875 Prince Edward (later Edward VII) registered his racing colours, and in 1877 had his first runner under Jockey Club Rules – this was his horse Aleb. Shortly afterwards the Prince began buying stock for the Sandringham Stud, which he had instituted in 1855. An enthusiastic owner-breeder, and a keen racegoer, 'Teddy' had mixed fortunes with his racehorses and, in fact, started off rather badly. But in 1896 his colt, Persimmon, won the Derby and was led in amidst unparalleled scenes of jubilation (*see* photograph facing page 84). Later, Persimmon went on to win the St Leger. In 1900, Diamond Jubilee, a colt by St Simon, won the Triple Crown and the Prince of Wales was the leading owner of that year with prize money (flat) totalling nearly £30,000.

In the same year, 1900, the Prince won the Grand National with his horse, Ambush II.

Prince Edward was a great favourite with the public, who delighted to see his horses win – in the days when gentlemen really did take their hats off for a royal victory.

In 1909 'Teddy', who by then had succeeded to the throne as Edward VII, had another classic winner, when Minoru (leased from Colonel Hall-Walker) won the Derby. In 1915 Colonel Hall-Walker (later Lord Wavertree) presented his famous Tully Stud in Ireland to the British nation. This became known as the National Stud.

In 1910, when Edward VII died, George V inherited the Royal Stud. In 1913 all hopes of another Royal Derby were shattered when a suffragette threw herself in front of the King's horse, Anmer, during the race. After that the royal colours did not feature very much until 1922, when Weathervane won the Royal Hunt Cup.

THE AMERICAN INVASION

In the early 1900s racing in America had virtually come to a standstill. Racing in the States was almost completely in the hands of gangsters and racketeers and gradually racing became illegal.

As race tracks in America closed down, more and more owners, trainers and jockeys crossed the Atlantic, and this led to what became known in racing circles as the 'American Invasion'. In 1897, Tod Sloan, the brilliant, if unorthodox American jockey, revolutionised race-riding in Britain, when he first appeared on British racecourses with his crouched forward style of riding.

Close on Sloan's heels came a horde of American owners, trainers, gamblers and crooks. One trainer, named Wishard, together with his cronies, evolved a method of buying horses and then doping them with stimulants before racing them. This operation proved to be so successful that in 1900 Wishard was the leading winning trainer.

The Hon George Lambton, quite rightly concerned for the future of

British racing, experimented with the use of drugs on race horses and passed on his findings to the Jockey Club, with the result that in 1903 doping became illegal.

THE JERSEY ACT

The closure of the American race tracks meant that a great number of American horses were available for export. The English racing authorities were concerned in case large numbers of American horses of doubtful pedigree should be introduced to this country. In 1909, therefore, it was announced in the *Stud Book* that they (the editors) had decided that, in the interests of the English *Stud Book*, no horse or mare could be admitted unless it could be traced to a strain already accepted in earlier volumes of the *Stud Book*.

As this measure proved to be only partially successful, the 'Jersey Act' was introduced in 1913. This came about after the Jockey Club, at the instigation of Lord Jersey (a Senior Steward) suggested to Messrs Weatherbys that, in future, the relevant passage should read as follows:

'In the interests of the English *Stud Book*, no horse or mare can, after this date, be considered as eligible for admission, unless it can be traced, without flaw, on both sires and dams side of its pedigree, to horses and mares already accepted in earlier volumes of the book.'

The Jersey Act caused an uproar amongst American breeders, as this was a condition impossible for many American horses to fulfil. They were, therefore, labelled half-bred.

The Derby winner of 1914, for example – Durbar II – was not eligible for the *Stud Book*, by virtue of his American-bred dam. Indeed, so many half-bred horses won good races that eventually the Jersey Act was repealed in 1949. The last word on the subject being as follows:–

'Any animal claiming admission from now onwards must be able to prove satisfactorily, some eight or nine crosses of pure blood, to trace back for at least a century, and to show such performances of its immediate family on the Turf as to warrant the belief in the purity of its blood.'

During the First World War racing was drastically curtailed and it was only by the continued efforts of the Jockey Club, anxious for the future of the British bloodstock, that there was any racing at all. During this period, substitute 'classics' were run at Newmarket, while National Hunt racing, which does not have the same significance in the breeding of horses, ceased altogether.

Following the war, the public, weary no doubt of wartime restrictions and economies, flocked back to the racecourses to enjoy the return of a full racing programme. With the boom, however, came the villains, attracted no doubt by the prospect of easy pickings, and very soon gang warfare was rife on racecourses throughout the country as rival gangs fought for control of bookmakers' pitches.

This state of affairs eventually led to strong action by the bookmakers who saw their living in danger. The Jockey Club, concerned for the future of racing, also took active steps to control this state of affairs and finally, in the twenties, the trouble was effectively stamped out.

Today there are still a few 'wide boys' to be encountered at racetracks and pickpockets continue to ply their trade, but happily these are few and far between.

Between the wars, breeding was dominated by two great owner-breeders – the Aga Khan, winner of five Derbys and Lord Derby, owner of the great Hyperion. The leading jockey of the day was undoubtedly Steve Donoghue.

The biggest single innovation, as far as racing was concerned, was the setting-up of the Racecourse Betting Control Board, and the introduction of the Tote in 1929. It was intended that this should skim off, for the benefit of racing, some of the enormous sums which were wagered annually on horseracing, but unfortunately the Tote was only partially successful in this (*see* Tote chapter).

With the outbreak of World War II, racing ceased altogether. Then, late in 1940, some racing was allowed to take place. Again, it was only by the sustained efforts of the Jockey Club that any racing took place at all. As in the First World War, substitute 'classics' were run at Newmarket and also, as in the First World War, National Hunt racing ceased altogether.

After the war, full-time racing started up again, but it was not long before the full effect of the war on the British bloodstock industry began to be felt. For a time, Classic after Classic went to foreign-bred horses, and it was not until the late fifties that the British bloodstock industry fully recovered its strength.

During the period since the end of World War II racing in Britain has undergone a great many changes and seen a great many innovations, such as the introduction of racecourse commentaries, the use of the patrol camera, the photo-finish camera, extensive television coverage, commercial sponsorship, starting stalls, the licensing of women trainers and women jockeys, the setting-up of the Horserace Betting Levy Board, the Turf Board, the introduction of off-course betting, and the introduction of the dreadful Betting Tax (racing receives approximately £7 million from the Levy Board annually, while the Government receives £70 million through the medium of the Tax).

However, racing continues to enjoy royal patronage, and Her Majesty the Queen and Her Majesty Queen Elizabeth the Queen Mother are both enthusiastic owners and keen racegoers. (The Queen Mother even has the 'Extel' race commentary and results service laid on at Clarence House.)

Since the war, the jockeys' championship tables have been dominated by Lester Piggott, and we have been privileged to see some wonderful horses run on British racecourses – horses such as Royal Palace, Ribot, Crepello, St Paddy, Ribero, Sky Diver, Sir Ivor, Nijinsky, Mill Reef, Brigadier Gerard, Grundy and Bustino on the Flat.

Alas, however, like every other industry, racing is having its problems – inflation, increased labour costs, industrial troubles and increased taxation are all making life difficult, and many trainers are finding it less and less easy to make ends meet. Owners, too, are feeling the pinch and while many of the richer owners are drastically cutting back on their racing commitments, others are being forced out of racing altogether because, contrary to popular belief, not all racehorse owners are millionaires.

In the labour field, experienced stable staff lag a long way behind in the wages stakes and, overall, the picture is a gloomy one. But it is to be hoped that all those who are concerned with the government, the organisation and the furtherance of the sport (Jockey Club, Levy Board, owners, trainers, bookmakers, et al) will unite to find a way out of present doldrums in order to keep British racing what it has always been – the envy of the racing world.

PRINCIPAL FLAT RACES

The flat racing season lasts from March until November. Foals and yearlings are not permitted to run in any races, and two-year-olds are not permitted to run distances of more than 5 furlongs before June 1st, distances of more than 6 furlongs before July 1st, or more than 7 furlongs before September 1st.

The principal races for two-year-olds are :–

Epsom – Summer Meeting

Woodcote Stakes	6 furlongs
Lonsdale Stakes	5 furlongs
Acorn Stakes	5 furlongs

Ascot – June Meeting

Coventry Stakes	6 furlongs
Queen Mary Stakes	5 furlongs
Norfolk Stakes	5 furlongs
Chesham Stakes	6 furlongs
Windsor Castle Stakes	5 furlongs

Sandown Park – July Meeting
National Stakes   5 furlongs

Newmarket – July Meeting
July Stakes   6 furlongs

Goodwood – July/August Meeting
Richmond Stakes   6 furlongs
Molecomb Stakes   5 furlongs   (fillies only)

York – August Meeting
Gimcrack Stakes   6 furlongs
Lowther Stakes   5 furlongs   (fillies only)

Kempton Park – September Meeting
Imperial Stakes   6 furlongs

Doncaster – September Meeting
Champagne Stakes   7 furlongs

Ascot – September Meeting
Royal Lodge Stakes   1 mile

Newmarket – October Meeting
Middle Park Stakes   6 furlongs
Cheveley Park Stakes   6 furlongs   (fillies only)
Dewhurst Stakes   7 furlongs

Ascot – October Meeting
Cornwallis Stakes   5 furlongs

Doncaster – October Meeting
William Hill Futurity   1 mile

The principal races for three-year-olds are:–

Newmarket – April/May Meeting
Two Thousand Guineas   Rowley Mile   colts carrying 9 stone/fillies
                        8st 9lbs
One Thousand Guineas   Rowley Mile (fillies only) 9 stone

Epsom – May/June Meeting
Derby Stakes   1 mile 4 furlongs   colts carrying 9 stone/fillies 8st 9lbs
Oaks Stakes   1 mile 4 furlongs   (fillies only) 9 stone

Ascot – June Meeting
St James' Palace Stakes   1 mile
Coronation Stakes   1 mile   (fillies only)

| King Edward VII Stakes | 1 mile 4 furlongs | |
| Ribblesdale Stakes | 1 mile 4 furlongs | (fillies only) |

Goodwood – July Meeting

| Gordon Stakes | 1 mile 3 furlongs | |
| Nassau Stakes | 1 mile 2 furlongs | (fillies only) |

York – August Meeting

| Great Voltigeur Sweepstakes | 1 mile 4 furlongs | |
| Yorkshire Oaks | 1 mile 4 furlongs | (fillies only) |

Doncaster – September Meeting

St Leger	1 mile 6 furlongs	colts carrying 9 stone/fillies
	8st 11lbs	
Park Hill Stakes	1 mile 6 furlongs	(fillies only)

Other races for three-year-olds:

Craven Stakes and Nell Gwyn Stakes at Newmarket
Greenham Stakes at Newbury
Two Thousand Guineas and One Thousand Guineas Trials at Kempton
Oaks Trial and Ladbroke Derby Trial at Newmarket
Blue Riband Trial Stakes and Princess Elizabeth Stakes at Epsom
Classic Trial Stakes at Sandown
St James' Stakes and Ebbisham Stakes at Epsom
Jersey Stakes at Ascot
Commonwealth Stakes at Sandown
Princess Royal Stakes (fillies only) at Ascot

WEIGHT FOR AGE RACES

Races in which three-year-olds, four-year-olds, and older horses may compete against each other on weight for age terms. The younger and less mature horses carry less weight than the more fully developed horses, according to the weight for age scale first drawn up by Admiral Rous in 1855 and subsequently modified by the Jockey Club.

The principal weight for age races are:–

Newmarket – Spring Meeting

Jockey Club Stakes   1 mile 4 furlongs

Epsom – May/June Meeting

Coronation Cup   1 mile 4 furlongs

Ascot – June Meeting

Gold Cup   2 miles 4 furlongs
(This race was founded in 1807 and it is run during the Royal Ascot

Meeting in June. After the Classics, the Gold Cup is regarded as one of the most important races in the Calendar.)
Hardwicke Stakes   1 mile 4 furlongs

Newmarket – July Meeting
Princess of Wales Stakes   1 mile 4 furlongs

Sandown Park – July Meeting
Eclipse Stakes   1 mile 2 furlongs

Ascot – July Meeting
King George VI and Queen Elizabeth Diamond Stakes   1 mile 4 furlongs
(The King George VI and Queen Elizabeth Diamond Stakes is a combination of two comparatively recent additions to the Calendar. The King George VI Stakes was originally a two-mile open race for three-year-olds, which was first run at Ascot in 1946; the Queen Elizabeth Stakes, a weight for age race, was first run over one and a half miles at Ascot in 1951 (Festival of Britain year). These two races were merged to form one of the most valuable races in the Calendar – a one and a half mile race for three-year-olds and upwards, run at Ascot each July. Three-year olds carry 8 stone 8 lbs., and older horses carry 9 stone 7 lbs. Fillies and mares are given a 3 lb allowance.)

Goodwood – June Meeting
Sussex Stakes   1 mile

Goodwood – July Meeting
Goodwood Cup   2 miles 5 furlongs

Ascot – September Meeting
Queen Elizabeth II Stakes   1 mile

Newmarket – October Meeting
Jockey Club Cup   1 mile 6 furlongs
Champion Stakes   1 mile 2 furlongs

   Other weight for age races include:–

Queen Anne Stakes, Queen's Vase, Churchill Stakes, Yorkshire Cup, Rous Memorial Stakes.

HANDICAP RACES
A race in which every horse taking part is given an equal chance of winning by virtue of weight allotment, calculated by the Jockey Club handicappers, and based mainly on each horse's previous form.
   The principal handicap races are:–

Doncaster – March Meeting
Lincolnshire   1 mile

Epsom – April Meeting
City and Suburban   1 mile 2 furlongs

Chester – May Meeting
Chester- Cup   2 miles 2 furlongs

Kempton Park – May Meeting
Great Jubilee   1 mile 2 furlongs

Ascot – June Meeting
Ascot Stakes   2 miles 4 furlongs
Royal Hunt Cup   1 mile

Goodwood – July Meeting
Steward's Cup   6 furlongs
Goodwood Stakes   2 miles 3 furlongs

York – August Meeting
Ebor Handicap   1 mile 6 furlongs

Doncaster – September Meeting
Portland Handicap   5 furlongs

Newmarket – Autumn Meeting
Cesarewitch   2 miles 2 furlongs
Cambridgeshire   1 mile 1 furlong
(these two races are known as the Autumn Double)

   Other handicap races include:–

Zetland Gold Cup at Redcar; Wokingham Stakes at Ascot; Ayr Gold Cup
at Ayr; Vaux Gold Tankard and William Hill Gold Cup at Redcar.

SPONSORSHIP

As will be seen, many of the races listed carry the names of commercial
enterprises of one sort or another. This has come about as the result of
the great increase in sponsorship which has taken place during recent
years. It is true that there have been instances of sponsorship in racing
for many years (Tattersalls, for example, have been sponsoring races
quietly for a very long time), but it was the introduction of televised
racing which really set the ball rolling.

   Prize money is the lifeblood of racing and given the present difficult
economic state, it is perhaps as well for racing that so many generous
sponsors are ready to put up prize money or to add to the prize money

for important races. Today there are upwards of three hundred sponsored races, some of the best known being the Benson & Hedges Gold Cup, the William Hill Gold Cup, the Whitbread Gold Cup. De Beers (of diamond fame) support the King George VI and Queen Elizabeth Diamond Stakes.

Bookmaking organisations have not been slow to sponsor races. William Hill, Ladbrokes, Joe Coral, have all given generously to racing. Of course it is in their interests to do so, but as they already contribute through the Levy, they are not obliged to sponsor races.

With the advent of ladies' races, sponsorship has increased even further, as commerce realised the publicity potential of such an innovation.

Of course, publicity can sometimes misfire, as on the occasion when a horse named Ovaltine won a race which was sponsored by a well-known whisky firm, but no doubt they benefited greatly from the coverage given to the matter by the Press.

There are still people who regard sponsored racing with a deal of suspicion, and it is true that some race cards are beginning to read more like grocery lists.In November 1975 it was announced by the Jockey Club that racehorses owned by commercial concerns could carry the name of the company or the company's product(s). One or two of the sponsored races could perhaps be better named, but there is no doubt that both racing and business have benefited greatly through their alliance.

The Racing Information Bureau has an advisory service which is ready to help and advise any potential sponsors who may wish to seek their assistance.

DERBY DAY

In 1537 Henry VIII built Hampton Court (Nonsuch Palace) near to the village of Epsom. His daughter Elizabeth I did not own Nonsuch, but bought it from the Earl of Arundel, who exchanged it for Lord's which was apparently worth the sum of £534!

There was some horse racing at Epsom during Elizabeth's time. 'On Monday a great supper was made for her, but before night she stood at her standing in the further park and saw a course.' Then, in 1603, Nonsuch passed to James I, a keen huntsman and rider, who organised races to be held there during the Court's residence.

In 1618 a cowman named Whicker noticed that his cows would not drink the water in one of the springs. It was discovered that the water had certain healing properties, and soon it was being used by Epsom villagers to heal cuts and sores. It was then found that, if taken internally, the waters had a purgative effect. Soon the fame of Epsom began to spread and people came from all over the country to take the waters. As the number of visitors grew, so too did the number of race meetings held there. In 1648, racing on the Downs was used as a cover for meetings of Charles I's Royalist supporters.

'After the King had addressed the two Houses of Parliament at Guildford, a meeting of Royalists was held on Banstead Downs, under pretence of a horse race.' After his Restoration to the throne, Charles II came to Epsom to take the waters with the Duchess of Cleveland, and also with Nell Gwynn. Epsom then became a meeting place for the rich and fashionable.

By 1776 Epsom, with its waters, downs and gaming houses, had become a major racing centre. Then, in 1779, following the first running of the Oaks, the Derby Stakes was instituted. When Sir Charles Bunbury and Edward Smith Stanley (the Earl of Derby) tossed a coin to decide the name of their new sweepstake, they little dreamed that they were naming what was to become the most famous race in the world and the supreme test for three-year old thoroughbred colts and fillies (geldings were excluded in 1904).

Like the Oaks and the St Leger races, the Derby was an innovation, inasmuch as it was for three-year old horses only and was run over the then short distance of one mile (altered to 1 mile 4 furlongs in 1784). Today, everybody has heard of the Derby, but for the first few years of its running it was just another race to all but racing aficionados.

But although the first few runnings of the Derby attracted little interest outside the racing world, it was not long before it started to find a wider public. The new shorter sweepstakes, the Derby in particular, attracted high-class entries setting new standards, until the Derby became the most important race in the Flat Race season.

As time passed and means of transport and communication improved, the crowds grew even larger. In 1829 a grandstand was built on the Epsom Course. Later, in 1927, this was replaced at a cost of a quarter of a million pounds.

It is Derby Day, with its Bank Holiday atmosphere, which sets Epsom apart from any other racecourse, and the race has a special aura which is all its own. Weeks before the race takes place, in pubs and clubs all over the country, the chances of each runner are discussed at length. As the race draws near, suddenly everybody is an expert. Confident predictions are made as to the outcome of the race by people who cannot tell one end of a horse from the other. Form, times, distances, owner, trainer and jockey — all these factors are discussed and taken into account, as the great British public tries to pick the winner.

There is something special about having picked the winner of the

Derby, which has nothing to do with any financial gain one might enjoy. On Derby Day the off-course betting shops do a roaring trade, with regular betting shop customers almost being trampled underfoot in the rush (or else becoming involved with old ladies who are determined to have a flutter and who don't know how to write out their bets). In all, millions of pounds are wagered on the Derby every year with bookmakers all over the country, and many factories, offices and clubs have their own Derby Sweepstake.

On Epsom Downs on the morning of the race the enormous crowd (well over half a million) slowly starts to build up as cars and coaches pour in to Epsom. Everywhere there is an air of expectation and excitement, with lines of bookmakers arriving to put up their stands. Television crews set up their cameras and other equipment; on the hill the fairground gets under way, with its steam organs, side shows, strip shows, candy floss, jellied eels, and all the fun of the fair. Nearby, in long rows of booths and caravans, fortune tellers, apparently all related to Rose Lee, wait for customers. As the morning wears on, the double-decker buses arrive on the course. These are usually specially chartered for small parties and whilst the top deck is used for watching the races, the lower deck serves the dual purpose of bar and buffet.

By lunchtime the crowd on the course is enormous. High in the grandstand the 'other half' enjoys luncheon in comparative comfort. The bars are less crowded than those on the course but, although both the dress and the manners are better tailored, the feeling of excited expectancy is the same.

Back on the course, enormous queues form for toilets, drinks, hot dogs and everything else. One of the highlights of the day is the arrival of the Royal party, and it is an impressive moment as the entire crowd stands in silence whilst a military band plays the National Anthem.

Then the business of the day really gets going. The bookmakers start shouting the odds and the first races seem to be over in a flash. And then it is time for the main event of the day – the Derby. While the horses parade in the paddock, the betting reaches its peak. Frenzied bookies shout the odds, and punters (the drunk, the sober and the bewildered) try to get the best value for their money.

Suddenly, there is a roar (and it is a great roar) as the race starts. As the horses round Tattenham Corner, the excitement reaches fever pitch. Then they're in the straight, and in no time at all the horses are past the winning post. The race is over, and the winner is being led in.

To watch the Epsom Derby, either from the stands or on the course, is to watch one of the most exciting races in the world. After the race the tension is over. Many of the crowd immediately start for home. There are more races to come but somehow they don't seem to matter.

'The Derby is lost, the Derby is won,
The race of all races has come and is gone' . . . until next year.

SOME FAMOUS DERBYS

1780. The first ever running of the Derby Stakes, won by Diomed, owned by Sir Charles Bunbury, one of the founders of the race. This first Derby was run over a distance of one mile (altered to 1 mile 4 furlongs in 1784) for a first prize of £1,065 15s.

1787. Won by Sir Peter Teazle, an unraced colt, owned by the 12th Earl of Derby.

1788. The first Royal Derby winner – Sir Thomas – owned by H.R.H. The Prince of Wales (later George IV). The horse was ridden by William South, who was then fifty-four years of age.

1797. The only Derby to be won by an unnamed horse. The property of the Duke of Bedford, this unnamed colt by Fidget out of a sister by Pharamond, had never run before.

1801. Won by Eleanor (owned by Sir Charles Bunbury) the first filly to win the Derby. She also won the Oaks.

1805. During the race, won by Cardinal Beaufort, one of the runners was brought down by a spectator. (This was to happen again in 1913, with tragic results.)

1813. Won by a black horse, Smolensko (owned by Sir Charles Bunbury). Smolensko, returned at even money, was heavily backed and cost the bookmakers a fortune. One bookmaker, Brogrove, shot himself.

1844. The sensational 'Running Rein' Derby. Running Rein, a four-year old, not only ran in the Derby but won it. The owner of the second horse (Orlando) objected. The stakes were withheld, and after a sensational court case, Orlando was awarded the race. This is the race which was said to have killed the notorious bookmaker, William Crockford, whose horse, Ratan, was nobbled.

1853. Won by West Australian, the first horse ever to win the Triple Crown.

1855. Won by Wild Dayrell, bred by Francis Popham, who could only get 100 guineas for him from Lord Henry Lennox. Later Popham and Lord Cavendish bought back the horse, which they trained themselves. Trained by amateurs, ridden by Bob Sherwood an inexperienced jockey, Wild Dayrell, against all the odds and despite an attempt to nobble him, won the Derby with comparative ease.

1867. Won by Hermit, owned by Mr Henry Chaplin. The Marquis of Hastings (the ill-starred Harry Hastings) eloped with Lady Florence Paget just prior to her marriage to Hermit's owner, Henry Chaplin. Hastings laid heavily against Chaplin's horse, and suffered tremendous losses from which he never completely recovered. He is reputed to have lost £120,000 during the time it took to run the race.

1877. Won by Silvio. The first of five Derbys to be won by the great jockey, Fred Archer. His other successes were on Bend Or (1880); Iroquois (1881): Melton (1885) and Ormonde (1886).

1884. A dead heat between St Gatien and Harvester.

1886. Won by Ormonde (Triple Crown winner).

1894. Won by the then unbeaten Ladas, owned by the 5th Earl of Rosebery. This was an extremely popular win as at that time Rosebery was Prime Minister of England.

1896. Won by Persimmon, owned by the Prince of Wales. Another popular win, which was greeted by unrivalled scenes of excitement at Epsom (*see* photograph facing page 84).

1897. Won by Galtee More, who was Irish bred (Triple Crown winner).

1900. Another Royal winner – Diamond Jubilee, owned by the Prince of Wales. He became a Triple Crown winner.

1909. Won by Minoru, owned by King Edward VII. The first Derby win by a reigning Monarch.

1913. Perhaps the most famous of all the runnings of the Derby. The favourite, Craganour, although first past the post was disqualified, and the race was given to the 100–1 outsider, Aboyeur. During the race a suffragette, Emily Davison, threw herself in front of the King's horse, Anmer, and was killed.

1921. Won by the ill-fated Humorist, which was found shortly after the race to have run with a tubercular lung. Two weeks later he bled to death in his stable.

1924. Won by Sansovino, owned by the 16th Earl of Derby. The first winner of the race to be owned by the family of its namesake since 1787.

1925. Won by Manna, the last of Steve Donoghue's six Derby wins, which included two winners of the 1915–1918 New Derby Stakes, run at Newmarket, together with Humorist (1921); Captain Cuttle (1922) and Papyrus (1923).

1927. Won by Call Boy. The first ever Derby to be broadcast by the B.B.C.

1936. Won by Mahmoud, owned by the Aga Khan, in the then record time of 2 minutes 33.8 seconds.

1953. Won by Pinza, owned by Sir Victor Sassoon. An extremely popular win as the jockey, Gordon Richards, won the race after twenty-eight attempts.

1954. Won by Never Say Die, ridden by eighteen-year-old, Lester Piggott. The first of Piggott's many Derby winners, which include Crepello (1957); St Paddy (1960); Sir Ivor (1968); Nijinsky (1970) and Roberto (1972).

DERBY WINNERS

*Triple Crown winners (Two Thousand Guineas, Derby and St Leger)

1780 Diomed	1818 Sam	1856 Ellington
1781 Young Eclipse	1819 Tiresias	1857 Blink Bonny
1782 Assassin	1820 Sailor	1858 Beadsman
1783 Saltram	1821 Gustavus	1859 Musjid
1784 Sergeant	1822 Moses	1860 Thormanby
1785 Aimwell	1823 Emilius	1861 Kettledrum
1786 Noble	1824 Cedric	1862 Caractacus
1787 Sir Peter	1825 Middleton	1863 Macaroni
Teazle	1826 Lapdog	1864 Blair Athol
1788 Sir Thomas	1827 Mameluke	*1865 Gladiateur
1789 Skyscraper	1828 Cadland	*1866 Lord Lyon
1790 Rhadamanthus	1829 Frederick	1867 Hermit
1791 Eager	1830 Priam	1868 Blue Gown
1792 John Bull	1831 Spaniel	1869 Pretender
1793 Waxy	1832 St Giles	1870 Kingcraft
1794 Daedalus	1833 Dangerous	1871 Favonius
1795 Spread Eagle	1834 Plenipotent-	1872 Cremorne
1796 Didelot	iary	1873 Doncaster
1797 Unnamed colt	1835 Mündig	1874 George
owned by	1836 Bay Middleton	Frederick
Duke of	1837 Phosphorus	1875 Galopin
Bedford	1838 Amato	1876 Kisber
1798 Sir Harry	1839 Bloomsbury	1877 Silvio
1799 Archduke	1840 Little Wonder	1878 Sefton
1800 Champion	1841 Coronation	1879 Sir Bevys
1801 Eleanor	1842 Attila	1880 Bend Or
1802 Tyrant	1843 Cotherstone	1881 Iroquois
1803 Ditto	1844 Orlando	1882 Shotover
1804 Hannibal	1845 The Merry	1883 St Blaise
1805 Cardinal	Monarch	1884 St Gatien/
Beaufort	1846 Pyrrhus the	Harvester
1806 Paris	First	(dead heat)
1807 Election	1847 Cossack	1885 Melton
1808 Pan	1848 Surplice	*1886 Ormonde
1809 Pope	1849 The Flying	1887 Merry
1810 Whalebone	Dutchman	Hampton
1811 Phantom	1850 Voltigeur	1888 Ayrshire
1812 Octavius	1851 Teddington	1889 Donovan
1813 Smolensko	1852 Daniel	1890 Sainfoin
1814 Blücher	O'Rourke	*1891 Common
1815 Whisker	*1853 West	1892 Sir Hugo
1816 Prince	Australian	*1893 Isinglass
Leopold	1854 Andover	1894 Ladas
1817 Azor	1855 Wild Dayrell	1895 Sir Visto

1896	Persimmon	1915		1933	Hyperion
*1897	Galtee More	1916	New Derby	1934	Windsor Lad
1898	Jeddah	1917	Stakes run	*1935	Bahram
*1899	Flying Fox	1918	at Newmarket	1936	Mahmoud
*1900	Diamond	1919	Grand Parade	1937	Mid-day Sun
	Jubilee	1920	Spion Kop	1938	Bois Roussel
1901	Volodyovski	1921	Humorist	1939	Blue Peter
1902	Ard Patrick	1922	Captain	1940	
*1903	Rock Sand		Cuttle	1941	Substitute
1904	St Amant	1923	Papyrus	1942	Derby run at
1905	Cicero	1924	Sansovino	1943	Newmarket
1906	Spearmint	1925	Manna	1944	
1907	Orby	1926	Coronach	1945	
1908	Signorinetta	1927	Call Boy	1946	Airborne
1909	Minoru	1928	Felstead	1947	Pearl Diver
1910	Lemberg	1929	Trigo	1948	My Love
1911	Sunstar	1930	Blenheim	1949	Nimbus
1912	Tagalie	1931	Cameronian	1950	Galcador
1913	Aboyeur	1932	April The	1951	Arctic
1914	Durbar II		Fifth		Prince

For full information on the years 1952–1976, please turn to page 38.

Pommern (1915), Gay Crusader (1917) and Gainsborough (1918) were also Triple Crown winners although the Derbys were run at Newmarket.

SOME CLASSIC STATISTICS

ONE THOUSAND GUINEAS
Newmarket, 1 mile, for 3-year-old fillies, first run 1814

Year	Winner	Jockey	Trainer	Time	S.P.
1952	Zabara	K. Gethin	V. Smyth	1.40.92	7–1
1953	Happy Laughter	E. Mercer	J. Jarvis	1.45.05	10–1
1954	Festoon	A. Breasley	N. Cannon	1.38.90	9–2
1955	Meld	W. Carr	C. B. Rochfort	1.42.16	11–4
1956	Honeylight	E. Britt	C. Elsey	1.38.01	100–6
1957	Rose Royale II	C. Smirke	A. Head (FR)	1.39.15	6–1
1958	Bella Paola	S. Boullenger	F. Mathet (FR)	1.38.75	8–11
1959	Petite Etoile	D. Smith	N. Murless	1.40.36	8–1
1960	Never Too Late II	R. Poincelet	E. Pollet (FR)	1.39.89	8–11
1961	Sweet Solera	W. Rickaby	R. Day	1.38.14	4–1
1962	Abermaid	W. Williamson	H. Wragg	1.39.36	100–6
1963	Hula Dancer	R. Poincelet	E. Pollet (FR)	1.42.34	1–2
1964	Pourparler	G. Bougoure	P. Prendergast (IRE)	1.38.82	11–2
1965	Night Off	W. Williamson	W. Wharton	1.45.43	9–2

1966	Glad Rags	P. Cook	M. V. O'Brien (IRE)	1.40.30	100–6
1967	Fleet	G. Moore	N. Murless	1.44.76	11–2
1968	Caergwrle	A. Barclay	N. Murless	1.40.38	4–1
1969	Full Dress II	R. Hutchinson	H. Wragg	1.44.53	7–1
1970	Humble Duty	L. Piggott	P. Walwyn	1.42.13	3–1
1971	Altesse Royale	Y. Saint-Martin	N. Murless	1.40.9	25–1
1972	Waterloo	E. Hide	J. Watts	1.39.49	8–1
1973	Mysterious	G. Lewis	N. Murless	1.42.12	11–1
1974	Highclere	J. Mercer	W. Hern	1.40.32	12–1
1975	Nocturnal Spree	J. Roe	H. V. S. Murless (IRE)	1.41.65	14–1
1976	Flying Water	Y. Saint-Martin	A. Penna (FR)	1.37.83	2–1

TWO THOUSAND GUINEAS
Newmarket, 1 mile, for 3-year-olds, first run 1809

Year	Winner	Jockey	Trainer	Time	S.P.
1952	Thunderhead II	R. Poincelet	E. Pollet (FR)	1.42.48	100–7
1953	Nearula	E. Britt	C. Elsey	1.38.26	2–1
1954	Darius	E. Mercer	H. Wragg	1.39.45	8–1
1955	Our Babu	D. Smith	G. Brooke	1.38.83	13–2
1956	Gilles de Retz	F. Barlow	G. Jerdein	1.38.76	50–1
1957	Crepello	L. Piggott	N. Murless	1.38.24	7–2
1958	Pall Mall	D. Smith	C. B. Rochfort	1.39.43	20–1
1959	Taboun	G. Moore	A. Head (FR)	1.42.42	5–2
1960	Martial	R. Hutchinson	P. Prendergast (IRE)	1.38.33	18–1
1961	Rockavon	N. Stirk	G. Boyd	1.39.46	66–1
1962	Privy Councillor	W. Rickaby	T. Waugh	1.38.74	100–6
1963	Only For Life	J. Lindley	J. Tree	1.45	33–1
1964	Baldric II	W. Pyers	E. Fellows (FR)	1.38.44	20–1
1965	Niksar	D. Keith	W. Nightingall	1.43.31	100–8
1966	Kashmir II	J. Lindley	C. Bartholomew (FR)	1.40.68	7–1
1967	Royal Palace	G. Moore	N. Murless	1.39.37	100–30
1968	Sir Ivor	L. Piggott	M. V. O'Brien (IRE)	1.39.26	11–8
1969	Right Tack	G. Lewis	J. Sutcliffe	1.41.65	15–2
1970	Nijinsky	L. Piggott	M. V. O'Brien (IRE)	1.41.54	4–7
1971	Brigadier Gerard	J. Mercer	W. Hern	1.39.20	11–2
1972	High Top	W. Carson	B. Cutsem	1.40.82	85–40
1973	Mon Fils	F. Durr	R. Hannon	1.42.97	50–1
1974	Nonoalco	Y. Saint-Martin	F. Boutin (FR)	1.39.58	19–2
1975	Bolkonski	G. Dettori	H. Cecil	1.39.49	33–1
1976	Wollow	G. Dettori	H. Cecil	1.38.09	Evens

THE DERBY

Epsom, 1 mile 4 furlongs, for 3-year-olds (colts 9 st : fillies 8 st 9 lbs), first run 1780.

Year	Winner	Jockey	Trainer	Time	S.P.
1952	Tulyar	C. Smirke	M. Marsh	2.32$\frac{2}{5}$	11–2
1953	Pinza	G. Richards	N. Bertie	2.35$\frac{3}{5}$	5–1
1954	Never Say Die	L. Piggott	J. Lawson	2.35$\frac{4}{5}$	33–1
1955	Phil Drake	F. Palmer	F. Mathet (FR)	2.39$\frac{4}{5}$	100–8
1956	Lavandin	W. Johnstone	A. Head (FR)	2.36$\frac{2}{5}$	7–1
1957	Crepello	L. Piggott	N. Murless	2.35$\frac{2}{5}$	6–4
1958	Hard Ridden	C. Smirke	J. Rogers (IRE)	2.41$\frac{1}{5}$	18–1
1959	Parthia	W. Carr	C. B. Rochfort	2.36	10–1
1960	St Paddy	L. Piggott	N. Murless	2.35$\frac{3}{5}$	7–1
1961	Psidium	R. Poincelet	H. Wragg	2.36$\frac{1}{2}$	66–1
1962	Larkspur	N. Sellwood	M. V. O'Brien (IRE)	2.37.3	22–1
1963	Relko	Y. Saint-Martin	F. Mathet (FR)	2.39.4	5–1
1964	Santa Claus	A. Breasley	J. Rogers (IRE)	2.41.98	15–8
1965	Sea Bird II	T. Glennon	E. Pollet (FR)	2.38.41	7–4
1966	Charlottown	A. Breasley	G. Smyth	2.37.63	5–1
1967	Royal Palace	G. Moore	N. Murless	2.38.36	7–4
1968	Sir Ivor	L. Piggott	M. V. O'Brien (IRE)	2.38.73	4–5
1969	Blakeney	E. Johnson	A. Budgett	2.40.30	15–2
★1970	Nijinsky	L. Piggott	M. V. O'Brien (IRE)	2.34.68	11–8
1971	Mill Reef	G. Lewis	I. Balding	2.37.14	100–30
1972	Roberto	L. Piggott	M. V. O'Brien (IRE)	2.36.09	3–1
1973	Morston	E. Hide	A. Budgett	2.35.92	25–1
1974	Snow Knight	B. Taylor	P. Nelson	2.35.04	50–1
1975	Grundy	P. Eddery	P. Walwyn	2.35.35	5–1
1976	Empery	L. Piggott	M. Zilber (FR)	2.35.69	10–1

THE OAKS

Epsom, 1 mile 4 furlongs, for 3-year-old fillies carrying 9 st, first run 1779.

Year	Winner	Jockey	Trainer	Time	S.P.
1952	Frieze	E. Britt	C. Elsey	2.35$\frac{3}{5}$	100–7
1953	Ambiguity	J. Mercer	J. Colling	2.36$\frac{4}{5}$	18–1

★Triple Crown winner

1954	Sun Cap	W. Johnstone	R. Carver (FR)	2.39$\frac{1}{5}$	100–8
1955	Meld	W. Carr	C. B. Rochfort	2.47$\frac{4}{5}$	7–4
1956	Sicarelle	F. Palmer	F. Mathet (FR)	2.42	3–1
1957	Carrozza	L. Piggott	N. Murless	2.37$\frac{2}{5}$	100–8
1958	Bella Paola	M. Garcia	F. Mathet (FR)	2.40$\frac{4}{5}$	6–4
1959	Petite Etoile	L. Piggott	N. Murless	2.35$\frac{4}{5}$	11–2
1960	Never Too Late II	R. Poincelet	E. Pollet (FR)	2.39$\frac{1}{5}$	6–5
1961	Sweet Solera	W. Rickaby	R. Day	2.39$\frac{2}{5}$	11–4
1962	Monade	Y. Saint-Martin	L. Lieux (FR)	2.38$\frac{1}{5}$	7–1
1963	Noblesse	G. Bougoure	P. Prendergast (IRE)	2.39$\frac{3}{5}$	4–11
1964	Homeward Bound	G. Starkey	J. Oxley	2.49.36	100–7
1965	Long Look	J. Purtell	M. V. O'Brien (IRE)	2.39.56	100–7
1966	Valoris	L. Piggott	M. V. O'Brien (IRE)	2.39.35	11–10
1967	Pia	E. Hide	W. Elsey	2.38.34	100–7
1968	La Lagune	G. Thiboeuf	F. Boutin (FR)	2.41.66	11–8
1969	Sleeping Partner	J. Gorton	D. Smith	2.39.94	100–6
1970	Lupe	A. Barclay	N. Murless	2.41.46	100–30
1971	Altesse Royale	G. Lewis	N. Murless	2.36.95	6–4
1972	Ginevra	A. Murray	R. Price	2.39.35	8–1
1973	Mysterious	G. Lewis	N. Murless	2.36.31	13–8
1974	Polygamy	P. Eddery	P. Walwyn	2.39.39	3–1
1975	Juliette Marny	L. Piggott	J. Tree	2.29.10	12–1
1976	Pawneese	Y. Saint-Martin	A. Penna (FR)	2.35.25	6–5

ST LEGER

Doncaster, 1 mile 6 furlongs 32 yards, for 3-year-olds, first run 1776.

Year	Winner	Jockey	Trainer	Time	S.P.
1952	Tulyar	C. Smirke	M. Marsh	3.7$\frac{4}{5}$	10–11
1953	Premonition	E. Smith	C. B. Rochfort	3.6$\frac{4}{5}$	10–1
1954	Never Say Die	C. Smirke	J. Lawson	3.10$\frac{3}{5}$	100–30
1955	Meld	W. Carr	C. B. Rochfort	3.14$\frac{3}{5}$	10–11
1956	Cambremer	F. Palmer	G. Bridgland (FR)	3.12$\frac{1}{5}$	8–1
1957	Ballymoss	T. Burns	M. V. O'Brien (IRE)	3.15$\frac{3}{5}$	8–1
1958	Alcide	W. Carr	C. B. Rochfort	3.6$\frac{2}{5}$	4–9
1959	Cantelo	E. Hide	C. Elsey	3.4$\frac{3}{5}$	100–7
1960	St Paddy	L. Piggott	N. Murless	3.13$\frac{1}{5}$	4–6
1961	Aurelius	L. Piggott	N. Murless	3.6$\frac{3}{5}$	9–2
1962	Hethersett	W. Carr	W. Hern	3.10$\frac{4}{5}$	100–8
1963	Ragusa	G. Bougoure	P. Prendergast (IRE)	3.5$\frac{4}{5}$	2–5

1964	Indiana	J. Lindley	J. Watts	3.5	100–7
1965	Provoke	J. Mercer	W. Hern	3.18$\frac{3}{5}$	28–1
1966	Sodium	F. Durr	G. Todd	3.9$\frac{4}{5}$	7–1
1967	Ribocco	L. Piggott	R. Houghton	3.5$\frac{2}{5}$	7–2
1968	Ribero	L. Piggott	R. Houghton	3.19$\frac{4}{5}$	100–30
1969	Intermezzo	R. Hutchinson	H. Wragg	3.11$\frac{4}{5}$	7–1
1970	Nijinsky	L. Piggott	M. V. O'Brien (IRE)	3.6$\frac{2}{5}$	2–7
1971	Athens Wood	L. Piggott	H. Thomson Jones	3.15	5–2
1972	Boucher	L. Piggott	M. V. O'Brien (IRE)	3.28.71	3–1
1973	Peleid	F. Durr	W. Elsey	3.8.21	28–1
1974	Bustino	J. Mercer	W. Hern	3.9.2	11–10
1975	Bruni	A. Murray	R. Price	3.5.31	9–1
1976	Crow	Y. Saint-Martin	A. Penna (FR)	3.13.17	6–1

SOME LEGENDARY RACEHORSES

ECLIPSE

'Eclipse first, the rest nowhere.' (Colonel Dennis O'Kelly)

Eclipse was the great great grandson of the Darley Arabian. He was bred by the Duke of Cumberland, and was foaled in 1764 (the year of the great eclipse of the sun). He did not race until he was five years old, but he won all of the twenty-six races and matches in which he took part.

Sir Theodore Cooke, writing about Eclipse in his *History of the Turf*, says: 'His excellence was not only owing to the races he won, but even more clearly to the astonishing ease with which he won them, and to the fact that in addition to the undoubted speed and stride, he possessed sound wind, an ability to carry heavy weight, and an endurance over long distances which could never be thoroughly tested, for its limit was never reached.'

Eclipse sired 335 winners of over £160,000 in stakes before he died in 1789. The principal lines which can be traced from Eclipse are those of the four famous stallions, Touchstone, Stockwell, Isonomy and Vedette.

GLADIATEUR

Gladiateur was owned by Comte Frédéric de Lagrange and was trained by Tom Jennings at Newmarket. Gladiateur was in the direct line of descent from Eclipse. His grandsire was The Emperor, who won the Ascot Gold Cup twice, and who was sold to France when he retired to stud.

Gladiateur's sire was Monarque, who won both the French Derby and the Goodwood Cup.

Gladiateur himself won twelve races, and is one of the twelve horses in the history of racing to have won the Triple Crown (in 1865). He is the only horse ever to have won the Grand Prix de Paris in the same year that he won the Triple Crown. In the following year, 1866, Gladiateur won the Ascot Gold Cup by 40 lengths!

At the end of his racing career, Gladiateur was sold to Mr William Blenkiron (owner of the Middle Park Stud) but, unfortunately, the horse died young and his line did not survive.

Gladiateur's success as a racehorse was quite remarkable in view of the fact that he suffered from almost chronic lameness because of swellings on his fetlock joints.

ORMONDE

Ormonde was bred and owned by the Duke of Westminster. He won the Triple Crown in 1886 and was never beaten in his sixteen races, which were run over almost every distance. His sire was Bend Or (winner of the Derby in 1880) and his dam was Lily Agnes, who was a daughter of Macaroni (winner of the Derby of 1863). Ormonde was trained by John Porter at Kingsclere, and was ridden in most of his races by Fred Archer.

Unfortunately, Ormonde was unsound in his wind and he was sold to an Argentine breeder in 1889. He was later re-sold to an American breeder. However, he was almost sterile and had to be destroyed in 1904.

One of his sons was Orme, who won fourteen races, and who produced two sons – Flying Fox (who won the Derby in 1899) and Orby (Derby winner of 1907).

Of Ormonde it was said: 'The English thoroughbred has, throughout the last century, or even further back still, been the most valuable of all animals. For example, the sum of 30,000 guineas – at a time when a guinea was worth 21 shillings – was refused for Ormonde.'

SCEPTRE

Sceptre was one of only two fillies to have won four classic races, namely, the Two Thousand Guineas, One Thousand Guineas, the Oaks and St Leger, all in 1902. She also won the Jockey Club Stakes, the Champion Stakes, Hardwicke Stakes, and finished third in the Ascot Gold Cup. She was fourth in the Derby and the Grand Prix de Paris, and was only narrowly beaten by Ard Patrick in the Eclipse Stakes.

Sceptre was bought by Mr Robert Sievier, at the then record price of 10,000 guineas as a yearling. She was trained by Sievier himself. She was later bought by Sir William Bass, as a four-year old, for 25,000 guineas. Her total winnings for thirteen races amounted to £38,225.

Sceptre was a daughter of Persimmon (Derby winner in 1896), out of Ornament, who was a full sister to Ormonde by Bend Or.

HYPERION

Hyperion was bred and owned by Lord Derby, and was trained by the Honourable George Lambton. He was by Gainsborough (Triple Crown winner 1918) and out of Selene, a very great brood mare. Hyperion was only 15 hands $1\frac{1}{2}$ inches in height and was a beautiful chestnut colour with four white socks. He was not generally well thought of before his Derby win, however, because he was so small and because four white socks were supposed to indicate a poor sort of horse.

However, in spite of this criticism, Hyperion managed to win the Chester Vase, the Derby, the Prince of Wales's Stakes and the St Leger in 1933. He also finished third in the Ascot Gold Cup, in 1934. His total winnings amounted to £29,509.

Hyperion was thirty years old when he died in 1960 after an extremely successful career at stud. His sons included Aureole, Owen Tudor, Abernant, Suncastle, Sun Chariot, Hypericum, Rising Light and Gulf Stream, together with many other sons and daughters who figure prominently in the Stud Book and in the list of great race winners.

RIBOT

Ribot was bred in Italy by the great breeder, Federico Tesio, in 1952, and was owned by the Marchesa Incisa della Rochetta. He ran in sixteen races, winning all of them, including the Prix de l'Arc de Triomphe (which he won twice) and the King George VI and Queen Elizabeth Stakes.

However, Ribot's greatest successes have not been on the race course but at stud, and he has become one of the outstanding classic sires of the century. He is in direct line of descent from St Simon through his son, Rabelais. Ribot's descendants include – Ribofillio, Ribot's Palace, Riboletta, Ribot Prince, Ribocco, Ribero, Boucher and Ragusa.

SEA BIRD II

Sea Bird II was born in 1962. He ran eight times, winning seven races, including the Derby, the Prix de l'Arc de Triomphe and the Grand Prix de St Cloud. He was bred and owned by M. Jean Ternynck, and was trained in France by Etienne Pollet. It was in the Prix de l'Arc de Triomphe race in 1965 that Sea Bird II achieved his really outstanding success. The field included five Derby winners, one of whom, Reliance, had never been beaten. Sea Bird II won the Arc by six lengths.

NIJINSKY

Nijinsky was bred in Canada from Canadian-bred stock. Northern Dancer, his sire, was a grandson of the famous Italian-bred sire, Nearco, and Nijinsky's dam was Flaming Page. Nijinsky's owner was the late Mr

Charles Engelhard who sent Nijinsky to Ireland for training at Vincent O'Brien's stables. The horse ran four races in Ireland as a two-year old, winning them all very easily. He then came to England to run in the Dewhurst Stakes, which he won by 3 lengths.

In 1970 Nijinsky won the Triple Crown, as well as the King George VI and Queen Elizabeth Stakes, making a total of ten wins in the ten races in which he ran. Nijinsky's first defeat was in the Prix de l'Arc de Triomphe, where he was beaten by a head by the French horse, Sassafras. He was also beaten in his last race, the Champion Stakes. Many people criticised the fact that Nijinsky was made to race when he had not completely recovered his fitness after a bad attack of ringworm.

However, these two defeats could not alter the fact that Nijinsky was a brilliant and extremely popular horse. He has now retired to stud in America, where it is hoped that his success as a sire will equal his success on the racecourse.

MILL REEF

Mill Reef, who is owned by Mr Paul Mellon, was bred in America. His sire was Never Bend, a son of Nasrullah, and his dam was Milan Mill. Mill Reef was brought to Ian Balding's stables at Kingsclere as a yearling in October 1969. He ran six times in England as a two-year old, winning the Coventry Stakes at Ascot, the Gimcrack Stakes at York, the Imperial Stakes at Kempton and the Dewhurst Stakes at Newmarket.

In his racing career, Mill Reef ran a total of fourteen races, winning twelve of them. His first defeat was when he went to France for the Prix Robert Papin, when he was beaten by a short head by My Swallow.

As a three-year-old, Mill Reef ran in the Two Thousand Guineas, but was beaten by Brigadier Gerard. However, in the 1970 Derby, Mill Reef won quite comfortably, beating some fairly stiff opposition. He then went on to win the Eclipse Stakes, the King George VI and Queen Elizabeth Stakes, and the Prix de l'Arc de Triomphe. As a four-year old, Mill Reef won the Prix Ganay in France and the Coronation Cup.

However, during exercising, Mill Reef broke his near foreleg and although he could never race again, a masterly operation enabled him to walk almost as well as ever.

Mill Reef is now at the National Stud, where he has already sired several winning progeny.

BRIGADIER GERARD

Brigadier Gerard, who was sired by Queen's Hussar out of La Paiva, was bred by Mr John Hislop at his stud in Berkshire. His ancestry can be traced back to Pretty Polly, a wonderful mare who won the One Thousand Guineas, the Oaks and the St Leger in 1904.

After Brigadier Gerard had won the Middle Park Stakes as a two-year-old, John Hislop received an offer of £250,000 for his horse, which he refused to accept. Brigadier Gerard ran in eighteen races, winning seventeen of them, and in all of his races he was ridden by that great jockey, Joe Mercer. Brigadier Gerard was not entered for the 1971 Derby, because he had not been bred for the distance, but he won the Two Thousand Guineas that year, very comfortably beating Mill Reef by 3 lengths.

As a four-year old, Brigadier Gerard suffered his only defeat – in the Benson & Hedges Gold Cup at York, when he was beaten by Roberto, winner of the 1972 Derby. Brigadier Gerard's last race was in the Champion Stakes at Newmarket, which he won in an impressive manner.

He has now retired to stud at the Egerton Stud at Newmarket.

CHAPTER TWO

National Hunt Racing

'Two horsemen, drunk or sober, in or out of their wits, fix upon a steeple or some other conspicuous distant object, to which they make a straight cut, over hedge, ditch and gate.'

(*Pownall*)

HISTORY AND DEVELOPMENT

Steeplechasing has its origins in Tudor times, when a popular form of entertainment amongst horsemen was the 'wild goose chase' (races over open country). The earliest actual steeplechases probably originated in the hunting field, with gentlemen riders trying to cut each other down and this led to challenge matches, in which gentlemen would ride their own horses across country from point A to point B, for a fixed sum of money.

In 1804 a three-horse steeplechase was ridden, with the riders wearing colours. In the same year the first military match was run. At first, gentlemen rode their own hunters, but later they employed professional riders to take their place. Gradually the idea sprang up of building fences on racecourses.

Hurdle races, incidentally, are supposed to have been invented by the Prince of Wales (later George IV) who, while out riding with a group of friends, began jumping over sheep pens. The first hurdle race was run at Bristol in 1821, under Flat Race rules.

As steeplechasing developed, sweepstakes were introduced, and this greatly increased the popularity of the sport. Robert Surtees, the great hunting novelist and creator of the hunting grocer, John Jorrocks, seems not to have approved of steeplechasing, maintaining that 'nine-tenths of steeplechasing and hare coursing matches are got up by innkeepers for the good of their houses'. He also wrote: 'Farmers, too, are easily satisfied with the benefits of an impossible mob careering over their farms, even though some of them are attired in the miscellaneous garb of hunting and racing costume. Indeed, it is just this mixture of two sports that spoils both – steeplechasing being neither hunting or racing'. Nevertheless, one innkeeper (or, rather, hotelier) whether for the benefit of his house or not, did get up a race which developed into one of the greatest racing spectacles ever. In 1836, William Lynn instigated the Grand Liverpool Steeplechase, which later (in 1847) became the Grand National.

This was not the first grand steeplechase, however, as the Cheltenham Grand Annual Steeplechase had already started in 1834. This race was won in the year 1837 by the indomitable Captain Becher, of Becher's Brook fame (*see* Grand National).

Captain Becher was the leading professional jockey of his time. As for his Captaincy (somehow one always imagines him to have been a dashing cavalry officer) – in fact, he held a commission in the Buckinghamshire Yeomanry, and later became an Inspector of Sacks for the Great Northern Railways.

Other well-known jockeys of the time were Jem Mason, who learned to ride in the hunting field and who, for some reason, always rode in white kid gloves (Mason won the Grand National on Lottery in 1839) – and Tom Oliver, who won the Grand National three times (on Gay Lad in 1842; Vanguard in 1843 and Peter Simple in 1853).

Amateur jockeys have always played an important part in National Hunt racing, and in the late nineteenth century there were many crack amateurs competing against professionals on equal terms – men like Mr George Ede who, riding as Mr Edwards, won the Grand National on The Lamb in 1868 and who, two years later, was killed during a race at Cheltenham – and Captain Roddy Owen, who won the Grand National in 1892 on Father O'Flynn.

In addition to these crack riders, there must have been a great many lesser riders, if we are to believe Surtees, who wrote: 'We know of no more humiliating sight than mis-shapen gentlemen playing at jockeys. What a farce to see the great bulky fellow go to the scale with their saddles strapped to their backs, as if to illustrate the impossibility of putting a round of beef upon a pudding plate.'

By the middle of the nineteenth century, steeplechases were being held all over the country – no doubt 'got up by innkeepers for the good of their house' – but also got up by a variety of ne'er-do-wells for the good of their own pockets. Fraud and scandal became commonplace and, with the coming of the railways, great crowds began to descend upon country race meetings. Surtees described these race meeting crowds in his great comic novel, *Mr Sponge's Sporting Tour* as . . . 'the same sort of people that one would expect to see if a balloon was to go up or a man to be hung'.

He went on to say: 'Grandiddle Junction, by its connection with the great network of railways, enabled all the patrons of this truly national sport to sweep down upon the spot like flocks of wolves.'

Crowds were a problem on racecourses, and racing in St Albans ceased because of the many complaints received from the inhabitants and because of lack of support from local farmers, who were angry at the destruction caused to their crops by the huge crowds who came to see the races.

In 1863 the Grand National Hunt Steeplechase Committee was formed by certain members of the Jockey Club, in an attempt to inject some order into the sport. Later, in 1867, the Jockey Club ruled that hurdle races were also to come under the G.N.H.S.C.'s jurisdiction. By 1870 there were firm rules laid down, and the sport had a recognised authority. But it took a lot of work on the part of the Committee, and a very long time before the sport developed into the well-ordered, well-organised National Hunt racing as we know it.

In 1969 the National Hunt Committee, which had developed from the original G.N.H.S.C., amalgamated with the Jockey Club, which is now responsible for both types of racing.

CHELTENHAM

In 1837 a Mr Rowlands got up a Grand National Hunt Steeplechase race at Market Harborough. This first meeting proved to be a failure but, undaunted by this, Mr Rowlands tried again. In the following year twelve hunts took part, and the meeting was a great success. In 1861 the race was moved to Cheltenham (now the headquarters of National Hunt racing).

Flat racing started in Cheltenham in 1815 and, despite the efforts of no less a person than the Dean of Carlisle, who preached against it, the meeting was very successful. In 1834 the Grand Annual Steeplechase was run there.

For many years, Mr Rowlands' Grand National Hunt Steeplechase was the only important conditions race at Cheltenham. Then, in the 1920s, the Cheltenham Gold Cup was instituted (1924) and later the Champion Hurdle (1927). In both of these races all entries carry equal weight so that the races are, therefore, a test of the very best horses.

In the 1940s the prize money at Cheltenham was greatly increased, and the present-day Cheltenham National Hunt Festival meeting, which is held in March each year, is the highlight of the National Hunt year. This meeting always attracts the very best steeplechasers and hurdlers and is always well-supported by a huge crowd, including a large contingent of Irish racing enthusiasts who come over to cheer on the high-class Irish challengers that the meeting always attracts.

Past winners of the Gold Cup include Miss Dorothy Paget's famous horse, Golden Miller, who won the race five times, and Anne, Duchess of Westminster's Arkle, who won the race three times in succession. Past winners of the Champion Hurdle include Mr Henry Alper's great horse, Persian War, who won the race three times – a feat only equalled by two other horses since the race began, Hatton's Grace and Sir Ken, all three winning in successive years.

Point-to-point races have always been popular amongst jumping enthusiasts, and the first hunt to organise such a meeting for its members was the Atherstone in 1870. Later, the Pytchley followed suit. There is even a record of a House of Commons Point-to-Point which was held in Warwickshire, but this was discontinued in 1892 after two riders had been killed.

During the two World Wars, racing ceased altogether (although substitute Grand Nationals were run at Gatwick during the First World War). But after the Second World War there was a boom in the sport. Since then National Hunt racing has greatly benefited from Royal patronage; both Her Majesty the Queen and Her Majesty Queen Elizabeth the Queen Mother have always taken a great interest in National Hunt racing. The Queen Mother is an enthusiastic and successful owner, and almost won the Grand National in 1956 with the unfortunate Devon Loch, which unaccountably fell when only 50 yards from the winning post.

During the 1950s two most important sponsored races were introduced into the National Hunt calendar – the Whitbread Gold Cup and the Hennessy Gold Cup, which have produced some splendid winners for these very valuable prizes.

National Hunt racing is now more popular than ever, and televised racing has greatly increased the number of people interested in the sport. Great horses, such as Arkle, Pendil, Bula, Mill House, Crisp, The Dikler, Spanish Steps, Red Rum, Captain Christy, L'Escargot and Comedy of Errors, are only some of the great jumping stars who have given pleasure to millions during recent years.

THE GRAND NATIONAL
'There is only one Grand National and that is at Aintree'.

(Mrs Mirabel Topham)

If the Derby is the most famous flat race in the world, the Grand National is without doubt the most famous steeplechase – a fascinating sporting spectacle, which is a gruelling challenge to both horse and rider, with the added element of real danger.

The first steeplechase run at Aintree was the 1837 Grand Liverpool Steeplechase, which was organised by a Liverpool hotelier, Mr William Lynn, as a 'Sweepstake of 10 sovereigns each with £100 added by the town of Liverpool, for horses of all denominations, 4 years – 11 st 5 lbs, 5 years – 11 st 7 lbs, 6 years and aged – 12 st. Gentlemen riders, over a country not exceeding 5 miles, to be chosen by the umpire.' This race was won by The Duke, ridden by Captain Becher.

In 1843 the name of the race was changed to the Liverpool and National Steeplechase, and then in 1847 to the Grand National Steeplechase. However, the first Grand National is generally considered to have been run on February 26th, 1839, when seventeen horses started from fifty-three entries, and the race was won by Lottery, ridden by Jem Mason.

It was in this race that Captain Becher achieved immortality, not for winning the race, but for falling off his horse and landing in a brook. Becher, riding Conrad, remounted and continued the race, only to fall into the brook a second time. Today, 138 years later, Becher's Brook is still the best-known jumping obstacle in the world. It is to the gallant Captain's eternal credit that, on emerging from the brook, he is supposed to have remarked that he had no idea how filthy water tasted without brandy.

These early steeplechases at Aintree were run over a distance of 4 miles, with twenty fences in each of two circuits, and two flights of hurdles in the straight. The course was mainly across country, including a half-field of plough. At a later stage, its two brooks were widened, and in 1840 a stone wall was added. Today, the Grand National is run over a distance of 4 miles 856 yards and is, therefore, the longest race of the National Hunt season. There are now thirty fences, including the huge open ditch called The Chair, the big drop fence known as Valentine's, the Canal Turn which has a sharp turn to the left on the landing side and, of course, Becher's Brook.

The long run-in after the last fence has often proved to be a critical factor in the race as, for example, in the 1956 running of the race when Devon Loch, owned by H.M. Queen Elizabeth the Queen Mother, and ridden by Dick Francis, came away after the last fence, looking to be a certain winner. Unbelievably, when only 50 yards from the winning post, Devon Loch suddenly spreadeagled and the eventual winner, E.S.B., swept past him. Various theories have been put forward as to the reason for Devon Loch's remarkable behaviour. It has been suggested that the horse tried to jump an imaginary fence, but Dick Francis, who should know best, is on record as saying that Devon Loch veered away from the sudden roar of the crowd. Whatever the reason, it was one of the most remarkable and one of the saddest moments in the history of the race. Dick Francis (now the successful author of eminently readable racing thrillers) has achieved his place in racing history as 'the man who didn't win the National'.

Another occasion when the long run-in played a deciding factor in the race was in the 1973 Grand National, when the gallant horse, Crisp, after leading throughout the race and giving an incredible display of jumping, found the long run-in just too much for him. He was finally overtaken, just before the winning post by Red Rum, who was ridden with relentless determination by Brian Fletcher. But if ever a horse deserved to win the Grand National it was Crisp, who was giving Red Rum 22 lbs. Both horses broke Golden Miller's record time of 9 minutes 20.4 seconds by some 18 seconds.

Red Rum (again ridden by Brian Fletcher) went on to win the 1974 National from the Irish-trained horse, L'Escargot, thus becoming one of the few horses ever to win the race twice. But, in 1975, Red Rum and Fletcher just failed to bring off the hat-trick when they finished second to L'Escargot, reversing the results of the year before. The 1976 season started poorly for Red Rum, to such an extent that many people were prepared to write him off as a 'has been'. Then this incredible horse, this time ridden by Tommy Stack, again finished second in the Grand National. His only consolation was in establishing a record, having finished first on two occasions and second on two occasions, in four consecutive years, in the world's most difficult steeplechase race.

GRAND NATIONAL WINNERS

1837 The Duke	1877 Austerlitz	★1915 Ally Sloper
1838 Sir William	1878 Shifnal	★1916 Vermouth
1839 Lottery	1879 The Liberator	★1917 Ballymacad
1840 Jerry	1880 Empress	★1918 Poethlyn
1841 Charity	1881 Woodbrook	1919 Poethlyn
1842 Gay Lad	1882 Seaman	1920 Troytown
1843 Vanguard	1883 Zoedone	1921 Shaun Spadah
1844 Discount	1884 Voluptuary	1922 Music Hall
1845 Cure-All	1885 Roquefort	1923 Sergeant
1846 Pioneer	1886 Old Joe	Murphy
1847 Matthew	1887 Gamecock	1924 Master Robert
1848 Chandler	1888 Playfair	1925 Double Chance
1849 Peter Simple	1889 Frigate	1926 Jack Horner
1850 Abd el Kadar	1890 Ilex	1927 Sprig
1851 Abd el Kadar	1891 Come Away	1928 Tipperary
1852 Miss Mowbray	1892 Father O'Flynn	Tim
1853 Peter Simple	1893 Cloister	1929 Gregalach
1854 Bourton	1894 Why Not	1930 Shaun Goilin
1855 Wanderer	1895 Wild Man from	1931 Grakle
1856 Free Trader	Borneo	1932 Forbra
1857 Emigrant	1896 The Soarer	1933 Kellsboro' Jack
1858 Little Charley	1897 Manifesto	1934 Golden Miller
1859 Half Caste	1898 Drogheda	1935 Reynoldstown
1860 Anatis	1899 Manifesto	1936 Reynoldstown
1861 Jealousy	1900 Ambush II	1937 Royal Mail
1862 The Huntsman	1901 Grudon	1938 Battleship
1863 Emblem	1902 Shannon Lass	1939 Workman
1864 Emblematic	1903 Drumcree	1940 Bogskar
1865 Alcibiade	1904 Moifaa	1941 ⎫
1866 Salamander	1905 Kirkland	1942 ⎪
1867 Cortolvin	1906 Ascetic's	1943 ⎬ World War II
1868 The Lamb	Silver	1944 ⎪ no race
1869 The Colonel	1907 Eremon	1945 ⎭
1870 The Colonel	1908 Rubio	1946 Lovely Cottage
1871 The Lamb	1909 Lutteur III	1947 Caughoo
1872 Casse Tete	1910 Jenkinstown	1948 Sheila's
1873 Disturbance	1911 Glenside	Cottage
1874 Reugny	1912 Jerry M	1949 Russian Hero
1875 Pathfinder	1913 Covertcoat	1950 Freebooter
1876 Regal	★1914 Sunloch	1951 Nickel Coin

For full information on the years 1952–1976, please turn to page 54.

★run at Gatwick

MAJOR N.H. STATISTICS

CHAMPION HURDLE
Cheltenham, 2 miles 200 yards, first run 1927

Year	Winner	Age and Weight st lbs	Jockey	Trainer	S.P.
1952	Sir Ken	5	11 12	T. Molony	W. Stephenson	3–1
1953	Sir Ken	6	12	T. Molony	W. Stephenson	2–5
1954	Sir Ken	7	12	T. Molony	W. Stephenson	4–9
1955	Clair Soleil	6	12	F. Winter	R. Price	5–2
1956	Doorknocker	8	12	H. Sprague	W. Hall	100–9
1957	Merry Deal	7	12	G. Underwood	A. Jones	28–1
1958	Bandalore	7	12	G. Slack	J. Wright	20–1
1959	Fare Time	6	12	F. Winter	R. Price	13–2
1960	Another Flash	6	12	H. Beasley	P. Sleator	11–4
1961	Eborneezer	6	12	F. Winter	R. Price	4–1
1962	Anzio	5	11 12	W. Robinson	F. Walwyn	11–2
1963	Winning Fair	8	12	Mr A. Lillingston	G. Spencer	100–9
1964	Magic Court	6	12	P. McCarron	T. Robson	100–6
1965	Kirriemuir	5	11 12	W. Robinson	F. Walwyn	50–1
1966	Salmon Spray	8	12	J. Haine	R. Turnell	4–1
1967	Saucy Kit	6	12	R. Edwards	M. Easterby	100–6
1968	Persian War	5	11 12	J. Uttley	C. Davies	4–1
1969	Persian War	6	12	J. Uttley	C. Davies	6–4
1970	Persian War	7	12	J. Uttley	C. Davies	5–4
1971	Bula	6	12	P. Kelleway	F. Winter	15–8
1972	Bula	7	12	P. Kelleway	F. Winter	8–11
1973	Comedy of Errors	6	12	W. Smith	F. Rimell	8–1
1974	Lanzarote	6	12	R. Pitman	F. Winter	7–4
1975	Comedy of Errors	8	12	K. White	F. Rimell	11–8
1976	Night Nurse	5	12	P. Broderick	M. Easterby	2–1

CHELTENHAM GOLD CUP
Cheltenham, about 3¼ miles, first run 1924. All to carry 12 st.

Year	Winner	Age	Jockey	Trainer	S.P.
1952	Mont Tremblant	6	D. Dick	F. Walwyn	8–1
1953	Knock Hard	9	T. Molony	M. V. O'Brien	11–2
1954	Four Ten	8	T. Cusack	J. Roberts	100–6
1955	Gay Donald	9	A. Grantham	J. Ford	33–1
1956	Limber Hill	9	J. Power	W. Dutton	11–8
1957	Linwell	9	M. Scudamore	C. Mallon	100–9
1958	Kerstin	8	S. Hayhurst	C. Bewicke	7–1
1959	Roddy Owen	10	H. Beasley	D. Morgan	5–1
1960	Pas Seul	7	W. Rees	R. Turnell	6–1
1961	Saffron Tartan	10	F. Winter	D. Butchers	2–1
1962	Mandarin	11	F. Winter	F. Walwyn	7–2
1963	Mill House	6	W. Robinson	F. Walwyn	7–2
1964	Arkle	7	P. Taaffe	T. Dreaper	7–4
1965	Arkle	8	P. Taaffe	T. Dreaper	30–100
1966	Arkle	9	P. Taaffe	T. Dreaper	1–10
1967	Woodland Venture	7	T. Biddlecombe	F. Rimell	100–8
1968	Fort Leney	10	P. Taaffe	T. Dreaper	11–2
1969	What A Myth	12	P. Kelleway	R. Price	8–1
1970	L'Escargot	7	T. Carberry	D. Moore	33–1
1971	L'Escargot	8	T. Carberry	D. Moore	7–2
1972	Glencaraig Lady	8	F. Berry	F. Flood	6–1
1973	The Dikler	10	R. Barry	F. Walwyn	9–1
1974	Captain Christy	7	H. Beasley	P. Taaffe	7–1
1975	Ten Up	8	T. Carberry	J. Dreaper	2–1
1976	Royal Frolic	7	J. Burke	F. Rimell	14–1

THE GRAND NATIONAL
Liverpool (Aintree), about 4 miles 856 yards, first run 1837.

Year	Winner	Age and Weight st lbs		Jockey	Trainer	Time	S.P.
1952	Teal	10	10 12	A. Thompson	N. Crump	$9.20\tfrac{3}{5}$	100–7
1953	Early Mist	8	11 2	B. Marshall	M. V. O'Brien	$9.22\tfrac{4}{5}$	20–1
1954	Royal Tan	10	11 7	B. Marshall	M. V. O'Brien	$9.32\tfrac{4}{5}$	8–1
1955	Quare Times	9	11	P. Taaffe	M. V. O'Brien	$10.19\tfrac{1}{5}$	100–9
1956	E.S.B.	10	11 3	D. Dick	F. Rimell	$9.21\tfrac{2}{5}$	100–7
1957	Sundew	11	11 7	F. Winter	F. Hudson	$9.42\tfrac{3}{5}$	20–1
1958	Mr What	8	10 6	A. Freeman	T. Taaffe	$9.49\tfrac{4}{5}$	18–1
1959	Oxo	8	10 13	M. Scudamore	W. Stephenson	$9.37\tfrac{3}{5}$	8–1
1960	Merryman II	9	10 12	G. Scott	N. Crump	9.27	13–2
1961	Nicolaus Silver	9	10 1	H. Beasley	F. Rimell	$9.22\tfrac{3}{5}$	28–1
1962	Kilmore	12	10 4	F. Winter	R. Price	9.50	28–1
1963	Ayala	9	10	P. Buckley	K. Piggott	$9.35\tfrac{4}{5}$	66–1
1964	Team Spirit	12	10 3	W. Robinson	F. Walwyn	$9.30\tfrac{3}{5}$	100–6
1965	Jay Trump	8	11 5	C. Smith	F. Winter	$9.52\tfrac{4}{5}$	50–1
1966	Anglo	8	10	T. Norman	F. Winter	$9.49\tfrac{3}{5}$	100–1
1967	Foinavon	9	10	J. Buckingham	J. Kempton	$9.28\tfrac{4}{5}$	100–7
1968	Red Alligator	9	10	B. Fletcher	D. Smith	$9.29\tfrac{4}{5}$	100–9
1969	Highland Wedding	12	10 4	E. Harty	G. Balding	9.38	15–1
1970	Gay Trip	8	11 5	P. Taaffe	F. Rimell	$9.34\tfrac{1}{2}$	28–1
1971	Specify	9	10 13	J. Cook	J. Sutcliffe	$10.8\tfrac{3}{4}$	14–1
1972	Well To Do	9	10 1	G. Thorner	T. Forster	9.1.90	9–1
1973	Red Rum	8	10 5	B. Fletcher	D. McCain	9.20.30	11–1
1974	Red Rum	9	12	B. Fletcher	D. McCain	9.31.10	13–2
1975	L'Escargot	12	11 3	T. Carberry	D. Moore	9.20	14–1
1976	Rag Trade	10	10 12	J. Burke	F. Rimell		

SOME GREAT CHASERS AND HURDLERS

GOLDEN MILLER

Golden Miller was bred in 1927 in Ireland, where he was sired by Goldcourt out of Miller's Pride. He was brought to England by Mr Carr for training as a three-year old. Golden Miller was not very well thought of by his trainer, Mr Briscoe, and showed no promise at all when he ran in a flat race in 1930. He was then taken out hunting, but still did not impress anyone with his abilities.

Golden Miller continued racing, this time over hurdles, and was then tried in a steeplechase, when he managed to finish second. Golden Miller was sold to the great English owner, Miss Dorothy Paget in 1932. It was decided that Golden Miller should concentrate entirely on steeplechasing, and he was entered for the 1932 Cheltenham Gold Cup. He won this race, winning it again in 1933, 1934, 1935 and 1936 (an amazing achievement); he also won fourteen of his nineteen other races.

Golden Miller achieved a remarkable double in 1934, when he won the Grand National in addition to the Cheltenham Gold Cup. He won the Grand National in record time and this record was not broken until Red Rum's win in 1973.

In the 1935 Grand National, after his hard-won victory in the Cheltenham Gold Cup, Golden Miller was unable to finish the course. He had also been entered for the Championship Chase at Aintree on the day after the Grand National but, sensibly, he refused to jump.

Golden Miller was sent to a new trainer, Owen Anthony, who gave him a good long rest, and at the end of December 1935 he won the Andover Handicap at Newbury and went on to win several more races in the next three seasons. In Golden Miller's last appearance in the Cheltenham Gold Cup he still managed to finish second. In all, he won twenty-eight of the fifty-three races in which he took part, and was placed in many of them.

MANDARIN

All too often these days one hears the remark that there are too many bad horses in training and that a great many of them should not be allowed to race. It is tempting to wonder just how many great, but late-developing, horses would be dismissed and thus lost to racing by the advocates of this philosophy.

Arkle, Red Rum and Mandarin are just three who showed very little promise at the start of their racing careers. Mandarin, a small bay horse, was bred in France in 1951 by Madame Hennessy, and was shipped across to England to be trained by Fulke Walwyn at Lambourn in 1954. At first, Mandarin showed little promise, and seemed to have some difficulty in jumping. During the 1955/56 season, although winning his second race, he was unplaced in five out of the nine hurdle races he ran in. All in all, he was rather unspectacular as a hurdler.

Surprisingly, it was decided to try the horse over fences, and to this end he was schooled by the skilful Michael Scudamore. This schooling proved so successful that Scudamore, who rode Mandarin seven times during the 1956/57 season, won three times and was placed second four times. Indeed, so much had Mandarin improved that at the end of that season he was a close second in the Whitbread Gold Cup.

By the following season it was beginning to dawn on the racing public that he was something rather special, and the small horse's gameness and courage was beginning to win him many admirers. In the 1957 Hennessy Gold Cup, Mandarin beat Linwell (winner of the Cheltenham Gold Cup) by 3 lengths. In that same season he won the King George VI Chase, the Golden Miller Chase, and at the end of the season finished second, once again, in the Whitbread Gold Cup.

Throughout 1959, however, ill-fortune dogged Mandarin. During the running of the King George VI Chase he fractured a bone in his hind leg. Even so, this game little horse managed to finish third. After a long rest and first-class treatment by Fulke Walwyn, Mandarin was back on the racecourse, but suffered mixed fortunes, coming third in the Cheltenham Gold Cup and although he started favourite for the Whitbread Gold Cup, was unplaced.

To many people it seemed as if Mandarin's best days were over, but his greatest triumphs were yet to come. It was in the 1961/62 season that Mandarin really came into his own – winning the Hennessy Gold Cup and then going on to win the Cheltenham Gold Cup, ridden by Fred Winter, with whom Mandarin's name will always be associated.

By 1962 Mandarin had notched up eighteen victories (out of fifty races) and had won some £30,000 in prize money. But it was at Auteuil, in France, in June 1962, that Mandarin really earned his place in racing history. During the running of the Grand Steeplechase de Paris (the French Grand National) he was again ridden by Fred Winter. Mandarin was well up with the leaders as they approached the fourth fence, when suddenly the rubber snaffle bit broke, leaving Winter with virtually no control over the horse. Nevertheless, showing remarkable skill and courage, Fred Winter, by use of the neck rein and the strength of his legs, managed to keep up with the leaders.

Very sportingly, the French jockeys helped by edging Mandarin round some of the more difficult bends. At the second to last fence, having amazingly negotiated and survived some nineteen fences, Mandarin was lying third. Over the last fence he was in the lead, and on the long run-in, after a desperately close finish, he managed to hold off a challenge from the French horse, Lumino, to win by a head. It is doubtful whether any other horse and rider could have achieved such a remarkable feat – the courage and gameness of the one and skill and nerve of the other resulting in an almost unbelievable victory. This was to be Mandarin's last race, and he enjoyed a well-deserved retirement at Lambourn until his death in July 1976.

MILL HOUSE

Mill House's career began in Ireland as a young hunter, but he then went into training with Tom Taaffe, Pat Taaffe's father. After winning on his first outing as a hurdler, Mill House was brought to England for training by Syd Dale at Epsom. He later went to Fulke Walwyn's stable, where he stayed for the remainder of his racing career.

Mill House's first season in England (1961/62) was not a great success, as he won only one of the three hurdle races in which he was entered. However, it was then decided to concentrate him on steeplechasing and by the end of the 1962/63 season, Mill House had won four of his races, including the Cheltenham Gold Cup (which he won by 20 lengths) and the Mandarin Chase at Newbury.

By this time, Mill House had become a great favourite with racegoers who were impressed with his tremendous jumping ability. In December 1963 he won the King George VI Chase at Kempton Park, going on to win the Gainsborough Chase at Sandown in February 1964. However, in the 1964 Cheltenham Gold Cup Mill House suffered his terrible defeat by Arkle and then, with a huge weight penalty, he was beaten by Dormant in the Whitbread Gold Cup. In the Hennessy Gold Cup at Newbury, poor Mill House was again beaten by Arkle.

Six weeks later Mill House won the Mandarin Chase, and then beat Arkle in his next race – the Gainsborough Chase at Sandown. By the end of 1965 it was apparent that Mill House had broken down, but Fulke Walwyn managed to treat Mill House's legs so that he was able to race in the Massey-Ferguson Gold Cup in December 1966. He then won the Gainsborough Chase (for the third successive year).

Mill House fell in the 1967 Cheltenham Gold Cup, and it was found that he had injured his back. However, he continued to race, winning the Whitbread Gold Cup in April 1967, before retiring from the racecourse.

ARKLE

One of the most famous horses in the world was Arkle who was born in Ireland in 1957. He was bred by Mrs Baker out of a steeplechase mare called Bright Cherry and he was sired by Archive, a not very distinguished horse in the Nearco line. Arkle was bought as a three-year old by Anne, Duchess of Westminster, and at four years old he was sent for training to Tom Dreaper at Kilsallaghan.

Arkle's racing career began with two flat races in Ireland, when he finished 3rd and 4th, respectively. As a five-year old, Arkle was entered for a 3-mile hurdle race, which he won with incredible ease. His English racing career began in October 1962 when he ran in a couple of races – one of which was the Honeybourne Chase at Cheltenham, which he won by 20 lengths against some very good horses.

Between February and October 1963, Arkle won the six races in which he ran, and in that November he raced against Mill House in the Hennessy Gold Cup at Newbury, which Mill House won. In the Cheltenham Gold Cup of March 1964, Arkle and Mill House met again, and this time it was Arkle who won. He then went on to win the Irish Grand National.

Arkle and Mill House next raced against each other in the 1964 Hennessy Gold Cup, when Arkle was carrying 12 st 7 lbs but still managed to win the race. In the Massey-Ferguson race a week later, when he was carrying yet another 3 lbs, Arkle managed to finish third. In 1965 Arkle again won the Cheltenham Gold Cup, again beating Mill House. Arkle then went on to win another six races. In 1966 Arkle won the Cheltenham Gold Cup for the third time, becoming one of the three horses to achieve this tremendous feat.

It was found that Arkle had fractured a bone in his foot (although he still managed to finish second in the King George VI Chase at Kempton Park in December 1966). After weeks of treatment, Arkle was sent back to Ireland for complete rest. It was hoped that he would be able to race again, but Anne, Duchess of Westminster wisely decided not to take the risk.

Arkle made his final appearance in England at the Horse of the Year Show at Wembley in October 1969, when he was again ridden by his jockey, Pat Taaffe. Unfortunately, Arkle had to be put down, as it was found that he was suffering considerable pain in his foot. But there are permanent reminders of this fabulous horse at Cheltenham racecourse, where he raced so magnificently, in the form of a life-size statue of Arkle and in the annual running of the Arkle Challenge Trophy.

RED RUM

Born on the 3rd May, 1965, Red Rum was bred by M. C. McEnery in County Kilkenny, Ireland. His pedigree suggested sprinting speed. His dam, Mared, a winner over 7 furlongs, was by Magic Red, a winner over 5 and 6 furlongs, and his sire, Quorum, finished second to Crepello in the 1957 Two Thousand Guineas.

Red Rum was sold as a yearling at Goff's September Sales, and was bought by Melton Mowbray trainer, Tim Molony, for a businessman, Mr M. Kingsley. It was Molony who considered Red Rum to be a bit too lively as a colt and had him gelded. Red Rum ran eight times on the flat as a 2-year old, dead-heating for first place on his début in a Liverpool selling race, and winning only one other race. During this period he was ridden by several different jockeys.

As a 3-year old, Red Rum ran again on the flat, winning first time out in a seller at Doncaster, and finishing second in the Earl of Sefton Stakes at Liverpool on Grand National day. Shortly afterwards, Mr Kingsley decided to sell Red Rum, and he was bought for £1,200 by the late Bobby Renton, on behalf of Mrs L. Brotherton, who once owned the 1950 Grand National winner, Freebooter, and who was at that time looking for a potential steeplechaser.

In his first season over hurdles, Red Rum ran consistently well, rounding off the season by winning three times in a row, when ridden by Paddy Broderick.

The following season was a poor one for Red Rum, who failed to win one of his fourteen races. It was then decided to send him steeplechasing. Red Rum immediately showed a natural aptitude for jumping the larger fences. He ran in twelve races that season, winning two and being placed in nine, including a fourth in the Mildmay of Flete Challenge Cup Handicap Chase at the Cheltenham N.H. Festival.

During the summer of 1971 his trainer, Bobby Renton, then eighty-four, decided to retire. Jockey Tommy Stack took over the stables for a time and rode Red Rum in two races, in one of which he finished second. Later the stables were taken over by Anthony Gillam, and Tommy Stack continued as stable jockey.

In 1972 Red Rum showed signs of foot trouble, which required prolonged treatment. He resumed racing in February and, after falling for the first time over fences in his first race, he then ran three good races, including coming fifth to Quick Reply in the Scottish Grand National.

About this time, his owner, Mrs Brotherton, decided to cut down on the number of steeplechasers she had in training, and Red Rum was sold at Doncaster August sales (1972). He was bought by trainer Donald 'Ginger' McCain, for Mr Noel Le Mare, a self-made millionaire, then in his eighties, whose ambition was to win the Grand National.

Red Rum, carefully trained by McCain with the National in view, won his first four races and was then sent to race at Ayr, where for the first time he was ridden by Brian Fletcher. The new combination won by 6 lengths. After a short rest, Red Rum ran in the Cumberland Grand National Trial Chase at Carlisle, finishing third.

Then, with only two months to go before his first National, he was placed twice in his next two races. Between races Red Rum was worked hard on the Southport Sands. This preparation was continued until the very day before the great Aintree Steeplechase, when Red Rum ran two fast 7-furlong gallops.

The field of thirty-eight runners for the 1973 Grand National included such top class chasers as the Australian horse Crisp, and the dual Cheltenham Gold Cup winner, L'Escargot. Red Rum carried 10 st 5 lbs, and started at 9–1.

The huge Crisp, ridden by Richard Pitman, ran the race of his life, and was going so well that as he started the second circuit, after jumping the water, the rest of the field were only at the Chair fence. After the 19th fence, Crisp was still in the lead, but was by now beginning to tire. Red Rum, ridden with tremendous determination by Brian Fletcher, set off in pursuit of the leader, and caught and passed the unlucky Crisp, to win by three-quarters of a length (9 min 1.9s) breaking Golden Miller's 38-year old record time for the race (9 min 20.2/5) by 18 seconds. L'Escargot finished third, 25 lengths behind.

When Red Rum returned to Aintree the following year, he carried top weight (12 stone) in a field of forty-two, and opened at 8–1 favourite (drifting to 11–1). Red Rum jumped his way to the front at Becher's Brook on the second circuit, and by the time he reached the fourth fence from home he was in the lead by 4 lengths. Here, he made his only mistake, hitting the fence hard but, quickly regaining his stride, went on to become one of the few horses in the history of steeplechasing to win the race twice. L'Escargot finished second, with Charles Dickens third.

Three weeks later, Red Rum, starting at 11–8, won the Scottish Grand National by 4 lengths from Lord Oaksey's mount, Proud Tarquin, thus becoming the first horse ever to win both races in the same year.

At the beginning of the 1974/75 season Ginger McCain found himself aiming at an unprecedented National hat-trick. During the early part of the season, Red Rum ran some good races, winning both the Joan Mackay Chase at Ayr and the Haydock Grand National Trial, each time conceding weight all round.

Red Rum started 7–2 favourite for the 1975 Grand National, again carrying top weight (12 stone in a field of thirty-one). Although he ran a brilliant race, this time the weight and the dead going told and he was beaten by 15 lengths by L'Escargot (ridden by Tommy Carberry) to whom he was conceding 11 lbs. This was the first time in the history of the race that the same two horses had taken 1st and 2nd places in consecutive years.

Red Rum's programme for the 1975/76 season followed the same pattern as in previous years. He ran in eight races and was placed in only four and many people began to write him off as a 'has been'. In the 1976

National, Red Rum (this time ridden by Tommy Stack) was set to carry 11 stone 10 lbs, and started at 10–1 in a field of thirty-two. Throughout the first circuit Red Rum kept his place, just tucked in behind the leaders. Then, three fences from home, he went into the lead. For a few moments it looked as if this remarkable horse was going to achieve the impossible and become the first horse in history to win the race three times. However Rag Trade, carrying 10 stone 12 lbs, began to close the gap, and finally passed Red Rum 200 yards from the winning post. With Red Rum coming back at him, and gaining ground, Rag Trade won by 2 lengths. Red Rum was once again second. Rag Trade, owned by Mr 'Teazy Weazy' Raymond, was a popular winner, but there can have been few people on the course, or amongst the millions who watched the race on television, who were not saddened by Red Rum's narrow failure to bring off the unique treble.

Even so, his current record of two firsts and two seconds in this most demanding of all steeplechases, in four consecutive years, is unequalled. If, as Ginger McCain has predicted, Red Rum runs at Aintree again in 1977, then the whole racing world will wish him the very best of luck.

CHAPTER THREE

Racehorse Owning

'At times racehorse owners are a great worry to trainers, but they pay the bill and they must be studied.'

(*H. S. Persse*)

In the early days of racing, owners were, for the most part, rich members of Royal or aristocratic families who raced their horses against one another in 'matches'. In these more democratic times, owners come from all walks of life, the common denominator being the love of the sport which they encourage and support. For, without the 11,500 or so registered owners in Great Britain today, there would be no racing and no racing industry.

Although a few owners do manage to show a profit each year, and although one reads in the press of enormous prizes being won on the Classic races (the 1976 Derby, for example, being run for a first prize of £111,825.50) very few owners are lucky enough to own a horse of Classic potential, never mind a classic winner.

For the most part, the rewards, if such they can be called, are almost non-existent. It has been calculated that the average prize money each year is somewhere in the region of £750 (total prize money divided by the number of horses in training) and as it costs well over £3,000 a year to keep a horse in training (with costs increasing all the time) it is virtually impossible for most winning owners to break even.

There has never been a worse time to consider taking up ownership than the present. Increased costs, Value Added Tax, Capital Transfer Tax, and galloping inflation are all taking their toll of the racing industry which employs many thousands of people.

During recent times, we have seen big owners either cutting down drastically on the number of horses they have in training or, as in the case of millionaire owner, Mr Ravi Tikkoo, taking their horses to be trained abroad. Some trainers and jockeys have also gone overseas, while others have left the business altogether. The most worrying aspect of the present situation is the fact that so much of the best British bloodstock is being sold abroad. This could result in largely second rate breeding stock being left in this country thus jeopardising the whole future of the breeding industry.

Furthermore, in order to avoid taxation, foreign buyers are now less likely to have their horses trained in England, preferring to ship them either to France or to Ireland where things seem so much better nowadays. In Ireland, for example, bloodstock is exempt from Value Added Tax, whilst in France, not only is V.A.T. charged only on the carcase value of a horse (as opposed to the price paid for it) but the average prize money is in the region of £4,000.

All in all, this is a somewhat depressing picture for British racing, and one which won't improve until the Government either offers some relief on V.A.T. or ploughs back some of the millions of pounds it makes out of racing, via the betting duty, each year. Perhaps the answer would have been to have made all off-course betting Tote betting, whilst keeping the on-course bookmakers – a system which seems to work extremely well in Australia. At the time of writing, suggestions are being put forward from all sides as to how the plight of British racing can be alleviated, and while there is great concern in all branches of the racing industry, there seems to be no sign of any concerted effort to improve matters.

For the newcomer interested in racehorse ownership the prospect is not an encouraging one.

BUYING A RACEHORSE

For those readers not completely discouraged by the introduction to this chapter who still wish to become racehorse owners, the first problem is, of course, when and where to acquire a horse. Unless one is a competent judge of horseflesh (and very few people are) it is most advisable to go either to a reputable bloodstock agency (who charges approximately 5 per cent commission) or to a licensed trainer. A beginner attempting to buy a horse at a bloodstock auction without expert advice would be taking a very great risk. Again, anyone wishing to purchase a horse privately, either through an advertisement or through a friend, is advised that it is absolutely essential to have an expert to examine the horse. (There is something about horse dealing which brings out the worst in almost everybody!)

As regards approaching a trainer, it would perhaps be as well, initially, to disregard the really big names in the racing world. The chances are that these trainers would already have full stables anyway and they could perhaps prove to be both rather awesome and expensive for the new owner. There are, however, dozens of very competent trainers with small yards who would be only too happy to take an interest in a prospective owner. Having acquired a horse, the new owner is going to need to find a trainer, so letting the trainer in at the buying stage would seem to make good sense.

One point to consider when approaching a trainer is the location of his stables and of the nearby racecourses. There is little point, for instance, in having a horse trained in Yorkshire, which will probably run at northern racecourses, if one lives in the south of England and can seldom manage to get to the stables or to see the horse run. The map on page 95 should be useful.

Having decided to buy a horse, the next question to consider is whether it should run in Flat races or in National Hunt races. This decision could, of course, affect both the initial outlay and the possible prize money for anyone lucky enough to own a winning horse.

As regards flat racing, the most common practice is to buy a yearling from one of the principal Autumn bloodstock sales (Newmarket or Doncaster). The average price for a reasonably well-bred yearling would probably be in the region of four or five thousand guineas. (Horses are always bid for in guineas; so much for decimalisation!). In addition to this price, there is a 5 per cent commission payable to an agent, if one has been employed. Four or five thousand guineas is, of course, at the lower end of the price scale. Exceptionally well-bred yearlings have fetched as much as 200,000 guineas.

In addition to the purchase price, it is as well to bear in mind that buying a yearling will result in further training and stabling costs, until such time as it is ready to race. Indeed, until the horse has raced, no one can have any idea of its racing temperament or of its true racing potential. Some of the very best bred horses have proved to be dismal failures on the racecourse; it's all very much of a gamble.

On the other hand, it is possible to buy an already trained two- or three-year old. Again, this could prove to be a somewhat hazardous undertaking and expert advice is absolutely essential. The first question to be asked is why the horse is being sold at all. A careful study of 'Horse for Sale' advertisements is a most instructive exercise and it soon becomes possible to read 'between the lines'. It is doubtful whether a bad horse has ever been advertised for sale, and many 'Horse for Sale' notices would qualify as major works of fiction. (The horse seller is both inventive and plausible). However, it is always just possible to pick up a good horse at a reasonable price and find that you have a real winner.

This is all part of the fascination of racing.

National Hunt horses are better bought when they have had some racing experience. Here again, a trainer or a bloodstock agent should be consulted. For an average to good horse, a price in the region of 3,000 guineas and upwards would be reasonable, although many people have had a lot of fun with National Hunt horses bought for very much less. It all depends upon what you can afford and where your interest lies.

While on the subject of National Hunt horses, it would be as well to mention that the prize money as compared with flat racing, for all but a few races, is absolutely pathetic. Very few owners of winning National Hunt horses can even manage to cover their costs. By and large, however, the whole atmosphere of National Hunt racing seems to be a much more sporting affair than the Flat racing scene, with people owning horses for the fun of it and treating it as an enjoyable hobby rather than as a business proposition.

Having bought a racehorse, the next thing a new owner should do is to get it insured. The premiums will, of course, depend upon the value of the animal and, here again, it is as well for a newcomer to ownership to take the best advice available.

REGISTRATION

If the horse has not already got a name, it will be necessary for the owner to choose one. The great tradition of naming horses has always been to incorporate or reflect the names of the sire or dam, e.g., Nijinsky: by Northern Dancer out of Flaming Page. But this is really a matter for the owner to decide. Names have to be registered with Weatherbys. See page 203 for full details. It is well worth while giving careful thought to the naming of a racehorse in order to avoid, in the first flush of enthusiasm, giving it a stupid name which neither the owner nor the horse will ever live down.

In order to race a horse, it is necessary to register with Weatherbys as an owner. Since March 1971, all owners have had to be registered. See page 204 for full details.

In addition to registering as an owner and registering a horse's name, it is also necessary to register the owner's racing colours. Although a new owner may know exactly what he or she wants, it is really a question of what is available since a great many other owners are already registered and have thus laid claim to certain colour combinations. See page 204 for full details. Registration costs about £2.50 and a set of racing colours costs in the region of £30.

OWNERS' ACCOUNTS

Another important point to remember is that it is a good idea for the new owner to open an account with Weatherbys in respect of fees and payments in connection with the horse. Weatherbys' Accounts Department handles over one million individual business transactions each year. See page 206, for full details.

COSTS INVOLVED

Having become a fully-fledged owner, with a fully insured and named horse, with racing colours registered, the next thing to consider is the sort of costs which will be payable. In the first place, training fees are likely to be in the region of £30 to £45 per week. Then there are jockeys' fees. For Flat racing, these are £14 per race; for National Hunt £17.25 per race. An additional £2 is payable for insurance. Entry and declaration fees are another item to take into account. These vary according to the amount of the prize money available for a particular race. They can run into hundreds of pounds, but for an ordinary race valued at, say, £600, the entry fee will be £3, with a declaration fee of £8: (entry fees eighteen days in advance; declaration fee payable when the horse is definitely declared to run at the four-day declaration stage).

Travelling expenses are also involved covering the transport of horses to and from race meetings. However, there is a subsidy scheme in operation for horses being transported long distances.

If an owner is lucky enough to win a race, he or she receives approximately 50% of the prize after all expenses have been paid. It is usual to give the stable lads a present, by way of showing appreciation for all the work they have put in in looking after the horse. It is also quite usual for a winning owner to 'push the boat out' by buying a bottle or two after the race.

The placing of a racehorse – i.e. deciding when and where it is to run – is a matter requiring great experience. Most owners tend to over-estimate their horse's potential, and would do well to remember the maxim of the great Admiral Rous: 'Keep yourself in the best company and your horses in the worst.'

There is little point in a new owner wishing to run his horse in the Champion Hurdle when his trainer knows very well that, by careful placing and a careful training schedule, it might pick up a decent hurdle race or two at somewhere like Folkestone or Devon and Exeter. Until an owner has sufficient experience of such matters, it is much better to take the trainer's advice – after all, that's what he is paid for.

PARTNERSHIPS

In order to meet the costs of owning a racehorse, it is not unusual for 2–4 people to form a partnership and thus to share the initial costs, training fees and other expenses involved in racehorse owning. All too often it is not the initial outlay of buying the horse which is the difficulty, but the meeting of the regular bills for training fees, veterinary bills, etc. Partnerships, however, can be tricky since both partners, in conjunction with, and on the advice of the trainer, have to agree on such matters as to which races to enter their horse, when and where it is to run, which jockey to put up, and so on. Before entering into such a partnership, therefore, it is wise to ensure (a) that the financial side is taken care of, and (b) that both partners are basically in agreement as to the way in which the horse's racing career is to develop. All too often there are reports in the sporting press that such and such a partnership has been dissolved. The reasons given, if any, are usually practical ones, but there is no doubt that on many occasions a clash of personalities has led to the winding-up of the partnership.

Perhaps before embarking upon such a venture it is as well to remember that old Yorkshire saying, to the effect that 'all folk are queer except thee and me, and I'm not so sure about thee.'

SYNDICATES

The ultimate in democratic racehorse owning is the syndicate – a system of multi-ownership, which was first given the go-ahead by the Racing Authorities in 1967. Under this system a number of people (*see* Jockey Club Rule No. 46) can form a syndicate in order to own a racehorse, sharing all expenses equally. In this way it is possible for people to enjoy the thrill of owning a racehorse, and seeing it race, at a comparatively small cost. But syndicates do have their drawbacks.

For example, if it is difficult for two people to agree in a partnership, how much more difficult when a syndicate consists of eight, ten or twelve persons (the present limit is twelve). Decisions do have to be taken where racehorse owning is concerned, and it is difficult for any one member of a syndicate to feel that he or she has sufficient power to take such decisions.

Of course, four members of the syndicate are now required to be registered as the owners but this, basically, does not give them any more say than their partners (always assuming that they all have equal shares). All too often the burden is thrown back onto the trainer. Many a trainer must have cursed the day he became involved with a syndicate, having been driven nearly mad by a succession of telephone calls and/or visits from each of the horse's 'owners' – each of them either wishing for information or trying to give advice to the trainer.

Again, cliques can form within the syndicate, with two or three people trying to run the whole show. This can lead to bad feeling and cause tremendous problems. But whatever the drawbacks, it is still a great feeling to be, in however small a way, a part of the Turf and to see one's horse run in the syndicate's colours.

Occasionally (and usually in strict rotation) it is possible for a member or members of the syndicate to stand in the paddock before the race and to watch the horse being led round, in company with the trainer and the jockey. The greatest thrill of all, of course, would be to lead your horse in as a winner.

One word of warning if you do decide to join a syndicate – owners are allowed a number of free admission tickets to the racecourse where their horse is running. If it should be your day to go along as representative owner, do make sure that the trainer has made clear arrangements concerning these tickets at the entrance gate. There are few more embarrassing experiences than having to stand at the entrance to a racecourse trying to convince some hard-faced (though usually icily polite) racecourse official that you really are part-owner and that you have the right to collect the admission ticket.

As regards becoming a member of a syndicate, this requires some thought. In the early days of syndication, and before the Jockey Club saw fit to tighten up the rules (in 1973) there was always the possibility of 'being taken for a ride'. This possibility is always with us, of course, but less so today than prior to 1973. All too often in those early days of syndication, horses were bought very cheaply and were then offered for sale in ten or twelve shares, expenses being apportioned in the same number of shares. Thus, groups of inexperienced enthusiasts were being made to pay well over the market price for a horse which had virtually no chance of winning a race or even of being placed. As ever, the unscrupulous few made things bad for the honest majority. So much so that when the Jockey Club did amend its Rules in order to ensure fair play in syndicates, many an honest bloodstock dealer suffered as the result of loss of business. (No person may be a member of or have an interest in more than twelve syndicates).

Shares in horses are to be found advertised in the sporting press: i.e., '$\frac{1}{4}$ shares in 3-year old, £175 per share, £34 per month expenses', and it is possible to become a member of a syndicate through a friend or through knowing a trainer.

A good way to join a syndicate is through the Racegoers' Club. This excellent organisation provides its members with a number of opportunities to join syndicates. In the Club's newsletter of Spring 1976, for example, there are three two-year-olds being offered to members – one at £400 per 12th-share, another at £382 per 12th-share, and a third at £327 per 12th-share (these prices to include all estimated expenses for the year 1976 of £200 per share). Anyone wishing to join a syndicate could do a lot worse than to write to the Secretary of the Racegoers' Club for full details of membership and syndication opportunities. (*See also* chapter on the Racegoers' Club.)

One final word. Whether you own your own racehorse or are a member of a partnership or syndicate, there is one hazard which must be mentioned. Friends! For some strange reason, anyone who knows that you own or have a part share in a racehorse will (a) imagine that this gives you some special inside knowledge or information as regards the selection of winners; (b) always back your horse, assuming that because he or she knows you they are bound to win money, and woe betide you when the horse does not win; (c) offer advice and criticism whenever you meet. You have been warned!!

THE RACEHORSE OWNERS' ASSOCIATION

It seems almost unbelievable that until comparatively recently racehorse owners, who after all supply the basic material upon which the whole racing industry is based, should have had little or no say in the government of racing. Then, in 1945, the Racehorse Owners' Association was formed. At first, this organisation was frowned upon by the Racing Authorities, but today it is well-established, with its offices at 42 Portman Square – the headquarters of the Jockey Club in London.

The objects of the R.O.A. are to encourage and ensure co-operative effort in all matters of interest to racehorse owners, to collaborate with and assist the Jockey Club (and the Levy Board) in their control of the sport; to obtain the views of owners concerning racing, to represent their views to the appropriate bodies, and also to circulate these views and other items of importance or interest to its members.

The R.O.A. now has some 2,950 members who, between them, are involved with half the total number of horses in training. The Association provides owner-members with regular information through its magazine *The Racehorse Owner*. Anyone who is fortunate enough to own a racehorse, or who is about to become an owner, would do well to consider joining the R.O.A. and thus be sure of representation where the future of racehorse ownership is concerned.

SOME CELEBRATED OWNERS

LORD GLASGOW (1792–1869)
'No one is unlucky who has an income of £150,000 a year'
                                                    (Lord Glasgow)

One of the least successful and the most eccentric owner-breeders in the history of racing was the 5th Earl of Glasgow. He was a Scottish peer, eccentric in dress and manner and famous for his short temper.

As a young man he served in the Navy, reaching the rank of Lieutenant-Commander. He was said to suffer from chronic neuralgia, as the result of a fall whilst he was in the Service. A memorable eccentric, Lord Glasgow once set fire to the bed of a servant who had forgotten to bring him his whisky night cap. On another occasion, he threw a waiter through an inn window and then requested the landlord to 'put him on the bill'.

Lord Glasgow was elected to the Jockey Club in 1839. He had a reputation for honesty, and Admiral Rous once said of him: 'I never met a man whose sole object was the improvement of horses except Lord Glasgow and the late Duke of Portland.'

Lord Glasgow supported racing for fifty years from 1819, with a singular lack of success, and bred any number of bad horses. He refused to name his horses and when required to do so, called them such things as, 'He hasn't got a name'; 'Give him a name'; 'He doesn't deserve a name'. He was also a terror to his trainers and his jockeys.

Lord Glasgow did have one good horse, however. This was Colonel Peel (named after a friend) which won the Two Thousand Guineas in 1864, but he could only come second to Blair Athol in the Derby and St Leger.

As a young man, Lord Glasgow would bet on anything. He once completely deflated Lord George Bentinck by offering him a bet of £90,000 to £30,000 against his (Bentinck's) horse Caper, which was entered for the Derby.

When he died, Lord Glasgow left his horses to be divided between two friends, none to be sold, and those not fit to race to be shot to prevent them falling into the hands of people who might ill-treat them.

Awkward to the last, Lord Glasgow also left a legacy to a certain Colonel Forester, whom he had regularly black-balled for membership of the Jockey Club.

THE 4TH MARQUIS OF HASTINGS (1841–1868)

Henry Charles Plantagenet Hastings, fourth and last Marquis of Hastings, is without doubt one of the saddest figures in the history of the Turf. Weak and foolish, with not the slightest sense of the value of money, he managed to lose his entire fortune in just six years.

Hastings began to take an interest in racing from the time of achieving his majority in 1862, when he was elected a member of the Jockey Club (he was also, incidentally, Master of the famous Quorn Hunt, but he was reputed to be neither a horseman nor a sportsman and as a Master was a complete failure).

His first horse was a moderate animal named Consternation. By 1865 he had some fifty horses in training. In 1864 Hastings eloped with, and married, Lady Florence Paget, a few days before she was to have been married to another keen racehorse owner, Henry Chaplin. Ironically enough, it was Chaplin's colt, Hermit, which was later to bring about Hastings' downfall.

1866 was a successful year as far as Harry Hastings' racing activities were concerned. He won the One Thousand Guineas with Repulse, the Cesarewitch with Lecturer (on which he won £70,000), and another of his horses, The Duke, won eleven races. The trouble was, however, that Hastings was a reckless gambler, often betting as much as £10,000 on a single race (in the days when the pound really was worth something). He also bet and regularly lost large sums of money playing cards and dice.

It was the Derby of 1867 which brought about his ruin. Hearing that Henry Chaplin's horse, Hermit, was favourite for the Derby, Hastings began to plunge so heavily that he soon stood to lose a fortune if the horse won. Hermit did not run in the Two Thousand Guineas that year, which was won by Vauban, which was later made favourite for the Derby. Then, prior to the Derby, Hermit broke a blood vessel, and its price drifted to 100 to 1. If Hastings had only thought to hedge his bets by having a substantial sum on the horse at this price, he could have saved himself. To everyone's surprise, and no doubt to Chaplin's delight, Hermit not only ran in the Derby of 1867, but also won it. In something like two and a half minutes, Hastings had lost £120,000.

In order to recover his losses, Hastings ran his brilliant filly, Lady Elizabeth, backing her heavily each time she ran. Lady Elizabeth had proved to be something of a banker for him since she won twelve times in thirteen races. By the autumn of that year (1867) the filly was badly in need of a rest. Hastings ran her in the Middle Park Stakes, which she failed to win, and he lost £40,000. Then, only two days later, he ran the filly in a match and, although she won, she was virtually ruined.

By 1868 Hastings (his health broken, and his fortune dissipated) was entirely at the mercy of the notorious moneylender, Henry Padwick. (Hastings is thought to have been the model for R. S. Surtees' character, Sir Harry Scattercash in *Mr Sponge's Sporting Tour*, where he is described as 'a young man with a strong tendency to delirium tremens; that, and consumption appeared to be running a match for his person'). It is thought that Hastings might have won the Derby in 1868 with his horse, The Earl, but, on Padwick's orders he was compelled to withdraw it from the race. Once again he trotted out the ill-used Lady Elizabeth, which was trained by John Day at Danebury. The filly started favourite, but came nowhere. However, Hastings, at his wits' end, insisted that she should run in the Oaks. For this piece of cruelty, he was heartily booed by the Epsom crowd.

The great Admiral Rous wrote to *The Times* concerning the running of the filly. He was threatened with a libel action by the trainer, the matter finally being settled out of court.

Hastings resigned from the Jockey Club, and died a few months later – at the age of twenty-six. Shortly before his death, he is reported to have said: 'Hermit's Derby broke my heart. I didn't show it, did I?'

ROBERT STANDISH SIEVIER (1860–1939)

Sievier was, by his own admission, born in a hansom cab. At the age of seventeen he was in South Africa, fighting in the Kaffir war. Two years later he returned to England, where he immediately embarked on a career as an actor.

Soon afterwards he began to take an interest in racing. As the result of information supplied to him by a pretty young barmaid, a girl friend of Mr Gretton, the owner of Isonomy, Sievier borrowed some money from an aunt. When Isonomy won the Manchester Cup, Sievier, a 30-shilling a week bit-player, found himself in possession of £3,000. But Sievier was a born gambler, and within a very short time he had not only lost the whole £3,000 but was also considerably in debt.

He then turned his attention to bookmaking. He was successful in this, winning another small fortune – which he promptly lost again. Sievier's next venture was to visit Australia where he set up as a bookmaker.

At that time Australian course bookmakers would only accept doubles, and winning bets were not paid until a settling day. Sievier, to the delight of the Australian racegoers, introduced the English system of betting and paying out after each race. Although he was popular with the racegoers, Sievier was far from popular with the bookmakers. Many threats were made against him, but none of them were actually carried out. When he returned to England he was a very rich man indeed.

By 1902 Bob Sievier had become well-known, even notorious, in racing circles. He had also become the owner of the great horse, Sceptre, for which he paid the then record price of 10,000 guineas. Sceptre, which Sievier trained himself, was one of the greatest mares in the history of the turf. In all, she ran twenty-five times, winning thirteen of her races, including every Classic except the Derby. See page 41.

In 1904 Sievier published his own newspaper, *The Winning Post*, which was in effect a scandal sheet and involved him in a number of court actions.

When Sievier died in 1939 he was virtually penniless. During his lifetime he had made several fortunes, but had managed to lose the lot by his extravagant life-style and his enormous gambles.

H.H. THE AGA KHAN (1877–1957)

Although famous as a racehorse owner in India, His Highness Sir Aga Mohammed Khan, spiritual leader of millions of Ismaili Muslims, did not begin racing in England until 1921. A multi-millionaire, he was persuaded to start his European operation by Colonel Hall Walker (later Lord Wavertree). Such was the scale and the success of his racing and breeding interprises that within three years he was the top owner in both England and France.

A popular figure on the English racing scene, the Aga Khan soon became one of the most important owners in the country, and his influence in racehorse breeding was tremendous. The Aga Khan's yearlings were bought for him by the Hon. George Lambton and, because money was no object where His Highness was concerned, he bought the best.

At first the Aga Khan's horses were trained by R. C. Dawson at Whatcombe. Then, after a quarrel with Dawson, Frank Butters became the Aga Khan's trainer in 1931. In 1949 he was replaced by Marcus Marsh. All of these trainers served the Aga Khan well, so much so that his record of Classic wins was as follows:–

The Oaks – twice; the Two Thousand Guineas – twice; the One Thousand Guineas – once; the St Leger – six times; and, incredibly, the Derby – five times! With a record like that, it is hardly surprising that the Aga Khan's colours (chocolate and green hoops) soon became the best-known on the racecourses of Great Britain.

But the Aga Khan's racing or, rather, his breeding and dealing activities were to make him extremely unpopular in some quarters and, indeed, were eventually to bring about the decline of his own stud farms. For although he was a multi-millionaire, the Aga Khan, it seems, could never resist a good offer. With almost frightening regularity, he began to sell his best stallions (some of the best in the world) to America. (All of the Aga Khan's winners went to stud at the end of their three-year old careers.)

When it was first announced that he was to sell Blenheim (the 1930 Derby winner and sire of the 1936 Derby winner, Mahmoud) to America, Lord Rosebery, a firm believer in keeping British bloodstock in England, called an extraordinary meeting of the Thoroughbred Breeders' Association. But nothing, it seems, could stop the Aga Khan's passion for dealing. He sold the Derby winner, Blenheim, for £45,000; Mahmoud for £21,000; Bahram for £40,000, all to America – a tremendous loss to British bloodstock.

The Aga Khan's Hindustan, which was sold to Japan in 1955, was virtually the beginning of racing in Japan. By 1971 the Japanese had imported seven Derby winners.

Small wonder that in the 1930s the Aga Khan's dealing activities offended the patriotic Lord Rosebery, who even went so far as to oppose the Aga Khan's membership of the Jockey Club. However, he was made an Honorary Member.

During the Second World War, the Aga Khan, having disposed of most of his bloodstock interests, spent the war years in Switzerland. After the war he returned to the British racing scene with all his usual flair, and was top owner from 1946 to 1949 (inclusive) and then again in 1952, the year in which he also won the Derby with Tulyar (later sold to Ireland for a quarter of a million pounds).

During this period, the Aga Khan again clashed with Lord Rosebery. In the first instance, he wrote to *The Times* complaining about the fact that too much British bloodstock was going to America. Here he was taken to task by Lord Rosebery, who quite rightly pointed out that the Aga Khan himself was one of the major offenders, having sold at that time no less than four Derby winners to America. Rosebery also pointed out that the Aga Khan, having removed his stud to France, for economic reasons, could hardly be of much benefit to British racing.

In 1956 the Aga Khan again wrote to *The Times*, suggesting that a Tote monopoly would be of benefit to British racing. As he pointed out, the whole of the racing industry, as carried out in Great Britain, seemed to be solely for the benefit of the bookmakers. Rosebery disagreed with him, saying that he was against monopolies and suggesting that a lightening of taxation was the answer to the problem.

(Perhaps, given the present plight of British racing, both men were right. A lightening of taxation (still much needed) and a properly organised Tote monopoly for off-course betting could have been of great benefit to the British racing industry.)

Towards the end of his life, the Aga Khan gradually began to dispose of his bloodstock interests in Europe, his stud farms having started to decline, as a direct result of his having sold his best stallions abroad.

6TH EARL OF ROSEBERY (1882–1974)

It is all too often forgotten by those who see fit to criticise the Jockey Club as being old-fashioned and its members as being out-of-date old fogies that, without the time and initiative given by many of its members throughout the years, British racing might be in a very much worse state than it is today. Indeed, there might not be any bloodstock industry or racing in the country at all.

One such member of the Jockey Club was the 6th Earl of Rosebery, a famous owner and breeder of racehorses. Lord Rosebery was born in 1882, the son of the 5th Earl who was leader of the Liberal Party and Prime Minister of England in 1894/1895.

The 5th Earl was himself famous as an owner and breeder, having bred three Derby winners, one of which, Ladas, won the Derby while the Earl was in office (1894). This proved to be an immensely popular victory. (How difficult to imagine any of today's leading politicians actually owning a Derby winner!)

As a young man, Lord Dalmeny (a courtesy title as heir to the earldom) was a noted sportsman. He was a fine cricketer, and from 1904 to 1907 was captain of Surrey Cricket Club. He was also a noted polo player, and was reserve member of the English team.

Lord Dalmeny, a keen amateur rider, registered his colours under both Jockey Club and National Hunt Rules in 1905. He was also an enthusiastic rider to hounds and was at one time Master of the Whaddon Chase Foxhounds. During World War I he served as Military Secretary to Field-Marshal Lord Allenby.

It is interesting to note that during the 1914/18 war, when the whole future of racing was threatened, it was the 5th Earl who was one of the main advocates of keeping some racing going in order to preserve British bloodstock. During the Second World War, it was his son, the 6th Earl (the 5th Earl having died in 1929) who carried on the tradition and who fought tirelessly to ensure that racing should be kept alive during the war years, having the foresight to see that when the war was over there would be a great demand for British bloodstock throughout the world.

During the 1920s and 30s, Lord Rosebery established himself as an owner and breeder of racehorses. In 1931 he won the St Leger with Sandwich and, together with his trainer, Jack Jarvis (later Sir Jack Jarvis) he formed the Sandwich Stud, which was later to produce many Classic winners.

In 1924 Lord Rosebery was elected to the Jockey Club. He became a Steward in 1929 and a Senior Steward (an office which he was to hold twice) in 1931. In 1924 he was Chairman of Tattersalls' Committee, and in 1932 he became President of the Thoroughbred Breeders' Association, an office which he was to hold for many years.

Throughout his life. Lord Rosebery was a great champion of British bloodstock, and an advocate of the theory that the very best mares and stallions should be kept in Britain and not sold abroad. At one time he took the Aga Khan to task for having dared to sell his stallion, Blenheim, the winner of the 1930 Derby, to America.

Lord Rosebery's most famous horse was Blue Peter, trained for him by Jarvis. Early in 1939 Blue Peter won his first race as a 3-year-old – the Blue Riband Trial Stakes at Epsom. He then went on to win the Two Thousand Guineas by half a length. Then, ridden by Ephraim Smith, and carrying the famous Rosebery colours (primrose and rose – the family name being Primrose) Blue Peter won the 1939 Derby by four lengths.

Later he won the Eclipse Stakes at Sandown Park, and looked all set to win the St Leger, with the Triple Crown in sight. But war was declared and racing was temporarily abandoned.

During the war, Lord Rosebery acted as Regional Commissioner for Scotland. In 1944 he won the substitute Derby, run at Newmarket with Ocean Swell (sired by Blue Peter) which also won both the Ascot Gold Cup and the Jockey Club Cup.

It was once said of Lord Rosebery that if he had had to earn his own living he would have become a millionaire. He was an energetic and talented organiser and administrator, who might have followed in his father's footsteps and have a successful career in politics. But, according to one authority, it was his father (who apparently did not like him) who thwarted his political career. Thus it came about that he mainly devoted his energies to racing, becoming one of racing's great 'elder statesmen', fighting all the time on behalf of British racing and British bloodstock.

In World War II, he fought to keep racing going. Later he fought the Government over the taxation on bloodstock. As President of the T.B.A., he fought to maintain the supremacy of British bloodstock.

As a Steward of the Jockey Club, the Earl served on committees concerned with such aspects of racing as the identification of horses, in order to prevent 'ringing' (i.e., one horse being run in place of another but under the same name), or how to prevent racehorses being doped. When a two-year old filly of his own was proved to have been doped (Snap in 1951) he immediately offered a reward of £1,000 and appealed to Scotland Yard to help stamp out this menace. This led to a great deal of publicity which, in turn, led to stricter security measures being introduced, with the result that the threat of doping was greatly reduced.

During the 1960s, Lord Rosebery had a run of bad luck where his horses were concerned. In 1964 his colt, Fighting Ship, broke down after winning the Henry II Stakes at Sandown Park. This was a blow since Fighting Ship was thought to have a good chance of winning the Ascot Gold Cup.

Then, in 1966, the Earl's colt, General Gordon (winner of the Chester Vase) broke a leg during his final Derby trial and had to be destroyed.

In 1969, however, Rosebery's luck changed for the better, when he managed to achieve one of his life-time ambitions by winning the Oaks with Sleeping Partner (a race his father had won in 1883 with Bonny Jean). It was in that same year, 1969, that Lord Rosebery was voted Racehorse Owner of the Year.

In 1974, the 6th Earl of Rosebery, who had devoted so much of his life to the improvement and furtherance of the cause of British racing, died at the age of ninety-two . . . on the very eve of the running of that year's Derby.

DOROTHY PAGET (1905–1960)

One of the greatest ever supporters of British racing, and without doubt one of the most eccentric owners in the history of the Turf was the Hon. Dorothy Paget. She was the younger daughter of Lord Queenborough and is said to have become a millionairess at the age of eleven.

Born in 1905, D.P., as she later became known, proved to be a difficult child and was expelled from no less than five girls' schools before her despairing parents sent her to finish her education in Paris where she settled down to some extent.

Fabulously wealthy (she was said to be receiving £250,000 per annum from investments) D.P. was inevitably courted by vast numbers of suitors but she showed no interest whatsoever in marriage or, for that matter, in men. Instead, she turned her attention to motor racing. She engaged the then famous racing driver, Sir Henry Birkin, to take charge of her £20,000 fleet of cars. This venture proved to be unsuccessful, however, and D.P. eventually lost interest in it. The fleet of cars was disbanded, but not before it had cost her somewhere in the region of £50,000.

Already a confirmed gambler, D.P. then turned her attention to horseracing and became one of the most famous owners and breeders of her time. She poured money into the sport, spending enormous sums on horses, which were good, bad and indifferent. Her racing outgoings were estimated to be in the region of £50,000 each season.

In 1936, for example, she paid the then record price of £15,000 for a yearling colt. Unlike her motor racing activities, however, D.P. did have one magnificent success where horseracing was concerned. She was the owner of the legendary Golden Miller, five times the winner of the Cheltenham Gold Cup and, in 1934, a Grand National winner. She also won a substitute Derby in 1943 with her horse, Straight Deal.

D.P.'s original trainer was Basil Briscoe, but the autocratic and unpredictable D.P. proved to be a difficult owner, to say the least. Briscoe was followed by a string of other trainers, including Fred Darling, Owen Anthony and Gordon Richards.

D.P. lived in a large house – Hermit's Wood at Chalfont St Giles – where she kept an army of female secretaries, each referred to by a different colour. They were busy, day and night, in typing, taking dictation, telephoning, organising her racing outings, and often running pointless messages.

Invariably dressed in unbecoming tweeds with sensible shoes and without make-up, Dorothy Paget became a familiar figure on the British racing scene. Her betting became notorious, and on one occasion she is reported to have bet £160,000 on a single race.

When Dorothy Paget died, at the age of fifty-four, her estate was valued at £3,803,380.

CHAPTER FOUR

Racehorse Training

'My horses understand me tolerably well; I converse with them at least
four hours every day.'

(Jonathan Swift, 1667–1745)

I n the early days of racing there was no such thing as the professional
or public racehorse trainer as we know him today. For the most part,
owners trained their own horses, assisted by stable grooms. Then, as
racing began to develop, competition became keener and the training of
racehorses became a specialised business. Gradually the stable grooms
assumed the overall responsibility for training horses and then, in the
early nineteenth century, the first public trainers appeared upon the
scene.

Many of the training methods used in the very first days of racing seem
today to be absolutely barbarous, and one wonders just how many good
horses were ruined as the result of such methods. One early remedy for a
difficult horse suggests that 'if a horse does not stand still or hesitates,
then rate him with a terrible voice and beat him with a good stick upon
the head between the ears'. Another method used with difficult horses
was – 'A catte tied under a horse's belly is a good specific against any
devilish masteries on the part of the horse'. These are, of course, rare
examples but, generally speaking, horses were purged, overworked,
sweated, over-galloped, and virtually run into the ground by the severe
training method of the times. Indeed, it is a wonder that any of them ever
got to the starting post at all, and it is hardly surprising that many early
sporting prints show racehorses looking as thin as greyhounds.

Gradually training methods improved as the first of the really expert trainers began to appear. Then, at the turn of the nineteenth century, during what has become known as the 'American invasion', new methods were introduced from across the Atlantic, when it was seen that the American horses were better fed, better shod, better trained and better housed in well-ventilated stables than their British counterparts. Today, however, British trainers and training methods are second to none.

TRAINING TODAY

Basically, the racehorse trainer's job is, by careful preparation, to bring a horse to the peak of its physical fitness and racing ability at a particular time, i.e., when it is due to race. In order to do this a trainer requires a high degree of experience, skill and patience, since horses are not machines (although punters often tend to forget this). Every horse requires individual attention as regards its feeding and the amount of work required to bring it to the peak of its racing fitness.

The profession of racehorse trainer is a curious one, taking in other people's horses to train for racing, trying to make a profit on the overall keep of the horses in his stable, and hoping for a share of any winning prize money that his horses collect.

Trainers are a varied and individualistic breed – each has his own methods and each tends to be a law unto himself. Prior to the Second World War, most trainers were employed by the very rich (a fast disappearing breed), labour costs were low, and the weekly cost of keeping a horse in training (£5 or £6) seems today to be a ridiculous figure. Indeed, if one considers the rate of price increases during the past forty years, today's average weekly figure, of between £30 and £45, for training a horse is still remarkably good value.

Since the war, however, things have changed drastically, and most trainers are now self-employed/freelancers, training for a great variety of owners, and very much at the mercy of the fluctuating financial conditions of the times. Labour costs have risen dramatically in recent years (and a good thing too, for many of the people who worked in racing stables were often exploited). Even so, it might have been better for racing if we had been spared the scenes which took place at Newmarket during Guineas week in 1975, when stable lads on strike attempted to prevent the running of the One Thousand Guineas race by blocking the course.

Whatever sympathy the racing public may have had for the lads' cause was quickly dispelled when jockey Willie Carson was pulled off his horse. The result was that hundreds of racegoers came down from the stands and a pitched battle took place prior to the running of the race. There was more trouble on the following day, when some 'genuis' decided to rip up the course with a bulldozer, in an unsuccessful attempt to stop the running of the Two Thousand Guineas.

Happily this dispute has now been resolved, but it did racing's image no good at all, and many a trainer must have been left with doubts as to the future of labour relations within the racing industry.

Of course, it is not only labour costs which have risen. During recent years there have been increases all across the board. Feed costs have rocketed, and veterinary charges, farrier charges, transport costs, etc., have all increased, and are continuing to do so, all of which makes it extremely difficult for the smaller trainer to survive. Indeed, during the past few years many have given up altogether.

As racing becomes more of an industry, and perhaps less of a sport, so the trainer is becoming more of a businessman. In addition to the care and attention he is required to give to the horses, he is also required to cope with the ever-increasing amount of business detail connected with the training and racing of horses.

For the very large training establishments with, say, over one hundred horses in training and strings of successes to their credit, things are perhaps easier. Success breeds success, and the few rich owners who do remain tend to gravitate towards the larger, more successful stables. Such a concern would usually have a racing manager to take care of the business side of things, leaving the trainer more or less free to concentrate on his horses. But for the smaller training establishment things are very different. The small trainer is required to be not only an expert where horses are concerned, but also a public relations man, something of a vet, something of a labour relations expert, something of an accountant, and God knows what else.

In the first place, he is an employer of labour – a head lad, a travelling head lad if he is lucky, stable lads and girls, and apprentices – all of whom have to be considered and paid. As with any other employer, the trainer is responsible for National Health Insurance stamps and P.A.Y.E.

OWNERS

In the days of the private trainer, i.e., the man who was employed to train for one or two owners, life was a great deal easier for the trainer. However, for the most part, those days have gone and now owners come from all walks of life, owning racehorses for many different reasons, and it is part of the trainer's job to keep his owners happy.

Owners, like the rest of us, are good, bad and indifferent. Some are knowledgeable about horses and racing; others less so. Some pay their bills promptly; others have to be chased. Some are content to leave the training and entry programme almost entirely to the trainer; others want to run things in their own way. Some are difficult; some are not. Some are never off the telephone; others don't bother. One trainer is supposed to have said that training horses was an easy business, but that training owners was another thing altogether.

Of course, there are and always have been difficult and autocratic trainers who regard owners as interfering bores. But is is the owner who foots the bill, and the sensible trainer will have established a good working relationship with his owners. It is in his interest, after all, that their horses stay in his yard, and it is in the owner's interest that his horses are cared for and trained as well as possible.

STABLE ROUTINE

A training stable routine is more or less as follows: early every morning the first string – i.e. those horses which are shortly due to race – will be ridden out for exercise. The trainer will no doubt be on the gallops to evaluate the general condition and fitness of his horses. Each horse will have had a training programme prepared for it, according to its individual requirements. Some horses require a great deal of work to bring them to racing fitness, others require much less, and the trainer will want to see for himself exactly how his horses are developing. Later in the morning, the second string will be exercised, and the rest of the day will be taken up with mucking-out, grooming, cleaning tack (each lad usually 'doing' and being responsible for two horses). Yearlings may have to be broken in, and taught to be ridden. Two-year olds will have to be schooled or hurdlers or jumpers schooled over fences. Then again, part of the day may be taken up with a visit from the vet or the farrier.

RACING

If it is a racing day, then the head lad will take over the responsibility for the yard while the trainer is at the races. A trustworthy and experienced head lad is essential to a trainer, both to maintain staff discipline and to take over the responsibility for the thousands of pounds' worth of horses kept in the yard during the trainer's absence. A great many head lads go on to become trainers in their own right. Assuming also that a trainer has a travelling head lad, the horses due to race that day will have already set off to the racecourse either early that morning or, if the course is a great distance away, the night before. However, most trainers prefer their horses to travel on the day of the race if possible.

A first-class travelling head lad is invaluable to a trainer. In the first place, he is responsible for getting the horses safely to the racecourse and for ensuring that they travel well. In cases where the trainer is unable to attend the meeting, or perhaps has runners at more than one meeting, the travelling head lad can declare horses on production of his Employee's Identity Card.

For most of us a day at the races is a pleasant day out, away from our normal routine. For the trainer it is often a hard and anxious day's work. Arriving at the racecourse, he will check that his horses have travelled well, supervise the saddling-up, ensure that the jockey has arrived, declare his horses (trainers or their representatives are required to make a formal declaration not less than forty-five minutes before each race, giving the name of the jockey and the weight at which he or she will ride). The rest of the trainer's time will be spent with his owners, discussing their horses' prospects, visiting the parade ring with them, giving the jockey any instructions he might need. During the race the trainer will watch how his horse runs and there is always the danger of something going wrong. His horse may be involved in an accident, have a fall, or may be involved in an objection or a Steward's Enquiry, resulting in the trainer having to appear before the Stewards of the meeting.

If a horse loses or does badly, the trainer will have to reassure his disgruntled owners. If it wins, especially if it is a famous horse, the trainer may be called upon to answer the questions put to him by racing reporters as to its running, its future prospects, etc. If the horse wins a Classic or a very valuable race, the trainer may even be faced with the horrors of a television interview before going off to the bar to celebrate with his triumphant owner.

Should the trainer have another runner at the same meeting, however, any celebrating will have to be cut short while the whole process is repeated. After the day's racing, the horses will be boxed and driven back to the yard.

The trainer, on returning to the yard, may have to deal with any problems which may have arisen during his absence, and will no doubt do a routine round of the stables before his working day is properly over. The chances are, however, that he will spend a greater part of the evening on the telephone, either discussing the day's running with the owners, discussing future prospects with other owners, booking jockeys for a forthcoming race meeting, or simply answering the questions of owners who have rung up to enquire after their horse's health.

ENTRIES AND DECLARATIONS

On non-racing days or, more usually, on Sundays (a day when most owners prefer to visit stables) the trainer will usually cope with his entries. This is perhaps the most difficult part of a trainer's job, and calls for a great degree of skill and experience. The placing of his horses in advance in races where they will have the best possible chance of winning or being placed is far from being an easy task, and many factors have to be taken into account. He has to consider which distance will suit the horse, which racecourse will suit the horse (some horses become course specialists), whether a horse is qualified for a certain race, which jockey is likely to be available, whether to enter a horse for more than one race, at different meetings, on a particular day, whether the course will suit the owner if he wishes to see his horse race.

Some trainers specialise in winning certain races, and the watchful punter will often keep a look-out for the horses of a trainer who is known to win a particular race year after year. Again, if a trainer has entered a horse for more than one meeting on the same day and has left his horse in all of them at the four-day declaration stage, then the trainer will most certainly have had his ear to the ground as to the likely opposition his horse will have to meet. Since most trainers know the form book backwards, the chances are that the horse will eventually run in that race which the trainer thinks he has the most chance of winning (another pointer which the experienced punter often looks for).

Of course, the really first-class horses, aimed at winning a Classic or a really valuable race, will have had a long-term training programme worked out for them, with a series of races mapped out as 'stepping stones' to the main objectives. These horses will be brought to the peak of their racing fitness as each of their races occurs. But, for the more moderate horses, the task of entries is somewhat trickier, as they are usually entered for a great number of races and have to be in a state of preparation so that they can be brought to racing form as and when it is decided to run them.

Entries are made three weeks in advance. Once an entry for a horse has been accepted and a weight allocated and published in the *Racing Calendar*, together with its age, weight, name of owner and trainer, its connections (owner and trainer) must then decide whether or not they wish to run the horse. A horse must be declared to run at the four-day declaration stage – that is, by noon four days before the race is due to take place. The stable then has the right to cancel the declaration up to 11.00 a.m. on the day before the race. Failure to run the horse after the final declaration stage, without a sufficiently good reason being given (such as a vet's certificate) could result in the trainer being fined.

The most usual reason for late withdrawals being made is a sudden change in the state of the going. It must be particularly galling to a trainer who has travelled to a racecourse with his horse only to find that the going has altered to such an extent that it is not in his owner's interest to run the horse. To be fined for being at the mercy of changing weather conditions does seem a little hard, especially as it also means that all of the time spent in preparing the horse for the particular race has been wasted. (The fixed penalty is not normally imposed if the going has changed suddenly and could not have been reasonably anticipated.)

The job of the modern trainer is an arduous one, involving long hours, a great deal of travelling, plus the added responsibility for the safety and welfare of horses worth many thousands of pounds. It requires skill, knowledge, hard work, patience and optimism. Above all, in these days of high taxation and inflation – optimism! In fact, for most trainers nowadays a secretary is essential to cope with the ever-increasing amount of paper-work involved in the business of training.

In addition to rising staff costs, there are, of course, many other expenses to be taken into account. In the first place, in order to become a trainer, one must have a yard. If a prospective trainer is wealthy, he may buy an establishment. If not, he will have to rent one. The yard has to be furnished with all the necessary equipment and tack (saddles, bridles, rugs, etc.), all of which, at today's prices, involves a great deal of capital outlay. He will then have to collect a number of owners (since the dual licence was introduced a minimum of twelve is needed) before applying to the Jockey Club for a licence to train. This will involve an inspection of his premises, taking into account such matters as security, etc.

A trainer's licence is renewable each year. Having obtained a licence to 'set up shop', the trainer is then faced with other expenses. In addition to his capital outlay, there are a variety of other costs to be considered – stable staff, accommodation, heating, lighting, running repairs, the cost of foodstuffs for his animals, telephone charges. Trainers spend endless hours on the telephone, making declarations, booking jockeys, discussing prospects and entries with owners, arranging transport. One trainer recently estimated that his yearly telephone bill was in the region of £2,000. Vet's bills, farrier's fees, transport costs, and gallops' fees (subject to V.A.T. on 1st July, 1976) are all passed onto the owners, and trainers are now obliged to charge V.A.T. on their training bills, thus adding another 8 per cent to the unfortunate owner's bill. In the case of transport costs, however, there is a transport subsidy scheme in operation through the Levy Board, in respect of horses transported over 50 miles (single distance).

SOME EARLY TRAINERS

TREGONWELL FRAMPTON (1648–1728)
Although not a trainer in the accepted sense of the word, no article on training would be complete without a mention of William Tregonwell Frampton, who was the leading authority of his time on all matters appertaining to racing and training.

1. The Prince of Wales (Edward VII) leading Persimmon into the weighing enclosure at Epsom after the 1896 Derby.

2. Empery, ridden by Lester Piggott, wins the 1976 Derby. Relkino was second, and Oats was third.

3. The start of a flat race.

4. A hard-fought finish: the Cementation Handicap at Ascot, finally won by Malleny.

5. A typical steeplechase.

6. A typical hurdle race.

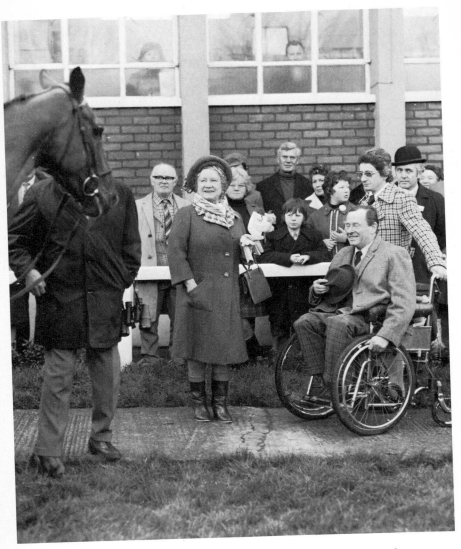

7. H.M. Queen Elizabeth the Queen Mother in the Windsor winning enclosure, with trainer Edward Courage. Her horse, Greystoke Pillar has just won the Langley Handicap Hurdle.

Frampton was born at Moreton in Dorset in 1648. He was the son of a country squire. A confirmed misogynist, his interest lay in racing, cockfighting, hawking and coursing. Frampton, who was both eccentric in manner and dress, and who was described as being of 'uncouth appearance', was an active and cunning racehorse owner, trainer, matchmaker, and a heavy gambler. He became the Royal trainer in 1688 and took up residence at Newmarket. During his lifetime he was 'keeper of the running horses' to four monarchs – King William III, Queen Anne, George I and George II.

Frampton's position would seem to have been that of a superior racing manager, although he was generally recognised as the arbiter in matters relating to racing and was, in fact, a sort of one-man Jockey Club.

Frampton was a shrewd matchmaker, and brought off many a racing coup. However, he did not always come off best. There was one occasion when he accepted a challenge from a Yorkshireman, Sir William Strickland, the owner of a horse named Merlin. Frampton agreed to race an unknown horse against Merlin, but before the actual match took place, a trial run was held between the two horses. This seems to have been the custom of the day, in order to evaluate the betting potential of the runners. On this occasion, Frampton ran his horse carrying a great deal of over-weight, as a result of which it was just beaten in the trial. Frampton and his associates, thinking that they were on to a good thing, immediately backed the Newmarket horse for all they were worth. Unfortunately for them, Sir William Strickland had arranged that his horse should also carry extra weight for the trial, and when the match was run, Merlin won easily. For once in his life, Frampton was completely taken in.

The match caused a great stir, and was even commemorated in verse:

Four and twenty Yorkshire knights
Came out of the North countree
And they came down to Newmarket
Frampton's horses for to see.

JOHN SCOTT (1827–1869)

Perhaps the first trainer of note – in the sense that we understand the term trainer – was John Scott, who was born at Chippenham, Wiltshire, in 1827. The son of a trainer, Scott started out as a jockey, but became too heavy and so turned to training, with a remarkable degree of success.

The best trainer of his day, Scott attracted the richest owners. These included the Marquess of Westminster, Lord Chesterfield and Lord Derby. At one time he is reported to have had over one-hundred horses in training. Scott's record of successes is impressive. In all, he won forty

Classic races, including sixteen St Legers, nine Oaks and six Derbys. Scott, who was known as the 'wizard of Whitewall', also trained Queen of Trumps, the first filly ever to win both the Oaks and the St Leger.

JOHN KENT

A notable contemporary of Scott was the southern trainer, John Kent, who trained for both the Duke of Richmond and Lord George Bentinck. Kent, a Newmarket man, was also the son of a trainer, and must have been a tremendous worker, for, in addition to having sixty horses in training, he also supervised a stud farm. It was Kent who was responsible for the implementation of Lord George Bentinck's improvements and innovations to Goodwood Racecourse – at one time employing over one hundred men to work on improving the gallops.

WILLIAM L'ANSON (d. 1881)

A contemporary of both Scott and Kent, William l'Anson was a Scotsman, who moved to Yorkshire in order to become a trainer. He is best remembered for having owned, bred and trained the great Blink Bonny which, in 1857, became the second filly in history to win the Derby and the Oaks. (The first was Sir Charles Bunbury's filly, Eleanor, in 1801.)

Blink Bonny was by Melbourne out of Queen Mary, a mare which originally cost only thirty guineas. Blink Bonny started favourite for the St Leger in 1857, but could only finish fourth to Imperieuse (which had finished fourth in the Oaks). The Stewards held an enquiry into Blink Bonny's running, and l'Anson was asked to explain her poor running. He had no explanation to give, but he could prove that the filly's losing of the race had cost him a great deal of money. Shortly afterwards, Blink Bonny ran in the Park Hill Stakes, which she won in a much faster time than the running of the 1857 St Leger (same course and distance). This led to a riot on the racecourse, and thereafter the Stewards ceased to announce the running times of races.

There is no doubt that the St Leger of that year was in some way 'fixed', and that Blink Bonny was robbed of the race, but nothing was ever proved.

In 1864 l'Anson had another great success when Blair Athol – one of Blink Bonny's three foals – won the Derby. L'Anson died in 1881. Before he did so, however, he founded the Blink Bonny Stud, in memory of his great filly.

THE DAYS OF DANEBURY

The Days of Danebury were perhaps the most unsavoury trainers of their times. Originally they trained for Lord George Bentinck who had invested a great deal of his own money in their Danebury stables. The break came, however, when old John Day wrote a letter to a friend, telling him to lay against a horse of Lord George's in a particular race as it had no chance of winning. At the same time, he wrote to Lord George telling him to back the horse. Unfortunately for Day, however, he put the letters into the wrong envelopes. Lord George Bentinck was certainly no angel when it came to racing and betting coups, but this was too much even for him, and he immediately removed his horses from Danebury and put them in the care of John Kent.

After this there was a bitter rivalry between the Days and Lord George, and they were always on the look-out for opportunities to do each other down. Throughout their long history as a training family, the Days seem always to have been mixed up in shady deals.

Among the owners they trained for was the notorious moneylender, Henry Padwick, who helped to ruin the 4th Marquis of Hastings, and it was Honest John who, when Hastings' fortunes were at their lowest ebb, failed to inform him that his brilliant filly, Lady Elizabeth, was broken down when she started favourite for the Derby of 1868.

Admiral Rous wrote to *The Times* about the filly's running, but John Day threatened to sue him, and the Admiral was forced to apologise. Public opinion at the time, however, was very much on the Admiral's side.

Honest John's sons were cast in the same mould as the old man. William Day was warned off for attempting to lame a horse which was thought to have a good chance in the Derby. The horse – John Gully's Old England – was in fact being trained by his father. John Day Junior was also warned off for giving false evidence before the Stewards in a case of bribery connected with the Derby of 1840. All in all, the Day family can hardly have been said to have been a credit to the Turf.

JOHN PORTER

The most successful trainer at the end of the nineteenth century was without doubt John Porter of Kingsclere. Porter, who originally came from Staffordshire, learned his business the hard way, working as a young man for a number of trainers, including Honest John Day, the notorious Danebury trainer.

In 1863 John Porter went to train for Sir Joseph Hawley, for whom he won the Derby in 1868 with Blue Gown. Sir Joseph Hawley was a great racing owner of his time. A member of the Jockey Club, he often clashed with Admiral Rous on matters of policy, especially concerning the running of two-year-olds.

Under Hawley's patronage, Porter went from strength to strength. In all, he trained over 1,000 winners. These included seven Derby and six

St Leger winners. Porter trained Ormonde and Flying Fox, both Triple Crown winners, for the Duke of Westminster, as well as the Triple Crown winner, Common, for Lord Alington.

Porter also trained for a time for Edward Albert, Prince of Wales, persuading him to buy one of the great mares of the time – Perdita II – dam of three great horses all by the unbeaten St Simon. These were Florizel II, Persimmon, which won the Derby in 1896, and the 1900 Triple Crown winner, Diamond Jubilee.

John Porter retired in 1905, but continued to take a keen interest in racing and was one of the founders of Newbury Racecourse.

MATTHEW DAWSON (1820–1897)

In complete contrast to the Days of Danebury, and once described as 'the straightest man that ever lived', was Matthew Dawson, the greatest trainer of his time.

Dawson was born in Scotland in 1820, one of seventeen children of George Dawson, also a trainer. Mat Dawson was an absolute autocrat where his training methods were concerned, never tolerating interference from an owner, and when one looks at his list of owners it is very impressive indeed.

During his sixty-year career, Dawson trained for the Duke of Newcastle, Lord Falmouth, Lord Lascelles, Lord Stamford, the Duke of Portland, Lord Rosebery, Lord Fitzwilliam, the Duke of St Albans, and many other of the richest and most powerful men in England at that time.

Dawson treated all men alike, from Duke to stable boy. He was apparently always extremely well-mannered, but would stand no nonsense from anybody and was, in consequence, greatly respected.

He trained at Heath House, Newmarket. Then, in 1885, he 'retired' to Melton House, Exning, but still continued to train for Lord Rosebery and Lord Fitzwilliam, until he died in 1897.

In all, Mat Dawson trained six Derby winners – Thormanby, Kingcraft, Silvio, Melton, Ladas, Sir Visto. He also trained the winners of five Oaks, five Two Thousand Guineas, three One Thousand Guineas, and six St Legers. It was Dawson also who trained the unbeaten St Simon, which won the Ascot Gold Cup in 1884 by 20 lengths, ridden by Fred Archer. Archer was Mat Dawson's star apprentice, and it was Dawson who described him as 'a tin-scraping young devil' – hence Archer's nickname the 'Tinman'.

Matthew Dawson seems to have earned the respect of all those who came into contact with him. One of his owners has written of him – 'His great and honourable career as a trainer must be thoroughly well known to every lover of the Turf. But perhaps only those who were personally acquainted with him knew the loyalty, kindness and geniality of his character. While fully aware of certain shady doings on the Turf, he never made use of them himself. One of the most generous men that ever lived, he was beloved and trusted by people of every class.'

THREE GREAT MODERN TRAINERS

CAPTAIN SIR CECIL BOYD ROCHFORT (b. 1887)

Cecil Boyd Rochfort, 'The Captain' as he later became known, was born in County Westmeath, in Ireland, in 1887. The son of a wealthy landowner, he was taught to ride at an early age.

Whilst at Eton, he became interested in horse racing, and later decided to make it his career. In 1906 he obtained the position of learner/assistant to the great Irish trainer, H. 'Atty' Persse, a famous amateur rider of his day, who was just starting to train horses in England.

C.B.R. remained with Persse until 1908, when he became assistant to Captain R. H. Dewhurst. Three years later, while still only twenty-one, C.B.R. was appointed Racing Manager to the multi-millionaire, Sir Ernest Cassel.

At this point World War I interrupted his career. During the war, C.B.R. served in the Scots Guards and was awarded the Croix de Guerre. In 1918 he returned to take up his position with Sir Ernest Cassel until, in 1921, following Sir Ernest's death, C.B.R. set up as a public trainer in his own right at Newmarket.

C.B.R., a dedicated professional, with a love of horses, a wide knowledge of breeding, and infinite patience, soon won the respect of the racing fraternity. Within a very short time he had successfully established himself as one of the foremost trainers of his day.

By 1937, when he first became leading trainer, he had built up a powerful and respected stable, with a first-class stable staff and sixty horses in training. His owners included Lord Derby, William Woodward (Chairman of the New York Jockey Club), Marshall Field III, a Chicago millionaire, Sir Humphrey de Trafford, and many others.

C.B.R. was to form strong ties with America through his American owners, making several trips there, often returning to England to implement aspects of American training methods which he had studied.

Following the death of W. H. Jarvis in 1942, C.B.R. was appointed trainer to King George VI, continuing to hold the Royal Appointment after the accession of Queen Elizabeth II, until he retired in 1968.

When Cecil Boyd Rochfort took up his appointment, the Royal racing fortunes were at a low ebb. C.B.R., however, brought about a revival, and during the nine seasons that he trained for King George VI, he produced fifty-seven winners. 1946 saw the first Royal Classic win for eighteen years, when Hypericum won the One Thousand Guineas.

Queen Elizabeth decided to continue to race on exactly the same lines as her father had done, and the home-bred horses from the Royal Stud were trained by C.B.R., whilst those horses leased by the Queen from the National Stud were trained by Noel Murless.

In 1952, C.B.R. became a Commander of the Royal Victorian Order (for personal services to the Sovereign). Appropriately enough, he received his Knighthood at Ascot on the first day of the Royal Meeting. By 1954 the Royal racing fortunes had improved to the extent that the Queen was leading owner for the year, while C.B.R. brought off the 'double' by being leading trainer.

During the sixteen years that Cecil Boyd Rochfort trained for the Queen, he produced 136 winners for her (prize money approximately £250,210), including Pall Mall – Two Thousand Guineas winner in 1958; Aureole – winner of the Coronation Cup at Epsom and the King George VI and Queen Elizabeth Stakes at Ascot, both in 1954; and Canisbay, winner of the Eclipse Stakes at Sandown Park in 1965.

In 1968, at the age of eighty-two, C.B.R. retired to Ireland. During his long and distinguished career, he had managed to win every major race in the Calendar. Perhaps the best horse he trained was Lady Zia Wernher's filly, Meld, winner of the 1955 One Thousand Guineas, The Oaks and St Leger. This St Leger was by way of being a milestone in Cecil Boyd Rochfort's career, since not only was it his fifth St Leger victory, but it also brought his winning owners' prize money to one million pounds!

During his career, Cecil Boyd Rochfort produced a total of 1,169 winners (winning prize money, not including place money, £1,651,514).

Leading Trainer:

1937	£61,012	1955	£74,423
1938	£51,359	1958	£84,186
1954	£65,325		

Classic Winners:

One Thousand Guineas	1933	Brown Betty
	1946	Hypericum
	1955	Meld
Two Thousand Guineas	1958	Pall Mall
The Derby	1959	Parthia
The Oaks	1944	Hycilla
	1955	Meld

St Leger

	1936	Boswell
	1941	Sun Castle
	1948	Black Tarquin
	1953	Premonition
	1955	Meld
	1958	Alcide

NOEL MURLESS (b.1910)

Charles Francis Noel Murless was born in Cheshire in 1910. His racing career started when he was attached to Frank Hartigan's stable, where he began riding under National Hunt Rules. Later he joined Frank's brother, Hubert, first at Penrith and then in Ireland.

Noel Murless first took out a Trainer's Licence in 1935. His stable at Hambleton, Yorkshire, proved so successful that he was later asked to take over from the famous Fred Darling at Beckhampton. Eventually he settled at Warren Place, Newmarket, the headquarters of racing, where he remained until the end of 1976.

At one time Noel Murless trained those horses leased by the Royal Family from the National Stud. His list of past and present owners was an impressive one and included H.M. the Queen, Lord Howard de Walden (the present Senior Steward of the Jockey Club); Mr. S. Joel, Lady Sassoon, Mr H. J. Joel, Prince Aly Khan, and many others.

If Noel Murless's list of owners was impressive, his list of winners and achievements in racing was even more so. He was nine times leading trainer on the Flat, and winner of eighteen English Classic races. His stable jockeys have included two of the greatest names in Flat racing – Gordon Richards and Lester Piggott.

A great lover of horses, who trained with patience and understanding, Noel Murless, now sixty-six years of age, retired at the end of the 1976 season after forty-one years as a top class trainer.

Leading Trainer:

1948	£66,542		1967	£256,899
1957	£116,898		1968	£141,508
1959	£145,727		1970	£199,524
1960	£118,327		1973	£132,984
1961	£95,972			

Classic Winners:

One Thousand Guineas	1948	Queenpot
	1959	Petite Etoile
	1967	Fleet

	1968	Caergwrle
	1971	Altesse Royale
	1973	Mysterious
Two Thousand Guineas	1957	Crepello
	1967	Royal Palace
The Derby	1957	Crepello
	1960	St Paddy
	1967	Royal Palace
The Oaks	1959	Petite Etoile
	1970	Lupe
	1971	Altesse Royale
	1973	Mysterious
St Leger	1949	Ridge Wood
	1960	St Paddy
	1961	Aurelius

FRED RIMELL (b.1913)

Thomas Frederick Rimell was born on June 24th, 1913. His father, Tom Rimell, was a successful trainer and trained Forbra, the 1932 Grand National winner.

Fred Rimell was apprenticed to his father and had his first ride on the Flat at the age of twelve. He rode his first winner, Rolie (owned and bred by his grandfather) at Chepstow, when he was thirteen. In all, Fred Rimell was to ride thirty-four winners on the Flat before weight problems forced him to turn his attention to National Hunt racing in 1931.

During his career as a jump jockey, he was to win the N.H. Jockeys' Championship four times (in 1938/39, 1939/40, 1944/45 and 1945/46). He rode in six Grand Nationals but, alas, only completed the course twice and never on the winner. In 1946, while riding a horse called Post Prince at Wincanton, Fred Rimell fell and broke his neck. Eight months later, riding Coloured Schoolboy in the 1947 Cheltenham Gold Cup, he fell again, breaking his neck for the second time. Fred Rimell decided to retire as a jockey and to set up as a trainer at Kinnersley in Worcestershire.

Like the great Fred Winter, Fred Rimell's riding experience and family background stood him in good stead and he achieved distinction as one of the foremost National Hunt trainers of his time. Fred Rimell has won the leading National Hunt trainer's title five times (1950/51; 1960/61; 1968/69, 1969/70 and 1975/76). To date, he has saddled well over 1,000 winners, including three Grand National winners – E.S.B., which went on to snatch the race from the unfortunate Devon Loch in 1956; Nicolaus Silver in 1961; and Gay Trip in 1970.

Fred Rimell has also trained two winners of the Welsh Grand National – Creeola II in 1957, and Glenn in 1968. He trained the Scottish Grand National winner, The Fossa, 1967; the Cheltenham Gold Cup winner, Woodland Venture in 1967; and four successive Mackeson Gold Cup winners – Jupiter Boy, 1968; Gay Trip, 1969; Chatham, 1970; and Gay Trip again in 1971. He also trained the great hurdler, Comedy of Errors, twice winner of the Champion Hurdle, 1973 and 1975.

At sixty-two, with fifty years of racing experience behind him, Fred Rimell is still at the very top of his profession. In the 1974/75 season he was second in the trainers' table, with a total of 62 winners, and was awarded the William Hill Golden Spurs award (decided by a panel of distinguished racing correspondents) for his contribution to racing. At the end of the 1975/76 season he was, once again, leading trainer, with 49 winners to his credit.

LICENSED TRAINERS

ADAM, N. M., Racecourse Farm, Bescaby, Melton Mowbray, Leicestershire.
Tel: Waltham-on-the-Wolds (066 478) 878   FLAT & N.H.

AKEHURST, R. P. J., Bourne House, Oxford Street, Lambourn, Berkshire.
Tel: Lambourn (0488) 71850.   FLAT

ALLINGHAM, P. B., Dog Kennel Farm, Lilley, Luton, Bedfordshire.
Tel: Offley (046 276) 337.   FLAT & N.H.

ANCIL, D. I., Thorpe Mandeville Manor, Banbury, Oxfordshire.
Tel: Sulgrave (029 576) 316.   FLAT & N.H.

ANGUS, N. J., Cree Lodge, Craigie Road, Ayr, Scotland.
Tel: Ayr (0292) 66232.   FLAT & N.H.

ARMSTRONG, R. W., St Gatien, Newmarket, Suffolk.
Tel: Newmarket (0638) 3333.   FLAT & N.H.

ARMYTAGE, R. C., Nelson House, East Ilsley, Newbury, Berkshire.
Tel: East Ilsley (063 528) 203.   FLAT & N.H.

ASHWORTH, P. H., 37 Burgh Wood, Banstead, Surrey.
Stables: Treadwell Stables, Aston Way, Epsom, Surrey.
Tel: (House) Burgh Heath (25) 54550; (Stables) Epsom (78) 20336.
     FLAT & N.H.

ATKINSON, W., Coledale Farm, Newtown Road, Carlisle, Cumbria.
Tel: Carlisle (0228) 25649.   FLAT & N.H.

BACH, G. F., Furze Hill Farm, Churt, Farnham, Surrey.
Tel: Headley Down (042 874) 2313.   N.H.

BACON, A. W., The Chase, Grove Coach Road, Retford, Nottinghamshire.
Tel: Retford (0777) 2638.   FLAT & N.H.

BAILEY, K., Brackley Grange, Brackley, Northamptonshire.
Tel: Brackley (028 03) 3486.   N.H.

BAILEY, P. G., Hall Place, Sparsholt, Wantage, Oxon.
Tel: Childrey (023 559) 288.   FLAT & N.H.

BALDING, A., Ryton House, Scrooby, Doncaster, Yorkshire.
Stables: Serlby Hall Stables, Doncaster, Yorkshire.
Tel: (House) Doncaster (0302) 710221; (Stables) Ranskill (077 782) 407.
                                                            FLAT & N.H.

BALDING, G. B., Fyfield House, Weyhill, Andover, Hampshire.
Tel: Weyhill (026 477) 2278.   FLAT & N.H.

BALDING, I. A., Park House, Kingsclere, Newbury, Berkshire.
Tel: (Office) Kingsclere (0635) 298210; (Private) Kingsclere 298274.
                                                                  FLAT

BARCLAY, A. T., Beckfoot, Annan, Dumfriesshire, Scotland.
Tel: Annan (046 12) 2815.   N.H.

BARCLAY, J., Belston Farm, by Ayr, Scotland.
Tel: Joppa (029 257) 226.   FLAT & N.H.

BARNES, T. A., Ellercrow, Ousby, Penrith, Cumbria.
Tel: Langwathby (076 881) 379.   N.H.

BARONS, D. H., Wotton Farm, Woodleigh, Kingsbridge, Devon.
Tel: Loddiswell (054 855) 326.   FLAT & N.H.

BARRATT, L. J., Bromwich Park, Maesbury, Oswestry, Shropshire.
Tel: Queen's Head (069 188) 209.   FLAT & N.H.

BASTIMAN, R., Byways Stables, Linton, Wetherby, Yorkshire.
Tel: Wetherby (0937) 2901.   FLAT & N.H.

BEESON, E. E. G., Hoddern Farm, Piddinghoe, Newhaven, Sussex.
Tel: Peacehaven (079 14) 3304.   FLAT & N.H.

BELL, C. H., Midshiels, Hawick, Roxburghshire, Scotland.
Tel: Denholm (045 487) 278.   FLAT & N.H.

BENSTEAD, C. J., The Limes, Shepherd's Walk, Epsom, Surrey.
Tel: Ashtead 73152.   FLAT & N.H.

BERRY, J., Moss Side Stables, Cockerham, near Lancaster, Lancashire.
Tel: Forton (0524) 791179.   FLAT & N.H.

TRAINING
CENTRES
INVERURIE
DUNBAR
BERWICK ON TWEED
KILWINNING
IRVINE
MONKTON
AYR
GALASHIELS
HAWICK
ALNWICK
LOCKERBIE
ANNAN
CARLISLE
RIDING MILL
NEWCASTLE
BISHOP AUCKLAND
LEASINGTHORNE
PENRITH
GREYSTOKE
RICHMOND
STOCKTON
DARLINGTON
HAMBLETON
THIRSK
MIDDLEHAM
SKIPTON
RIPON
MALTON
BRIDLINGTON
BOLTON LE SANDS
SCOTFORTH
KIRBY OVERBLOW
YORK
WETHERBY
TADCASTER
BEVERLEY
NOSTELL
ASKERN
BOLTON
FLOCKTON
DONCASTER
NORLEY
BAWTRY
LINCOLN
TARPORLEY
SOUTHWELL
MALPAS
MARKET DRAYTON
WALTHAM
OSWESTRY
DUNSTALL
MELTON MOWBRAY
MARKET DEEPING
ALREWAS
NORWICH
UPPINGHAM
WYMONDHAM
SHREWSBURY
ATTLEBOROUGH
WYTHALL
LUDLOW
STETCHWORTH
LEINTWARDINE
WARWICK
GUILSBOROUGH
NEWMARKET
KINNERSLEY
HILL CROOME
BANBURY
DENTON
UPTON-ON-SEVERN
BRACKLEY
ROYSTON
BISHOPS CLEEVE
PRESTBURY
CHELTENHAM
BLETCHLEY
ANDOVERSFORD
WITHINGTON
ASTON TIRROLD
WANTAGE
BLEWBURY
COWBRIDGE
CARDIFF
WEST ILSLEY
EAST ILSLEY
LAMBOURN
COMPTON
BARRY
SOUTHFLEET
MARLBOROUGH
ASHSTEAD
EPSOM
DEVIZES
KINGSCLERE
HEADLEY
REIGATE
TONBRIDGE
WARMINSTER
DORKING
CHARING
WEYHILL
ALRESFORD
CRANLEIGH
STOCKBRIDGE
WINCHESTER
HORSHAM
FOLKESTONE
WHITSBURY
UPHAM
PETWORTH
LEWES
CATSFIELD
CHARD
FINDON
HONITON
BLANDFORD
ARUNDEL
KINGSTEIGNTON
POOLE
WEYMOUTH
KINGSBRIDGE

BETHELL, J. D. W., Lower Whatcombe House, Whatcombe, Wantage, Berkshire.
Tel: Chaddleworth (04872) 372.   FLAT

BEVAN, P. J., The Stables, Black Pit Farm, Kingston, Uttoxeter, Staffordshire.
Tel: Dapple Heath (088 921) 647 or 670.   FLAT & N.H.

BEWICKE, Major C., Downs House, Chilton, Didcot, Oxfordshire.
Tel: Rowstock (023 583) 333; (Office) 355   FLAT & N.H.

BIRCH, A., The Limes, Rocester, Uttoxeter, Staffordshire.
Tel: Rocester (088 923) 356.   N.H.

BISSIL, J. P., Enville Hall, Enville, near Stourbridge, Worcestershire.
Tel: Kinver (038 483) 2460.   N.H.

BLACKSHAW, H. F., Warwick Lodge, Middleham, Leyburn, Yorkshire.
Tel: Middleham (096 92) 3295.   FLAT & N.H.

BLAGRAVE, H. H. G., The Grange, Beckhampton, Marlborough, Wiltshire.
Tel: (House) Avebury (067 23) 218; (Office) Avebury 345.   FLAT

BLAKENEY, R. E., Calehil Stud, Charing, Ashford, Kent.
Tel: Charing (023 371) 2667.   N.H.

BLOOM, J., Downham Lodge, Wymondham, Norfolk.
Tel: Wymondham (057 284) 3176.   N.H.

BLUM, G., Hackness Villa, Exeter Road, Newmarket, Suffolk.
Tel: Newmarket (0683) 2734.   FLAT & N.H.

BOLTON, M. J., Cromwell Hill Farm, Felcourt, East Grinstead, Sussex.
Tel: Dormans Park (034 287) 403.   FLAT & N.H.

BOOTHMAN, C., Holme Farm, Biggin, South Milford, Yorkshire.
Tel: South Milford (097 768) 2481.   N.H.

BOSLEY, J. R., Lower Haddon Farm, Bampton, Oxfordshire.
Tel: Bampton Castle (099 385) 212   N.H.

BOSS, R., Coronation House, Station Approach, Newmarket, Suffolk.
Tel: Newmarket (0638) 3286.   FLAT

BOWER, J. R., Border Stud Farm, Little Plealey, Pontesbury, near Shrewbury, Shropshire.
Tel: Pontesbury (074 376) 502.   N.H.

BRADLEY, J. M., Meads Farm, Sedbury Park, Chepstow, Monmouthshire.
Tel: Chepstow (029 12) 2486.   FLAT & N.H.

BRENNAN, J. J., Compton Rise, Withington, Nr Cheltenham, Gloucestershire.
Tel: Withington (024 289) 212.   N.H.

BRIDGE, S. L., Branthill Farm, Belbroughton, Stourbridge, Worcestershire.
Tel: Belbroughton (056 284) 284.   N.H.

BRIDGWATER, K. S., Elvers Green Cottage, Elvers Green Lane, Knowle, Solihull, Warwickshire.
Tel: Knowle (056 45) 77026.   FLAT

BRITTAIN, C. E., Carlburg, Bury Road, Newmarket, Suffolk.
Tel: Newmarket (0638) 3739.   FLAT

BROOKSHAW, S. J., Lostford Manor, Ternhill, Market Drayton, Shropshire.
Tel: Ternhill (068 083) 272.   FLAT & N.H.

BUDGETT, A. M., Whatcombe, Wantage, Oxfordshire.
Tel: Chaddleworth (048 82) 234.   FLAT

BUXTON, W. S., Lowdham Lodge, Lowdham, Nottinghamshire.
Tel: Lowdham (060 745) 2244.   N.H.

CALLAGHAN, N. A., Flat 1, Amberley House, Bury Road, Newmarket, Suffolk.
Tel: Newmarket (0638) 4040.   FLAT

CALVER, P., Hockely House Stud, Cheriton, Alresford, Hampshire.
Tel: Bramdean (096 279) 527.   FLAT & N.H.

CALVERT, J. B., Hambleton House, Hambleton, Thirsk, Yorkshire.
Tel: Sutton (Thirsk) (084 56) 373.   FLAT & N.H.

CAMACHO, M., The Manor, Towton, Tadcaster, Yorkshire.
Tel: Tadcaster (093 785) 3294.   FLAT

CAMBIDGE, B. R., Weston Park Farm, Weston-under-Lizard, Shifnal, Shropshire.
Tel: Weston-under-Lizard (095 276) 249.   FLAT & N.H.

CANDY, H., Kingstone Warren, near Wantage, Oxfordshire.
Tel: Uffington (036 780) 276.   FLAT

CANN, J. F., Newland, Cullompton, Devon.
Tel: Cullompton (088 43) 2284.   FLAT & N.H.

CARR, E. J., Hambleton Lodge, Hambleton, Thirsk, Yorkshire.
Tel: Sutton (Thirsk) (084 56) 288.   FLAT & N.H.

CARR, F., Whitewall Stables, Welham Road, Norton, Malton, Yorkshire.
Tel: Malton (0653) 2695.   FLAT & N.H.

CARTER, R., Beechamwell Hall, Swaffham, Norfolk.
Tel: Gooderstone (036 621) 226.   N.H.

CECIL, H. R. A., Marriott Stables, Hamilton Road, Newmarket, Suffolk.
Tel: (Office) Newmarket (0638) 2192; (Home) Newmarket 730300.
                                                            FLAT

CHAMPNEYS, Major E. G. S., Church Farm, Upper Lambourn,
Newbury, Berkshire.
Tel: Lambourn (0488) 71495.   N.H.

CHAPMAN, D. W., Mowbray House Farm, Stillington, Yorkshire.
Tel: Easingwold (0347) 21683.   FLAT & N.H.

CHARLES, W., Guys Cliffe Training Stables, Coventry Road, Warwickshire.
Tel: Warwick (0926) 43878.   N.H.

CHESMORE, Mrs S., Strathendrick Stud, Drymen, Stirlingshire,
Scotland.
Tel: Drymen (036 06) 596.   N.H.

CLAY, R. H., Oaklands, Shareshill, near Wolverhampton, Staffordshire.
Tel: Cheslyn Hay (0922) 412746.   FLAT & N.H.

CLAY, W., Lees Hill Farm, Kingstone, Uttoxeter, Staffordshire.
Tel: Uttoxeter (088 93) 2068.   FLAT & N.H.

COLE, P. F. I., Hill House, Folly Road, Lambourn, Berkshire.
Tel: Lambourn (0488) 71632.   FLAT & N.H.

COLE, S. N., Woad Farm Stables, Newport Pagnell, Buckinghamshire.
Tel: Newport Pagnell (0908) 611149.   FLAT & N.H.

COLLINGRIDGE, H. J., 44 Croft Road, Newmarket, Suffolk.
Tel: Newmarket (0638) 5454.   FLAT & N.H.

COLLINGWOOD, E. E., Thorngill, Middleham, Leyburn, Yorkshire.
Tel: Coverdale (096 94) 653.   FLAT & N.H.

CORBETT, T. A., Lagrange, Fordham Road, Newmarket, Suffolk.
Tel: (House) Newmarket (0638) 2417; (Office) Newmarket 2614.
                                                            FLAT

CORRIE, T. F. M., Leighton Hall, Shrewsbury, Shropshire.
Tel: Cressage (095 289) 224.   FLAT & N.H.

COTTRELL, L. G., The Paddocks, Dulford, Cullompton, Devonshire.
Tel: Kentisbeare (088 46) 320.   FLAT & N.H.

COUSINS, E., Sandy Brow Stables, Tarporley, Cheshire.
Tel: Little Budworth (082 921) 316.   FLAT & N.H.

COUSINS, J. H. E., Hala Carr, Scotforth, Lancaster, Lancashire.
Tel: Carnforth (052 473) 2780.   FLAT & N.H.

CRAIG, T., Tilton House Stables, West Barns, East Lothian, Scotland.
Tel: Dunbar (036 82) 2583.   FLAT & N.H.

CRAWFORD, W. H., Huntingdon, Haddington, East Lothian, Scotland.
Tel: Haddington (062 082) 2229.   N.H.

CROSS, R. F., Chatton Park, Chatton, Alnwick, Northumberland.
Tel: Chatton (066 85) 247.   FLAT & N.H.

CROSS, V. B., Chattis Hill, Stockbridge, Hampshire.
Tel: Stockbridge (026 481) 515.   FLAT & N.H.

CROSSLEY, C. C., New Hall Farm, Neston, Wirral, Cheshire.
Tel: Neston (051 336) 2382.   FLAT & N.H.

CRUMP, N. F., Warwick House, Middleham, Leyburn, Yorkshire.
Tel: Middleham (096 92) 3269.   FLAT & N.H.

CUMANI, L., Bedford House, Bury Road, Newmarket, Suffolk.
Tel: Newmarket (0638) 61569 and 5432.   FLAT

CUNARD, Sir Guy, The Garden House, Wintringham, Malton,
Yorkshire.
Tel: Rillington (094 42) 286.   N.H.

CUNDELL, P. D., Roden House, Compton, Newbury, Berkshire.
Tel: Compton (063 522) 26718.   FLAT & N.H.

DALE, D., Wishanger Racing Stables, Frensham Lane, Wishanger,
Churt, Farnham, Surrey.
Tel: Headley Down (042 874) 3464.   FLAT & N.H.

DALTON, A., Somerville Lodge, Fordham Road, Newmarket, Suffolk.
Tel: Newmarket, (0638) 3741.   FLAT & N.H.

DARTNALL, D. J. A., Old Park Farm Stud, Trelleck Grange, Chepstow,
Monmouthshire.
Tel: Tintern (029 18) 279.   FLAT & N.H.

DAVIES, C. H., Oakgrove, St Arvans, Chepstow, Monmouthshire.
Tel: Chepstow (029 12) 2876.   N.H.

DAVISON, A. R., Tillingdown Farm, Tillingdown Lane, Caterham,
Surrey.
Tel: Caterham 48163.   FLAT & N.H.

DENT, A., The Woodland Bungalow, Willingham Road, Market Rasen,
Lincolnshire.
Tel: Market Rasen (067 32) 3689.   FLAT & N.H.

DEVER, F., Robin Hood Farm, Eakring Road, Bilsthorpe, Newark,
Nottinghamshire.
Tel: Bilsthorpe (062 371) 276.   FLAT & N.H.

DICKINSON, A. E., Ribblesdale Stables, Gisburn, Clitheroe, Lancashire.
Tel: Gisburn (020 05) 227. N.H.

DINGWALL, Mrs L. G., Lucerne, 38 Panorama Road, Sandbanks, Poole,
Dorset.
Tel: Canford Cliffs, (0202) 70165. FLAT & N.H.

DOCKER, L. O. J., Windyshields Racing Stables, Cranley Estate,
Cleghorn, Lanarkshire.
Tel: Carstairs (05587) 277. FLAT & N.H.

DOIDGE, G. C., The Lodge, Mothercombe, Plymouth, Devonshire.
Tel: Holbeton (075 530) 228. N.H.

DOYLE, D. A., 1 Boston Road, Wetherby, Yorkshire.
Tel: Wetherby (0937) 2420. FLAT & N.H.

DUDGEON, I. M., Chitterne Stables, Chitterne, Warminster, Wiltshire.
Tel: Codford St Mary (098 55) 477. FLAT & N.H.

DUNLOP, J. L., Castle Stables, Arundel, Sussex.
Tel: (Office) Arundel (0903) 882194; (Home) Arundel 882106. FLAT

DREAPER, J., Greenogue, Kilsallaghan, County Dublin, Eire.
Tel: Dublin (0001) 50187.

EASTERBY, M. H., Habton Grange, Great Habton, Malton, Yorkshire.
Tel: Kirby Misperton (065 386) 600. FLAT & N.H.

EASTERBY, M. W., New House Farm, Sheriff Hutton, Yorkshire.
Tel: Sheriff Hutton (034 77) 368. FLAT & N.H.

EDMUNDS, J., Houndsfield Farm, Houndsfield Lane, Wythall,
Birmingham.
Tel: Wythall (0564) 822334. N.H.

EDWARDS, D. R., Blakely Stud, Stanton, Shrewsbury, Shropshire.
Tel: Hodnet (063 084) 374. N.H.

EDWARDS, J. A. C., Hill Barn, Aymestry, Leominster, Herefordshire.
Tel: Kingsland (056 881) 533. FLAT

ELSEY, C. W. C., Highfield, Malton, Yorkshire.
Tel: Malton (0653) 3149. FLAT

ETHERINGTON, J., Wold House, Lampton Road, Norton, Malton,
Yorkshire.
Tel: Malton (0653) 2842. FLAT

EVANS, J. S., Grange Farm, Empshott, Liss, Hampshire.
Tel: Blackmoor (042 07) 340. FLAT & N.H.

FAIRBAIRN, G. B., Hallington Hall, Hallington, Newcastle-upon-Tyne,
Northumberland.
Tel: Great Whittington (043 472) 215. N.H.

FAIRHURST, T., The Cottage, Middleham, Leyburn, Yorkshire.
Tel: Middleham (096 92) 3362. FLAT & N.H.

FELGATE, P. S., The Stables, Aslockton, Nottinghamshire.
Tel: Whatton (0949) 50335. N.H.

FINCH, Mrs A., Corner Farm, Sedgehill, Shaftesbury, Dorset.
Tel: East Knoyle (074 783) 305 N.H.

FINCH, R. E. G., Wissington Grange Stud, Nayland, Colchester, Essex.
Tel: Nayland (0206) 262238. FLAT & N.H.

FISHER, A. L., Hermitage Stables, Gaddesby, Leicestershire.
Tel: Syston (053 723) 3306. N.H.

FISHER, W. E., Bathway Farm, Chewton Mendip, Bath, Somerset.
Tel: Chewton Mendip (076 121) 283. N.H.

FITZALAN-HOWARD, Lady Anne, Everingham Park, York.
Tel: Holme-on-Spalding Moor (069 63) 203. N.H.

FITZGERALD, J. G., Norton Grange, Norton, Malton, Yorkshire.
Tel: Malton (0653) 2718. FLAT & N.H.

FORSTER, Captain T. A., Old Manor House, Letcombe Bassett, Wantage,
Berkshire.
Tel: Wantage (023 57) 3092. FLAT & N.H.

FRANCIS, G. T., Clouds Stables, East Knoyle, Salisbury, Wiltshire.
Tel: East Knoyle (074 783) 219. N.H.

FRANCIS, M. E. D., Crocker's Farm, Coldharbour, Dorking, Surrey.
Tel: Dorking (0306) 6223. FLAT & N.H.

FRANCIS, W. D., Cliffe Bank, Carden, Malpas, Cheshire.
Tel: Tilston (082 98) 208. N.H.

FREEMAN, F. G., Upper Shockerwick Farm, Upper Shockerwick, Bath,
Avon.
Tel: Box (022 121) 2456. FLAT

GADD, G. J., Cherhill Stables, Cherhill, Calne, Wiltshire.
Tel: Calne (0249) 814723. N.H.

GANDOLFO, D. R., The Downs, Manor Road, Wantage, Berkshire.
Tel: Wantage (023 57) 3242. FLAT & N.H.

GATES, T. l'Anson, South Ella, 82 Prince Edward's Road, Lewes,
Sussex.
Tel: Lewes (079 16) 4250. FLAT & N.H.

GIBSON, J. H., Glenfall Farm, Charlton Kings, Cheltenham, Gloucestershire.
Tel: Cheltenham (0242) 20302. N.H.

GIFFORD, J. T., The Downs, Findon, Worthing, Sussex.
Tel: Findon (090 671) 2226.   N.H.

GILBERT, J. C., Postlip Stables, Winchcombe, Cheltenham, Gloucestershire.
Tel: Winchcombe (0242) 602194.   N.H.

GILLAM, T. A., Wheatlands House, Roecliffe, Boroughbridge, Yorkshire.
Tel: Boroughbridge (090 12) 2592.
Stables: Oxclose, Ripon, Yorkshire.
Tel: Bishop Monkton (076 581) 436.   N.H.

GODDARD, E. C., Tunmore Cottage, The Street, West Horsley, Surrey.
Tel: East Horsley (048 65) 3166, 4188.   FLAT & N.H.

GOODWILL, A. W., Sackville House, Newmarket, Suffolk.
Tel: Newmarket (0638) 3218.   FLAT & N.H.

GOSLING, T., Priam Lodge, Burgh Heath Road, Epsom, Surrey.
Tel: Epsom 22080.   FLAT

GOSWELL, M. O., Mannamead Stables, Beaconsfield Road, Epsom, Surrey.   FLAT & N.H.

GRAY, W. H., York Road Stables, Beverley, East Yorkshire.
Tel: Beverley (0482) 882490.   FLAT

GREEN, P. T. G., Manor House, Gunthorpe, Nottinghamshire.
Tel: Lowdham (060 745) 2275.   N.H.

HAIGH, W. W., White House Stables, Clifton, Penrith, Cumberland.
Tel: Penrith (0768) 4485.   FLAT & N.H.

HAINE, J., Cross Farm, Haresfield, Gloucestershire.
Tel: Hardwicke (045 272) 256.   N.H.

HALL, L. A., Sarum Lodge, Littleton, Winchester, Hampshire.
Tel: Winchester (0962) 880341.   FLAT

HALL, N., Sherholt Lodge, Dunstall, Burton-on-Trent, Staffordshire.
Tel: Burton-under-Needwood 2279.   FLAT & N.H.

HALL, S., Spigot Lodge, Middleham, Leyburn, Yorkshire.
Tel: Leyburn (096 92) 3350.   FLAT & N.H.

HALL, Miss S. E., Brecongill, Middleham, Leyburn, Yorkshire.
Tel: Coverdale (096 94) 223.   FLAT & N.H.

HANBURY, B., Eve Lodge Stables, Hamilton Road, Newmarket, Suffolk.
Tel: Newmarket (0638) 3193.   FLAT

HANLEY, D. L., Delamere Stables, Baydon Road, Lambourn, Berkshire.
Tel: Lambourn (0488) 71700; (Head Lad) Lambourn 71316.

FLAT & N.H.

HANNON, R. M., East Everleigh Stables, East Everleigh, Marlborough, Wiltshire.
Tel: Collingbourne Ducis (026 485) 254. FLAT & N.H.

HANSON, J., Crackhill Farm, Sicklinehall, Wetherby, Yorkshire.
Tel: Wetherby (0937) 2841 FLAT & N.H.

HARDY, J., Staunton Grange Stud, Staunton, Nottinghamshire.
Tel: Long Bennington (040 05) 212. FLAT & N.H.

HARRIS, J. L., Eastwell Hall Stables, Eastwell, Melton Mowbray, Leicestershire.
Tel: Harby (094 98) 671. N.H.

HARTY, C. B., Springfield House, Clondalkin, County Dublin, Eire.
Tel: Dublin (0001) 592703.

HARWOOD, G., Coombelands Racing Stables, Pulborough, Sussex.
Tel: Pulborough (079 82) 2335. FLAT & N.H.

HASLAM, P. C., Lynchet Stables, Upper Lambourn, Berkshire.
Tel: Lambourn (0488) 71455. FLAT & N.H.

HASSEL, C. M., Cairns, Northend, Exning, Newmarket, Suffolk.
Tel: Exning (063 877) 321. N.H.

HAYNES, M. J., Tattenham Corner Stables, Epsom Downs, Epsom, Surrey.
Tel: Burgh Heath (25) 51140. FLAT & N.H.

HAYWARD, J. E., The Lemon's Farm, Ewhurst, Surrey. FLAT & N.H.

HEAD, R. A., Rhonehurst, Upper Lambourn, Newbury, Berkshire.
Tel: Lambourn (0488) 71411. N.H.

HEALEY, T. W., Deerhurst, Lydart, Monmouthshire.
Tel: Monmouth (0600) 3884. N.H.

HERN, Major W. R., West Ilsley Stables, Newbury, Berkshire.
Tel: (Stables) East Ilsley (063 528) 219; (Private) East Ilsley 251. FLAT

HILLS, B. W., South Bank, Lambourn, Berkshire.
Tel: Lambourn (0488) 71548. N.H.

HINDLEY, J. J., Kremlin House Stables, Fordham Road, Newmarket, Suffolk.
Tel: Newmarket (0638) 4141. FLAT

HOBBS, B., Palace House, Palace Street, Newmarket, Suffolk.
Tel: Newmarket (0638) 2129. FLAT

HOLDEN, W., Priors House, Exning, Newmarket, Suffolk.
Tel: Exning (063 877) 384.   FLAT & N.H.

HOLLINSHEAD, R., Longdon Lodge Farm, Upper Longdon, Rugeley,
Staffordshire.
Tel: Armitage (0543) 490298.   FLAT & N.H.

HOLMES, D. H., Spring Cottage Stables, Langton Road, Norton, Malton,
Yorkshire.
Tel: Malton (0653) 2140.   FLAT & N.H.

HOLT, L., Tunworth Down Stables, Tunworth, Basingstoke, Hampshire.
Tel: Long Sutton (025 681) 376.   FLAT & N.H.

HOUGHTON, R. F. Johnson, Woodway, Blewbury, Didcot, Berkshire.
Tel: Blewbury (0235) 85480.   FLAT

HUNT, J., Wood House Racing Stables, Mattersey, Doncaster,
Yorkshire.
Tel: Wiseton (077 786) 379.   FLAT

HUNTER, G. H., Kennet House, East Ilsley, Newbury, Berkshire.
Tel: East Ilsley (063 528) 250.   FLAT

HURLEY, M., Osborne Lodge, Kildare, Eire.
Tel: Kildare 21490.

INGHAM, S. W. H., Thirty Acre Barn, Roman Road, Headley, Surrey.
Tel: Ashtead (07) 72859.   FLAT & N.H.

IVORY, K. T., Harper Lodge Farm, Harper Lane, Radlett, Hertfordshire.
Tel: Radlett (779) 6081.   FLAT & N.H.

JAMES, C. J., Mask Cottage, East Garson, Near Newbury, Berkshire.
Tel: Great Shefford (048 839) 280.   N.H.

JAMES, M. B. C., Warren Stables, Prees Heath, Whitchurch, Shropshire.
Tel: Whitchurch (0948) 3155.   FLAT & N.H.

JAMES, S. S., Montpelier House Stables, East Ilsley, Newbury,
Berkshire.
Tel: East Ilsley (063 528) 248.   FLAT & N.H.

JARVIS, A. P., Grange Farm, Featherbed Lane, Withybrook, Coventry,
Warwickshire.
Tel: Wolvey (045 523) 566.   FLAT & N.H.

JARVIS, M. A., Carlburg Stables, Bury Road, Newmarket, Suffolk.
Tel: Newmarket (0638) 2915.   FLAT

JARVIS, R., Phantom House, Fordham Road, Newmarket, Suffolk.
Tel: Newmarket (0638) 2677.   FLAT

JERMY, D. C., New Lodge Stables, Little Woodcote Lane, Carshalton, Surrey.
Tel: 01-668 3765. FLAT & N.H.

JOHNSON, J. A. T., Berkley House, Upper Lambourn, Newbury, Berkshire.
Tel: Lambourn (0488) 71368. FLAT

JONES, A. W., Pentre David, Oswestry, Shropshire.
Tel: Gobowen (069 182) 324. FLAT & N.H.

JONES, Dr Arthur, Craig Cefn Park, Swansea, Glamorganshire.
Tel: Clydach (044 15) 3504. FLAT & N.H.

JONES, C. I., Kinnerley Stables, Kinnerley, Oswestry, Shropshire.
Tel: Knockin (069 185) 511. FLAT & N.H.

JONES, D. H., Garth Paddock, Efail Isaf, Pontypridd, Glamorganshire.
Tel: Newton Llantwit (044 362) 2515. FLAT & N.H.

JONES, E., Hazel Slade House, Hednesford, Staffordshire.
Tel: Hednesford (054 38) 2721. N.H.

JONES, H. Thomson, Rose Hall, Exning, Newmarket, Suffolk.
Tel: Newmarket (0638) 4884. FLAT & N.H.

JONES, Herbert, Sutton Stables, Norton, Malton, Yorkshire.
Tel: Malton (0653) 2630. FLAT

JONES, T. M., Brook Farm, Albury, Guildford, Surrey.
Tel: Shere (048 641) 2604. N.H.

JORDON, I. D., Whorlton Hall, Westerhope, Newcastle-upon-Tyne, Northumberland.
Tel: Newcastle-upon-Tyne (0632) 869143. FLAT & N.H.

KEARNEY, P. J., Harnham Cottage, Withington, Cheltenham, Gloucestershire.
Tel: Withington (024 289) 253. FLAT & N.H.

KEENOR, R. F., Bealey Court, Chulmleigh, Devon.
Tel: Chulmleigh (076 98) 432. N.H.

KEITH, D., The Red House, Littleton, Winchester, Hampshire.
Tel: Winchester (0962) 880808. FLAT

KEMP, A. R., Forcett Barns, Forcett, Richmond, Yorkshire.
Tel: East Layton (032 570) 397. N.H.

KENNARD, Mrs E., Blakes Stables, Bicknoller, Taunton, Somerset.
Tel: Williton (098 43) 588. N.H.

KENNARD, L. G., Crendo House, Bishops Lydeard, Taunton, Somerset.
Tel: Bishops Lydeard (082 343) 550. FLAT & N.H.

KENT, D. W. J., Lynch Farm, Funtingdon, Chichester, Sussex.
Tel: West Ashling (024 358) 231.   N.H.

KERR, K. R., M.R.C.V.S., Summerseat, Clonee, County Meath, Eire.
Tel: Clonee 255231.

KERNICK, S. G., Leighton, 1 Church Street, Kingsteignton, Devon.
Tel: Newton Abbot (0626) 5899.   FLAT

KERSEY, T., Bleak House Stables, Packham Road, West Melton,
Rotherham, Yorkshire.
Tel: Rotherham (0709) 873166.   FLAT & N.H.

KILLORAN, M., Windmill Bungalow, Seven Springs, Cheltenham,
Gloucestershire.
Tel: Cobberley (024 287) 344.   N.H.

KINDERSLEY, G., Parsonage Farm, East Garston, Newbury, Berkshire.
Tel: Great Shefford (048 839) 264.   N.H.

LAMB, C. R., East Fleetham, Seahouses, Northumberland.
Tel: Seahouses (066 572) 260.   FLAT & N.H.

LAY, V. M., Rectory Farm, Broughton, Banbury, Oxfordshire.
Tel: Banbury (0295) 3209.   N.H.

LEIGH, J. P., Mount House, Long Lane, Willoughton, Gainsborough,
Lincolnshire.
Tel: Hemswell (042 773) 210.   N.H.

LOMAX, Mrs R. A., Downs House, Baydon, Marlborough, Wiltshire.
Tel: Aldbourne (067 24) 288.   FLAT & N.H.

LONG, J. E., Rose and Crown Stables, Elham, Canterbury, Kent.
Tel: Elham (030 384) 229.   N.H.

LUNNESS, B. W., 57 King Edward Road, Newmarket, Suffolk.
Stables: Machell Place Stables, Newmarket, Suffolk.
Tel: Newmarket (0638) 3926.   FLAT

MAGNER, E., Red House Farm, Racecourse, Doncaster, Yorkshire.
Tel: Doncaster (0302) 49787.   FLAT & N.H.

MAGNIER, C., Rathvale, Athboy, County Meath, Eire.
Tel: Trim 32218.

MAKIN, P. J., Little Paddocks, Ogbourne Maisey, Marlborough,
Wiltshire.
Tel: Marlborough (067 25) 2973.   FLAT & N.H.

MANN, W. G., Cottage Stables, Bishops Itchington, Leamington Spa,
Warwickshire.
Tel: Harbury (092 688) 659.   N.H.

MARKS, D., Lethornes, Lambourn, Berkshire.
Tel: Lambourn (0488) 71767.   FLAT & N.H.

MARSHALL, W. C., Eve Lodge Stables, Newmarket.   FLAT & N.H.

MASON, R. E. G., Guilsborough Hall, Guilsborough, Northamptonshire.
Tel: Guilsborough (060 122) 381.   FLAT & N.H.

MASSON, M. J., Barn Stables, De Montfort Road, Lewes, Sussex.
Tel: Lewes (079 16) 4984.   FLAT & N.H.

MATTHEWS, S. G., Wellow Manor, East Wellow, Romsey, Hampshire.
Tel: West Wellow (0794) 22254.   FLAT & N.H.

MAXWELL, F., Lambourn House, Lambourn, Berkshire.
Tel: Lambourn (0488) 71653.   FLAT

McCAIN, D., 10 Upper Aughton Road, Birkdale, Southport, Lancashire.
Tel: Southport (0704) 66007/69677.   FLAT & N.H.

McCARTAN, C., Baltrasna, Kells, County Meath, Eire.
Tel: Moynalty 9.

McCOURT, M., Antwick Stud, Letcombe Regis, Wantage, Berkshire.
Tel: Wantage (023 57) 4456.   FLAT & N.H.

McCREERY, P. D., Capdoo, Clane, Co. Kildare, Eire.
Tel: Naas 68148.

McGRATH, S., Glencairn Stables, Sandyford, County Dublin, Eire.
Tel: Dublin (0001) 984852.

McMAHON, B. A., Woodside Farm, Hopwas Hill, Tamworth,
Staffordshire.
Tel: Tamworth (0827) 62901.   N.H.

MELLOR, S. T. E., Linkslade, Mile End, Lambourn, Berkshire.
Tel: Lambourn (0488) 71485.   FLAT & N.H.

METCALFE, P. E. A., Sand Lane House, Oldstead, Coxwold, Yorkshire.
Tel: Coxwold (034 76) 278.   FLAT

MILLER, C. J. Vernon, Alscot Park Stables, Stratford-on-Avon,
Warwickshire.
Tel: Alderminster (078 987) 296232.   FLAT & N.H.

MILNER, G. P., Heath Paddocks, Press Heath, Whitchurch, Shropshire.
Tel: Whitchurch (0948) 3527.   FLAT & N.H.

MITCHELL, P., Downs House, Epsom Downs, Epsom, Surrey.
Tel: Ashtead (27) 73729.   FLAT & N.H.

MITCHELL, V. J., Carburton Stables, Carburton, Worksop, Nottinghamshire.
Tel: Worksop (0909) 5962.   FLAT

MOLONY, T., Manor House, Wymondham, Melton Mowbray, Leicestershire.
Tel: Wymondham (057 284) 273.   FLAT

MOORE, A., Ingleside Racing Stables, 10 Holtview Road, Woodingdean, Brighton, Sussex.
Tel: Brighton (0273) 681679.   N.H.

MOORE, D. L., Ballysax Manor, Curragh Camp, County Kildare, Eire.
Tel: Curragh 41344.

MORLEY, M. F. D., Greenfarm House, Timworth, Bury St Edmunds, Suffolk.
Tel: Culford (028 484) 278.   FLAT & N.H.

MORRIS, H., Maesewaylod, Erbistock, Wrexham, Denbighshire, North Wales.
Tel: Overton-on-Dee (097 873) 349.
Stables: Deeside Stables, Bangor-on-Dee.   N.H.

MORRIS, Miss S. O., Holemmor Farm, Eleighwater, Chard, Somerset.
Tel: Chard (046 06) 3379.   N.H.

MUGGERIDGE, F. M., Lark Cottage Stables, Sherfield English, Romsey, Hampshire.
Tel: West Wellow (0794) 22430.   N.H.

MULHALL, J., Oak House Stables, 60a Tadcaster Road, York, Yorkshire.
Tel: York (0904) 66321.   FLAT & N.H.

MULLINS, P., Doninga, Goresbridge, County Kilkenny, Eire.
Tel: Carlow 25121.

MURLESS, N., Warren Place, Newmarket, Suffolk.
Tel: (Office) Newmarket (0638) 2024; (House) Newmarket 2387. FLAT

MURPHY, R. C. R., Eyton Hall, Wellington, Shropshire.
Tel: Wellington (0952) 2209.   FLAT & N.H.

MURRAY, W. F., Leyburn House, Middleham, Leyburn, Yorkshire.
Tel: Leyburn (096 92) 2220.   FLAT

NAGLE, Mrs F., Westerlands, Petworth, Sussex.
Tel: Graffham (079 86) 220.   FLAT

NAUGHTON, M. P., High Gingerfield Lodge, Hurgill Road, Richmond, Yorkshire.
Tel: Richmond (0748) 2803.   N.H.

NEAVES, A. S., Arnolds Oak Farm, Eastling, Faversham, Kent.
Tel: Eastling (079 589) 274.   FLAT & N.H.

NELSON, Major P. M., Kingsdown, Upper Lambourn, Berkshire.
Tel: Lambourn (0488) 71391.   FLAT

NESBITT, S., Newby Hall Stables, Skelton-on-Ure, Ripon, Yorkshire.
Tel: Boroughbridge (090 12) 2037.   FLAT & N.H.

NEVILLE, M., Ballymee House, Doneraile, County Cork, Eire.
Tel: Mallow 24135.

NICHOLSON, D., Cotswold House, Condicote, Stow-on-the-Wold, Gloucestershire.
Tel: Stow-on-the-Wold (0451) 30417.   FLAT & N.H.

NICHOLSON, H. C. D., Park Corner, Prestbury, Cheltenham, Gloucestershire.
Tel: Cheltenham (0242) 28763.   FLAT & N.H.

NORRIS, P., Cherryfield, The Curragh, County Kildare, Eire.
Tel: Curragh 41243.

NORTON, S. G., Throstle Nest, Silkstone Common, Barnsley, Yorkshire.
Tel: Silkstone (022 679) 8497.   FLAT & N.H.

O'BRIEN, A. S., The Grove, Golden, County Tipperary, Eire.
Tel: 062-54129.

O'BRIEN, M. V., Ballydoyle House, Cashel, County Tipperary, Eire.
Tel: Cashel 203–4.

O'DONOGHUE, J., Priory Racing Stables, Reigate, Surrey.
Tel: Reigate (073 72) 45241.   N.H.

O'GORMAN, W. A., Graham Place, Newmarket, Suffolk.
Tel: Newmarket (0638) 3330.   FLAT & N.H.

O'GRADY, E. J., Killeens, Ballynonty, Thurles, County Tipperary, Eire.
Tel: Killenaule 8.

OLD, J. A. B., Glebe Farm, Ashmore (Dorset), near Salisbury, Wiltshire.
Tel: Fontmell Magna (074 781) 648.   N.H.

OLIVER, J. K. M., Hassendean Bank, Hawick, Roxburghshire, Scotland.
Tel: Denholm (045 087) 216.   N.H.

OLIVER, M. E., New House Farm, Elmley Lovett, Droitwich, Worcestershire.
Tel: Hartlebury (029 96) 500.   N.H.

O'NEILL, H., Westbrook Stables, Westbrook Hall, Warnham, Sussex.
Tel: Slinfold (040 374) 790500   N.H.

O'NEILL, O., Cleeve Lodge, Cleeve Hill, Cheltenham, Gloucestershire.
Tel: Bishops Cleeve (024 267) 3275.   FLAT & N.H.

OSBORNE, P. D., Brownstone, Curragh, County Kildare, Eire.
Tel: Kildare (045) 21421.

O'TOOLE, M. A., Maddenstown, Kildare, Eire.
Tel: Curragh 045.

OUGHTON, Mrs D. R., The Vale, Findon, Worthing, Sussex.
Tel: Findon (090 671) 2113. FLAT & N.H.

OX, J. R., Lisnawilly, Dundalk, County Louth, Eire.

OXX, J., Currabeg, Kildare, County Kildare, Eire.
Tel: (045) 21310.

PALMER, S. T., Willow Farm Stables, Normanton, Bottesford,
Nottinghamshire.
Tel: Bottesford (0949) 42767. N.H.

PAYNE, H. W., Burcott Farm, Wells, Somerset.
Tel: Wells (0749) 72419. N.H.

PAYNE, K., Kingsley House, Middleham, Leyburn, Yorkshire.
Tel: Leyburn (096 92) 3254. FLAT & N.H.

PAYNE, W. J., Eastbury Cottage, Eastbury, Berkshire.
Tel: Lambourn (0488) 71722. FLAT

PEACOCK, J. H., Fair Lea Training Stables, Caynham, Ludlow,
Shropshire.
Tel: Ludlow (0584) 2708. FLAT & N.H.

PEACOCK, R. D., Manor House, Middleham, Leyburn, Yorkshire.
Tel: Leyburn, (096 92) 3291. FLAT

PEACOCK, R. E., Tilstone Paddocks, Tilstone Fearnall, Tarporley,
Cheshire.
Tel: Tarporley (082 93) 2716. FLAT & N.H.

PERRETT, A. C. J., Yew Trees, Shipton Cliffe, Cheltenham, Gloucestershire.
Tel: Andoversford (024 282) 244. N.H.

PETER-HOBLYN, G. H., Hill House, East Ilsley, Newbury, Berkshire.
Tel: East Ilsley (063 528) 253. FLAT & N.H.

PIPE, K. A., Benshayne Farm, Culmstock, Cullompton, Devon.
Tel: Craddock (088 44) 713. N.H.

PITT, A. J., Wendover Stables, Burgh Heath Road, Epsom, Surrey.
Tel: Epsom (78) 25034. FLAT & N.H.

PLANT, D. G., The Cottage, Willow Farm, Sealand Road, Deeside,
Flintshire. FLAT

POSTON, P. J., Raylands, Rayes Lane, Newmarket, Suffolk.
Tel: Newmarket (0638) 2319. FLAT

POTTS, A. W., Manor Stables, Horkstow, Barton-on-Humber, South
Humberside.
Tel: Saxby-All-Saints (065 261) 750. N.H.

POWER, J., French Furze, The Curragh, County Kildare, Eire.
Tel: Kildare (045) 41406.

POWNEY, J., Saville House, St. Mary's Square, Newmarket. Suffolk.
Tel: Newmarket (0638) 3343. FLAT & N.H.

PRENDERGAST, K., Frindale, Friarstown, County Kildare, Eire.
Tel: 045 21387.

PRENDERGAST, P. J. Jnr., Meadow Court, Maddenstown, Curragh,
County Kildare, Eire.
Tel: Kildare (045) 21461.

PRENDERGAST, P. J., Melitta Lodge, Kildare, Eire.
Tel: Kildare (045) 21288/21275.

PRESCOTT, Sir Mark, Heath House, Moulton Road, Newmarket,
Suffolk.
Tel: Newmarket (0638) 2117. FLAT

PRICE, Captain H. R., Soldiers Field, Findon, Worthing, Sussex.
Tel: Findon (090 671) 2388. FLAT & N.H.

PRITCHARD-GORDON, G. A., Shalfleet, Bury Road, Newmarket,
Suffolk.
Tel: (Stables) Newmarket (0638) 2824; (Home) Newmarket 4685.
FLAT & N.H.

PULLEN, J. R. F., Redfields Racing Stables, Redfields Lane, Church
Crookham, Hampshire.
Tel: Aldershot (0252) 850567. N.H.

QUARTERMAINE, D. J., Chase Stables, Fosse House, Ettington,
Warwickshire.
Tel: Stratford-on-Avon (0789) 740001. N.H.

RANSOM, P. B., Chapel Farm, Wigmore, near Leominster, Herefordshire.
Tel: Wigmore (056 886) 253. N.H.

REAVEY, E. J. B., Orchard Stables, East Hendred, Wantage, Berkshire.
Tel: East Hendred (023 588) 297. FLAT

RICHARDS, G. W., The Stables, Greystoke, Penrith, Cumbria.
Tel: Greystoke (085 33) 392. FLAT & N.H.

RICHMOND, B. A., Hall Stables, Navenby, Wellingore, Lincolnshire.
Tel: Navenby (052 283) 578. FLAT & N.H.

RIMELL, T. F., Kinnersley, Severn Stoke, Worcestershire.
Tel: Severn Stoke (090 567) 233. FLAT & N.H.

RINGER, D. S., Saffron House, 10 The Avenue, Newmarket, Suffolk.
Tel: Newmarket (0638) 2653. FLAT & N.H.

RIPLEY, G., Glebe Farm, Shaddoxhurst, Ashford, Kent.
Tel: Ham Street (023 373) 2462. N.H.

ROBINSON, G. N., Haggeston, Beal, Berwick-on-Tweed, Northumberland.
Tel: Beal (028 981) 237. FLAT & N.H.

ROBINSON, G. W., Stepaside, The Curragh, County Kildare, Eire.
Tel: Curragh (045) 41368.

ROBINSON, P. J., Fitzroy House Stables, Black Bear Lane, Newmarket, Suffolk.
Tel: (Office) Newmarket (0638) 2090 (Home) Newmarket 3226. FLAT

ROHAN, H. P., Grove Cottage, Norton, Malton, Yorkshire.
Tel: Malton (0653) 2337/8. FLAT & N.H.

RUMSEY, A. J., Upper Whittimere Farm, Bobbington, Stourbridge, Worcestershire.
Tel: Bobbington (038 488) 269. N.H.

SALAMAN, M., The Bungalow, Court Farm, Llangattock, Crickhowell, Powys.
Tel: Crickhowell (0873) 810326. FLAT & N.H.

SASSE, D. J. G., Frenchmans Yard, Upper Lambourn, Berkshire.
Tel: Lambourn (0488) 71902. FLAT & N.H.

SCUDAMORE, M. J., Prothither, Hoarwithy, Herefordshire.
Tel: Carey (043 270) 253. N.H.

SHEDDEN, L. H., The Grange, Wetherby, Yorkshire.
Tel: Wetherby (0937) 2122. FLAT & N.H.

SIMPSON, Mrs J. B., Cowfold Farm, Heighlington, Darlington, Co Durham.
Tel: Aycliffe (032 571) 2263. N.H.

SIMPSON, R., Priors Court Stables, Sutton Courteney, Abingdon, Oxfordshire.
Tel: Sutton Courteney (023 582) 609. FLAT

SINCLAIR, Miss A. V., The Nunnery Stables, De Montfort Road, Lewes, Sussex.
Tel: (Home) Lewes (079 16) 3851; (Office) Lewes 6619. FLAT & N.H.

SLEATOR, P., Grange Con, County Wicklow, Eire.
Tel: Grange Con 4.

SMALL, L. G., East Farm, Charlton Adam, Somerton, Somerset.
Tel: Charlton Mackrell (045 822) 213. N.H.

SMITH, A., Pasture Terrace, Beverley, East Yorkshire. FLAT & N.H.

SMITH, Denys, Holdforth Farm, Bishop Auckland, County Durham.
Tel: Bishop Auckland (0388) 3317.   FLAT & N.H.

SMITH, Douglas, Loder Stables, Hamilton Road, Newmarket, Suffolk.
Tel: (Office) Newmarket (0638) 2036; (Private) Newmarket 2841.
                                                                FLAT

SMYLY, Capt. R. M., Kingswood House, Lambourn, Berkshire.
Tel: Lambourn (0488) 71403.
                                                                FLAT

SMYTH, G. R., Heath House, Lewes, Sussex.
Tel: Lewes (079 16) 4581.
                                                                FLAT

SMYTH, H. E., Valence, 38 Downs Road, Epsom, Surrey.
Tel: Epsom (78) 21446
Stables: Down Cottage, Burgh Heath Road, Epsom Surrey.
Tel: Epsom 23664.
                                                                FLAT

SMYTH, R. V., Clear Height, Downs Road, Epsom, Surrey.
Tel: Epsom (78) 20053.   FLAT & N.H.

SPEARING, J. L., 1 Orchard Villas, Sherriffs Lench, Harvington,
Evesham, Worcestershire.
Tel: Harvington (038 671) 342.   N.H.

STEPHENSON, W., The Ridings, London Road, Royston, Hertfordshire.
Tel: Royston (0763) 43386.   FLAT & N.H.

STEPHENSON, W. A., Crawleas, Leasingthorpe, Bishop Auckland,
County Durham.
Tel: Rushyford (038 886) 213.   FLAT & N.H.

STEVENS, A. G. M., Lucknam Park, Colerne, Chippenham, Wiltshire.
Tel: Box (022 121) 2777/2828.   FLAT & N.H.

STOUTE, M. R., Beech Hurst, Bury Road, Newmarket, Suffolk.
Tel: Newmarket (0638) 3801.   FLAT

STURDY, R. C., Elston House, Shrewton, Salisbury, Wiltshire.
Tel: Shrewton (098 062) 222.   FLAT & N.H.

SUPPLE, S. H., Clock House Stables, Green Street Green, Dartford, Kent.
Tel: Longfield (047 47) 3915.   FLAT & N.H.

SUTCLIFFE, J. Jnr, Woodruffe House, Headley Road, Epsom, Surrey.
Tel: Ashtead (27) 72825.   FLAT & N.H.

SUTHERLAND, F., Aghinagh House, Killinardrish, County Cork, Eire.
Tel: Killinardrish 23.

SWAINSON, Captain W. J. H., The Farm, Westmancote, Bredon,
Tewkesbury, Gloucestershire.
Tel: Bredon (068 47) 332.   FLAT & N.H.

SWIFT, B. C., Loretta Lodge, Headley, Surrey.
Tel: Leatherhead (53) 77209. FLAT & N.H.

TAAFFE, P., Alasty, Straffan, County Kildare, Eire.
Tel: Straffan 288424.

TATE, F. M., Winterfold Farm, Chaddesley Corbett, Kidderminster, Worcestershire.
Tel: Chaddesley Corbett (056 283) 243. FLAT & N.H.

TAYLOR, P. M., Dunroamin, High Street, Lambourn, Berkshire.
Tel: Lambourn (0488) 71667. FLAT & N.H.

TAYLOR, T., Elkar House, Aldershawe, Lichfield, Staffordshire.
Tel: Lichfield (054 32) 51611. FLAT & N.H.

THOM, D. T., Harraton Court, Exning, Newmarket, Suffolk.
Tel: Exning (063 877) 288. FLAT

THOMPSON, B., Grove Stud Farm, Leighton Buzzard, Bedfordshire.
Tel: Leighton Buzzard (052 53) 3771. N.H.

THOMPSON, V., Link House Farm, Newtown-by-Sea, Embleton, Alnwick, Northumberland.
Tel: Embleton (066 576) 272. N.H.

THORNE, J., Lilstock Farm, Kilve, Bridgewater, Somerset.
Tel: Holford (027 874) 216. FLAT & N.H.

TINKLER, C. H., Whitegates, Boltby, Thirsk, Yorkshire.
Tel: Upsall (084 54) 336. N.H.

TITTERINGTON, R., The Green, Skelton, Penrith, Cumberland.
Tel: Skelton (0287) 363. FLAT & N.H.

TOFT, G., King's Arms Stables, North-Bar-Within, Beverley, East Yorkshire.
Tel: Beverley (0482) 885105. FLAT & N.H.

TREE, A. J., Beckhampton House, Marlborough, Wiltshire.
Tel: (Office) Avebury (067 23) 204; (Home) Avebury 244. FLAT

TURNELL, A. R., Ogbourne, Maisey Lodge, Marlborough, Wiltshire.
Tel: Marlborough (067 25) 2542. FLAT & N.H.

TURNER, J. A. M., 53 Clifford Moor Road, Boston Spa, Wetherby, Yorkshire.
Tel: Boston Spa (0937) 843324.
Stables: Crackhill Farm, Sicklinghall, Wetherby.
Tel: Wetherby (0937) 2841. FLAT & N.H.

TWIBELL, J., Hall Farm, Dinnington, Sheffield, Yorkshire.
Tel: Dinnington (090 978) 2338. N.H.

UNDERHILL, S., Grafton Court Stables, Temple Grafton, Alcester, Leicestershire.
Tel: Bidford-on-Avon (078 988) 374. N.H.

UNDERWOOD, D. B., Centaur Place Farm, Foxburrow Hill, Bramley, Surrey.
Tel: Bramley (048 647) 3147. N.H.

UPTON, Captain P. J., Rectory House, Sparsholt, Wantage, Berkshire.
Tel: Childrey (023 559) 654. N.H.

VALLANCE, Lt Colonel G. R. A., Lynes House, Bishops Cannings, Devizes, Wiltshire.
Tel: Cannings (038 086) 285. N.H.

VANCE, M., Whitechurch Stud, Straffan, County Kildare, Eire.
Tel: Dublin (0001) 288415.

VERGETTE, G. M., Market Deeping, Peterborough, Northamptonshire.
Tel: Market Deeping (0778) 342226. FLAT & N.H.

VIBERT, R. J., Framptons House, East Hendred, Wantage, Berkshire.
Tel: East Hendred (023 588) 247. FLAT & N.H.

VICKERS, J. R. P., Newton Grange, Sadberge, Darlington, County Durham.
Tel: Dinsdale (032 573) 2450/2438. FLAT

VIGORS, N. A. C., The Old Manor, Upper Lambourn, Newbury, Berkshire.
Tel: Lambourn (0488) 71657. FLAT & N.H.

WAINWRIGHT, S., Grove Yard Stables, Longton Road, Norton, Malton, Yorkshire.
Tel: Malton (0653) 3489. FLAT & N.H.

WAKLEY, N. J. W., Hunters Lodge, Churchinford, Taunton, Somerset.
Tel: Church Stanton 253. N.H.

WALKER, I. S., Leveretts, Windmill Hill, Exning, Newmarket, Suffolk.
Tel: Exning (063 877) 219. FLAT

WALKER, T. F., Gennel House, Flaxton, Yorkshire.
Tel: Flaxton Moor (090 486) 314. FLAT & N.H.

WALL, R., Little Olivers Farm, Olivers Lane, Colchester, Essex.
Tel: Colchester (0206) 330232. N.H.

WALLACE, G., M.B.E., Kirby House Stables, Woolsthorpe-by-Belvoir, Grantham, Lincolnshire.
Tel: Knipton (047 682) 312. FLAT & N.H.

WALWYN, F. T. T., Saxon House Stables, Lambourn, Berkshire.
Tel: Lambourn (0488) 71555. FLAT & N.H.

WALWYN, P. T., Seven Barrows, Lambourn, Newbury, Berkshire.
Tel: Lambourn (0488) 71347. FLAT

WARD, R. C., Fir Tree Stables, Doncaster, Yorkshire.
Tel: Doncaster (0302) 700574. FLAT & N.H.

WARDLE, I. P., Windwhistle Stables, East Horrington, Wells, Somerset.
Tel: Wells (0749) 73167. N.H.

WARING, Mrs B. H., Southey Farm, Wrangway, Wellington, Somerset.
Tel: Wellington (082 347) 2660. N.H.

WATSON, A., Southfield Farm, West Marton, Skipton-in-Craven, Yorkshire.
Tel: Earby (028 282) 2228. N.H.

WATTS, J. W., Hurgill Lodge, Richmond, Yorkshire.
Tel: Richmond (0748) 2287. FLAT

WATTS, W. C., 27 Fourth Avenue, Bridlington, East Yorkshire.
Tel: Bridlington (0262) 3719. FLAT

WAUGH, T. A., Sefton Cottage, Bury Road, Newmarket, Suffolk.
Tel: Newmarket (0638) 2233. FLAT

WEBB, H. J. M., Peartree Farm, Great Coxwell, Faringdon, Berkshire.
Tel: Faringdon (0367) 20173. N.H.

WEBBER, J., Cropredy Lawn, Mollington, Banbury, Oxfordshire.
Tel: Cropredy (029 575) 226. N.H.

WEEDEN, D. E., Calder Park, Hamilton Road, Newmarket, Suffolk.
Tel: Newmarket (0638) 5050. FLAT & N.H.

WELCH, J. T., Cowarth Park Stables, Ascot, Berkshire.
Tel: Ascot (0990) 22395. N.H.

WELD, D. K. M.V.B., M.R.C.V.S., Rosewell House, Curragh, County Kildare, Eire.
Tel: Curragh 41273.

WESTBROOK, H. C., 66 Old Station Road, Newmarket, Suffolk.
Tel: Newmarket (0638) 3657. FLAT

WEYMES, E., Ashgill, Coverdale, Middleham, Yorkshire.
Tel: Coverdale (096 94) 229. FLAT & N.H.

WHARTON, H., Low Farm Stables, Almholme, Arksey, Bentley, Doncaster, Yorkshire.
Tel: Doncaster (0302) 54126. FLAT & N.H.

WHARTON, W., Shipmans Barn Stud, Melton Mowbray, Leicestershire.
Tel: Waltham-on-the-Wolds (066 478) 258. FLAT & N.H.

WHELAN, D., 18 Woodcote Hurst, Epsom, Surrey.
Tel: Epsom (78) 21482.

FLAT

WHISTON, W. R., Beech House, Wollerton, Market Drayton, Shropshire.
Tel: Hodnet (063 084) 203.

N.H.

WHITFIELD, Mrs N., Upper Diddlesfold, Haslemere, Surrey.
Tel: Northchapel (042 878) 438.

N.H.

WIGHTMAN, W. G. R., Ower Farm, Upham, Southampton, Hampshire.
Tel: Bishops Waltham (048 93) 2565.

FLAT & N.H.

WILES, F. J., Langley Holme Stables, Barnsley Road, Flockton, Wakefield, Yorkshire.
Tel: Flockton (092 481) 468.

FLAT & N.H.

WILKINSON, B. E., Mooredge, Park Lane, Middleham, Yorkshire.
Tel: Middleham (096 92) 3385.

FLAT & N.H.

WILLIAMS, D. H., Middlethorpe Hall Stables, Middlethorpe, Yorkshire.
Tel: York (0904) 28639.

FLAT & N.H.

WILLIAMS, H. F., Stork House, Lambourn, Berkshire.
Tel: Lambourn (0488) 71423.

FLAT & N.H.

WILLIAMS, W. R., The Stables, Old Racecourse, Buckfastleigh, South Devon.
Tel: Buckfastleigh (036 44) 3590.

FLAT & N.H.

WILLIS, H., Morestead Farm Stables, Morestead, Winchester, Hampshire.
Tel: Twyford (Hampshire) (0962) 713483.

N.H.

WILMOT, Miss N., Binfield Grove, Binfield, Berkshire.
Tel: Bracknell (0344) 3326.

FLAT

WILSON, R., College House, Lambourn, Berkshire.
Tel: Lambourn (0488) 71636.

FLAT & N.H.

WINT, Miss P., Hargate House Farm, Hilton, Derbyshire.
Tel: Etwall (028 373) 2387.

N.H.

WINTER, F. T., Uplands, Lambourn, Newbury, Berkshire.
Tel: Lambourn (0488) 71438.

N.H.

WINTER, J. R., Highfield, Bury Road, Newmarket, Suffolk.
Tel: Newmarket (0638) 3898.

FLAT

WISE, B. J., Linbury Stables, Jevington, Polegate, Sussex.
Tel: Polegate (032 12) 3331.

FLAT & N.H.

WOODMAN, S., Parkers Barn Stables, East Lavant, Chichester, Sussex.
Tel: Chichester (0243) 527136.   FLAT & N.H.

WRAGG, H., Abington Place, Bury Road, Newmarket, Suffolk.
Tel: Newmarket (0638) 2328.   FLAT

WRIGHT, J. S., Bredenbury Court Stables, Bromyard, Herefordshire.
Tel: Bromyard (088 52) 3239.   N.H.

YARDLEY, F., Glebe Farm, Stone, Kidderminster, Worcestershire.
Tel: Kidderminster (0562) 3537.   N.H.

YARNOLD, T. H., Bank Farm, Kyre. Tenbury Wells, Worcestershire.
                                        N.H.

YEOMAN, D., Middlethorpe Hall Stables, Middlethorpe, Yorkshire.
Tel: York (0904) 28693.   FLAT & N.H.

CHAPTER FIVE

Jockeys

'There is no secret so close as that between a rider and his horse.'

(R. S. Surtees)

In its early days, racing was confined to matches and to races run in heats. For the most part, gentlemen rode their own horses and, although there were grooms and boys known as riders who exercised horses, there were no jockeys as we know them today. But as the pattern of racing changed, stakes and prize money began to increase, and competition between owners became keener. Weight and riding skill began to play a greater part in the business of racing, and racehorse owners began to employ men to ride for them.

According to one early authority: 'The history of jockeys, in fact, may be said to commence with John Singleton, whose register is still in the church chest of Melbourne, near Pocklington, and bears the date – May 10th, 1715.'

Singleton began life as a cowherd and later on he became engaged/apprenticed to a Mr Read 'on the terms of sleeping in the stable and eating what he could get'. Later he began riding races for rich farmers and was often paid in sheep – these Mr Read reared for him. Singleton became especially interested in breeding horses for racing and crossing English mares with Arab stallions. One horse, Lucy, which was bred by Mr Read and Singleton, did so well that Singleton was approached by the Marquess of Rockingham who offered him the position of jockey and trainer at a salary of £40 per year.

Singleton was perhaps the first nationally-known professional jockey, and 'The Druid' says that 'no jockey ever had so many pictures taken (i.e., painted) of him'. Singleton remained with the Rockingham Stud as Manager until he retired in 1774.

About the time that Singleton retired, another jockey was beginning to make his mark. This was Sam Chifney who was born in Norfolk in 1753, and who began riding races in 1770 when he became attached to a stable at Newmarket. Chifney, it seems, had every confidence in his own ability. He once wrote: 'In 1773 I could ride horses in a better manner in a race than any other person known in my time.'

Chifney was apparently every bit as good as he claimed, and in July 1790 he was retained 'for life' to ride for the Prince of Wales (later George IV) at a fee of 200 guineas a year. This appointment was to prove short-lived, however. Following the notorious incident concerning the running of the Prince of Wales's horse Escape in October 1791 (*see* Jockey Club chapter) the Stewards of the Jockey Club warned the Prince that if he suffered Chifney to ride his horses no gentleman would start against him. The Prince, furious, withdrew his patronage of the Turf and settled 200 guineas a year on Chifney for life (the Prince's life, that is).

After this, Chifney went steadily downhill. He sold the annuity which the Prince had given him and moved from Newmarket to London, where he hoped to make his fortune by promoting the 'Chifney bit' which he had invented. However, he proved unsuccessful in this and was eventually committed to the Fleet Debtors' Prison, where he remained until he died in 1807, at the age of fifty-four.

In these days of high-speed transport, when a jockey can ride at Newmarket in the afternoon and Doncaster in the evening of the same day, it is difficult to imagine the rigours of life as experienced by the early jockeys. For example, John Day, writing in *The Racehorse in Training* of 1923 tells of how 'for two successive years when a boy, my grandfather, after taking part in Exeter races, rode his pony through the night to ride there [Stockbridge] the following day' – a distance of 100 miles!

Robert Black, writing in *The Jockey Club and Its Founders* (1891) tells us that Frank Collinson, who won the Derby in 1808, died as the result of sleeping in a damp bed on the way to Epsom. Jockeys suffered in other ways also – some being cheated out of their fees by owners. Even as late as 1880 the Jockey Club was legislating concerning the payment of jockeys' fees. Often the jockeys fell foul of crooked owners or trainers or of the legions of villains who infested racing at the time.

Not that all jockeys were saints by any means. Sam Chifney was suspected of having been concerned in many shady deals. And one Harry Edwards, although a brilliant jockey, was said to have cheated himself into abject poverty. In the early days of racing, riding could be a very rough business indeed, and jockeys were up to all manner of tricks to win races. There are horrific stories of horses being almost cut to pieces by whip and spur. Jockeys at that time were not only allowed to own and run racehorses, but they were also allowed to bet – and many of them did so, very heavily indeed.

Of course, there were plenty of honest jockeys, men such as Frank Buckle and Jem Robinson. Buckle, who was born in 1766, was known as the 'Pocket Hercules'. He won the Derby five times, the Oaks nine times, and the St Leger twice. When Buckle died in 1832, the following verse was written about him:–

'No better rider ever crossed a horse;
Honour his guide, he died without remorse.
Jockeys, attend – from his example learn
The meed that honest worth is sure to earn.'

In 1824 Jem Robinson wagered that he would win the Derby, the Oaks and get married all in the same week. He did so, and won £1,000. In all, Robinson won the Derby six times. He was the son of a farmer, and became a protégé of Frank Buckle. In 1850 Robinson (at the age of sixty) ran the great horse Voltigeur to a dead heat in the St Leger, riding a horse called Russborough. In addition to his Derby successes, Robinson won the St Leger twice, the Oaks twice, and the Two Thousand Guineas nine times.

Another notable jockey of the early nineteenth century was Will Scott, the foremost northern jockey of the time. Described by the trainer Matthew Dawson as a 'good rough jockey', Scott had an incredible record of success. He won the Derby four times, the Oaks three times, and the St Leger nine times. Scott was a drinker, to say the least, and by his own admission, from the time he was twenty, he had never spent a sober evening.

In 1879 the Jockey Club Rules Committee introduced rulings concerning jockeys, and thereafter jockeys were not allowed to own and run racehorses or to bet on horse races. Furthermore, they were now to be licensed by the Jockey Club.

Riding is even more stringently controlled nowadays and since the advent of the patrol camera, the slightest infringement of the rules can result in a Stewards' Enquiry, and the offending jockeys are often fined or suspended from riding for some time.

A study of an early print or painting of racehorses in action shows the jockeys riding in a long-legged, upright manner. This was the normal method of riding until the arrival of the American jockey, Tod Sloan.

SOME FAMOUS JOCKEYS

FRED ARCHER (1857–1886)

Fred Archer was born in Cheltenham in 1857, the son of a National Hunt jockey, William Archer. At the age of eleven, Fred was apprenticed to Matthew Dawson at Heath House, Newmarket. Although he was sensitive and delicate, he soon won his master's admiration because he could ride anything. He had won a steeplechase at Bangor before he had his first ride on the flat.

Archer's first victory under Jockey Club rules was on Athol Daisy in a nursery race at Chesterfield in September 1870. In this, his first season, he had two wins from fifteen rides. The next season he had three winners from forty rides. Archer went on to win the Cesarewitch in his next season, although his other successes were still rather limited. When Tom French died in 1874, the way was left open for Fred Archer to ride Lord Falmouth's strong string of horses in training with Dawson. He immediately became champion jockey – a position which he held for the rest of his life.

Gradually, Archer began to have trouble with his weight. Although in 1875 he was able to weigh in at 7 stone 2 lbs, by 1879 he had difficulty in keeping to 8 stone 7 lbs. He had grown to 5 feet $8\frac{1}{2}$ inches in height, and was apparently very attractive to women. He married in 1883, but unfortunately his young child and his wife both died in 1884 – an incident which affected him deeply. He later considered remarrying; it is said that he thought of marrying the Duchess of Montrose, but refused when he realised he would not become a Duke.

In 1884 over forty-one per cent of Archer's rides were winners. In 1885, after the loss of his family, he threw himself into his work, reaching an all-time record at that time of 246 winners from 667 rides. He was then undisputedly the greatest jockey that had ever lived. In 1885, when he reached this record, his wins included the Two Thousand Guineas, the Oaks, Derby, St Leger, and the Grand Prix de Paris.

During his career, Fred Archer rode some remarkable races. One of the finest races he ever rode was on Bend Or in the 1880 Derby. A short while before the race, a horse called Muley Edris attacked and trampled Archer on the gallops. If it had not been for the horse slipping and running away in fright, Archer would probably have been killed. As it was, he could not move his arm, and the enforced rest, together with the wasting necessary to keep his weight in check, made great demands on Archer's health. Despite being unable to use his whip, he won the Derby.

One of the best horses he ever rode was St Simon. One day Archer rode the horse at a gallop, using spurs because the horse was not moving freely. St Simon took off with him, and ran into another string which had started off up the gallops a couple of furlongs in front. Archer was only able to stop the horse at the end of the Limekilns Gallop.

Archer was a great judge of horses, and immediately developed a mutual understanding with any animal he rode. He would tell owners that a horse would win next time out if he rode it – he also told them not to run their horses if he thought he could win on something else. He was gentle, modest and fearless, but he was also unscrupulous and won some clever races. If he knew that a horse running against him hated to run alone, he would keep well clear of it until it was worked up and fighting, and would then catch up with it and pass it just before the winning post.

Although Archer was practically illiterate, he was very intelligent. He was also fond of money – hence his nickname – 'The Tinman'. It was Fred Archer's increasing weight problem which brought about his death in 1886; the effort of trying to get down to 8 stone 6 lbs from 9 st 4 lbs to ride St Mirin in the Cambridgeshire – the only important race he never won – proved to be too much for him. Even though Archer used featherweight silks and saddle, he still had to put up 1 lb overweight, and was beaten by a short head. Soon after this he developed a chill and then typhoid fever. He eventually shot himself, on the anniversary of his wife's death.

Another jockey worth mentioning is George Fordham – 'The Demon' – reputed to be one of the greatest jockeys ever. A contemporary description of him reads as follows: 'Fordham, with his little short legs looking almost pinned at the knee to the saddle, on which he appeared propped up rather than sitting down, flourishing his whip and riding more with his body and shoulders than his legs, yet getting every ounce of his horse to the very last stride on the post.'

Fordham rode fifteen Classic winners (and was champion jockey thirteen times), and there were many people who thought him a better jockey than Fred Archer.

Other jockeys of the period were Tom Cannon (winner of thirteen Classic races), and Tiny Wells (winner of eight Classic races, including three Derbys – on Beadsman, Musjid, and Blue Gown, which were all owned by Sir Joseph Hawley). It was Wells who refused to tell Queen Victoria his weight, when asked. His reply to her was: 'Please, Ma'am, the master told me never to say how much I weighed.'

TOD SLOAN (d.1933)

Sloan was born in Indiana. He was given the names James Foreman Sloan but, because he had extremely short legs, he became known as Toad and then Tod.

Sloan had an unhappy childhood, his mother having died when he was five years old. As he grew older, Tod's brother, Cash, insisted on his working in stables, no doubt because of his small stature. Tod was afraid of horses and he himself said that at that stage of his career he was so bad that he was only allowed to ride those horses which the trainers wanted to lose.

One day, whether by accident or design, Tod Sloan adopted a new style of riding – a forward crouch with short reins and shortened stirrup leathers. This style was once described as 'the monkey on a stick', and it has since been attributed to both the American Red Indian and the American Negro riders.

In 1897 Sloan came to England to ride. At first, his style of riding was a source of both dismay and amusement. Then it was realised that Sloan was beginning to win a great many races. His original style of riding, plus his experience of the starting gate (at that time a recent innovation as far as English racing was concerned) enabled him to get a head start on his English rivals. Soon other jockeys started to use the Sloan style of riding, and the whole concept of race riding was changed.

Although he was a brilliant jockey, Sloan was less attractive as a person. It seems that he was wild and unstable, and quite unable to cope with his success. He was constantly rude to people especially, it seems, to his friends. He tried to bribe other jockeys to let him win races, and he also bet very heavily. It was this which brought about his downfall.

Sloan had bet very heavily on the 1900 Cambridgeshire race, which he lost, riding Codaman. In the weighing room after the race, Sloan insulted the winning jockey. Sloan was called before the Stewards, and in 1901 he was politely advised against applying for a licence to ride in England again. After this, Sloan gradually sank into oblivion, until he died in the charity ward of a Los Angeles hospital in 1933.

Without doubt, the three most famous flat race jockeys of the twentieth century to date are Steve Donoghue, Gordon Richards and Lester Piggott. This is not to denigrate the many other good jockeys of the period – men such as Joe Childs, Harry Wragg, Charlie Smirke, Harry Carr, Charlie Elliott, etc., and, more recently, Willie Carson, Pat Eddery, Frankie Durr, Paul Cook, Sandy Barclay, Eric Eldin, Ron Hutchinson, Geoff Lewis, all of whom are very fine jockeys indeed. But the above named trio are outstanding, having what is known in the theatre as 'star quality'.

STEVE DONOGHUE (1884–1945)

Donoghue was born in Warrington in 1884, the son of a steelworker, who spent most of his money backing the wrong horses. Steve Donoghue became a steelworker at the age of twelve, but one day, after having walked to Chester to see the races, he decided he wanted to be a jockey. However, his first job did not last very long – the first time he rode a thoroughbred out at exercise with John Porter's string, he fell off. The horse had bolted, disrupting the string which contained Flying Fox, the red-hot favourite for that year's Derby.

Donoghue returned to Warrington, but left hurriedly when he feared that he had killed another boy in a street fight. He went to Newmarket, where his riding potential was soon realised. Donoghue then went to France, where he rode his first winner on 25th April, 1904.

In 1906, he left for Ireland, returning to England in 1910 to concentrate on riding the very best English horses. He was offered the retainer to Fred Darling's stable, which trained Lord Woolavington's horses; he rode these until he chose to ride Papyrus instead of Lord Woolavington's Knockando in the 1923 Derby. In 1920 Donoghue was riding Abbots Trace in Spion Kop's Derby, when he was brought down by Sarchedon, which suddenly swerved. Luckily, this fall had no serious consequences, and Donoghue went on to win a Derby hat-trick – winning in 1921 on the one-lunged horse, Humorist; in 1922 on the massive Captain Cuttle; and in 1923 on Papyrus, on whom he set an Epsom record. In 1925, Donoghue won the Derby again, on Manna.

Apart from these good horses, Donoghue had two legendary animals to ride – Brown Jack, who won twenty-five of his sixty-five races, and who established himself as a great character; and The Tetrarch, who retired unbeaten after rapping a fetlock before the Derby. (Donoghue did not think The Tetrarch would have stayed the Derby course and distance, in any case).

Steve Donoghue recorded some remarkable incidents – once he turned down a Royal retainer; another time he went on a short holiday to Paris, where he won the Grand Prix de Paris on Admiral Drake (a ride he was offered only a few hours before the race). He had some bad luck, too, in connection with the colt, April the Fifth, owned by Tom Walls. Donoghue told Walls that the colt would do well in the Derby, but when Donoghue was asked to ride him in the Two Thousand Guineas, he refused because he was riding Firdaussi. April the Fifth finished a creditable sixth in that race. Walls again asked Donoghue to ride his colt in the Derby, but he chose to ride Firdaussi instead, and April the Fifth won the Derby by three-quarters of a length from Dastur. Unfortunately, April the Fifth injured a knee, and finished thirteenth in the St Leger. The race was won by Firdaussi, who started at 20 to 1 – this time Donoghue was not riding him.

Steve Donoghue topped the jockeys' table for ten years, sharing first place in 1928 with Charlie Elliott. After his retirement from riding,

Donoghue turned to training, but was not very successful.

He was a brave, skilful, generous, and very popular man, although he was rather casual about business matters. After his death in 1945, he was very much missed by all who had known him.

GORDON RICHARDS (b.1904)

Gordon Richards was born in Shropshire in 1904. He went to work at Martin Hartigan's stables, and first learned the art of riding racehorses from Steve Donoghue. Gordon Richards started as a jockey in 1920, and he retired from riding in 1954, when he became a trainer.

Gordon Richards was Champion Jockey twenty-six times, but, somehow he never rode the winner of the Derby until the last year of his jockeyship, when he stormed home on Pinza, beating the Queen's horse, Aureole. He also won the King George VI and Queen Elizabeth Stakes in the same year, again on Pinza.

Gordon Richards won thirteen other Classic races, on Sugare, Chumleigh, Turkham, Sun Chariot and Tehran in the St Leger; on Rose of England and Sun Chariot in the Oaks; on Pasch, Big Game and Tudor Minstrel in the Two Thousand Guineas; and on Sun Chariot, Queenpot and Belle of All in the One Thousand Guineas. Gordon Richards was first jockey to the Beckhampton Stable for many years, but he also held a retainer from Fitzroy House Stable.

One of the proudest moments in Richards' life must have been when, in 1933, he won his 247th race of the season, beating Fred Archer's previous record of 246 winners, which he had set up in 1885. However, he surpassed this magnificent total in 1947, when he rode a total of 269 winners in one season. During his career as a jockey, Richards rode a total of 4,870 winners, out of 21,828 rides.

In 1926 Gordon Richards became seriously ill with consumption, but luckily for him, and for us, he recovered his health completely, returning to the Turf as a jockey in 1927. He went on to become one of the most popular and highly respected jockeys ever to ride in England. He was knighted in 1953 for his services to racing, and retired in 1970.

LESTER PIGGOTT (b.1935)

In 1948 a young apprentice jockey rode his first winner at the precocious age of thirteen. Twenty-eight years later, riding the French colt Empery, that same jockey became the first in racing's history to win the Derby seven times. During those twenty-eight years Lester Piggott, eight times Champion Jockey, had become certainly the most famous and arguably the best jockey of all time.

Lester Piggott came of a racing family : his grandfather, Ernest Piggott, rode two Grand National winners, and his father, Keith, was a well-known jump jockey and trainer. Lester's mother was a member of the famous Rickaby racing family.

Lester Piggott's early racing career was a stormy one, to say the least. Apprenticed to his father, he was a brilliant, if occasionally reckless rider, dominated always by the will to win. This recklessness brought him to the attention of the Stewards on more than one occasion. At the age of eighteen, he rode his first Derby winner, Never Say Die. Shortly afterwards, as the result of his riding Never Say Die in the King Edward VII Stakes at Ascot, Lester Piggott was suspended for the rest of the Ascot Meeting and was reported to the Stewards of the Jockey Club.

Eventually it was announced that he had been suspended for the rest of the season for dangerous and erratic riding, since he had continued to 'show complete disregard for the Rules of Racing and for the safety of others jockeys' despite having had previous warnings. It was also announced that before his licence would be renewed he had to serve six months' apprenticeship with a trainer other than his father. Subsequently, he went to Jack Jarvis (Lord Rosebery's trainer) and he was to have a long association with Noel Murless' stable before going freelance in 1967.

At the same time, some people thought that the Stewards had been rather hard on the young jockey and that he hadn't been the only one at fault in the running of the race that led to his suspension. However, the suspension seemed to do the trick as far as his recklessness was concerned. Thereafter, although still as determined to win as ever, he managed to combine his skill, verve and determination with a professional caution and a respect for the Rules. Although he has since (and no doubt will again) come up against the Racing authorities, he has never allowed his nerve or confidence to be in any way diminished, nor has his will to win evaporated over the years. It is impossible to leave him out of the reckoning in whatever race and on whatever horse he is riding, for Lester Piggott is a master, perhaps one should say *the master*, where racing tactics are concerned.

A superb judge of horses, he can play a waiting game, tucking his horse in at the rear or middle of the field. Then, at exactly the right moment, he manages to get his horse to produce a sudden, devastating burst of speed to win his race in the last few, expertly judged, strides. A fine example of this was in the 1968 Derby when he produced Sir Ivor in an electrifying burst of speed to the astonishment of the crowd who thought that Sandy Barclay had already won the race on Connaught.

Piggott often plays the 'waiting game' in front of the field. Many a jockey lying in a comfortable second or third position, waiting for Lester's horse to 'come back to the field', has suddenly realised that Piggott has, in fact, expertly slipped the field and gone on to win.

Lester Piggott is often described as looking dour; the 'enigmatic Lester Piggott' is a phrase often found in the racing columns of the Press. Yet behind that often expressionless countenance there must be a brain like a computer when it comes to matters of judgement of pace, distance, balance and timing. Critics of Piggott's racing style (and it is still possible for him to have critics even though he has been Champion Jockey nine times) say that he rides too short, i.e., with his stirrups too high up, that he is perched on top of the horse and is thus unable to control it properly. It is true that many a young jockey has tried to copy Lester, without success, but Lester is unique. Where riding style is concerned, he can do as he likes, and whatever his critics may say, his record is always there to confound them.

Again, much has been made of the fact that Piggott rides with his bottom high in the air (a very useful pointer when you are trying to pick him out in a race). Apparently, when asked why he rode with his bottom so high, he is reputed to have answered: 'Well, there's nowhere else to put it.'

Lester's popularity amongst racegoers, or rather amongst punters, is debatable; some love him, some hate him, but all respect him. To most of the habitués of the off-course betting shops, Lester Piggott is 'The Guv'nor' – the best.

During the past few years, Piggott has tended to ride rather less in England and more abroad, especially in France, where the prize money is better. Indeed, Lester has rather the same sort of reputation as Fred Archer (the Tinman) when it comes to money – of only really riding his best when the prize is greatest. This is, of course, nonsense. Lester Piggott, being the best jockey, is always in demand all over the world to ride the best horses in the richest races. He is also the right man for the big occasion, always appearing to be absolutely cool and collected before the start of any big race. Always in perfect control of the horse he is to ride and apparently absolutely nerveless, it is small wonder that the owner or trainer with a potential Classic winner should try to engage Lester to ride for him.

While on the subject of money, there are many stories which suggest Piggott is downright mean – an image which some people think he deliberately fosters (as he is not without humour). He is reputed to read only the Form Book, the *Sporting Life* and the *Financial Times*, and to have an encyclopaedic knowledge where racing form is concerned. Although he was taken up by the Press in a big way during his early years (and of course today it is hardly possible to read a racing column without some mention of his name) Lester Piggott has somehow managed to avoid that awful exposure which the media has given to some sportsmen which, in some instances, has seriously affected their careers.

Lester was born slightly deaf and with a cleft palate – not a good subject to interview. He was never a great conversationalist and no doubt was not always over-anxious to be interviewed. But luckily, during his formative years, television was still in its infancy and had not yet become the terrifying force it is today. More recently Lester Piggott has been seen in television interviews as, for example, when he spoke to Lord Oaksey after his historic Derby win on Empery. He is also seen to smile more often these days (he can afford to), although there was a time when a smiling Lester Piggott was a rarity.

From time to time there are rumours that he is to retire as a jockey to take up training. It will be a sad day for British racegoers when the magic and excitement that he brings to racing is no longer to be seen on the racecourse. But one suspects that if he trains with the same determination to win and the same skill that he shows when riding races, his name will continue to appear in the racing press just as frequently as it does today.

During his racing career, Lester Piggott has ridden well over 3,000 winners in Britain. His best season was in 1966 when he rode 191. Only one other jockey has ridden more – Sir Gordon Richards, who won 4,870 races. To list all of Piggott's winners would need a separate volume. The following, therefore, is Lester Piggott's record in the English Classic races – a remarkable record by any standards, and one which it is hoped is a long way from being completed, as it is hard to imagine the British racing scene without this remarkable man.

	Owner	Price	Trainer
ONE THOUSAND GUINEAS			
1970 Humble Duty	Jean, Lady Ashcombe	3–1	P. Walwyn
TWO THOUSAND GUINEAS			
1957 Crepello	Sir Victor Sassoon	7–2	N. Murless
1968 Sir Ivor	R. R. Guest	11–8	M. V. O'Brien
1970 Nijinsky (CAN)	C. W. Engelhard	4–7	M. V. O'Brien
DERBY			
1954 Never Say Die	Mr R. S. Clark	33–1	J. Lawson
1957 Crepello	Sir Victor Sassoon	6–4	N. Murless
1960 St Paddy	Sir Victor Sassoon	7–1	N. Murless
1968 Sir Ivor	R. R. Guest	4–5	M. V. O'Brien
1970 Nijinsky (CAN)	C. W. Engelhard	11–8	M. V. O'Brien
1972 Roberto	J. W. Galbreath	3–1	M. V. O'Brien
1976 Empery (USA)	N. B. Hunt	10–1	M. Zilber

OAKS

1957 Carrozza	H.M. The Queen	100–8	N. Murless
1959 Petite Etoile	Prince Aly Khan	11–2	N. Murless
1966 Valoris	C. Clore	11–10	M. V. O'Brien
1975 Juliette Marny	J. Morrison	12–1	J. Tree

ST LEGER

1960 St Paddy	Sir Victor Sassoon	4–6	N. Murless
1961 Aurelius	Mrs V. Lilley	9–2	N. Murless
1967 Ribocco	C. W. Engelhard	7–2	R. Houghton
1968 Ribero	C. W. Engelhard	100–30	R. Houghton
1970 Nijinsky (CAN)	C. W. Engelhard	2–7	M. V. O'Brien
1971 Athens Wood	Mrs J. Rogerson	5–2	H. Thomson Jones
1972 Boucher (USA)	O. Phipps	3–1	M. V. O'Brien

CHAMPION APPRENTICE

Year	Winners
1950	52
1951	51

CHAMPION JOCKEY

Year	Winners	Year	Winners	Year	Winners
1960	170	1966	191	1969	163
1964	140	1967	117	1970	162
1965	166	1968	139	1971	162

FAMOUS NATIONAL HUNT JOCKEYS

FRED WINTER (b.1926)

What Lester Piggott is to flat racing, so Fred Winter is to National Hunt racing. His skill, horsemanship and courage have established him for all time in the history of racing as the greatest jump jockey the sport has yet seen.

Four times Champion National Hunt jockey, he had over nine hundred winners to his credit, including two Grand Nationals, three Champion Hurdles, two Cheltenham Gold Cups, three King George VI Chases, and an historic Grand Steeplechase de Paris. Fred Winter rode his first winner in May 1940 at Salisbury. He was then just fourteen years of age and seemed all set for a successful career as a flat race jockey. However, the advent of World War II, plus increasing weight problems, combined to direct his career towards National Hunt racing.

During the war, after training as a parachutist, Fred Winter served as a lieutenant in the West Kent Regiment. After being demobbed, he turned his attention to jumping and, in his first season, 1947/48, he rode two winners out of nine rides.

At the beginning of the following season, he suffered a terrible blow when, as the result of a fall in a hurdle race at Wye racecourse, he broke his back. This injury, which would have been enough to discourage most people, kept him off the racecourse for over a year. But, by September 1949, he was once again riding over jumps.

During the 1949/50 season, he rode 18 winners out of 131 rides, and by the end of that season he had quite firmly established himself among the top flight of up and coming jump jockeys. His skill and determination had by this time attracted the attention of trainer Captain Ryan Price, for whom he was to ride over the next sixteen years.

During the 1950/51 season, Fred Winter rode in his first Grand National (the race with which his name was later to become so strongly associated) riding Glen Fire, which unfortunately fell at the Canal Turn. During this season he became one of the top jump jockeys, riding winners regularly. He wasn't far behind the Champion Jockey but had been out of action quite a lot of the time due to injuries caused by falls. Throughout his riding career, this incredibly tough and courageous man suffered and survived over three hundred falls.

During the 1952/53 season, despite some hundred falls, he rode a record 121 winners and this time he did become Champion Jockey. Then, at the beginning of the following season, a serious fall resulted in a broken leg, and Fred Winter was again out of action for a year.

Remarkably, he was back on the racecourse in July to ride in the 1954/55 season, and not only won the Champion Hurdle on Clair Soleil, but only just failed to beat Tim Molony in that season's Championship, the final tally of winners being Molony 67 – Winter 65.

The following season, however, Fred Winter regained the Championship, and in the 1956/57 season he not only became Champion Jockey for the third time, but also won his first Grand National – on Sundew. In the 1958/59 season he was robbed of the title as the result of another crashing fall, which this time resulted in a fractured skull.

Back again in the 1959/60 season, this extraordinary man, who must surely be made of india-rubber, survived a further thirty falls, and went on to achieve the seven hundredth win of his career. During the following season, which was a great one for Fred Winter, he won his third Champion Hurdle – on Eborneezer, and the Cheltenham Gold Cup – on Saffron Tartan. The 1961/62 season also brought its successes, when Fred Winter won the Cheltenham Gold Cup on Madame Peggy Hennessy's great horse, Mandarin; the Grand National (the first ever for Captain Ryan Price) on Kilmore; and also achieved his eight hundredth winner.

There are some horse and jockey partnerships which have become legendary, e.g., Lester Piggott and Nijinsky; Brian Fletcher and Red

Rum; Joe Mercer and Brigadier Gerard, but none more so than Fred Winter and Mandarin. Mention the name of either Fred Winter or Mandarin in any conversation with racing enthusiasts, and someone is bound to mention their great partnership.

In 1962, Mandarin, owned by Madame Hennessy, trained by Fulke Walwyn, and ridden by Fred Winter, won the Cheltenham Gold Cup by a length, after a terrific battle with the Irish horse, Fortria who was ridden by Pat Taaffe. In June that same year, Mandarin was entered for the gruelling Grand Steeplechase de Paris – the French Grand National. The story of this astonishing race is recounted under the Mandarin section, page 55.

In 1963 Fred Winter was awarded the C.B.E. for his services to racing. In 1964, at the age of thirty-seven, and after seventeen hard seasons, he decided to retire from riding. He had recently suffered a punctured lung following a fall at Chepstow, and this may have influenced his decision.

Fred Winter decided to become a trainer. Today it is difficult to imagine his being anything else. Indeed, it sometimes seems that there are two Fred Winters – the jockey and the trainer – so successful has he been in both careers.

In his first two seasons as a trainer, he won the Grand National twice: in 1965 with Jay Trump, and in 1966 with Anglo. Since then his name has been associated with many famous horses, including Bula, Pendil and the 1973 Grand National runner-up, Crisp, and in 1974 this amazing man was the leading National Hunt trainer for the fourth successive year.

STAN MELLOR (b.1938)

One of the most popular and respected figures in National Hunt racing, and one of the foremost jump jockeys of his time is Stan Mellor. The son of a northern timber merchant, Stan Mellor became interested in riding at an early age, and by the time he was ten years old he was a regular winner in junior show jumping competitions.

When he was fifteen he was apprenticed to the Tarporley trainer, George Owen (a one-time professional jump jockey who won the 1939 Cheltenham Gold Cup on Brendan's Cottage). Owen seems to have had a flair for training apprentices, for he also produced Dick Francis and Tim Brookshaw, both Champion Jockeys.

After riding as an amateur for a year in order to gain race riding experience, Stan Mellor turned professional at sixteen. He won his first race at Wolverhampton, riding Straight Border.

A skilful horseman, with courage and with perfect timing where jumping was concerned (no doubt as the result of his earlier show jumping experience), Mellor soon established himself among the top rank of jump jockeys. At the end of the 1959/60 National Hunt season he succeeded Tim Brookshaw as Champion Jockey, with a total of 68 winners. He was again Champion Jockey in the following season, with 117 winners, and in the 1961/62 season he brought off the 'hat-trick' with 80 winners.

In 1963 it looked as though Stan Mellor's riding career had come to an end when he suffered a crashing fall when riding Eastern Harvest in the Schweppes Gold Trophy at Liverpool; he fractured his jaw in *sixteen* places.

But National Hunt jockeys seem to be made of different stuff from the rest of us, and Stan Mellor was soon riding again. He not only managed to break Fred Winter's record of 923 winners, but went on to become the first jump jockey ever to ride over 1,000 winners.

A veteran of well over 5,000 rides, it comes as a surprise to find that Stan Mellor never won the Grand National. However, he does have the distinction of having beaten Arkle, when riding Stalbridge Colonist in the Hennessy Gold Cup.

In 1969 Stan Mellor was awarded the M.B.E. for his services to racing. He also received the Derby Award as National Hunt Jockey of the Year. Greatly respected throughout the racing world for his courage and good humour, Stan Mellor was at one time Chairman of the National Hunt Jockeys' Association. Later, when this was amalgamated with the Flat Racing Association, he was elected Vice-President of the Jockeys' Association.

At the end of the 1971/72 season, Stan Mellor retired in order to train at Lambourn, and has been very successful in his new career.

TERRY BIDDLECOMBE (b.1941)

Terry Biddlecombe was born in Gloucester in 1941. His father, Walter Biddlecombe, a farmer, was himself at one time a well-known point-to-point rider and show jumper.

Terry Biddlecombe rode his first winner under Rules as an amateur in 1958 when he was only seventeen. Riding a novice hurdler, Burnella, at Wincanton, he managed to snatch victory by a head from the great Fred Winter on Piper.

Having ridden 22 winners as an amateur, Terry Biddlecombe turned professional in 1959, achieving his first professional win at Market Rasen on Bonnie Warrior.

At the start of the 1963/64 season, Terry Biddlecombe became stable jockey to Fred Rimell, thus forming one of the most formidable partnerships in National Hunt racing. Biddlecombe won the Jockeys' Championship in the 1964/65 season with 114 winners. The following season he was again Champion, this time with 102 winners.

In 1967 he won the Cheltenham Gold Cup on Woodland Venture, beating such first-class jumpers as Fort Leney, Mill House and What a Myth. In 1969 and again in 1971, he won the Mackeson Gold Cup on Gay Trip. Unfortunately, injuries resulting from a bad fall, caused him to miss the ride on Gay Trip in the 1970 Grand National. Characteristically, it was Terry Biddlecombe himself who suggested that Pat Taaffe should have the ride, and he was delighted when Gay Trip won. Two years later, he had his chance to ride Gay Trip in the National and they finished second.

At the end of the 1968/69 season, Terry Biddlecombe was Champion Jockey again, sharing the title with his brother-in-law, Bob Davies, with a total of 77 winners.

Five feet 11 inches is very tall for a jockey, and throughout his career, Terry Biddlecombe was beset by weight problems, continually having to 'waste' in order to make the necessary riding weight of 10 stone 7 lbs., or thereabouts.

During his career, he suffered and survived over 300 falls and at one time or another has either dislocated or broken almost every bone in his body. Nevertheless, Terry Biddlecombe shared the indomitable spirit of people like Fred Winter and Stan Mellor, and kept coming back for more. His courage and skill have earned him the respect of both his fellow jockeys and racegoers alike.

In 1974, his weight having become an increasing problem, Terry Biddlecombe decided to retire after sixteen years as a first rate jockey, with over 900 wins to his credit.

CHAMPION JOCKEYS

FLAT RACING

Season	Rider	Number of Winners
1952	G. Richards	231
1953	G. Richards	191
1954	D. Smith	129
1955	D. Smith	168
1956	D. Smith	155
1957	A. Breasley	173
1958	D. Smith	165
1959	D. Smith	157
1960	L. Piggott	170
1961	A. Breasley	171
1962	A. Breasley	179
1963	A. Breasley	176

1964	L. Piggott	140
1965	L. Piggott	166
1966	L. Piggott	191
1967	L. Piggott	117
1968	L. Piggott	139
1969	L. Piggott	163
1970	L. Piggott	162
1971	L. Piggott	162
1972	W. Carson	132
1973	W. Carson	163
1974	P. Eddery	148
1975	P. Eddery	164
1976	P. Eddery	162

NATIONAL HUNT

Season	Rider	Number of Winners
1951–52	T. Molony	99
1952–53	F. Winter	121
1953–54	R. Francis	76
1954–55	T. Molony	67
1955–56	F. Winter	74
1956–57	F. Winter	80
1957–58	F. Winter	82
1958–59	T. Brookshaw	83
1959–60	S. Mellor	68
1960–61	S. Mellor	117
1961–62	S. Mellor	80
1962–63	J. Gifford	70
1963–64	J. Gifford	94
1964–65	T. Biddlecombe	114
1965–66	T. Biddlecombe	102
1966–67	J. Gifford	122
1967–68	J. Gifford	82
1968–69	{ T. Biddlecombe { B. R. Davies	77
1969–70	B. R. Davies	91
1970–71	G. Thorner	74
1971–72	B. R. Davies	89
1972–73	R. Barry	125
1973–74	R. Barry	94
1974–75	T. Stack	82
1975–76	J. Francome	96

LADY JOCKEYS

' "Now women are mostly troublesome cattle to deal with," said Coggins.'

(*S. Lower, 1797–1868*)

Prior to 1971 the only race that women were permitted to ride in was the Newmarket Town Plate, which was not under Rules. For some time the Jockey Club had been thinking about the idea of women's races, mainly for flat racing stable girls, who had no chance of riding except in point-to-point races.

When Mrs Judy Goodhew, the wife of a Kent Permit Holder, applied for a licence to ride over hurdles, she was promptly turned down, but a few weeks later the Jockey Club announced its intention of experimenting with ladies' races during the 1972 flat racing season.

In all, six races were planned for that season, but the response from racecourses and sponsors was so great that the number of races planned was doubled before the season had started. All ladies' races were to be for 3-year old horses and upwards, to be started from stalls, and to be run over distances of one mile or a mile and a half. The prize money was limited to £1,000, and there were to be no handicap races. Furthermore, races were to be in addition to the normal six-race card and, finally, races were not to be divided – if the safety limit for the number of entries was exceeded, then horses were to be balloted out.

When it was first announced that there were to be ladies' races, the media went wild – all the obvious jokes were made ad nauseum, and all the obvious newspaper articles duly appeared. Happily, the racing press took a saner view, but the fact that girls had ridden in point-to-points, hunted, and ridden out for stables for years was conveniently forgotten. What the media seemed to want was a bunch of pretty girls leaping about with horses. What they got was a number of very determined young ladies (albeit pretty ones) who were anxious to gain experience in the very specialised field of race riding.

On Saturday, 6th May, 1972 racing history was made when the first-ever ladies' race in Britain (women riders have been part of the racing scene for some time in America, Europe and Japan) was run at Kempton Park. Twenty-one runners took part, and the race was won by twenty-three-year old Meriel Tufnell, riding her mother's horse, Scorched Earth (50 to 1). Meriel Tufnell also went on to win the *Daily Mirror* sponsored Ladies' Championship.

Altogether, some ninety girls rode in this first series of ladies' races and, because of the girls' lack of racing experience, these races were somewhat curious to watch. Invariably the horses were strung out in a procession, there seemed to be no rhythm to the race, and the horses appeared to bucket about all over the place. This is not to denigrate the women riders, but it is obviously one thing to be an experienced rider and quite another to be an experienced jockey.

Within a very short time, however, the best of the women riders were beginning to ride with something like the economy of style of their male counterparts. They no longer went wide at the bends, and began to ride their finishes with much more style and expertise.

In 1973, twenty ladies' races were run, each on a different course, all over distances of a mile or a mile and a half. The basic weight was raised from 9 stone to 9 stone 7 lbs, and an allowance of 5 lbs was recommended for girls riding for their own stables who had not previously ridden a winner. In 1973, the champion lady jockey was Linda Goodwill, who had been runner-up to Meriel Tufnell in 1972.

In 1973 the Jockey Club granted 150 licences to girls, permitting them to ride in races.

Women were permitted to ride against men in 1974 (in amateur races), and in 1975 women were allowed to apply for Professional Jockey's Licences.

At the time of writing there are four girls holding professional licences but, so far, in one and a half seasons' racing, although they have managed to gain several places, they have yet to ride a winner. In 1976 the first National Hunt Amateur Permits were issued to lady jockeys, Mrs Muriel Naughton being the first woman to ride over fences. Over forty women jockeys have since ridden under National Hunt Rules, and between them they have won ten races, all of these being against professional jockeys.

THE SEX DISCRIMINATION ACT

The Sex Discrimination Act, which came into force on the 29th December 1975, now means that women may ride on equal terms with men, both on the flat and over fences and hurdles, provided that they hold the appropriate Amateur Riders Permit or Professional Licence.

On the flat, women may now hold a professional licence which allows them to compete against male professional jockeys, or an Amateur Riders Permit which will allow them to ride against male amateurs in Amateur Riders Races. If they are members of the Lady Jockeys Association, they are able to get a special permit which will allow them to ride in races confined to members of the L.J.A., which will be the only 'Ladies Only' races to be run on the flat.

Ironically, with the introduction of the Sex Discrimination Act, 'Ladies Only' flat races were ruled out. However, after negotiations had taken place between the Lady Jockeys Association, the Senior Steward of the Jockey Club and the Minister for Sport, Mr Denis Howell, it was agreed to follow the advice of the Equal Opportunities Commission. This determined that as a voluntary body (under Section 31 of the Act) it would be open to the Lady Jockeys Association to run single sex races for the Association's own members.

Before the Act, girls paid to work in racing stables had been able to ride in the 'Ladies Only' races. However, after the Act was brought into force, it was thought that they would have to be regarded as 'professionals' in the same way as male stable employees. These girls may now ride in the races put on by the Lady Jockeys Association.

The Rules of Racing have also been amended so that both men and women may return to amateur status if they have not worked 'professionally' in the sport for twelve months.

Over fences and hurdles, women, like men, may either ride professionally, or with an Amateur Riders Permit.

From the 1st July 1977, Amateur Riders Permits for both men and women will be issued in two categories. Category A Permits will be required for all amateur flat races, steeplechases and hurdle races. Category B Permits will be needed for steeplechases and hurdle races which are open to professional jockeys. The granting of a Category B Permit will be dependant upon the Licensing Stewards being fully satisfied that the applicant has sufficient experience to ride against professionals.

The introduction of ladies' races in 1972 gave horse racing a great boost as far as publicity is concerned. It also attracted sponsorship, and brought many more girls into stable work, enticed no doubt, by the prospect of riding in races. But, to some extent, the novelty of the ladies-only flat races has now worn off, and they tend to be regarded by the general public as being very much on a level with apprentice races – to be taken seriously as races, but not really worth having a bet on. In the off-course betting shops, ladies' races are still regarded with a good deal of suspicion by the dyed-in-the-wool punters.

However, since the advent of the first ladies' races, lady jockeys have been making their presence felt in all spheres of racing but, in view of the comparative strength for weight of the sexes, it is debatable whether we shall ever see a Derby or a Grand National winner ridden by a woman.

It will probably be a long time before a really great lady jockey does emerge, although anyone who saw the degree of skill and determination with which Miss Charlotte Brew tackled the difficult Aintree fences in March 1976 or the professional pre-race coolness of Miss Johanna Morgan at the start of the Irish Sweeps Derby, can have no doubts that lady jockeys are here to stay.

LADIES MAKE RACING HISTORY

1. At Kempton Park on May 6th, 1972, Miss Meriel Tufnell won the first ever ladies' race, riding Scorched Earth (50–1). Miss Tufnell went on to become the first ever Lady Champion Jockey.

2. At Kempton Park on April 30th, 1974, Miss Rosemary Rooney, riding Onward Taroo, won the first ever Ladies' International race in England.

3. Professional licences for flat racing were first issued to women in 1975. The first lady to turn professional was Miss Linda Goodwill.

4. At Stratford-upon-Avon on February 7th, 1976, Miss Diana Thorne became the first woman to win against men in a National Hunt race, when she rode Ben Ruler in her first ride under National Hunt Rules.

5. At the Aintree Meeting in April 1976, Miss Charlotte Brew became the first woman to ride round the testing Aintree course, when she finished a creditable fourth on Barony Fort in the Greenall Whitley Foxhunters' Chase.

6. At Phoenix Park, Ireland, on March 17th (St Patrick's Day), 1976 Miss Johanna Morgan, riding Mount Eaton, beat Lester Piggott by half a length in the G.T.X. Spring Handicap.

7. At Edinburgh on April 12th, 1976, Lady Kilmany, Joint-Master of the Fife Hunt, and a well-known and successful point-to-point rider, became the first woman to act as a local Steward.

8. At the Curragh, Ireland, on June 26th, 1976, Miss Johanna Morgan became the first woman to ride in a European Classic race, when she rode the unplaced Riot Helmet in the Irish Sweeps Derby.

LADY JOCKEYS' ASSOCIATION OF GREAT BRITAIN

This Association was formed at the end of 1972 season, Great Britain being the first country to form such an association. Basically, the L.J.A. formed itself, although it received a lot of help from the Jockeys' Association and the Amateur Riders' Association of Great Britain, neither of which the girls are permitted to join.

The current Secretary of the Lady Jockeys' Association is Mrs Vivien Kay. The Honorary Treasurer is Joy Gibson, and the first Chairman was Meriel Tufnell, the first champion lady jockey. Full membership is open only to those girls who have weighed out for a Flat Race. Only full members have a vote, ensuring that the Association is actually controlled by the girls themselves. Associate membership is open to anyone.

THE INJURED JOCKEYS' FUND

'As long as men ride horses at racing speed, falls and injuries will happen.'

(Lord Oaksey, 1973)

Harriet, Lady Ashburton, writing in the early nineteenth century, commented upon the wonderful freemasonry to be found amongst the racing fraternity, describing them as 'the only people who really hold together'. Anyone who doubts that this spirit of camaraderie still exists in racing need look no further than the Injured Jockeys' Fund.

Following the serious injuries to the National Hunt jockeys, Paddy Farrell and Tim Brookshaw, during the winter season of 1963/64, an appeal was made to set up a fund for the benefit of these two jockeys. Public response to this appeal proved to be so generous that when the Farrell/Brookshaw Fund was closed in 1964, it was decided that any further donations were to be used to found a new charity fund called 'The Injured National Hunt Jockeys' Fund'. This was set up in order to make grants or weekly payments to any injured National Hunt jockeys or their families. The initial appeal for this new Fund realised approximately £6,000 and donations, both large and small, have been forthcoming ever since. In fact, by 1976, somewhere in the region of £226,000 had been distributed in various ways to more than sixty jockeys and their families, and the Fund is currently paying out some £300 every week.

In addition to the financial assistance that the Fund has been able to offer to injured or permanently disabled jockeys, the Trustees have used the Fund to further the interests of injured jockeys in many other ways. They have, for instance, been able to obtain legal advice where questions concerning compensation have arisen. Also, jockeys have been encouraged and financed to undertake vocational training schemes, in cases where their injuries were such that they have been forced to seek other employment.

The Trustees of the Fund are in constant touch with the Horserace Betting Levy Board and have paid the expenses of several jockeys who have attended the Medical Rehabilitation Centre under a scheme devised and initiated by the Board's one-time Chairman, Lord Wigg.

Recently the name of the Fund has been changed to the 'Injured Jockeys' Fund' and under its new Trust Deed, the Fund is now able to assist all jockeys, whether they be engaged in Flat racing or in National Hunt racing.

The Fund's main source of income to date has come from the Christmas cards sold on its behalf every year. Since its inception, however, money has been raised by a variety of people in any number of imaginative ways. For example, in December 1964 a special performance of *Our Man Crichton* was held at the Shaftesbury Theatre, in the presence of Her Majesty Queen Elizabeth the Queen Mother; this raised over £11,000 for the Fund. Mr Tim Durant paid over to the Fund the sum he won in respect of a wager made by a bookmaker against his completing the course in the 1968 Grand National. During an outbreak of foot and mouth disease the *Evening Standard* newspaper organised a computerised version of the King George VI Chase and presented a cheque for £1,000 to the fund. One final example of just how much voluntary effort goes into raising money for the Fund – during the summer of 1967 the National Hunt Jockeys' Cricket Team collected over £500. Supporters of the Injured Jockeys' Fund have also raised money by means of raffles, dances and special events organised by race courses, and in this way they attempt to repay, in some small measure, those jockeys who, while giving racegoers so much pleasure, have suffered fearful physical injury.

INFORMATION

Any communications concerning the Fund should be addressed to the Secretary, The Injured Jockeys' Fund, Market Place, Ely, Cambridgeshire, or to any of the Trustees: Mr E. R. Courage, C.B.E.; Lord Oaksey; Mrs Lester Piggott; Mr F. T. Winter, C.B.E.; Wing Commander P. D. O. Vaux; Mr R. J. McCreery and J. A. T. Barstow, D.S.O., T.D.

CHAPTER SIX

The Jockey Club

'I don't pretend to know much, but I can judge men and horses.'
(*Lord George Bentinck, 1802–1848*)

The exact date of the founding of the Jockey Club is unknown. The first recorded reference to the Club, however, appeared in 1752 in *Sporting Kalendar*, published by Mr Pond, a Newmarket auctioneer. 'A contribution plate will be run for at Newmarket on Wednesday, April 1st, 1752, by horses the property of noblemen and gentlemen belonging to the Jockey Club at the Star and Garter, Pall Mall.'

This then was the Club's first London meeting place. Subsequently Mr Richard Tattersall, founder of the firm of bloodstock auctioneers, provided the Club with two rooms and a cook at his Hyde Park premises, which were opened in 1766. Later, however, Mr Weatherby's rooms in Old Burlington Street became the Club's headquarters. Although the first mention of the Jockey Club relates to its London meeting place, it is thought that the Club originated some time before 1752 at Newmarket – 'as a pleasant and convenient assembly of gentlemen of like tastes and background, who raced at Newmarket and who wanted a club to meet in.'

It was in 1752, however, that the Club acquired the site of the original Coffee House at Newmarket. The Jockey Club Rooms at Newmarket continue to this day on the same site, with the original coffee house (which consisted of alcoves set round a courtyard) roofed over and built into the existing building.

The term 'Jockey' in the eighteenth century meant, in fact, 'rider', as all riders were amateurs, being for the most part gentlemen owners, in the early days of racing.

The Jockey Club was hardly the dignified, authoritarian body which we know today. Primarily, the Club was a social one, with no aspirations to becoming the ruling body of the Turf, and membership appears to have been general. Early records provide us with instances of bouts of fisticuffs having taken place within the Club. In 1767 two members were accused by a Mr Brereton (described by Lady Sarah Bunbury as a 'sad vulgar') of having cheated at cards. Following this incident, admission to the rooms was restricted to Jockey Club members and members of the Rooms, who had to be approved by a ballot among the Club's members.

In the very early days of racing there were few rules and racing was confined to matches and to races run in heats. There was no Stud Book giving a controlling register of horses, so runners had to be produced on the spot some time before a race, standing at a local inn so that they could be identified. The starter was chosen from amongst the more respectable of the persons present at the time. Sometimes prison sentences were given for foul riding and brawls were commonplace.

Disputes could be settled either through the courts or through a mediator. In Queen Anne's reign the general arbiter in matters affecting racing was William Tregonwell Frampton, Keeper of the Running Horses at Newmarket. Frequently the Monarch was called upon to settle disputes arising from racing: King Charles II, for example, himself a keen rider of races, was often called upon to mediate, and there is on record an account of his being called in to settle the matter of a false start which occurred at Newmarket in 1682.

The first ever rules of racing are thought to be those which appeared in 1664, in connection with the first running of the Newmarket Town Plate. In 1740 Parliament attempted to impose some control over racing and an Act was introduced 'to restrain and prevent the excessive increase of horse races and the more effectual preventing of excessive and deceitful gaming'. This had little effect, however, as at the time it was virtually impossible to enforce.

The first rules affecting racing generally were published in Mr Pond's *Sporting Kalendar* in 1751. The early Jockey Club rules of the 1750s were concerned only with racing at Newmarket, and the first mention of Jockey Club conditions for a race appeared in 1752. Gradually, however, the power of the Jockey Club began to assert itself and the Club's members, by virtue of their wealth and position, were able to command a degree of respect, and so they began to introduce some sort of order into the sport.

Before long, difficult disputes in connection with racing were being referred to 'the judgement of Newmarket', and subsequently more and more rulings were introduced. For example, in 1756 the Jockey Club abolished the system of running races in heats followed by a final race, and declared that all horses would run against each other in single races. In 1758 the first rulings concerning the weighing-in of jockeys were introduced, and in 1762 there appears the first mention concerning the colours to be worn by riders.

In 1770 the Club appointed its first Stewards, and in 1772 the first official Judge was appointed. When in 1773 Mr James Weatherby, already Keeper of the Match Book, was appointed Secretary to the Jockey Club, racing was well on the way to becoming an organised sport.

Three great names dominate the early history of the Jockey Club: Sir Charles Bunbury, Lord George Bentinck and Admiral Rous, and it is largely due to these three men that the whole system of horse racing in Britain as we know it came about.

Sir Charles Bunbury (1740–1821) was perhaps the most important and influential figure in racing during the later part of the eighteenth century. He was much associated with Turf reform, and was for forty years Perpetual President of the Jockey Club. Born in 1740, the son of the Rector of Mildenhall, he became Member of Parliament for Suffolk in 1761, and in 1762 he married 'the most beautiful woman in England' – Lady Sarah Lennox, the daughter of the 2nd Duke of Richmond. Lady Sarah first appeared at Court at the age of sixteen, and it was said that the Prince of Wales (later George III) fell madly in love with her and proposed marriage. She accepted, but there was so much powerful opposition to the match that it was called off. Lady Sarah then married Sir Charles Bunbury, who succeeded his father as 6th Baronet in 1764. Five years afterwards, however, Lady Sarah left her husband for Lord William Gordon.

Sir Charles Bunbury was made a Steward of the Jockey Club in 1770. He was the owner of many fine racehorses, including Diomed, winner of the first ever Derby in 1780. He is, however, commemorated by the Bunbury Mile course at Newmarket.

In addition to Diomed, Sir Charles also owned Eleanor, the first filly to win both the Derby and the Oaks (1801), and Smolensko, the first colt to win both the Derby and the Two Thousand Guineas (1813). He also bred the unbeaten horse, Highflyer, which was subsequently sold to Lord Bolingbroke and later sold by him to Mr Richard Tattersall. Tattersall had such a high regard for the horse that he named his country house Highflyer Hall. It was Sir Charles Bunbury who, in 1773, invited Mr James Weatherby, the son of a Newcastle solicitor, to act as Keeper of the Match Book and Secretary to the Jockey Club, thereby starting a

Weatherby tradition which has benefited racing for over two hundred years.

Perhaps the most famous, or notorious, incident to occur during Sir Charles Bunbury's reign as 'Dictator of the Turf', was that which concerned the running of the Prince of Wales' (later George IV) horse, Escape. In 1791 Escape was entered in a two-mile race to be run at Newmarket – the Sixty Guinea Stakes. In all, there were four horses in the race and Escape, ridden by Sam Chifney, was 2 to 1 favourite. The Prince's horse finished last of the four. The following day, however, Escape won a four-mile race at Newmarket, at odds of 5 to 1, thereby creating a great scandal, as it was held by some who were present that the horse had been deliberately 'pulled' on the first day in order to obtain a better price on the second. It was also rumoured that His Royal Highness had made a considerable fortune by this stratagem.

Sam Chifney was called before the Stewards and whereas the other two Stewards concerned – Mr Dutton and Mr Panton – seemed disposed to accept Chifney's explanation that the horse needed the earlier race to bring it to peak fitness, Sir Charles Bunbury did not accept this. It was he who later informed the Prince that 'if he suffered Mr Chifney to ride his horses, no gentleman would start against him'. The Prince of Wales was greatly upset by the whole affair, so much so that he not only withdrew his patronage of the turf, but even went so far as to sell his entire stable and stud. It was many years before a reconciliation could be effected between the Prince and the Jockey Club.

There has always been a great deal of speculation concerning the incident, and it has been suggested that the Turf authorities were 'after' Chifney, who was thought to be a villain. However, if the Turf authorities were to function properly there had to be an enquiry into the running of Escape on the two occasions. Whatever the rights and wrongs of the matter, it must have greatly strengthened the position of the Jockey Club once it was seen that, where the good name of racing was concerned, they were not prepared to kotow, even to so great a patron as the Prince of Wales.

Sir Charles Bunbury died in 1821 and by the 1840s his position as 'Dictator of the Turf' had been filled by Lord George Bentinck (1802–1848), the son of the 4th Duke of Portland who, in 1827, brought about the right of the Jockey Club to 'warn persons off Newmarket Heath', when he brought a successful action against one S. Hawkins in consequence of his having used unbecoming language to Lord Wharncliffe on the Heath.

Lord George Bentinck, who was later to become known as the 'Napoleon of the Turf', was a well-known and respected rider, owner and backer of horses. At one time, it is estimated, he owned some 130 horses, and the upkeep of his stable and stud cost £40,000 a year. One contemporary said of him that 'he never did things by halves', and this certainly applied to his betting activities, for he was perhaps the biggest backer of horses in his day, winning and losing enormous sums of money. In 1845, for example, he is reputed to have won over £100,000.

Lord George was responsible for the introduction of a number of reforms into racing. As manager and controller of Goodwood racecourse, he introduced the flag start. This was regarded as a most useful innovation and was quickly copied by other racecourses. Prior to its introduction, races had been started in a most haphazard fashion. The St Leger of 1827, for example, had seven false starts, and when the field did eventually get away the favourite Mameluke, was facing in the wrong direction. Following the race the starter was dismissed, but by then the damage had been done and the notorious bookmaker, William Crockford, who is thought to have bribed not only the starter but also several of the jockeys, had 'cleaned up' and later opened a gaming club on the proceeds.

It was Lord George Bentinck who also introduced the principal that races should start punctually. His other reforms included the numbering of horses taking part in a race, as well as the parading of horses in the paddock prior to each race. Another innovation which Lord George developed was that of conveying horses to race meetings by cart or box. Previously they had either been led or ridden to the course. Then, in 1836, Lord George employed a coachmaker to construct an enormous horse box to carry his horse, Ellis, to Doncaster, where it won the St Leger.

As well as introducing new ideas for the benefit of racing, Bentinck also did away with some outdated customs, such as the time-honoured and extremely dubious custom whereby the winning owner was required to give the Judge a present.

By the early part of the nineteenth century horse racing was well on the way to becoming a national sport. The number of race courses had greatly increased, and so had the number of races and racehorses. Touts and bookmakers had, by this time, appeared on the scene in ever-increasing numbers, as also had rogues and villains, which the Turf has always attracted. Racing, as a private sport between gentlemen prepared to back their own horses, was rapidly becoming a thing of the past, and the 'sharp boys', ever in attendance when the prospect of easy money seems likely, had moved in with a vengeance. Coups and frauds were perpetrated shamelessly and fancied horses were 'nobbled' or even destroyed.

In 1812 a tout, named Daniel Dawson, was publicly hanged for poisoning racehorses with arsenic, but even the threat of such drastic penalties as hanging hardly seemed to deter the villains. Bribery and corruption were rampant in every class, and one contemporary wrote: 'I grow more and more disgusted with the atmosphere of villainy I am forced to breathe. It is not easy to keep oneself undefiled. It is monstrous to see high-bred and high-born gentlemen mixed up in schemes which are neither more nor less than a system of plunder. The sport of horse racing has a peculiar and irresistible charm for persons of unblemished probity. What a pity it is that it makes just as strong an appeal to the riff-raff of every town and city.'

Perhaps the greatest Turf scandal at this time happened in 1844 and was concerned with the running of the Derby of that year. This scandal, incidentally, showed just how much still needed to be done in the way of Turf reform – even though the Jockey Club had, by this time, been in existence some ninety-two years and had already introduced a great many worthwhile reforms. It was Lord George Bentinck who was responsible for bringing to light the whole sordid business and who helped to put matters to right.

In 1843 a horse called Running Rein ran in and won a race for two-year-olds at Newmarket. The Duke of Rutland, owner of the second horse in the race objected on the grounds that Running Rein was, in fact, a three-year-old and therefore not eligible to run. An enquiry was held, but nothing could be proved and so the matter was dropped. The following year, 1844, Running Rein was entered for the Derby. Now the Derby is a race confined to three-year-olds, and to run a four or even a five-year-old horse against a three-year-old is to give the older horse every advantage, by virtue of its greater development and maturity. Before the race there was an objection to Running Rein taking part but, and this seems unbelievable today, no action was taken. So not only did Running Rein run in the Derby, but it also won, or rather, it was first past the post. Immediately after the race, however, the owner of the second horse, Orlando, lodged an objection. The owner of this horse was Colonel Peel, the younger brother of the Prime Minister Sir Robert Peel, and he was acting on the advice of Lord George Bentinck when he lodged his objection.

The Stewards advised Weatherbys, the stakeholders, to withhold the stake money and this they did, paying the money into Court. This meant that the owner of Running Rein, a Mr Wood, (who, incidentally, was nowhere to be seen after the race) would have to bring an action against Colonel Peel in order to claim the stake money, and this he did. The case was heard in the Court of Exchequer on July 1st, 1844, and it was largely as the result of information supplied by Lord George Bentinck who had, it seems, engaged in a great deal of detective work, that the Jury awarded the race to Orlando and the stake money to Colonel Peel. Running Rein, which had conveniently disappeared, was, in fact, a four-year-old named Maccabaeus who was thought to have died in 1843. During the uproar that followed the Derby of 1844, further discoveries came to light, which must have given the Jockey Club a great deal to think about.

The favourite – The Ugly Buck – was thought to have been interfered with during the running of the race. The second favourite – Ratan – owned by the notorious bookmaker, William Crockford, had been 'nobbled', and Ratan's jockey, Sam Rogers, was subsequently 'warned off'. Another entry – Leander – was found to have been at least a four-year-old, and its owners were also 'warned off'. Altogether, the Running Rein Derby proved to be one of the most unsavoury episodes in the history of the Turf.

Following the scandal of the Derby of 1844, the Jockey Club decided to prosecute in all cases of suspected fraud, whether or not action was taken by others. The resolution commented that such frauds 'are calculated to inflict an injury upon the Turf by bringing racing into disrepute, and by deterring honourable men from entering into competition in which they run the risk of being encountered by such dishonest rivals'.

As a result of his work in helping to uncover the truth concerning the Running Rein scandal, Lord George Bentinck was presented with a sum of money, raised by public subscription, in appreciation of his efforts. Characteristically, he presented this money to the Jockey Club in order to start a fund for the relief of distressed jockeys.

In 1846, encouraged by his friend Disraeli, Lord George Bentinck decided to devote himself entirely to politics. He sold his horses, for the incredibly low sum of £10,000, and withdrew from the Turf. Two years later he died, as the result of a heart attack.

The last member of this trinity of 'Turf dictators' was the celebrated Admiral Rous (1795–1877). Born in January 1795, Henry John Rous was the second son of the 1st Earl of Stradbroke. After being educated at Westminster, he entered the Royal Navy and served as a midshipman aboard the *Repulse* and later aboard the *Victory*. He saw a great deal of action, and was highly commended for gallantry when in command of a yawl which attacked several large gunboats. In 1821, during a period ashore, he was elected a member of the Jockey Club.

From 1835 onwards Rous, on the retired list, devoted his energies towards the improvement of racing. In 1838 he was elected a Steward of the Jockey Club, and from then until his death in 1877 he gradually became a sort of permanent Senior Steward and Treasurer, by a process of continual re-election. And, indeed, never before or since has one man had so much power in connection with horse racing in this country. A man of high moral principles, Admiral Rous disliked heavy betting.

Nevertheless, he realised that horse racing and betting are inseparable. 'Racing has always been, and will always be a gambling speculation.'

In 1855 Admiral Rous had published his *Law and Practice of Horseracing*. In 1855 he was appointed Public Handicapper – an office which he had previously refused and which he had strong views upon. 'A public handicapper should be a man of independent circumstances in every sense of the word, and beyond suspicion of accepting illicit compensation for favours received; attached to no stable, a good judge of the dispositions of owners and trainers; he should be a spectator of every race of any importance in the United Kingdom; and his station should be at the distance post, where horses are pulled, not at the winning post where they are extended; he should never make a bet and he should treat all remarks which may be made about his handicaps with the utmost indifference. . . Such a man is not to be found.'

If such a man was not to be found, Admiral Rous was certainly the best possible substitute. He attended race meetings and gallops, and worked assiduously in order that he might correctly assess the respective merits of the horses he was called upon to handicap. As the result of the experience he gained in this field, he was later to introduce the 'Weight for Age Scale' which, with few modifications, is still in use today. In 1865, at a public dinner given in his honour, Admiral Rous was presented with his own portrait and three pieces of silver plate, in recognition of his services to the Turf for over twenty-five years.

During his term of office, the Admiral had improved the financial position of the Club out of all recognition, in addition to having greatly enhanced its prestige throughout the racing world. He died in 1877 at the age of eighty-two.

Sir Charles Bunbury, Lord George Bentinck and Admiral Rous were the three great dictators of the turf during the Jockey Club's formative years. Following the death of Admiral Rous no single person was ever again to wield quite so much power with the Club.

During the early days of racing administration and control there were, of course, many other nobles and gentlemen who also played their part in the establishment of the Jockey Club as the undisputed ruling body of the Turf. One was Sir Joseph Hawley, often a keen opponent of Admiral Rous where matters of racing legislation were concerned. The 5th Earl of Glasgow, an eccentric and often violent man, is described elsewhere. Another of the early Jockey Club members was the 5th Duke of Richmond, who, in 1845, introduced the 'Manly Sports Bill', which was to do away with the restrictive laws imposed on betting during Queen Anne's reign.

Lord Rosebery became the first Prime Minister in office to win the

Derby in 1894 with his horse Ladas. The 1st Duke of Westminster, owner and breeder respectively of the legendary horses Ormonde and Sceptre, was the winner of four Derbys. Lord Palmerston, Sir John Astley, 3rd Earl of Durham, 17th Earl of Derby and many others, have all played their part in shaping the history of British racing.

In our own time, Lord Willoughby de Broke, the late Duke of Norfolk and Major-General Sir Randle Feilden will be remembered as notable Turf administrators. Indeed, the latter has often been compared to Admiral Rous and Lord George Bentinck because of the many reforms he introduced to racing during his term of office as Senior Steward of the Jockey Club.

By the middle of the nineteenth century, the Jockey Club was firmly established as the governing body where racing was concerned. It was so firmly established, in fact, that when, in 1860, Parliament attempted to introduce legislation concerning the weights to be carried by certain racehorses, the Jockey Club was successfully able to combat the Bill, which was subsequently withdrawn.

In 1858 a committee was formed to revise the existing Rules of Racing. This was done again in 1870 and, indeed, since that time the Rules of Racing have been subject to constant amendment and revision in order to meet the ever changing needs of horse racing in Britain.

In 1859, for example, a rule was introduced which forbade the running of yearlings. In 1879 jockeys were licensed. 1889 saw the compulsory registration of colours. 1905 was the year when trainers were first licensed. In 1912 Rule 86 declared that nominations did not become void on the death of the nominator. (Incidentally, the previous ruling formed the basis of the plot of Edgar Wallace's famous racing novel *The Calendar*). In 1913 a rule came into effect that no horse of three years or upwards could run unnamed – a rule which would have infuriated Lord Glasgow. Recent years have seen the amalgamation of the Flat and Jumping Rules, the licensing of women as trainers, a revision of the rules of owning in respect of syndicated horses, and latterly the licensing of women jockeys.

The Jockey Club has often been criticised for being ultra-conservative and, as a self-electing body, for drawing on too narrow a circle for its members. There is no doubt that since its inception the Club has, for the most part, been made up of members drawn from what used to be known as the upper classes. This is hardly surprising, because in the early days of racing the owning, racing and breeding of racehorses was the prerogative of the aristocracy and of the very rich. (It is hardly a poor man's hobby today). What more natural than that the owners and breeders should have banded together to safeguard their own and others' interest in the sport?

The First World War and the years that followed saw the breaking down of many of the social barriers and conventions which had hitherto existed. The Second World War completed this process. What has often been referred to as the 'well ordered society', with all its artificial distinctions of rank and privilege, and the tremendous gulf between the 'haves' and 'have nots', eventually became, for better or for worse, the Welfare State. What is remarkable is that, despite all the great social changes which have occurred during the past fifty years, the Jockey Club still remains an outpost of rank and privilege. The view is often expressed that it still excludes from its ranks many people whose influence and experience would be of great benefit to racing.

It was during the two World Wars that the work of the Jockey Club was seen to its very best effect. Indeed, without the efforts of the Club, it is difficult to imagine exactly what would have become of British bloodstock and of the whole racing industry.

Throughout the four years of World War I there was very little racing in Britain. That there was any at all was mainly due to the efforts of those leading members of the Jockey Club who ensured that a minimum of racing should take place in order to preserve the bloodstock industry.

In March 1915 a meeting of the Jockey Club was held in London to consider the whole question of racing in wartime, following the appearance in *The Times* of letters from three prominent Club members – The Duke of Portland, Lord Dunraven and the Hon. F. W. Lambton – advocating a complete suspension of racing until the end of the war. The Duke of Portland had, it seemed, believed a totally unfounded rumour to the effect that wounded soldiers were to be moved out of the Epsom stands so that the Derby could be run. The Duke, who did not attend the meeting of the Jockey Club, prepared a long statement which was read out to those members who had assembled. Lord Durham, strongly backed by the former Prime Minister Lord Rosebery, was in favour of a modified continuance of racing. It was finally resolved that 'racing should be carried out where local conditions permit and the feeling of the locality is not averse to the meeting being held'. In the following May, however, representations were made by the Government to the Jockey Club, which issued a notice to the effect that all fixtures, except those at Newmarket, were to be cancelled.

In 1916 the Stewards, after much lobbying, were able to get permission to start racing again at Gatwick, Newbury, Lingfield and Windsor. Then, in 1917, the Government announced that there was to be a complete ban on racing until the war was over. After representations had been made to Lloyd George, on behalf of the bloodstock industry, it was finally agreed that there should be some forty-nine days' racing that year.

When the First World War came to an end, it soon became obvious that the old order was changing and that there was a new and more democratic spirit abroad. The pre-war 'well-ordered' Edwardian society had gone for ever and social barriers were rapidly being lowered. In 1919 the Jockey Club appointed a Committee under the chairmanship of Lord Hamilton of Dalzell, to enquire into the long-term future of racing in Britain and to consider schemes which would attract a larger racegoing public.

While the long-term aspects of racing were being considered, however, there was an immediate problem to be dealt with. In 1919, when a full programme of racing was resumed, the public, in a mood of post-war elation, flocked to the racecourses – there was no shortage of money and racing enjoyed a boom. With the crowds and the money, however, came the racketeers and the race gangs who forced bookmakers to pay 'protection' money with threats of violence.

At that time there were no official regulations concerning the allocation of bookmakers' pitches and rival gangs vied for control of the best positions on the course. Very often territorial disputes arose, which led to open and extremely violent gang warfare. In 1921, the bookmakers, realising that their livelihood was at stake, banded together to form the Bookmakers' Protection Association which, with the co-operation of the Jockey Club and the newly-formed 'Flying Squad', began to combat the activities of the racecourse gangs.

Then, in 1923, the Jockey Club appointed its own officials, under the leadership of Major G. P. Wymer, D.C.M., in order to protect the public and to supervise security arrangements on all racecourses. The gangs were very soon expelled from the courses, and the trouble was effectively stamped out.

In 1930 the authority of the Jockey Club was challenged in the Law Courts in connection with the famous racing/doping scandal, which became known as the Don Pat case.

The circumstances were as follows:

In 1930 a horse named Don Pat, trained by Mr Charles Chapman, ran in to win a race at Kempton Park. After the race, a dope test was administered which was found to be positive. An enquiry followed, as a result of which Mr Chapman had his Trainer's Licence revoked and he was 'warned off'. There was no suggestion that Mr Chapman was in any way responsible for the actual doping of the horse; his crime was that of having allowed the doping to take place. The result of the enquiry was published in the *Racing Calendar*, in such a manner as to suggest that Mr Chapman had, in fact, been a party to the doping. *The Times* published an account of the affair, which included a copy of the notice in the *Calendar*.

Mr Chapman then brought an action against the Stewards of the Jockey Club and also against *The Times* for repeating the notice. The Jury in the case returned a verdict in favour of Mr Chapman, awarding him the sum of £13,000 against the Stewards and Messrs. Weatherby, in respect of the notice in the *Calendar*, and £3,000 against *The Times*. The Jockey Club immediately appealed against the decision and, after a four-day deliberation, the Appeal Court decided that both the Stewards and Weatherbys were protected and that the case against them could not, therefore, be maintained. The Appeal Court also found that damages in both cases were too high and a new trial was ordered in respect of *The Times*. This case, however, never came to Court.

The whole affair caused a great furore at the time, and although Mr Chapman was eventually to be deprived of the damages awarded to him, his character was vindicated in his fight against both the Jockey Club and the Press.

The whole question of doping has always been a difficult one. 'Racing', as Admiral Rous once said, 'will always be a gambling proposition.' And gambling propositions, unfortunately, will always attract the unscrupulous and the greedy.

Throughout the whole history of racing there are to be found instances where horses have been doped, either to stop them from winning or to improve their performance. It is surprising, therefore, that it was not until 1904 that the Jockey Club began to consider seriously the whole question of doping.

For the most part, the doping of horses in the early days of racing must have been a pretty crude business. But, by the beginning of the nineteenth century, the art of introducing chemical stimulants to racehorses had begun in earnest. This type of doping is thought to have been brought to this country from America and it soon threatened to become a dangerous problem in Britain.

The Hon. George Lambton, trainer to Lord Derby and brother of the 3rd Earl of Durham, tried, unsuccessfully, to bring to the attention of the Jockey Club the full extent and implications of the doping of racehorses in this country. He then provided a most successful demonstration of just how effective doping methods could be by doping a number of indifferent horses, four of whom won races.

Shortly afterwards, the Jockey Club introduced a rule to the effect that – 'If any person shall administer or cause to be administered, for the purpose of affecting the speed of a horse, drug or stimulants internally, or by hypodermic or other method, he shall be warned off the Turf.'

But doping has always been extremely difficult to prove and so, in 1945, the onus was put on the trainer, when a rule was introduced which stated that – 'If in any case it shall be found that any drug or stimulant has been administered to a horse for the purpose of affecting its speed in a race, the licence of the trainer of the horse shall be withdrawn, and he shall be declared a disqualified person.' A number of trainers lost their licences as the result of this rule which, if it was expedient, was hardly fair to trainers.

In 1960 a Committee was set up, under the late Duke of Norfolk, to enquire into the whole question of detecting the presence of drugs in racehorses and the operation and efficiency of the then existing rules to prevent doping. This Committee found that doping, which had become a serious menace at the beginning of the century, was far less prevalent in the sixties. Since it was decided that it was almost impossible to prevent a really determined person from doping a racehorse, the Committee decided to concentrate their attention on deterrents. It recommended the setting-up of the present Research Laboratory at the Equine Research Station at Newmarket, where routine and special tests are carried out, as well as research into the effects of drugs. The Committee also recommended alterations to the then existing penalties for trainers whose horses had been doped.

A further Committee, known as the F. W. P. Committee from the names of its members (Major-General Sir Randle Fielden, Lord Willoughby de Broke and the Hon J. Philipps) was set up in August 1963 to examine the physical arrangements for protecting racehorses from dopers. This Committee's aims were to ensure that the task of would-be dopers was made as difficult as possible, and to make easier the investigations into a case of doping, by narrowing down the number of individuals who had had access to the horse. Detailed recommendations were made, with special reference to the security of racehorse stables and the control and identification of all persons entering them, and to the security of horses while in transport to the course. The automatic withdrawal of the trainer's licence, should one of his horses be found to have been doped, was amended on June 1st 1964, although a trainer's licence may still be withdrawn if circumstances warrant it.

Probably the most important step in racing which occurred in the period between the two World Wars was the establishment of the Totalisator, which was brought into being in order to plough back into racing some of the tremendous amounts of money wagered on the sport.

The introduction of the Tote was initially brought about by the efforts of Lord Hamilton of Dalzell, who was the prime mover in the Jockey Club's decision to advocate the introduction of the Tote on British racecourses. The Tote was legalised through the Racecourse Betting Act of 1928, having been introduced as a Private Member's Bill by Sir Ralph Glynn.

During the Second World War racing was again severely curtailed and, again, it was only by the efforts of the Jockey Club that any took place at all. In 1941, the Jockey Club provided a splendid example of British imperturbability by setting up a Committee, under Lord Ilchester, to study all aspects of the future of British racing. This Committee came up with a great many far-reaching recommendations concerning the future of racing, many of which, alas, were never implemented.

Following World War II, racing experienced a boom. This was to be short-lived, however, and for many years racing in Britain was to lag behind that of other countries. In the first place, the war had greatly affected the bloodstock industry and, for a time, foreign horses swept the board. Also, there was a great deal of resistance to innovation, both as regards race procedure and racecourse facilities. Much of this resistance, it must be said, came from within the Jockey Club itself. Today, however, British racing as a spectator sport is second to none, thanks to the introduction of many new features, including the patrol camera, the photo-finish camera, racecourse commentaries, starting stalls, televised racing, sponsored racing, the licensing of women trainers and women jockeys.

The life-blood of racing is, of course, the prize money. Sponsorship of races by commercial concerns (especially since the introduction of televised racing) has done much to help the sport. One could wish, however, that the Jockey Club had power to impose some restriction on the names given to certain of the sponsored races.

As regards racecourse facilities, many courses in Britain still leave a lot to be desired. At the time of writing, there is a great deal of talk about streamlining our racecourses – of doing away with the smaller courses, etc. It would be a great pity, however, if British racing ever became streamlined to such a degree that all the character was removed from it. Biggest is not always best!

If the Tote was the major financial innovation where racing was concerned between the wars, then there is no doubt that the setting-up of the Horserace Betting Levy Board in 1961 was one of the most important things ever to happen to the racing industry. In November 1959, an inter-departmental committee (under the chairmanship of Mr Leslie E. Peppiatt) was appointed by the Rt. Hon. R. A. Butler, 'to consider whether it is desirable and practicable that persons engaged in betting transactions on horse races, otherwise than by means of the Totalisator, should be required to make a contribution for purposes conducive to the improvement of breeds of horses or the sport of horse racing; and if so, to advise on its amount and the means of securing it.'

The Stewards of the Jockey Club and the Stewards of the National Hunt Committee, who had been strongly in favour of such a committee being set up, presented a memorandum to the Peppiatt Committee. This memorandum was supported by the Racecourse Association, the Racehorse Owners' Association, the Thoroughbred Breeders' Association, the Racecourse Betting Control Board, whose members also gave independent evidence before the Committee.

In this, the Jockey Club and the National Hunt Committee strongly supported a contribution for these purposes from those engaged in betting, giving as their main points:–

(a) It is equitable that they should contribute;

(b) It is harmful to racing in this country if they do not;

(c) A contribution will bring benefit to racing and to the ancillary trades connected with it.

The Peppiatt Committee reported back to the Government in April 1960, and the key phrase in their report was – '. . . there is almost unanimous opinion, on all sides of the racing industry (including the bookmakers), that a Levy is required. . .'

The Horserace Betting Levy Board Bill became law on September 1st 1961, and the first Levy Scheme came into effect on April 1st 1962, as a result of which much-needed financial aid began to flow into the racing industry.

THE JOCKEY CLUB TODAY

There is no doubt that if those 'gentlemen of like tastes and background', who first gathered together at Newmarket (and who put into effect and operated the Newmarket Rules) were to be faced with the sheer volume and complexity of racing in Britain today, they would wonder what had hit them. For, from the simple beginnings of one gentleman racing his horse against another, racing has become a complex, multi-million pound industry. In 1975, for example, there were 952 racing fixtures at which 5537 races were run, with a total of 58,888 runners.

With the rapid development of racing since the end of World War II, the Jockey Club has come to accept that its unilateral role should be augmented with other authorities and controls. Today, the Jockey Club remains solely responsible for the conduct of racing, under a Royal Charter granted in 1970. The executive power of the Club is vested in nine Stewards. It controls every aspect of the conduct of racing, including the framing of races, the construction and safety of tracks, the allocation of prize money and the security of racing; this includes licensing as 'fit persons' all those closely engaged in the industry, including trainers and jockeys. The Jockey Club is also responsible for disciplining those who have infringed the Rules of Racing.

The Jockey Club is not responsible for the running of racecourses, except Newmarket, with which it has a special relationship, nor for the collection of money fed back into racing from the betting levy, which is administered by the Horserace Betting Levy Board.

In 1969 the Jockey Club amalgamated with the National Hunt Committee and is now responsible for both types of racing. The administrative work of the Jockey Club remains the business of Messrs. Weatherby.

The various boards and committees which govern, control and promote racing are as follows:–

THE HORSERACE BETTING LEVY BOARD
The Horserace Betting Levy Bill became law on September 1st 1961, and the first Levy Scheme came into effect on April 1st 1962. The Levy Board determines and collects the levy from bookmakers and the Totalisator. The money is applied for the purposes laid down in the Act, i.e., the improvement of breeds of horses, the encouragement of veterinary science and education, and the improvement of horse racing.

The charts on pages 158–9 will give some insight into the scope and complexity of the activity of the Board and also of the benefits which it provides for the racing industry.

The Chairman of the Levy Board is appointed by the Home Secretary, who also appoints two independent members. The Chairman of the Totalisator Board and the Bookmakers' Committee are both ex-officio members of the Board. There are three members appointed by the Jockey Club.

THE JOINT RACING BOARD
Under the co-chairmanship of the Senior Steward of the Jockey Club and the Chairman of the Levy Board, the Joint Racing Board meets monthly. It is the most important policy-making body in racing. Other members of the Board are the two deputy Senior Stewards and the two Government-appointed members of the Levy Board.

THE RACECOURSE ASSOCIATION
The Racecourse Association represents the interests of the sixty-one racecourses in Britain. The R.C.A. is represented on many of the Jockey Club and Levy Board subsidiary committees. It maintains a close watch on any aspect of racing which is liable to affect the individual racecourses.

THE RACEHORSE OWNERS' ASSOCIATION
This Association represents 75 per cent of racehorse owners in Britain, ensuring that the views of owners are heard and considered by the Jockey Club.

SOURCES AND ALLOCATION OF LEVY BOARD FUNDS
1st APRIL 1975 – 31st MARCH 1976

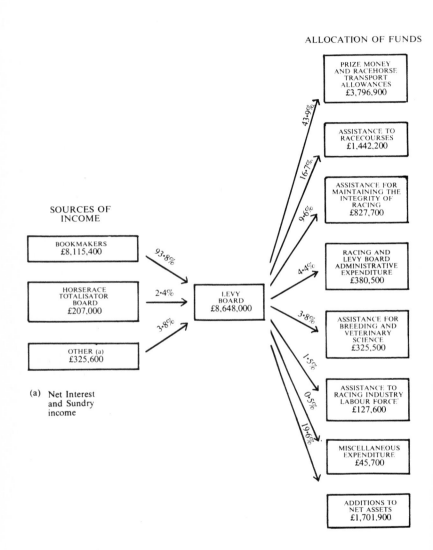

ALLOCATION OF FUNDS

PRIZE MONEY
AND RACEHORSE
TRANSPORT
ALLOWANCES
£3,796,900

ASSISTANCE TO
RACECOURSES
£1,442,200

ASSISTANCE FOR
MAINTAINING THE
INTEGRITY OF
RACING
£827,700

SOURCES OF
INCOME

BOOKMAKERS
£8,115,400

HORSERACE
TOTALISATOR
BOARD
£207,000

OTHER (a)
£325,600

LEVY
BOARD
£8,648,000

RACING AND
LEVY BOARD
ADMINISTRATIVE
EXPENDITURE
£380,500

ASSISTANCE FOR
BREEDING AND
VETERINARY
SCIENCE
£325,500

ASSISTANCE TO
RACING INDUSTRY
LABOUR FORCE
£127,600

MISCELLANEOUS
EXPENDITURE
£45,700

ADDITIONS TO
NET ASSETS
£1,701,900

(a) Net Interest
and Sundry
income

93·8% 2·4% 3·8%

43·9% 16·7% 9·6% 4·4% 3·8% 1·5% 0·5% 1·6%

SOURCES AND ALLOCATION OF LEVY BOARD FUNDS
SEPTEMBER 1961 - 31st MARCH 1976

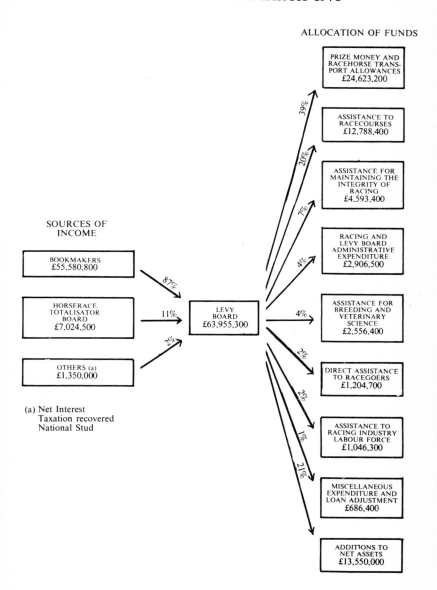

ALLOCATION OF FUNDS

PRIZE MONEY AND RACEHORSE TRANS-PORT ALLOWANCES £24,623,200

ASSISTANCE TO RACECOURSES £12,788,400

ASSISTANCE FOR MAINTAINING THE INTEGRITY OF RACING £4,593,400

RACING AND LEVY BOARD ADMINISTRATIVE EXPENDITURE £2,906,500

ASSISTANCE FOR BREEDING AND VETERINARY SCIENCE £2,556,400

DIRECT ASSISTANCE TO RACEGOERS £1,204,700

ASSISTANCE TO RACING INDUSTRY LABOUR FORCE £1,046,300

MISCELLANEOUS EXPENDITURE AND LOAN ADJUSTMENT £686,400

ADDITIONS TO NET ASSETS £13,550,000

SOURCES OF INCOME

BOOKMAKERS £55,580,800

HORSERACE TOTALISATOR BOARD £7,024,500

OTHERS (a) £1,350,000

LEVY BOARD £63,955,300

(a) Net Interest
Taxation recovered
National Stud

39% 20% 7% 4% 4% 2% 2% 1% 21%

87% 11% 2%

RACING INDUSTRY LIAISON COMMITTEE

In May 1976, the above Committee was set up in order to improve communications within the racing industry. A fully representative advisory body, R.I.L.C. replaced the Racing Policy Committee and the Joint Associations Liaison Committee. R.I.L.C. is composed of all the major elements in the racing and breeding industries, and represents the collective or individual views of all the organisations represented on it to both the Stewards of the Jockey Club and the Horserace Betting Levy Board.

RACECOURSE SECURITY SERVICES LIMITED

A company, limited by guarantee, on which the Jockey Club, the Horserace Betting Levy Board, Racecourse Association and the Horserace Anti-Doping Committee are represented to co-ordinate all matters relating to security in racing.

THE RACING INFORMATION BUREAU

The Public Relations Office of the Racecourse Association, the Horserace Betting Levy Board and the Jockey Club, the function of which is to publicise and promote racing to all media, including national and provincial press, television and radio. The Bureau has already proved of tremendous value in encouraging more people to go racing; it has also explained and promoted the aims and functions of the Jockey Club, the Levy Board and the racecourses to the racing public.

Like most governing bodies, the Jockey Club receives its fair share of criticism. It is often accused of being too slow to act, of being too authoritarian, etc. Occasionally a controversial or, perhaps, unpopular decision will make the headlines, causing the Jockey Club to come under fire from both the public and the popular press. There is no doubt, however, that the control and administration of British racing is in the capable hands of men who care about racing and, indeed, about the future of racing. Those of us who attend an occasional race meeting or who enjoy a 'flutter' at the nearest betting shop would do well to consider the enormous benefits which the Jockey Club has brought to racing.

For over two hundred years the Jockey Club has served racing well. Above all, in that time it has managed to preserve the integrity of British racing. If it had done nothing else, this in itself would be a remarkable achievement. Today the whole future of racing in Britain is a matter of concern to both the racing public and to everyone working in or connected with the industry. The present economic situation is creating, and will no doubt continue to create, problems. Many changes have been made and are being made in the control of racing, and much serious thought will have to be given to the future of the sport if it is to survive. But the most important task before the Jockey Club is that of reform and change without losing the integrity of British racing.

EXTRACTS FROM THE RULES OF RACING

THE JOCKEY CLUB
(Incorporated by Royal Charter, 1970)
1976

PATRONS:
Her Majesty The Queen
Her Majesty Queen Elizabeth the Queen Mother

STEWARDS:
Lord Howard de Walden (Senior Steward)
Capt. H. M. Gosling (Deputy Senior Steward)
R. N. Richmond-Watson, Esq (Deputy Senior Steward)
Lt-Col P. H. G. Bengough
Jocelyn Hambro, Esq
Major E. M. Cameron
Sir John Thomson
Lord Manton
Mr J. B. Sumner

PART 1

STEWARDS OF THE JOCKEY CLUB AND STEWARDS OF MEETINGS

STEWARDS OF THE JOCKEY CLUB

1. The Stewards of the Jockey Club have power, at their discretion.

   (i) To grant or to refuse to grant licences to Race-courses and to make it a condition of a licence being granted that

   (a) the Racecourse shall be a member of the association of Racecourses currently approved by the Jockey Club.

   (b) facilities shall be afforded on the Race-course for the operation of the Totalisator.

   (ii) To withdraw licences to Race-courses.

(iii) To fix the dates on which all meetings shall be held and in the case of emergency or expediency to order the abandonment of any race or Race Meeting or to make any alteration in the date of any such Meeting and to supervise and make such alterations as they may think advisable in the programme of, or the conditions of any race at, any Meeting.

(iv) To authorise Point-to-Point fixtures, to authorise the publication of 'Jockey Club Regulations for Point-to-Point Steeple Chases' and to make any alterations to them from time to time that they consider necessary.

(v) To prohibit the advertisement of any race or meeting in the Racing Calendar, or call upon the Stewards to alter or expunge any conditions, even after advertisement.

(vi) To grant or to refuse to grant and to renew or to refuse to renew licences to officials, jockeys, and trainers and permits to trainers and amateur riders. Every application for renewal of any licence or permit shall be treated and regarded in all respects and for all purposes as if it were the first application by the applicant for such a licence or permit.

STEWARDS OF MEETINGS

10.   There must be at least three Stewards for every Meeting appointed by the Racecourse Executive and approved by the Stewards of the Jockey Club, and each Steward may appoint a deputy at any time.

11.   Should there not be three Stewards or their deputies present, the Clerk of the Course shall, without delay, see that any vacancy or vacancies are filled, so that there shall be three persons to act, and shall notify conspicuously such appointment.

POWERS OF THE STEWARDS OF MEETINGS

12.   The Stewards have control over, and have free access to, all stands, rooms, enclosures, and other places used for the purposes of the Meeting.

13.   The Stewards shall exclude from all places under their control every disqualified person, and all such persons or description of persons as they may, from time to time, be required by the Stewards of the Jockey Club to exclude.

14. The Stewards of a Meeting have full power—

   (i) to make (and, if necessary, to vary) all such arrangements for the conduct of the meeting as they think fit, and to dispense with the Starting Gate or Starting Stalls, as provided in Rule 28.

   (ii) Under exceptional circumstances or if the weather or ground be in an unfit state to cancel a parade or to abandon a day's racing or to abandon any races or to postpone any races to the following day or days within the original fixture, provided that all the races originally advertised for any day shall be included in that day's programme.

   Should the Stewards abandon a day's racing on the grounds specified above a Certificate must be drawn up stating the day and the hour when the decision to abandon was arrived at. The decision to abandon should not normally be taken before 8 a.m. on the day preceding the day's racing in question but in exceptional circumstances where the Stewards are entirely satisfied that no racing can possibly take place, the decision may be taken by noon two days prior to that on which the day's racing has been advertised to take place. The Certificate must be signed by two of the Stewards or by one Steward and the Clerk of the Course and without delay despatched to the Racing Calendar Office.

   (iii) To leave out or to alter any (but not more than two) fences or flights of hurdles in the circuit of the course if their retention would necessitate the abandonment of the day's racing, but the original advertised distance of a race must not be decreased.

   Should the Stewards authorise the abandonment or postponement of any races, the deletion of any fences or flights of hurdles or vary in any way the programme as originally advertised they shall without delay report to the Racing Calendar Office their reasons for so doing.

   (iv) To determine all questions arising in reference to racing at the meeting whether during the course of or subsequent to the meeting except as otherwise provided in these Rules and subject to appeal under Rule 176.

   (v) To call for proof (see Rule 170 (i)) that a horse is neither itself disqualified in any respect, nor nominated by, nor the property, wholly or in part, of a disqualified person; and in default of such proof being given to their satisfaction they may declare the horse disqualified. They have power to prevent from running any horse which cannot be shown to be qualified under these Rules or under the conditions of the race.

15.   (i) When in the opinion of the Stewards any person has committed any breach of the Rules of Racing they have power at their discretion to impose upon such person a fine not exceeding £100. Save that where any Rule prescribes a maximum penalty they may not impose any greater penalty or any penalty of some other kind and save that where any Rule prescribes a mandatory penalty they shall impose that penalty. Save as aforesaid the powers given by this Rule are not and are not to be construed as being in any way or in any instance limited or excluded by reason of the fact that some Rules do while others do not prescribe penalties for their breach.

(ii) When in the opinion of the Stewards there is a reasonable suspicion that any person has committed any breach of the Rules of Racing which in their opinion ought to be considered by the Stewards of the Jockey Club, or where in their opinion any person has committed any breach of the Rules of Racing and in their opinion some fine or punishment in excess of £100 ought to be imposed upon such person, they have power at their discretion to report the matter to the Stewards of the Jockey Club.

16.   In addition to their foregoing powers, the Stewards have the powers of suspension conferred on them in Rule 153 (iv) (a).

17.   The Stewards, as such, shall not entertain any disputes relating to bets.

PART 2

OFFICIALS

CLERK OF THE COURSE

23.   The Clerk of the Course, or his authorised substitute, is the sole person responsible to the Stewards for the general arrangements of the Meeting, and the proper construction and maintenance of the Course and fences, he shall see that the Course is properly measured and marked and shall:–

(i) Arrange for the publication, under the sanction of the Stewards, of a daily official card of the races, containing the conditions of each race, as published in the Racing

Calendar, the names of the horses engaged together with the saddle cloth number allotted to them by the Racing Calendar Office, their pedigrees or descriptions, and such other particulars as the Stewards of the Jockey Club may require. He shall send a copy of each day's card to the Racing Calendar Office.

A horse may appear on the card in the name of the owner instead of that of the nominator and the Stewards may, in special circumstances, grant permission for a horse to run in the name of the trainer or of some other person. The Clerk of the Course shall, in such latter case, make a report to the Racing Calendar Office, stating the grounds upon which the permission was granted.

(ii) See that a parade ring is provided in the paddock. All horses running at the meeting shall be saddled in the paddock and brought into the parade ring a reasonable time before the signal to mount is given. The attendants shall be provided with badges bearing numbers corresponding with those on the card. In the case of any horse not being brought into the parade ring, or a badge not being exhibited, the trainer shall be reported to the Stewards. No horse shall be admitted to the paddock unless he has been declared to run under Rule 124, or is advertised on the race card for sale. The parade ring shall be reserved strictly for those horses which are about to run. No person shall, without special leave from the Stewards, be allowed access to the parade ring except officials of the meeting and owners, trainers and riders of horses about to run in the next race. Any person refusing to leave shall be reported to the Stewards. For the purpose of this Rule, the Stewards shall determine whether or not the Race-course Stabling forms part of the paddock.

(iii) See that a clean number-cloth, of a pattern approved by the Stewards of the Jockey Club, is provided for every horse for which a rider presents himself to be weighed out.

(iv) Have in his possession, for the information of the Stewards, a list of persons disqualified and of persons warned off, and of trainers and riders reported, also a copy of the latest Monthly Forfeit List, and he shall not allow any horse which, or the owner or nominator of which, is in the Forfeit List to start for any race.

(v) Make a return to the Racing Calendar Office of any Deputy Steward or official appointed, of all complaints to and decisions of the Stewards, of any accident during the course of a flat race and the result of the enquiry into the accident, which must be held by the Stewards, of all fines inflicted, and of all horses sold or claimed.

THE JUDGE

26. (i) The Judge, or his authorised substitute, must occupy the judge's box at the time the horses pass the winning-post, or the race shall be void. He must announce his decision immediately, or after consulting the photograph, and shall determine the winner according to that part of the horse's head, excluding the ears, which is first past the winning post, the remaining placings being determined in a similar manner. Such decision shall be final, unless an objection to the winner, or any placed horses, is made and sustained; provided that this Rule shall not prevent a Judge from correcting any mistake, such correction being subject to confirmation by the Stewards.

(ii) The Judge shall, at the close of each day's racing, sign and send a report of the result of each race to the Racing Calendar Office.

STARTER AND STARTING

28. (i) The Starter shall obtain a list of runners for each race from the Clerk of the Scales in the Weighing Room.

(ii) Every horse shall be at the Post ready to start at the appointed time. In races confined to apprentices horses shall not be led to the Start.

(iv) The horses must be started by the Official Starter or his authorised substitute.

(a) all Flat races shall be started from Starting Stalls, or, if they are not available, with a flag.

(b) all Steeple Chases and Hurdle races shall be started by a Starting Gate approved by the Stewards of the Jockey Club unless they have given special permission for a flag to be used.

Except that, in the case of emergency, by permission of the Stewards or the Starter, any race may be started with a flag.

(v) The Starter shall call over the names of the runners and for Flat races assign the horses to the places drawn by lot, all horses taking their place at the Start in the order drawn for them. The rider who has drawn No. 1 must always be placed on the left and other riders must take their places in consecutive numbers from the left.

(vi) The Starter shall give all orders necessary for securing a fair start. The horses must be started, as far as possible, in a line, but they may be started at such reasonable distance behind the Starting Post as the Starter thinks necessary.

(viii) In a start from Starting Stalls the Starter has full power to remove an unruly horse but no horse shall be permitted to start from outside the Stalls, nor is it permitted for a horse to be held in the Stalls. A horse which refuses to enter the Stalls, or a horse which enters and through its unruly behaviour damages its Stall shall be withdrawn by the Starter.

(ix) The Starter shall order the white flag denoting that the horses are under Starter's orders to be hoisted:

(a) for races started from Starting Stalls when all the horses are in the Stalls.

(b) for races started from a Starting Gate when he has mounted his rostrum.

(c) for races started by Flag when he has taken up his position to start the race.

PART 3

HORSES

AGE

30. The age of a horse shall be reckoned as beginning on the 1st January in the year in which he is foaled.

REGISTRATION OF NAMES

31. (i) A name cannot be registered for a horse before it is a yearling unless the horse is foaled elsewhere than in Great Britain, Ireland or the Channel Islands, or is outside these countries at the date of registration.

(ii) A name may only be registered for a horse by application to the Racing Calendar Office on the prescribed form signed by or on behalf of the owner or owners of the horse unless otherwise ordered by the Stewards of the Jockey Club.

(ix) A name may not be changed for any horse:
  (a) that is more than three years old, or
  (b) whose name has been registered by another recognised Turf Authority except with the permission of that Turf Authority, or
  (c) that has been entered under the Rules of any recognised Turf Authority, or
  (d) whose registered name has already been published in the official Stud Book or Register of Non-Thoroughbred Mares, of any recognised Turf Authority.

(x) A change of name must be applied for in the same way as a registration of name.

(xi) If the same name be simultaneously claimed for two horses, the order of priority shall be determined by lot at the Racing Calendar Office.

(xii) Every provision contained in this Rule shall be subject to the power conferred upon the Stewards of the Jockey Club by Rule 1 (vii) to accept or to refuse to accept or to cancel any registration under these Rules, notwithstanding any contrary implication which may be contained in any such provision.

(xiii) A list of names registered and changes of names shall be published in the Racing Calendar.

PART 4

OWNERS, RECOGNISED CLUBS AND COMPANIES, SYNDICATES, PARTNERSHIPS, LEASES, COLOURS

OWNERS

40. The Stewards of the Jockey Club shall maintain a register of the names of owners of horses. The name of an owner may only be registered by application to the Registry Office on the prescribed form signed by the owner unless otherwise ordered by the Stewards of the Jockey Club. Except in the case of a recognised Company a fee of £5.40 (including V.A.T.) must accompany each application. No Company other than a recognised Company may be registered as an owner.

Registration will be effective on and after the Monday following acceptance of the application. If any registered owner shall become a disqualified person his registration shall thereupon become void and if the Stewards of the Jockey Club shall register the name of a person previously warned off or disqualified the registration shall be void. The registration of ownership shall lapse if a registered owner shall not have a horse returned as in training under these rules for two consecutive calendar years. The registration of the name of a recognised Company shall become void if the Company ceases to be a recognised Company within the meaning of the Rules.

42. (i) A recognised Club may enter and run a horse under its own name provided that the legal ownership of the horse is vested in a body of not more than four trustees on behalf of the Club each of whom has been and is approved by the Stewards of the Jockey Club and each of whose names has been and is registered at the Registry Office. The Stewards of the Jockey Club shall not approve trustees and their names may not be registered unless the Stewards of the Jockey Club have approved any trust deed or other document appointing the trustees and establishing their powers and unless any amendment or addition to or deletion from the trust deed or other document required by the Stewards of the Jockey Club has been duly made by the Club. Without prejudice to the foregoing the Stewards may at their absolute discretion refuse to approve any trustee without assigning any reason therefor and they may at their absolute discretion at any time and without assigning any reason therefor withdraw the approval of any trustee and cancel the registration of his name.

(ii) The horse shall be entered in the name of one of the trustees, but there will be no objection to the horse running under the name of the Club.

(iii) The trustees shall for the purposes of these Rules be treated as though they are joint owners and are subject to all the liabilities, duties and privileges of joint ownership.

(iv) The Stewards of the Jockey Club take no cognisance of any disputes arising between the trustees and the members of the Club.

(v) Other than having the privilege of running the horse under the name of the Club no privilege of ownership shall attach to any member of the Club other than the trustees.

45. (i) A 'recognised Company' shall only be entitled to exercise the powers of an owner through its registered agent.

(ii) A registered agent means a person who is appointed as such by the 'recognised Company', in writing and under its Seal and whose appointment has been approved and registered by the Stewards of the Jockey Club at the Registry Office.

(iii) The Stewards of the Jockey Club shall have complete discretion whether to approve and register any person as a registered agent save that they shall not approve and register any person unless they are satisfied that:–

(a) he is not a disqualified person;
(b) he has been duly appointed to act as a registered agent by the 'recognised Company'.

SYNDICATES

46. (i) A syndicate of not more than 12 persons may share an interest in a horse provided that

(a) in the case of syndicate agreements registered on or after September 1st, 1973 the legal possession of the horse is vested in not less than three and not more than four members of the syndicate as lessees of the horse from the syndicate and

(b) in the case of syndicate agreements registered before September 1st, 1973 the legal possession of the horse is vested in not more than four members of the syndicate as lessees of the horse from or trustees of the horse for the syndicate.

(ii) The members of the syndicate in whom legal possession of the horse is vested (whether as lessees or trustees) shall be treated and are hereinafter referred to as joint owners and shall be subject to all the liabilities, duties and privileges of joint ownership. Either the joint owners of the horse or its trainer must have the control and management of the horse.

(iii) The names of the members of the syndicate and of the joint owners shall be lodged at the Registry Office together with a copy of the agreement between them signed by each member and such further information as the Stewards of the Jockey Club may from time to time require. A registration fee of £27.00 (including V.A.T.) shall be paid at the time the agreement is lodged which will be refunded if registration thereof is refused. Subject to the provisions of sub-Rule (vii) hereof registration of the agreement will automatically lapse and a new agreement must be lodged in the event of any change in the membership, shareholding or terms of the syndicate or in the legal possession of the horse.

(iv) The agreement shall include the following details:

    (a) the name and address of each member of the syndicate and the share each member has in the horse.

    (b) a statement setting out all financial arrangements agreed between the members and in particular the method of calculating and the timing of payment of any contributions due from members towards training and other expenses.

    (c) a declaration that each member has read the Rules of Racing dealing with syndicates and the current Jockey Club instructions relating thereto.

    (d) a term imposing upon the joint owners an obligation to keep proper books of account and to send to each member and to the Registry Office a copy of the Annual Accounts duly certified as audited by an Accountant having the qualifications required by Section 161 of the Companies Act, 1948.

(v) If the Stewards of the Jockey Club approve the membership of the syndicate and the syndicate agreement the syndicate agreement will be registered and the Registry Office will forward to each member of the syndicate a copy of the agreement.

(vi) The Stewards of the Jockey Club may order the books of account and all other bills, proceeds, vouchers and other documents relating to a syndicate to be examined by such person or persons as they may appoint. If the necessary facilities for such examination are not forthcoming within 14 days of written notice being served on the joint owners, the registration of the syndicate agreement shall automatically lapse. Notice shall be deemed to be served on the joint owners 24 hours after being posted to the last address notified to the Registry Office or, if no address has been notified, then to the address given for them in the agreement.

(vii) No horse in which a syndicate is interested may be entered for any race unless a syndicate agreement in respect thereof current at the date of entry, and no such horse may start in any race unless a syndicate agreement in respect thereof current at the date of the race, has been registered and unless that registration is currently in force. For the purposes of this sub-rule an agreement shall be deemed to be current notwithstanding that either

(a) a member of the syndicate other than a joint owner has disposed of the whole or part of his share since the agreement was registered provided that no share of any one such member is disposed of more than once in any period of 28 days and provided that notification of each such disposition signed by the transferor and by the transferee and containing a declaration by the transferee that he possesses a copy of the agreement and that he has read the Rules of Racing dealing with syndicates and the current Jockey Club Instructions relating thereto is lodged at the Registry Office within 48 hours of the disposition, or

(b) a member of the syndicate has died provided that written notification of the death is lodged with the Registry Office within 28 days thereof.

and provided that if the Stewards of the Jockey Club by written notice served in accordance with sub-rule (vi) hereof upon the joint owners call for a new formal agreement to be lodged at the Registry Office then at the expiration of 28 days after the date of such notice or such longer period as may be stated in that notice the registration of the agreement previously lodged shall be cancelled and that agreement shall cease to be current within the meaning of this sub-rule.

(viii) When a horse in which a syndicate is interested is sold or transferred it shall not be eligible to run until there has been lodged at the Registry Office a memorandum recording the sale and signed (a) in the case of agreements registered before September 1st, 1973 by all members of the syndicate and (b) in the case of agreements registered after that date by the joint owners.

(ix) No person may be a member of, or have any interest in, more than 12 syndicates.

(x) The Stewards may at their absolute discretion at any time and without assigning any reason therefor withdraw their approval of any member of a syndicate in which event the registration of the syndicate agreement in respect of that horse will be cancelled and the horse shall cease to be eligible to be entered for or run in any race until a fresh registration in respect of that horse has been accepted by the Stewards.

(xi) A horse in which a syndicate is interested shall not be eligible to be entered for or to run in any race whilst any member of the syndicate is a disqualified person and in the event of any such member becoming a disqualified person the registration of any syndicate agreement in respect of that horse shall automatically lapse.

(xii) For the avoidance of any doubt it is hereby expressly declared that nothing in this Rule affects or derogates from the powers of the Stewards of the Jockey Club under Rule 1(vii).

RACING COLOURS

48. (i) Every owner, or part-owner in whose name a horse is to run, is required to register colours annually by application at the Racing Calendar Office and any new registration must be made on the form prescribed by the Stewards of the Jockey Club and comply with the instructions contained thereon. Colours so registered shall not be taken by any other person. All disputes as to the right to particular colours shall be settled by the Stewards of the Jockey Club.

(ii) If any owner runs a horse when his colours are not registered he shall be fined £10 by the Stewards of the Jockey Club unless the circumstances under which this occurred are acceptable to them.
In the case of horses trained abroad a declaration of colours to the Overnight Declarations Office by the time fixed for declaration of runners in the conditions of the race is acceptable in lieu of a registration.

(iii) When an owner has more than one runner in the same race distinguishing caps may be declared at scale, but the owner of any horse which otherwise runs in colours other than those registered in his name or declared under sub-rule (ii) above shall be fined not less than £5 or more than £25 unless the Owner and/or his representative satisfies the Stewards on the day of racing that this is due to circumstances outside their reasonable control.

PART 5

TRAINERS

50. Every trainer in Great Britain of a horse running under these Rules must obtain from the Stewards of the Jockey Club either :–

  (i) A licence, to be applied for annually, which may be granted subject to such restrictions as the Stewards of the Jockey Club consider necessary, or

  (ii) In the case of persons training only those horses which are the sole property of themselves, or of their spouses, parents, sons or daughters (or the Executors or Administrators of such persons) for Steeple Chases and Hurdle races a permit to train, to be applied for each season and which may be granted subject to such restrictions as the Stewards of the Jockey Club consider necessary.

except that, for the purposes of Hunters' Steeple Chases and the Grand Military Gold Cup, a horse may also be trained privately without licence or permit by the proprietor of the stable from whence the horse was regularly and fairly hunted during the current season, but in that event the owner shall be treated as trainer for all purposes under these Rules.

51. Every trainer shall conduct his business properly and with due regard to the interest of his owners. Any negligent or improper conduct in respect of his business shall constitute an offence under these Rules punishable by the Stewards of the Jockey Club by virtue of the powers contained in Rule 2.

52. (i) Any trainer who has not received settlement of an account for training fees due from an owner for whom he trains or has trained horses under a written agreement within three months of the date of despatch of the account may report the matter to the Stewards of the Jockey Club. Such report shall be in writing, signed by the trainer concerned, giving details of the name and address of the owner, the nature and the amount of the debt and the date upon which the account was rendered.

  (iii) Should the owner fail to make the payment or should the Stewards of the Jockey Club consider that his explanation is not satisfactory the amount due will, after thirty days have elapsed from the date of the despatch of the notification, be considered to be arrears due under these Rules and his name will be added to the Unpaid Forfeit List.

(iv) It shall be a breach of the Rules of Racing for a trainer to submit an unjustified or frivolous report.

53. Where any horse has run in any race under these Rules and has been found, on examination under Rule 14 (vi), to have received any amount of any substance (other than a normal nutrient), being a substance which by its nature could affect the racing performance of a horse the trainer of the horse in question shall be fined not less than £100 and, at the discretion of the Stewards of the Jockey Club, his licence or permit may be withdrawn. However, the Stewards may waive the fine if they are satisfied that the substance was administered unknowingly and that the trainer had taken all reasonable precautions to avoid a breach of this Rule.

PART 6

RIDERS

LICENCES AND PERMITS

60. Subject to the provisions of Rule 61, no person shall ride in any race under these Rules unless he or she has obtained from the Stewards of the Jockey Club, subject to such restrictions as they consider necessary, a licence or permit as follows:—

(i) For Flat races:—

(a) a Flat race permit to ride as an amateur to be applied for each season on the prescribed form. Holders of these permits may only ride in Amateur Riders' races.

(b) a Flat race jockey's licence to be applied for each season on the prescribed form.

(c) a Flat race apprentice jockey's licence. Such licences must be applied for each season jointly by the master and the apprentice on the prescribed form and they are only granted in respect of lads who have, of their own free will, and with the consent of their parents or guardians, bound themselves for a period of not less than three years to a trainer, licensed to train horses for Flat races under these Rules, are over sixteen, but under twenty-four years of age, and have never, at the time of the first application for an apprentice licence, ridden as full jockeys under the Rules of any recognised Turf Authority.

On attaining the age of twenty-four no lad may ride as an apprentice.

(ii) For Steeple Chases and Hurdle races:—

    (a) a Steeple Chase and Hurdle race permit to ride as an Amateur to be applied for each season on the prescribed form.

    (b) a Steeple Chase and Hurdle race jockey's licence, to be applied for each season on the prescribed form.

61.   (i) This Rule only applies to riders who are the holders of a current licence or permit issued by a recognised Turf Authority and who are not the holders of a licence or permit to ride granted by the Stewards of the Jockey Club.

    (ii) Subject to sub-Rule (iii) upon production of his current licence or permit, any rider to whom this Rule applies shall be entitled to ride in any race under these Rules subject to such restrictions or conditions as the Stewards of the Jockey Club may consider necessary.

    (iii) In their absolute discretion, the Stewards of the Jockey Club may refuse to permit a rider to whom this Rule applies to ride in any or any particular race or races under these Rules.

    (iv) It shall be an offence for any rider to whom this Rule applies to ride in any or any particular race or races (as the case may be) under these Rules after he has been duly notified of the decision of the Stewards of the Jockey Club refusing him permission to ride therein.

62.   (i) The following persons are not eligible to hold Amateur Riders' permits:—

    (a) a person who has ever held a professional rider's licence from any recognised Turf Authority.

    (b) a person who has ever been paid directly or indirectly for riding in a race.

    (c) a person whose principal paid occupation is or at any time within the last three years has been to ride or groom for a licensed or permitted trainer.

    (d) a person who is or who within the last three years has been paid as a groom in private, livery or Horse Dealers' stables or as a Hunt Servant.

    (ii) During the term of his licence a jockey or an apprentice jockey may not—

(a) be the owner or part-owner of any horse being entered or run under these Rules with the exception of horses taking part in Hunters' Steeple Chases only, or

(b) bet on horse racing or receive presents in connection with a race from persons other than the owner of the horse he rides in that race.

And any rider who may be proved to the satisfaction of the Stewards of the Jockey Club to have contravened any of the above conditions appropriate to his or her licence or permit will have his licence or permit withdrawn.

FEES

63. The following fees are payable in respect of each licence or permit to ride :–

(i) Flat race or Steeple Chase and Hurdle race Amateur riders' permit – £5.40 (including V.A.T.).

(ii) Flat race jockey's licence – £10.80 (including V.A.T.) of which £1 is to be applied as the jockey's subscription to the Bentinck Benevolent Fund.

(iii) Flat race apprentice jockey's licence – £5.40 (including V.A.T.) of which £1 is to be applied as the jockey's subscription to the Bentinck Benevolent Fund.

(iv) Steeple Chase and Hurdle race jockey's licence – £5.40 (including V.A.T.) of which £2 is to be applied as the jockey's subscription to the Rendlesham Benevolent Fund.

65. Any horse ridden in a race in contravention of Rules 60 or 61 of these Rules shall, on objection, be liable to be disqualified by the Stewards of the Jockey Club.

66. (i) An amateur rider or jockey whose permit or licence has been suspended by the Stewards of the Jockey Club or by any other recognised Turf Authority shall not ride in any race during the period of his suspension.

(ii) If an amateur rider or jockey becomes a disqualified person his permit or licence is thereby revoked.

67. A list of the amateur riders, and licensed jockeys shall be published in the Racing Calendar.

PART 9

PROGRAMMES, HANDICAPS AND SELLING RACES

SELLING RACES

96.   The following Rules relating to selling races apply to all selling races but in optional selling races they apply only to horses which run as entered to be sold.

(i) In selling races, the selling price shall be equal to the guaranteed prize money or £1000, whichever is the least.

(ii) In all selling races the winner shall be offered for sale by auction immediately after the race except as provided in Rule 98 (i) and the surplus over the selling price shall go to the Race-course except that the winning owner shall be paid 10% of any surplus between the selling price and £1000 and 25% of any further surplus.

(iii) In the case of a dead-heat, each of the horses dividing is a winner for the purposes of the Rules relating to claiming and selling, and if a selling race, both shall be put up to auction, and any surplus shall go to the Race-course.

(iv) If a horse walk over (or there be no second horse placed) for a selling race, the winner is still liable to be sold.

(v) No person shall prevent or seek to prevent any other person from bidding for the winner of a selling race, whether by offering any consideration or guarantee or by means of a threat or otherwise; and no person shall accept or offer to accept, any consideration or guarantee or other inducement to refrain from bidding. Any person so offending shall be fined £100 or reported to the Stewards of the Jockey Club.

(vi) If sold, or bought in, the horse shall not leave the place of sale without permission of the auctioneer, and a written order given for his delivery to the actual bidder who alone shall be responsible for the price; and if the horse be not paid for, or the price secured to the satisfaction of the auctioneer within a quarter of an hour, he may put the horse up a second time, and the purchaser at the first sale shall be responsible for any deficiency arising from the second, and shall be treated as a defaulter until it is paid. Whoever issues the delivery order for a horse sold, bought in, or claimed, is responsible for the money and shall pay it over to the Stakeholder for payment in accordance with Rule 27 (v) to the person or persons entitled.

PART 14

WEIGHING-OUT, EXHIBITING NUMBERS, &c.

WEIGHING-OUT

141.   (i) No rider shall be weighed out (except as provided below) for any race unless the name of the race and of the horse and the rider have been given in writing to the Clerk of the Course not less than three-quarters of an hour before the time fixed for the race. Such declaration may only be made by the owner, trainer, employee of the trainer on production of his Stable Employees' Identity Card, or other person on production of a written authorisation by the owner or trainer and available only for the day of the race. When a horse is owned by a 'recognised Company' declaration may also be made by a registered agent of the Company or by another person on production of a written authorisation signed by such registered agent and available only for the day of the race.

(ii) The trainer is responsible that the horse carries the correct weight in accordance with the conditions of the race. The trainer is required to declare the weight his horse will carry or the colours to be worn by the rider if either is different from those appearing on the racecard to the Clerk of the Scales before the rider weighs out. Failure to make such declarations will render the trainer liable to a fine of not less than £5. Riders' allowances will not be taken into consideration when declaring a weight under this sub-Rule.

(iii) Should a rider, who has been declared, not present himself to be weighed, another rider may, with the permission of the Stewards, be substituted provided always that he can be weighed within the time specified in section (iv) of this Rule, but unless they are satisfied, after enquiry, that the absence of the rider was due to unavoidable circumstances, they shall, after dealing with the case under their powers, make a report to the Stewards of the Jockey Club.

(iv) Every rider must be weighed for a specified horse by the Clerk of the Scales, at the appointed place, not less than a quarter of an hour before the time fixed for the race. In exceptional cases, the Stewards may extend the time allowed for declaring runners under this Rule, weighing, declaring weight, and for exhibiting the numbers.

142.   If a rider intends to carry over-weight, he must declare the amount thereof at the time of weighing out or, if in doubt as to his proper weight, he may declare the weight he intends to carry.

When weighing out or weighing in the rider must put into the scale and include in his weight everything that the horse is to carry or has carried except the skull cap, whip, bridle, rings, plates and anything worn on the horse's legs.

143.   If a rider after he has been weighed for a specified horse, and before he has come under Starter's Orders, is prevented by accident or illness from riding in the race, another jockey may be substituted provided there is no unreasonable delay.

PART 15

RUNNING, VOID RACES, WALKING OVER AND DEAD HEATS

BEFORE THE RACE

151.   (i) Every horse which runs in a race shall be run on its merits, whether its owner runs another horse in the race or not.

(ii) The rider of every horse shall take all reasonable and permissible measures throughout the race to ensure that his horse is given a full opportunity to win or of obtaining the best possible placing.

(iii) It shall be the duty of a trainer to ensure that adequate instructions are given to the rider of any horse in his care and no owner, registered agent of a recognised Company, or trainer shall give any instruction to the rider of any horse which if obeyed could or would prevent the horse from winning a race or of obtaining the best possible placing, neither shall they, its rider or any other person prevent or try to prevent in any way any horse from winning a race or of obtaining the best possible placing.

THE RACE

152.   (i) Any horse getting away from its rider in a Steeple Chase or Hurdle race, may be remounted, but should it have run out of the course or continued in the race before being caught it shall be brought back to the part of the course where it parted from its rider, and shall continue by jumping all fences or hurdles from that point. Any rider so losing his horse may be assisted in catching it and remounting it without risk of disqualification.

(ii) If a horse having refused any fence, or hurdle, in a Steeple Chase or Hurdle race, has been led over it by any of the by-standers, or has been given a lead over by any horseman not riding in the race, the horse shall, on an objection under Rule 170 (iv), be disqualified.

(iii) If a horse run the wrong side of a direction post or flag, or miss a fence or hurdle, his rider shall turn back and ride the course correctly from such point, or he shall pull up. He shall not otherwise continue in the race, or his horse shall, on an objection under Rule 170 (iv) be disqualified.

IMPROPER RIDING

153. (i) A horse shall on an objection under Rule 170 (iv) be disqualified if his rider causes interference in any part of a race by dangerous, reckless, careless or improper riding.

(ii) A horse shall, on an objection under Rule 170 (iv), be disqualified if he or his rider interfere with any horse or rider in any part of a Flat race or at or after the last obstacle in a Steeplechase or Hurdle race unless

(a) the Stewards are satisfied that the interference was accidental when they may at their discretion and in lieu of disqualification alter the placings of any or all of the first four horses, or

(b) the Stewards are satisfied that the interference was both accidental and had no effect on the result of the race when they may overrule the objection and order that the placings shall remain unchanged.

(iii) The rider of any horse who, in the opinion of the Stewards of the Meeting or the Stewards of the Jockey Club, has been guilty of dangerous, reckless, careless or improper riding shall be guilty of an offence.

VOID RACES

154. (i) If a race has been run by all the horses at wrong weights, or over a wrong course, or distance, or before the appointed time, or if the Judge is not in the box at the time the horses pass the winning post, the Stewards shall order a Flat race to be run again the same day if practicable, but if otherwise, or in the case of a Steeple Chase or Hurdle race, it shall be void.

(ii) If no qualified horse cover the course in accordance with these Rules the race may be declared void.

PART 16

WEIGHING-IN

160. (i) Immediately after pulling up, the riders of the horses placed first, second, and third in each race must ride their horses to the place appointed for unsaddling, and the horses shall remain there until ordered to be taken away by the Clerk of the Scales. The other riders may dismount within a reasonable distance. Every rider must present himself to be weighed by the Clerk of the Scales at once, and, if he fail to complete the course, report the reason. If a rider be prevented from riding back to weigh in by reason of accident or illness, by which he or his horse is disabled, he may walk or be carried to the scales.

(ii) In cases where the Judge, in consulting the photograph, has not announced his decision before the jockeys return to weigh in, they may dismount either inside or within a reasonable distance of the place appointed for unsaddling the winner. In such cases the Clerk of the Scales shall weigh in all jockeys until such time as the Judge's decision is announced.

(iii) If a rider does not present himself to be weighed in, or dismount before reaching the place appointed for that purpose, or touch (except accidentally) any person or thing other than his own equipment before weighing in his horse shall, on an objection under Rule 170 (iv), be disqualified, unless he can satisfy the Stewards that he was justified by extraordinary circumstances.

PART 17

DISPUTES, OBJECTIONS AND APPEALS

DISPUTES AND OBJECTIONS

170. (i) If an objection to a horse engaged in a race be made not later than half-past ten in the morning of the day of the race, the Stewards may require his qualification to be proved before the race; and in default of such proof being given to their satisfaction they may declare him disqualified.

(ii) An objection to the distance of a course officially designated must be made before a race.

(iii) An objection to any decision of the Clerk of the Scales must be made at once.

(iv) An objection to a horse on the grounds of a cross, jostle, or any act on the part of his rider, or of his not having run the proper course, or of the race having been run on a wrong course, or of any other matter occurring in the race, or before weighing in, or on the ground that the rider did not present himself to weigh in, or that he could not draw the weight at which he weighed out, must be made within five minutes after the winner has been weighed in, or, within five minutes of the time the Judge has announced his decision on all placings, whichever be later (see also Rule 171 (iii)). The Stewards may extend the above period if they are satisfied that it could not have been made within that time. No objection on any other ground than these shall be heard within this time.

(v) An objection on any other ground than those laid down in Rule 170 (iv) shall be received within fourteen days of the conclusion of a Meeting. No objection under this paragraph may be heard until the signal has been hoisted in accordance with Rule 162.

(vi) In cases of fraud, or wilful misstatement, there shall be no limit to the time for objecting, provided the Stewards of the Jockey Club are satisfied there has been no unnecessary delay on the part of the objector. Such objection shall not be heard until the signal has been hoisted in accordance with Rule 162.

(vii) Nothing in this Rule shall restrict the operation at any time of Rules 1, 2, and 15.

PART 18

DISQUALIFICATION OF HORSES

180.

(i) Any horse which has been the subject of fraudulent practice may, at the discretion of the Stewards of the Jockey Club, be disqualified for such time and for such races as they shall determine.

(ii) Where a horse has been the subject of an examination under Rule 14 (vi) and has been found to have received any amount of any substance (other than a normal nutrient) being a substance which by its nature could affect the racing performance of a horse the horse shall be disqualified for the race in question and may, at the discretion of the Stewards of the Jockey Club, be disqualified for such time and for such races as they shall determine.

181.   A horse is not qualified to be entered or start for any race:–

   (i) If he has run at any unrecognised meeting.

   (ii) If and so long as he is in the ownership or part ownership of a disqualified person, or so long as any disqualified person has any interest in such horse's winnings in such race.

   (iii) If and so long as he is in the stable of, or under the care and management of, a disqualified person, but when such a person, other than the owner or part owner, incurs disqualification under Rule 137 or Rule 203 the horse shall be qualified to be entered or run until 14 days have elapsed from the date of publication in the Forfeit List, see Rule 137, or from the date of the disqualification under Rule 203.

   (iv) If and so long as he is in the Forfeit List.

   (v) In any case in which he is by these Rules or by the conditions of the race declared to be disqualified.

   (vi) If he has been declared disqualified by the Stewards of the Jockey Club.

   (vii) If he is the property of an owner whose name has not been duly registered under Rule 40, except in the case of a horse trained outside Great Britain coming to Great Britain for the purpose of a particular race.

   (viii) If he is a horse in which a syndicate is interested and if there is no syndicate agreement of which registration is currently in force in accordance with Rule 46.

   (ix) If he is the property of a recognised Company and that Company has no registered agent.

PART 20

PROHIBITED PRACTICES AND DISQUALIFICATIONS OF PERSONS

200.   Any person who administers or allows or causes to be administered or connives at the administration to a horse of any amount of any substance (other than a normal nutrient), being a substance which by its nature could affect the racing performance of a horse, shall be guilty of a breach of the Rules and may be declared a disqualified person or otherwise penalised by the Stewards of the Jockey Club in accordance with their powers under Rule 2 of these Rules.

201.   Any person may be declared a disqualified person or otherwise penalised by the Stewards of the Jockey Club in accordance with their powers under Rule 2 of these Rules who:

  (i) Gives or offers, or promises directly or indirectly, any bribe in any form to any person having official duties in relation to a race or racehorse, or to any trainer, rider, agent or other person having charge of, or access to, any racehorse; or

  (ii) Being a person having official duties in relation to a race, or being a trainer, rider, agent or other person having charge of, or access to, any racehorse, accepts or offers to accept any bribe in any form; or

 (iii) Wilfully enters or causes to be entered for any race, or causes to start in any race, a horse which he knows or believes to be disqualified; or

 (iv) Surreptitiously obtains information respecting a trial from any person or persons engaged in it, or in the service of the owner or trainer of the horses tried, or respecting any horse in training from any person in such service; or

  (v) Deliberately misleads or by any overt act endeavours to mislead the Stewards of a Meeting or the Stewards of the Jockey Club at any enquiry; or

 (vi) Is guilty of or conspires with any other person for the commission of, or connives at any other person being guilty of, any corrupt (or fraudulent) practice in relation to racing in this or any other country, or is convicted of any criminal offence in relation to racing in this or any other country.

and any such act shall constitute a breach of these Rules.

202. When a person is warned off, and so long as his exclusion continues, he is a disqualified person.

205. A disqualified person, so long as his disqualification lasts, shall not:–

  (i) Act as Steward or Official at any recognised Meeting.

 (ii) Act as authorised agent under these Rules.

(iii) Enter, run, train, or ride a horse in any race at any recognised Meeting, or ride in trials. If any entry made by a person disqualified or warned off be mistakenly or inadvertently accepted, the same shall despite such acceptance be void and the horse shall not be qualified to be entered or to start.

 (iv) Enter any Race-course, Stand, or Enclosure.

  (v) Except with permission of the Stewards of the Jockey Club be employed in any Racing Stable.

CHAPTER SEVEN

Tattersalls

'Who has not heard of Tattersalls?'
(*Bailey's Magazine*, 1870)

The names Tattersall and Weatherby are synonymous with horse racing in this country and it is a curious coincidence that British racing should contain two such famous families. Both are steeped in the traditions of the Turf, and both enjoy reputations for honesty and integrity, and each has a tradition going back over two hundred years.

The firm of Tattersalls was founded by Richard Tattersall (1724–1795) who was born at Hurstwood. From an early age Richard Tattersall showed a keen interest in horses and when in 1745 he left home – rumour has it after an argument with his father who refused to let him join the Jacobite Rebels – he went to London where he obtained employment at Beevor's Horse Repository in St Martin's Lane. Subsequently he became head ostler at Beevors and may even have acquired an interest in the firm.

In 1753 Richard Tattersall entered the service of Evelyn Pierrepont, the 2nd Duke of Kingston, where he eventually obtained the position of Stud Manager. By the year 1766 Tattersall had acquired sufficient capital to be able to purchase the lease of some land at Hyde Park Corner, the property of the Earl of Grosvenor. Here he built the premises which were eventually to become famous throughout the world and he set himself up as an auctioneer of bloodstock. Tattersall's business flourished, and he rapidly acquired the reputation for honesty and straight dealing. Soon his customers included many of the leading noblemen of the day, and he also attracted the notice of royalty; he was asked to procure many horses for the King of France.

In 1779 Tattersall fitted up two rooms which he made available, together with the services of a cook, for the use of members of the Jockey Club. These rooms soon became an important meeting place for the racing fraternity.

Tattersall's premises at this time consisted of a house and an office, coach houses, kennels, stables and exercise yards, and covered in all some ten acres. The main buildings consisted of offices and a sumptuous dining room, where 'Old Tatt', as he had become known, entertained his guests at his celebrated Monday Dinners. There were also the rooms set aside for the Jockey Club; later a Subscription Room was added, and it was here that the placing and paying, or not paying, of bets took place.

In that same year of 1779, Tattersall achieved one of his ambitions when he purchased from Lord Bolingbroke a horse which he had had his eye on for some time. This was the famous stallion, Highflyer, for which 'Old Tatt' paid £800 – no small sum in those days. However, the shrewd horse dealer knew what he was about, and recovered his money handsomely, for Highflyer ran eight times in all and was never beaten; he also proved to be most successful at stud. In 1793, when Highflyer died at the age of twenty, 'Old Tatt' was heartbroken and the following epitaph, from an anonymous correspondent, appeared in the *Sporting Magazine*:

> Here lieth the perfect and beautiful symmetry of the much lamented Highflyer, by whom, and his wonderful offspring, the celebrated Tattersall acquired a noble fortune, but was not ashamed to acknowledge it.

'Old Tatt' would no doubt have been delighted to know that Highflyer is still commemorated today by the Highflyer Stakes – a five furlong race for two-year-olds run at Thirsk.

By 1788 the firm of Tattersalls was well and truly established. Sometime earlier 'Old Tatt' had acquired sixty acres of grassland near Ely and here he built his country house – Highflyer Hall – where he later entertained the Prince of Wales (to become George IV), Charles Fox and many other notable personalities of the day, with 'some of the best port in England'. It was in 1788 that 'Old Tatt' purchased the *Morning Post*, which he owned jointly with the Prince of Wales, but, alas, his flair for judging horseflesh was not matched by his acumen as a newspaper proprietor, and the *Post* proved to be a losing venture.

Richard Tattersall died in February 1795 and he was buried in St George's Church, Hanover Square. In fifty years he had established what was to become the most famous bloodstock agency in the world and had acquired, both for himself and for his business, a reputation for integrity which was second to none.

'Old Tatt' was succeeded by his son, Edmund (1758–1810) who, for some years prior to his father's death, had been a partner in the business. Edmund, although a keen hunter and sportsman, seems to have lacked some of his father's initiative and drive when it came to making money – not that he was in any way foolish where money was concerned. Neither, it seems, did Edmund share his father's interest in breeding horses, as one of his first acts on taking over the firm was to sell the breeding stud. Edmund Tattersall did, however, consolidate his father's business and also industriously built up the firm's overseas connections, practically founding Tattersalls' foreign business organisation.

It was during Edmund's 'reign' at Hyde Park Corner that there occurred a difference of opinion between the Prince of Wales and the Jockey Club. The Prince took the matter to heart and withdrew his patronage of racing. Edmund, a firm friend of His Royal Highness, did well to avoid being drawn into the conflict and thus either losing business or risking the good name of Tattersalls.

Edmund Tattersall died of a brain fever in 1810. He left a wife and three children: Richard, Edmund and George, and it was Richard (1785–1859) who succeeded to command the business. In this Richard was later assisted by his brother Edmund, but George Tattersall, having unsuccessfully tried farming on his own account, took over the running of the family farm at Dawley. He never became a partner in the business.

Richard Tattersall seems to have possessed all his grandfather's flair and business acumen and consolidated Tattersalls' business interests both in Britain and abroad. Within a week of his father's death Richard, then aged twenty-five, was firmly in control, as witness this advertisement, which appeared in the *Morning Post* on February 18th, 1810:

> Messrs Tattersalls beg leave humbly to solicit the Nobility, Gentry and Public at large, a continuation of those favours so amply bestowed upon their deceased father, trusting their conduct in business will be found as to render them not unworthy of the confidence with which they may be honoured. They will continue to sell at Hyde Park Corner every Monday and Thursday in the winter months and at Newmarket during the meeting.

And continue to sell they did. In fact, since the time when 'Old Tatt' first founded Tattersalls until the present day, they have managed to carry on their business quietly and efficiently, despite wars, revolutions and riots, and amidst all the upsets which Europe has undergone during

8. Early morning exercise on the gallops at Malton, Yorkshire.

9. Red Rum exercising on the sands at Southport, his lad Billy Ellison up.

10. *left* Lester Piggott on Flying Legs, 1968.   11. *right* Grundy after winning the King George VI and Queen Elizabeth Diamond Stakes at Ascot, 1975. Pat Eddery up.

12. Brigadier Gerard after winning the same race in 1972, with Joe Mercer up.

13. *left* Mill House, ridden by David Nicholson, returns to the winner's enclosure after the 1967 Whitbread Gold Cup.   14. *right* Edward Courage greets Bill Smith after winning the National Hunt Two Mile Champion Chase on Royal Relief at the Cheltenham Festival Meeting, 1972.

15. A rather untypical departure. Graham Thorner loses touch with Retrospect at Stratford in 1973.

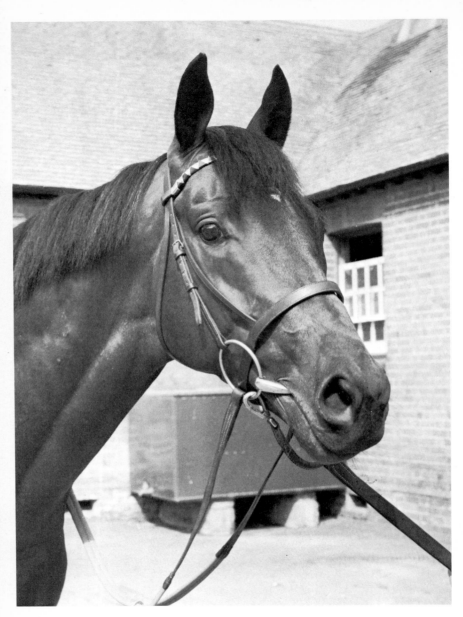

16. Mill Reef at his Kingsclere stables in 1971.

the past two hundred years. Indeed, in a small way, they have even had a hand in clearing away some of the debris resulting from those upsets, as witness an item sold at Tattersalls in November 1818: 'The four brown barouche geldings, taken with military carriage, of the ex-Emperor Napoleon, at the battle of Waterloo.'

Although based in London, Tattersalls also conducted sales in other parts of the country. Richard Tattersall delighted in travelling about the country and conducting sales, attending to the dispersal of major stud farms and attending race meetings. Always a popular and respected man, it was said of him that he was 'free of the road' – meaning that no highwayman would dream of molesting him.

Perhaps the best known of the out-of-town sales were held at Newmarket in the High Street, near the Jockey Club Rooms. In 1860, however, Tattersalls obtained some land behind Queensbury House and here they continued to function until 1870, when they moved to Park Paddocks, Newmarket, where they have continued to hold sales to this day.

It was in 1818 that Richard Tattersall opened his new Subscription Rooms at the 'Corner', anxious, it is thought, to separate the betting men from his regular customers. Interest in betting was spreading at this time and there were many disputes concerning the payment, or otherwise, of bets. 'The number of levanters on settling day at Tattersalls [settling day was invariably a Monday] after the Epsom Meeting was unprecedented; defaulters of every description were found from £10 up to £10,000; several who had lost thousands did not make their appearance at all.'

Richard, or 'Old Dick' as he became known, was reluctant to injure his business by becoming too much associated with the betting ring. It is, incidentally, strange that the name of Tattersall should be so closely associated with betting matters when, in fact, they have always been principally bloodstock auctioneers. Even today the main betting ring on any racecourse in Britain is known as 'Tattersalls' enclosure', although these have absolutely no connection with the firm of Tattersalls. In order to discourage members of the public from ringing up to discuss betting disputes, Tattersalls' London office at Knightsbridge Green has an ex-directory telephone number. Tattersalls the Auctioneers are in no way – other than by historical association – connected with Tattersalls' Committee, the recognised arbiters in all matters relating to betting.

The formation of Tattersalls' Committee came about, early in the nineteenth century, when the Jockey Club decided that they would no longer concern themselves with betting disputes, but that in future all betting disputes would be settled by referees. Following discussions with 'Old Dick' Tattersall, it was agreed that those persons in such disputes should meet either at the London or the Newmarket Subscription Rooms.

In 1851 Richard Tattersall's brother Edmund died and 'Old Dick' entered into a new partnership agreement with his son, 'Young Richard', who had in fact been a partner in the firm since 1840. There was also a third partner, Edmund Tattersall, 'Old Dick's' nephew. In 1855 'Old Dick' had virtually retired from the business and in 1859 he died of a heart attack whilst he was at Dover.

It was under 'Young Richard' Tattersall's leadership that Tattersalls finally moved from Hyde Park Corner, finding that the lease was due to expire and that the owner was not disposed to grant a new one. The firm looked for and found new premises at Knightsbridge Green, and so ended Tattersalls' ninety-nine year association with Hyde Park Corner. The premises and effects were pulled down and they moved to the new site, where Tattersalls still have their London office today. The family house, however, must have been retained, as Sommerville Tattersall was born there in 1863.

An interesting, if somewhat disapproving description of Tattersalls' Hyde Park Corner premises has been left us by George de Sala in his book *Twice Around the Clock*, which was first published in 1858:

> My business lies close to Hyde Park Corner, close to St George's Hospital. We have but to turn down Lower Grosvenor Place and lo and behold, we are at our destination – Tattersalls. I suppose that the British Empire could not progress prosperously without Tattersalls, so I suppose we must cry 'Tattersalls and our ancient constitution! Tattersalls and liberty!' And, indeed, of the last there seems in reality to be much liberty and equality, and fraternity, in all connected with horseracing, and at Tattersalls, though the resort of the most patrician turfites, the democratic element is noticeably strong.
>
> So long as both parties pay their bets, Dukes and dustmen seem to meet upon a cheerful footing, man to man, at this peculiarly national establishment. This is the famous 'Ring', which you have heard so much about, and the building that resembles a dissenting chapel is none other than Messrs. Tattersalls subscription room. Now cast your eyes to the right and you will see a low archway passing through which a hand points to where Mr Rarey, the horse tamer had his offices, while on the other side is a counting house, somewhat dark and mysterious in aspect, where the names and prices of more racers and hunters than you or I have ever heard of are entered in Tattersalls bulky ledgers.
>
> Beyond the archway stretches a spacious courtyard, the centre

of which is occupied by a species of temple, circular in form, with painted wooden pillars, and a cupola surmounted by a bust of George IV.

It is said that Richard Tattersall ('Old Tatt') erected this bust in gratitude for having been made a kind of almoner 'for the relief of certain decayed turfites' by George IV, when he was still the Prince of Wales. De Sala also mentions Tattersalls' famous fox: 'Beneath the cupola is the figure of a fox – very cunning and foxy indeed.' The statue of the fox under the rotunda can almost be said to be Tattersalls' trade mark. It was originally erected at Hyde Park Corner and was later moved to Knightsbridge. Subsequently, at the instigation of Captain Kenneth Watt, the present-day senior partner, it was moved to Park Paddocks, Newmarket, where it stands today outside the new sales ring.

Tattersalls' move from Hyde Park Corner to the Albert Gate, Knightsbridge, took place on April 10th, 1865. It was celebrated by a testimonial dinner, at which the principal guest was perhaps the most famous administrator in the history of the Turf – Admiral Rous. Shortly after the move to Knightsbridge, however, 'Young Richard' Tattersall developed a serious illness, and in 1869 he and Edmund took the unprecedented step of introducing a stranger – one Thomas Pain – into the partnership. Soon afterwards Richard was forced to retire and on May 3rd 1870 he died, at the age of fifty-eight.

Tattersalls' Knightsbridge premises covered two acres in all – it included a glass-covered yard, subscription rooms, a room set aside for the use of the Jockey Club, seventy-five open boxes and twenty-five stalls for brood mares.

One description of the clientele at the new Tattersalls appeared in *Bailey's Magazine*, 1870:

> We selected the 5th of September, when Count Lagrange's stud was to be sold, for our visit. As usual, the place was filled with all sorts and conditions of men – a curious collection of humanity within a small compass. There were Peers and peasants, leading dealers and petty copers, the real old-fashioned sportsmen, who run their horses for their own amusement, and the slang horse owner from the top of the Haymarket. The vicinity of the rostrum is soon occupied by a set of loafers, who steadily stick there from eleven to four, many of whom must have a job to pay their washing bills, small as they are, and certainly cannot want either a thoroughbred or a weight carrier. As a lounge, Tattersalls is not what it was, and except on great sale days the class of men present has much deteriorated, for gentlemen now go straight to the rooms which are shut off from the yard, so that on some days the

occupants of the latter place have a seedy and regular St Martin's Lane look about them.

This rather tight-laced description, harking back as it does to the days when horseracing was, for the most part, the prerogative of the nobility, reflects the social changes which were gradually taking place. Better means of transport, improved communications systems, the introduction of electricity, the legalization of the Trades Unions, the passing of the Elementary Education Act — all these things and many more, meant that a social revolution was taking place, and the Sport of Kings was well on the way to becoming a national sport.

As early as 1810 'Old Dick' Tattersall had made unsuccessful attempts to keep the seedier elements out — even going so far as to display a notice which read: 'Messrs. Tattersalls trust gentlemen will not encourage dog stealers who frequent this yard.' This notice was removed the next morning by persons unknown. But racing, and indeed anything to do with the buying and selling of racehorses, has always attracted a motley crowd, and this is part of its attraction. Anyone who doubts this has only to spend ten minutes looking around at the variety of types and characters to be found on any modern race course.

'All men are equal on the turf and under it,' ran the old maxim, and even when racing was solely in the hands of the nobility there must have been vast numbers of grooms, stable lads, touts, backers and layers, plus the inevitable hangers-on in the offing, and a goodly percentage of these people must have gravitated towards Tattersalls. R. S. Surtees, the great sporting writer wrote of Tattersalls in a book published in 1865.:

> What dilapidated specimens of humanity one sees down at Tattersalls on a full Monday morning in the height of the London season. Men in every stage of sporting decay, from the roseate groom of yesterday's dismissal, down to the threadbare scarecrow, who does not look as if he has had a square meal for a month. Were ever such queerly cut clothes so oddly put on such shaggy heads, such extraordinary coats, so rich in oddly placed pockets made for holding the mythical never coming coin. What sticks — what legs — what sticks of legs, and yet these incongruous garments often cover those who have been clad, if not in the purple, at all events in hunting pink. Men who have been hailed by My Lord and noticed by Sir Harry, now only perhaps too happy to lead a newly purchased horse all the way to Hackney or Hoxton for a shilling.

But whatever the changes in the social clime, Tattersalls' business continued to build steadily, and under the leadership of Edmund Tattersall (1816–1898) the organisation continued to prosper and to expand.

Edmund was the son of George Tattersall, the farmer, and in 1851, at the age of thirty-five, he began to assist his uncle, Richard Tattersall, at the Hyde Park Corner premises. When Richard died in May 1870, Edmund became the senior partner and it was he who gradually perfected and streamlined the organisation of the new Tattersalls at Knightsbridge. Edmund Tattersall was succeeded by his son, Sommerville ('Sommy') Tattersall, who had been admitted to the firm in 1885 and who had, in fact, taken over the responsibilities of Tattersalls some years before his father died in 1898.

Sommerville Tattersall (1863–1942) was born in the old house at Hyde Park Corner, and was christened at St George's Church, Hanover Square. He was educated at Eton, and at the age of twenty-one he began to help his father in the family business. Sommerville Tattersall was a man of many interests. He was a shrewd and respected auctioneer, and a good judge of horses – very much in the family tradition. He was also extremely interested in music, and numbered among his friends Sir Thomas Beecham, Sir Edward Elgar and Sir Henry Wood. 'Sommy' was also a keen mountaineer and spent much time climbing in Switzerland. Like 'Old Tatt' he was interested in racehorse owning and, for this purpose, used the pseudonym 'Mr Preston'.

In 1904 there were three members of the family in partnership – Sommerville, his brother Harry George, and Rupert Tattersall. In 1905, however, Harry George resigned after a quarrel with Sommerville, and Sommerville and Rupert then carried on the business until a Mr Gerald Deane was taken into the firm to assist them.

During the First World War Gerald Deane joined the Army and did not return to the firm until the war ended. Rupert Tattersall also enlisted in the Army as a Private in the 'Sportsmans' Brigade', later being commissioned in the Rifle Brigade. He was severely wounded, as a result of which it was impossible for him to continue with the firm when the war ended. Sommerville Tattersall had carried on the business as best he could, but the war was a bad time for Tattersalls and turnover had slumped alarmingly. 'Sommy' also devoted much time to racing politics, and when the Government attempted to stop all racing he joined forces with the Jockey Club in an attempt to save the British bloodstock industry.

Sommerville Tattersall was always greatly concerned with maintaining the standards of British bloodstock, as witness the following story (which appears in Vincent Orchard's excellent history of the family – *Tattersalls*) concerning the sale of the famous horse, Sceptre. *

*Extract from *Tattersalls* by Vincent Orchard is reproduced by kind permission of the Estate of the late Vincent Orchard.

When that immortal mare was in the ring Mr Tattersall remarked: 'We ought to keep Sceptre and her daughter (Maid of the Mist) in England. I shall look upon English racing people as unpatriotic, like some of our politicians, if they let her go.' The mare advanced to 6,800 guineas. That bid was made for France by Baron Maurice de Rothschild. Then there was a long pause. Mr Tattersall again and again swept the crowded ring, gently enquiring if anyone would make a final bid. No one took the Baron's place. Finally and quietly came the announcement that 7,000 guineas was bid for Sceptre. The Baron made no more, nor did anyone increase that bid. The hammer fell. Messrs Tattersall were announced as the purchasers of Sceptre.

Sommerville Tattersall was the last member of the family to be associated with the business. His nephew, Edmund Harry, who was invalided out of the Army after a distinguished military career, asked Sommerville to take him into the business, but Sommerville refused and gave no reason for his refusal. Sommerville Tattersall (who, incidentally, never married) died in London in October 1942. His Estate was valued at £161,228. The only person not mentioned in his Will was Edmund Harry Tattersall, the surviving male member of the family, in direct line from the firm's founder, Richard Tattersall.

Following the death of Sommerville Tattersall the business was carried on by Major Gerald Deane, who had become a partner in the firm in 1914. 1942 witnessed the tragic death of another member of the firm, when Major Terence Watt, who had joined the firm in 1937, was killed while on active service. His son, Mr Michael Watt, is now a partner in the firm.

The present-day senior partner is Captain Kenneth Watt, who joined Major Deane as partner at the end of the Second World War, becoming senior partner when Major Deane died in 1951. The other present-day partners are Mr John Coventry, a former Worcestershire cricket captain, and Mr Bruce Deane, the son of Major Gerald Deane.

In 1966 Tattersalls celebrated their bi-centenary and, to mark the occasion, a unique new sales ring, designed by Professor Sir Albert Richardson, was built at Park Paddocks, Newmarket. Here Tattersalls continue to hold sales of bloodstock, which are attended by the foremost breeders, owners and trainers in the world. Long may they continue to do so!

TATTERSALLS' COMMITTEE

'It has been said that the love of money is the root of all evil. The want of money is so quite as truly.'

(Samuel Butler, 1835–1902)

Since the early part of the nineteenth century (various authorities give the date as 1843, 1834 and 1832), when the Jockey Club gave up making decisions in matters concerning betting, Tattersalls' Committee has been the recognised tribunal before which all persons interested in betting disputes or claims in connection with horse racing may present their disputes or claims for adjudication. The Committee is recognised by the ruling Turf authorities and is also recognised by Her Majesty's Judges, who have laid down that Tattersalls' Committee is the right and proper tribunal for the hearing of betting disputes. In this respect, it must be remembered that debts incurred as the result of gaming are not recoverable through the Law Courts.

In 1928 the Committee was recognised by Parliament in the Racecourse Betting Act, when it was empowered to appoint one of its members to sit on the Racecourse Betting Control Board. Tattersalls' Committee report their findings to the interested parties only, and these findings are only made public in very special cases, where a general ruling as to the destination of bets is required. Reports of default are made privately to the Stewards of the Jockey Club.

The charges made by Tattersalls' Committee for hearing and determining a claim are nominal and fees, which are payable on the lodgement of a claim, range from £1 for a claim of up to £25, to £30 for a claim of over £5,000. Tattersalls' Committee do not ask either the complainant or the respondent to sign any formal submission or agreement to be bound by the Committee's decision.

At their meetings the Committee hear the evidence of the parties who are present before them, or read letters and/or statements from them if the parties are not present. The Committee hear the evidence of witnesses, read any documentary evidence, and inspect any betting books or slips, and generally give the matter before them their utmost consideration. If the Committee are satisfied that a complainant has established his claim, they make an order for payment of the amount claimed. If this order is not complied with, after giving notice to the respondent, they will, at the request of the complainant, report the respondent to the Stewards of the Jockey Club. The Stewards treat such persons who are reported to them by Tattersalls' Committee as 'disqualified persons', under the Rules of Racing, until the report is withdrawn.

There is no appeal against the decision of Tattersalls' Committee, but upon an application being made to the Committee in any case to admit or hear further evidence, the Committee may, at its discretion, re-hear such case as provided for in Rule 1 of the Rules on Betting. Tattersalls' Committee usually consists of a Chairman – at present the Hon. James Morrison – and twelve members (two of whom are appointed by the Jockey Club).

The Committee elects its own members to fill vacancies, subject to the Jockey Club's approval. Members of the Committee are not paid; neither do they receive any expenses. Tattersalls' Committee issue the Rules on Betting, and from time to time give rulings as to the destination of bets in peculiar circumstances.

RULES ON BETTING

(As authorised by Tattersalls' Committee on the 8th day of February 1886, and last revised on 26th March, 1976)

CHAIRMAN:
The Hon. James Morrison, T.D.

MEMBERS OF COMMITTEE:
Brigadier M. Gordon-Watson, O.B.E., M.C.
Mr Charles W. Layfield
Mr Herbert Finney
Mr T. E. S. Egerton
Mr Geoffrey Hamlyn
Major General J. M. Spencer-Smith, C.B., O.B.E., M.C.
Mr H. A. F. Ward-Jackson, M.A.
Mr. R. U. Gaskell
Mr Francis W. Habbershaw
Mr Joseph Ward Hill
Sir Thomas Pilkington, Bart

SECRETARY:
Mr William J. Guard
P.O. Box 13
7/9 Hatherley Road, Reading, RG1 5QD
Telephone: 0734 65402

1. Tattersalls' Committee have authority to settle all questions relating to bets, commissions for bets and any matters arising either directly or indirectly out of wagers or gaming transactions on horse-racing, to adjudicate on all cases of default, and at their discretion, to report defaulters to the Jockey Club. If a defaulter is a partnership or limited Company all or any of the partners or their agents and all or any of the

Shareholders, Directors, Officers or Agents of the defaulting Company may be reported to the Jockey Club.

Upon an application being made to the Committee in any case to admit or hear further evidence, the Committee may at its discretion decide to re-hear such case and upon such re-hearing may admit such further evidence and uphold, reverse or amend its original decision or adjudication as it may think fit.

2. In all bets there must be a possibility to win when the bet is made.

3. No betting first past the post will be recognised by the Committee.

4. All bets are P.P. – play or pay – with the following exceptions:

(A) Single Ante-Post bets, being made before the day on which the race is run, will be void if the race is abandoned, declared void, or if the conditions of the race are altered after bets are made, or on a horse balloted out under Jockey Club Rule 125, but in any such circumstances accumulative Ante-Post bets (win or place) will stand and be settled at the Ante-Post price(s) laid on the remaining horse(s).

(B) Bets other than Ante-Post bets will be void if the race is abandoned, declared void or postponed to another day, or if they are on a horse which does not come under Starter's Orders. Bets 'on the distance' are void if the first or second horse is disqualified.

(C) In the case of bets made at a price on the day of the race before it has been officially notified that a horse has been withdrawn before coming under Starter's Orders, the liability of a layer against any horse remaining in the race, win or place, will be reduced in accordance with the following scale depending on the odds current against the withdrawn horse at the time of such official notification:

(a)   if the current odds are 3/5 (8/13) or longer odds on by 60p in the £.

(b)   if shorter odds on than 3/5 (8/13) up to and including evens by 50p in the £.

(c)   if over evens up to and including 6/4 by 40p in the £.

(d)   if over 6/4 up to and including 5/2 by 30p in the £.

(e)   if over 5/2 up to and including 4/1 by 20p in the £.

(f)   if over 4/1 up to and including 10/1 by 10p in the £.

(g)   if over 10/1 the liability would be unchanged.

(h)   in the case of two or more horses being withdrawn before coming under Starter's Orders, the total reduction shall not exceed 75p in the £.

Bets made at Starting Price are not affected, except in cases where insufficient time arises for a fresh market to be formed, when the same scale of reductions will apply. In the event of the withdrawal of one or more runners in circumstances which would lead to only one runner and therefore a 'walkover', all bets on the race will be void. The race will be considered a 'walkover' for the purpose of settling bets.

For the purpose of this Rule, the non-appearance of the number of a declared runner in the Number Board shall be held to be an official notification of the withdrawal of such horse before coming under Starter's Orders.

(D) In the event of an announcement being made that the provisions of Rule 4(C) do not apply on the grounds that no market had been formed at the time of withdrawal of a declared runner or in the event of the number of a declared runner not appearing in the number board, all bets (other than Ante-Post bets) made at a price prior to either eventuality shall be settled at Starting Price.

(E) In the event of a horse or horses being withdrawn under Jockey Club Rule No. 125 (limitation of the number of runners in a race), all Ante-Post bets on such horse(s) shall be void and the liability of a layer against any horse(s) remaining in the race, win or place, will be reduced in accordance with a rate to be announced before the race by Tattersalls' Committee, dependent on the odds current against the withdrawn horse(s) at the time of such official withdrawal.

5. When the All Right Signal has been hoisted over the Number Board as provided for in Rule 162 of the Rules of Racing, or such other Rule being in identical terms which may be substituted for it, the bets go to the horses as officially shewn on the Board, and no objection or disqualification made subsequent to the hoisting of such Signal shall disturb the destination of the bets.

6. Bets made on one horse against another or that one horse beats another, are determined if either of them should win. Bets made between horses 1, 2, 3 are determined by the places assigned by the Judge. Unless agreed by the parties it is not indispensable that both horses should start.

7. In the event of a dead-heat, and in 'double events' if either is decided in the backer's favour and the other results in a dead-heat, the money betted must be put together and equally divided, except in the event of a dead-heat in a match in which case bets are void. In 'double-events' if both horses backed run dead-heats the money betted must be put together and divided in the proportion of one-fourth to the backer and three-fourths to the layer.

8. If a bet is made on one of the horses that runs a dead-heat against a beaten horse the backer of the horse that ran the dead-heat wins half his

bet. If odds are laid on one horse against another 1, 2, 3, and they run a dead-heat for any of such places, the money betted must be put together and equally divided.

9. If odds are laid without mentioning the horse, the bet must be determined by the state of the odds at the time it was made. Bets made after a race that a horse will be disqualified, stand, even if no objection be made.

10. Any bet made from signal or indication when the race has been determined, shall be considered fraudulent and void.

11. Subject to Rule 4(A) accumulative bets are not determined until the last race has been run.

12. Bets made on horses winning any number of races within the year shall be understood to mean between the 1st January and the 31st December, both dates inclusive.

13. In the event of a race being ordered to run over again, or of a false start or breakaway, starting price bets shall be regulated by the price current at the time of the original 'Off', false start or breakaway. All bets in favour of any horse which started on the first, but did not go to the post on the second occasion in the case of a race run over again, or in favour of any horse not returning to the post (by permission) in the case of a false start or breakaway are lost.

14. No bet can be declared off except by mutual consent but on any allegation of fraud or corrupt practice, the Committee may investigate the case and may declare the bet void. Either of the bettors may demand stakes to be made on proving to the satisfaction of the Committee, or any two of them, that he has just cause for doing so, and, if ordered, the bets must be covered or sufficient security given within the time specified in such order, in default whereof the bets will be off.

15. The Committee will not necessarily enforce the full settlement of a compromised account. Before giving a decision they may require the books of the debtor and a statement of his accounts to be submitted to them; and they may order the account to be settled if they think a reasonable offer is made, and on such terms as they may decide.

16. All bets made after a photo finish has been signalled shall be settled in the same way as if they had been made on the result of the race.

17. If any extraordinary occasion should arise, or in cases of notorious and palpable fraud, any of the before-mentioned rules may be suspended by the Committee, and any of the before-mentioned rules may be altered or added to by a simple majority of the whole Committee.

FOOTNOTE
Tattersalls' Committee: Rules on Betting 4(E)

When it is known that one or more horses has been withdrawn under Jockey Club Rule 125, the Committee will assess the market price(s) of the horse(s) withdrawn and announce a deduction based on the table displayed hereon. The 'percentages' of all relevant prices must be added and the overall deduction rounded off to a practical deduction in £, to the nearest p.

For example, if three horses were withdrawn at, say,

$$9 \text{ to } 2 = 18\%$$
$$8 \text{ to } 1 = 11\%$$
$$22 \text{ to } 1 = 4.3\%$$

Total would be 33.3% and a deduction of 33p would be announced. *The maximum deduction is to be limited to 75p in the £.*

CHAPTER EIGHT

Weatherbys

'That, sir, which you suppose to be a Bible, is no other than a book of matches, fairly entered and kept here for annual use.'

(P. Parsons, 1771)

Take a typical scene at any race meeting – the parade in the paddock prior to the race – the horses being led round and round by stable lads or girls. In the centre of the paddock apprehensive owners and trainers discuss their horses' prospects and the possible outcome of the race. On the rails the racegoers attempt to study horses and race-cards simultaneously, as they try to pick a winner. The jockeys, wearing a variety of brightly coloured racing silks, enter to receive their last-minute instructions before mounting and making their way to the start. Everything happens smoothly and efficiently and most racegoers take the scene for granted.

But if you stop to consider how it all happens, you begin to realise just how much hard work and behind-the-scenes organisation goes into producing an afternoon's racing. Consider also that there are race meetings held almost every day throughout the year in Britain, and you become aware just how tremendous the volume of that work must be. For, in addition to all the effort put into producing the horses in peak condition on that particular day by the trainers and their staff, plus the work carried out by the Clerk of the Course and his staff, there is also the sheer volume of paperwork connected with each race meeting.

For instance, what gives an owner the right to a particular set of racing colours? Who registers the owners? Who registers the colours? Who is responsible for the entry fees, forfeit fees, jockeys' fees, owners' bills, and the thousand other details which have to be attended to if racing in this country is to function smoothly? There is, indeed, a fantastic amount of paper work connected with the administration and organisation of racing in Britain, and the bulk of this work is carried out by one organisation — Weatherbys Ltd. — once aptly called 'the Civil Servants of Racing'.

Weatherbys' connection with horse racing began early in the reign of George III, when Captain Cook was preparing for his second round-the-world voyage and the first mutterings were being heard of the French Revolution. Horse racing in Britain was, at that time, a disorganised sport, over which the Jockey Club was only just beginning to exert its authority. Then, in 1773 Sir Charles Bunbury, who was known as the Perpetual President of the Jockey Club, invited a Mr James Weatherby, the son of a Newcastle solicitor, to become Keeper of the Match Book.

Three years later, in 1773, James Weatherby became Secretary to the Jockey Club. Since then there has been a continuous line of Weatherbys serving the Jockey Club. Indeed, as Dorothy Laird, the racing historian, has pointed out: 'There has hardly been a major change in the conduct of British racing during the whole of these two centuries with which Weatherbys have not been closely involved.'

As the Jockey Club developed, until it eventually became the ruling body of the Turf, so Weatherbys organisation developed with it. Not only have Weatherbys kept pace with all the changes which have taken place in racing during the past two centuries, they have also been responsible for the implementation of a great many of the improvements, which have resulted in British racing becoming second to none.

It was James Weatherby who first published a definitive *Racing Calendar* in 1773. This *Calendar*, later bought by the Jockey Club in 1901, has become the official organ of the Jockey Club and is still published by Weatherbys today.

It was a Weatherby — another James — who founded the *General Stud Book*, which has remained the property of Weatherbys since 1796, and which has been described as 'the most complete record of any living species, the *Stud Book* of the thoroughbred horse'. It was Edward Weatherby who, a century ago, worked with the celebrated Admiral Rous to produce the first modern Rules of Racing.

Indeed, it is hard to find any aspect of horse racing in Britain with which the Weatherby family is not in some way connected. But, despite its long traditional association with racing and with the Jockey Club, there is nothing old-fashioned about the organisation, and it is the computer and not the quill pen which symbolises the business today. For Weatherbys are in no way hampered (as might easily have been the case) by their two-hundred year association with racing. Rather than becoming 'precious' about it, they have built upon their connection gradually, extending their business commitments and responsibilities and assimilating modern business methods and techniques.

In 1964, for example, they moved their printing works to Wellingborough in Northamptonshire, where a computer was installed to deal with the production of copy for the *Stud Book* and for the *Racing Calendar*. Then, in 1970, a specially designed building, also at Wellingborough, was opened by the Queen Mother, and it is here that the bulk of Weatherbys' work is carried out today, at what has been described as 'the most advanced technical centre that any racing industry in the world can boast.'

TODAY'S RACING DEPARTMENT

Work carried out by Weatherbys' Racing Department includes:

REGISTRATION OF HORSE NAMES

Names, of not more than eighteen characters, including spaces, are applied for by owners and checked for availability against the list of registered names. Included in this list are all names currently in use, and 'protected' names of past famous horses and Classic winners. Details of the horses for which names have been applied are checked against the *General Stud Book* records to prove the identity of the animals concerned.

PASSPORTS

The Racing Department is responsible for issuing passports for all horses as they come into training. These passports, produced on an internationally agreed format, provide identification of all horses when travelling abroad for racing purposes.

HORSES IN TRAINING LIST

Once a month a list of horses in training is produced, together with the names of owners and trainers and the map grid reference number of the stable where the horse is training. This last piece of information, coupled with the grid reference for all racecourses, can enable the computer to calculate in a fraction of a second the travel allowance that an owner is entitled to when a horse runs in a race. Also printed each month are individual lists of horses in each stable, which have been updated with information supplied by the trainer. These are sent to the trainer so that he can delete any which may have left his charge and add any new arrivals.

REGISTRATION OF OWNERS

Since March 1971 it has been necessary for all owners to be registered. Applications for registration, with references and information on an owner's business connections, previous involvement in racing, etc., are processed at the Jockey Club headquarters in Portman Square. The list of owners is updated continuously and printed out every six weeks.

At March 1976, the approximate number of owners was 11,500, compared with about 6,500 in 1952.

REGISTRATION OF COLOURS

The Racing Department maintains a card index file with all colours listed under the basic colour of the jacket. In 1975, 10,470 colours were registered. If colours are not re-registered within a year, they lapse and are available to other applicants.

TRAINERS' LICENCES AND PERMITS

The Racing Department maintains the lists of licensed trainers, permit holders and jockeys, once licences have been issued by the Jockey Club.

HORSE RECORDS

Performance records of all horses in training are an important part of the information maintained in the Racing Department. Until 1972 all this information – date of race, course, distance, placing, value of prize money won – was kept on index cards, but it is now being transferred to magnetic discs to make possible the instantaneous printing of the complete racing record of a horse; the production for inclusion in the racecard of the past form figures for any runner; and the checking of a horse's credentials against race conditions to decide whether it is qualified and what weight it shall carry.

ENTRIES

The Racing Department is responsible for handling the huge amount of race entries received each week. Since the entry fee for English races was lowered the total number of entries handled has increased from 203,000 in 1962 to 355,246 in 1975 – 217,385 on the Flat and 137,861 N.H. After withdrawals, 30,944 horses raced on the Flat and 27,944 horses raced in N.H. races. In the peak week of the year (that in which the entries for the sixteen Easter Bank Holiday meetings are received) a total of some 16,000 entries have to be processed. For each entry received, the Racing Department must first make sure that the person signing the entry form has authority to act for the owner.

Once the entries for a race have been assembled, the weights for races other than handicaps can be added by computer, by comparing the performances, age and other qualifications of each entry with the conditions of each race.

HANDICAPS

From the start of flat racing in 1973, a central handicap has been maintained for all horses in training, revised every Tuesday to include new ratings based on the opinions of the Jockey Club's official handicappers on the results of races up to the previous Saturday.

Individual handicappers are responsible for the rating of horses in three divisions – sprinters, middle distance horses and stayers – with an additional handicapper dealing with the weights for two-year-old nurseries. The computer takes no part in the assessing of weights for horses, but prints out the entries for handicaps in weight order from the ratings supplied by the handicappers.

THE RACING CALENDAR

An editorial department, adjacent to the Racing Department, deals with the production of the *Racing Calendar*. This publication is essential to the smooth running of racing and includes notices issued by the Stewards of the Jockey Club, by Clerks of Courses and local Stewards, fixture lists, lists of licences issued to trainers, jockeys, and racing officials, registered colours and names of thoroughbreds and entries and weights for races.

The *Racing Calendar* was published by Weatherbys and was their sole property until 1901, when they sold the title of this important publication to the governing body of racing, the Jockey Club.

DECLARATIONS

Once an entry for a horse has been accepted, a weight allocated and published in the *Racing Calendar*, together with its age, weight, name of owner and trainer (all of which can now be assembled by the computer from its various files), the decision must be taken by its connections as to whether or not they wish to run the horse. It is the Declarations Department that deals with the assemblage of the final list of runners for publication in newspapers and in the racecard, after this decision has been taken.

Today a horse must be declared a runner at the four-day stage – by 12.00 p.m. four days before the event – and the stable has the right to cancel the declaration up to 11.00 a.m. the day before the race.

The Declarations Department has twenty telephone lines handling declarations to run, and eight dealing with cancellations. Declarations and cancellations can also be sent in on the Telex.

Both declarations to run and cancellations are received by operators wearing headsets and are written on to carbon copy pads. The moment an operator answers an incoming call from a trainer, a recording device starts to operate, so that, in the event of a query or if the operator is unsure about a message after a trainer has rung off, the message can be played back. The time of receiving the message is also spoken on to the tape at the end of transmission.

The person in charge of the Declarations Department is responsible for assembling on to a master list the names of horses declared to run, together with those declared to run in blinkers (from the start of flat racing in 1972), and at 11.00 a.m. no further cancellations can be accepted. If a Flat racing meeting is being dealt with, the draw for places is then made, using a simple device with numbered table tennis balls blown through a chute by compressed air and placed in numbered holes.

The lists of withdrawn horses and the draw for the main meeting of the day are usually available for distribution to the press by 11.15 a.m., though a little later if it is necessary to divide a large field because of the safety factor for the course. As soon as the final lists of withdrawals and the draw are completed, an operator cuts a perforated tape which is fed through telex machines for transmission to first the Press Association in London, for onward transmission to newspapers throughout England, Wales, Scotland and Ireland, to racecard printers and to the printers of wall lists for betting shops.

Weatherbys' own printing works at Wellingborough in fact deal with the production of racecards for forty-three of the sixty-one British racecourses, so that in the majority of cases the final list of runners is handed over to the printing works, instead of being sent to printers in other parts of the country.

ACCOUNTS DEPARTMENT

Almost every action in connection with a race involves an accountancy procedure – entry fee, forfeit fee, declaration to run, jockey's fee and percentage, the percentage to the trainer and stable yard, travel allowance, allocation of prize money, and fines and registration fees payable to the Jockey Club.

The computer is provided with the result of each race, and from this information debits owners' accounts with entry fees or credits them with prize money, credits jockeys' accounts with riding fees, deals with payments of retainers, payments to the apprentices training scheme, payments of the Newmarket Heath Tax and payments or receipts for overseas racing.

Owners' accounts are mailed every three months, or more frequently on request. The accounts department handles over a million individual transactions every year.

PRINTING DEPARTMENT

Weatherbys have for many years maintained a printing department, to handle the many racing publications including the *Calendar* and race-cards, and in recent years it has become a separate company.

SECRETARIAT DEPARTMENT

Weatherbys' Secretariat personnel are based in London at the Registry Office of the Jockey Club. They provide a direct service to the Stewards of the Jockey Club on the day-to-day matters which affect racing administration.

i. *Administration of Levy Board Prize Money Scheme*

Since 1962 when money from the Levy Board was first channelled into racing to increase prize money, an annual review takes place in consultation with the Horserace Betting Levy Board. The scheme is constantly up-dated and promulgation and administration is carried out by Weatherbys' Secretariat.

ii. *Race Planning, including International Pattern Races*

The Secretariat maintains full statistical information of race programmes in order to assist the committees responsible to the Jockey Club for race planning. A constant review is made of all Pattern races (the principal weight-for-age races) both nationally and internationally.

iii. *Racecourse Finance*

Statistics are maintained of the racing finances of all racecourses. The Secretariat provides the necessary information for the Stewards of the Jockey Club to approve the prize money given by each racecourse.

iv. *Preparation and Co-ordination of Annual Fixture List*

In consultation with Clerks of Courses, the Levy Board, Racecourse Technical Services, television authorities and bookmakers, the annual fixture list is prepared for approval by the Stewards of the Jockey Club.

v. *Trainers' and Jockeys' Licences and Permits*

All licences and permits are processed through the Secretariat. On an average, over 3000 applications are dealt with annually.

vi. *Point-to-Points*

All point-to-point steeplechases, involving 190 meetings, over 3,000 registered hunters and 1,150 races, run between February and May, are administered by a member of Weatherbys as Jockey Club Point-to-Point Controller and Weatherbys' staff at Portman Square.

vii. *Owners' Registrations*

Applications for registration as an owner are processed by the Secretariat and forwarded to the Racing Department at Wellingborough.

viii. *Overseas Visitors*

A service is given to members of racing authorities of other countries who wish to go racing in this country.

ix. *Racing Charities*

The Bentinck Benevolent Fund, the Beresford Trust and the Rendlesham Benevolent Fund are administered by the Secretariat. There are over 300 recipients of these charities.

GENERAL STUD BOOK

In addition to the administrative duties directly concerning with racing, the Weatherby organisation is also responsible for the upkeep of the *General Stud Book*, which contains the pedigrees of all thoroughbred horses, and these must be registered with Weatherbys as soon as the foals are born. The *Stud Book* Department's work also includes the production of certificates for horses going abroad, and a register of non-thoroughbred brood mares is also maintained. The Department is able to produce, on request, five-generation pedigrees and racing performances, for use in sales catalogues, etc.

In 1971 Weatherbys launched, in association with the *Stud and Stable* magazine, the *Statistical Record*. This publication, which is produced four times each year, provides breeding and racing statistics unique, not only in the British Isles, but in the world. With the co-operation of some fifty-two countries, the *Statistical Record* provides a world-wide review of the performances of British bloodstock.

In 1972 Weatherbys decided to finance a four-year programme, costing £16,000, for the use of blood typing as an additional means of checking the identity of horses for which application for inclusion in the *General Stud Book* had been made. The taking of blood samples from stallions, mares and foals is now a requirement before a foal can be registered in the *Stud Book*.

Unlike Tattersalls, which has no surviving member of the original family on its Board, Weatherbys are still going strong. One wit recently suggested that this is the result of the family's close association with breeding. There are at present four members of the family actively engaged in the business of the firm. Christopher Weatherby, who was formerly a stockbroker and became a partner of Weatherbys in 1968, is Chairman; Simon Weatherby is Secretary to the Jockey Club; Charles Weatherby is the Jockey Club's Head of Administration; and James Weatherby is Point-to-Point Controller.

There is no doubt that when the shrewd Sir Charles Bunbury invited James Weatherby to become Keeper of the Match Book in 1773, he did British racing an inestimable service and one which it is hoped will continue for another two hundred years at least.

CHAPTER NINE

Bookmakers and Bookmaking

'Gentle Jesus, bless this house.
Only one-fifth the odds will be paid a place.'

(Notice in an Irish betting shop)

Without a doubt the most maligned people on the British racing scene are the bookmakers, and the old image of the fat, red-nosed, loud-mouthed, check-suited and cigar-smoking bookmaker still persists. One reason for the bookmakers' unpopularity is easy to understand. The punter who has had a run of bad luck or who has made a miscalculation in his winnings, or for a dozen similar reasons, will blame the bookie for his ill-fortune. Such people often forget that they don't have to bet. In the past there were plenty of dishonest bookies and 'welshers', who either disappeared with the stake monies or failed to pay up when required to do so. But another, and possibly more justified reason for the bookies' tarnished image, is that for many years they lived quite happily off racing without putting back any money into the sport. Indeed, the Horserace Totalisator Board, which was set up in 1929, ploughed back millions of pounds into racing before the bookmakers were required by law to contribute a penny.

Then, in 1961, the Horserace Betting Levy Act was introduced. 'An Act to provide for contributions for purposes connected with the advancement of horseracing from persons engaged by way of business in effecting betting transactions on horseraces and for connected purposes.' With the introduction of this Act the bookmakers were obliged, not unjustly, to contribute towards the upkeep of racing.

Between the years 1961 to 1975 they have contributed £40,329,600. Even so, there are many people who are of the opinion that the Act could have been framed a good deal more tightly in order to obtain more money from the bookmakers.

It would be unfair, however, to present all bookmakers as leeches, taking all they can get from racing without giving anything in return. Messrs. William Hill and Ladbrokes, for example, have put back a great deal of money into racing by way of sponsorship in recent years, and the Joe Coral Organisation did much to prevent the threatened closure of Folkestone Racecourse by sponsoring special race days. And while such sponsorship is obviously of inestimable value in the fields of advertising and public relations, it would be unfair to suggest that all such sponsorship is only intended to fatten the goose that lays the golden egg.

Many people feel that bookmakers should be done away with altogether and that a Tote monopoly should be introduced, but such a possibility seems remote. For one thing, the Tote has never really been very popular with the betting public (although there are signs that this attitude is changing). Perhaps the Tote is too impersonal, and perhaps the uncertainty of the Tote returns, as against the certain odds given by the bookmakers, has something to do with this. (The returns on the Tote are based upon the amount of money in the 'pool', which is then shared out amongst the number of people with winning tickets). But, whatever the reasons, the bulk of betting money goes to the bookmakers.

For example, during the year ended 30 April 1976, the turnover of the Horserace Totalisator Board, as published in their annual accounts was £28 million for on-course betting (including greyhounds); and £21 million off-course betting (other than horseracing); whereas other turnover figures for the same year, calculated from Customs and Excise Betting Duty receipts were: on-course bookmakers £60,859,200; off-course bookmakers £1,287,383,333.

With regard to the latter figure, however, it is not possible to say how much of this represents betting on horseracing alone, as the total is calculated from Customs and Excise Duty figures which are not separated into Duty receipts to show how much of the money comes from horseracing, greyhound racing or other sources. But, un-doubtedly, horseracing accounts for the bulk of the money.

One of the effects of the introduction of a Tote monopoly would surely be to drive bookmaking underground, which would create an atmosphere where all manner of villainy and corruption could thrive. On the other hand, such a monopoly could be of inestimable benefit to racing if the Government of the day did not insist on taking the lion's share of the profits. But, for the time being, it looks as if the bookmaker is here to stay and, whatever one's personal opinion of bookmakers may be, there is no doubt that they add a tremendous amount to the interest and flavour of British racing.

SOMETHING OF THE HISTORY OF BOOKMAKING

The English have always been a nation of gamblers. Anyone who doubts this has only to read a little social history or, indeed, to consider the average amount of money wagered annually on horseracing in Britain — a matter of some 250 million pounds. Today, this amount consists of the millions of small bets made on racecourses and in betting shops throughout the country. Modern economics have become such that the days of the really great gamblers are over, gamblers such as Colonel Mellish, George Osbaldeston, the Marquis of Hastings and Lord Glasgow.

Colonel Mellish lost £20,000 on one race in 1804 and he was said never to open his mouth under £500. George Osbaldeston's losses on the Turf were estimated to be in the region of £200,000. The notorious Marquis of Hastings, who was probably the most reckless bettor in the history of racing, literally lost a fortune (£120,000) in two and a half minutes or so on the running of the 1867 Derby. The eccentric Lord Glasgow once offered to lay Lord George Bentinck £90,000 to £30,000 against his horse, Gaper, winning the Derby – a bet which that noble lord wisely declined to accept.

Again, by comparison with the betting habits of our forebears, betting today seems a very dull business. In the eighteenth and early nineteenth centuries, eccentric bets were practically a craze. For example, a Mr Charles Piggott backed his father's life against the life of a Mr Codrington's father. A Mr Ireland bet a Mr Jones that he could not cover 100 yards in less than 30 hops. Colonel Mellish staked £40,000 on the single throw of a dice, and lost. In the year 1750 the Marquis of Queensbury bet that he could have a letter carried 50 miles in one hour. He won his bet by having the letter placed inside a cricket ball, which was then thrown round a circle of twenty-four men.

In the early days of horse racing in Britain it was, for the most part, a matter of rough and ready matches between horses belonging to rich gentlemen and noblemen, who raced against each other for a small prize or stake. Betting was a matter of wagers between individuals, who bet on their own and each other's horses. No doubt there was also some 'fringe' betting, as it is hard to believe that the stable connections and hangers-on could have resisted the opportunity of betting amongst themselves. However, there were no bookmakers as we know them today.

By the seventeenth century racing had begun to develop into some sort of organised sport and serious betting began to be allied to racing. As the number of race meetings increased and the fields became larger, so too did the amounts wagered. In these early days there was no authority to control the sport and all manner of villainy took place. During the reign of Queen Anne an attempt was made to curtail betting. A Statute was passed, as the result of the havoc caused by betting on a match won by Old Merlin, wherein it was stated that 'penalties were enjoined against anyone who should win over £10 from any person or persons at one time.' As this meant that prizes for races were also limited to £10, this Statute was, in effect, a nonsense. No gentleman was going to spend his time or money rearing thoroughbred stock to race for such a paltry sum as £10.

Racing continued to develop during the early eighteenth century and the amounts wagered increased accordingly. Even so, it was not until 1790 that the first bookmaker of whom there is any record appeared. This was one William Ogden, who began laying odds against more than one runner in a race – very much in the manner of a modern bookmaker.

By 1804 numerous 'legs' (as bookmakers were then known) began to appear on the racecourses, offering odds on all the runners in a race. The scale of betting immediately soared to astronomic proportions. In 1806, for example, it has been estimated that upwards of one million guineas was wagered on the St Leger race. As always, when the prospect of easy money appears, so too do the villains. The racecourses began to be invaded by hordes of card sharpers, swindlers, pickpockets and all manner of crooks and parasites. Racing itself began to suffer, and horses were doped, lamed and even killed in order to line the pockets of the unscrupulous 'legs'.

One of most successful bookmakers was William Crockford, the fishmonger's son, who became a millionaire as the result of his often nefarious gambling activities. Another such was his arch-rival, John Gully, a prize fighter who became a bookmaker before turning 'respectable' and becoming a Member of Parliament.

Crockford was born at Temple Bar, London, in 1775. He became interested in gambling at an early age, having won a large sum of money from a local butcher in a game of cribbage. He graduated to the part-ownership of several shady gambling dens. By 1809 he was established as a bookmaker and racehorse owner, and in 1819 his horse, Sultan, came second in the Derby to the Duke of Portland's horse, Tiresias.

Crockford is thought to have laid the basis of his fortune when he bribed the starter and several of the jockeys in the St Leger of 1827. The favourite for this race, Mameluke, had been secretly bought from Lord Jersey by John Gully, who had backed the horse with Crockford for a considerable sum of money. It is believed that Gully stood to win some £45,000 if his horse won. However, Crockford found out that Gully owned the horse and, knowing it to be a bad-tempered animal, arranged for it to be bumped and jostled at every opportunity before the race. When the race eventually started, after seven false starts, Mameluke was facing in the wrong direction. Even so, it only just lost the race, finishing second.

This incident is said to have resulted in the following conversation between the two villains:

Crockford: 'Is it conwenient for you to settle, Mr Gully?'

Gully: 'It is always conwenient, Mr Crockford, but it is not always pleasant.'

Although Crockford had scored off Gully on this occasion, he was later to find that he had made a bad enemy.

Crockford's greatest achievement was to establish the most fashionable gaming club in Europe – Crockford's – which was built at a cost of £94,000. It became the centre of gaming for European high society and through it 'Crocky' is thought to have beggared at least half the English aristocracy. (Today, incidentally, the Club is owned by the Joe Coral Group).

When Crockford retired in 1840, he had only one ambition left – to win the Derby. In 1844 he stood a good chance of doing just that with his horse, Ratan, which had already won the Criterion Stakes at Newmarket. Unfortunately, Crockford reckoned without his old enemy, Gully. Ratan was successfully 'nobbled', finishing seventh in that notorious Derby of that year. Enquiries made by Lord George Bentinck revealed that Sam Rogers, Ratan's jockey, had been seen in the company of Gully. As a result of this, Rogers was later 'warned off'.

When the news of the result of the race was brought to Crockford he collapsed and died shortly afterwards. His last words were said to have been: 'I have been done! That was not Ratan's right running.'

Crockford's arch-enemy, John Gully, was the son of a Bristol butcher. He achieved fame as a young man when he fought a 64-round contest with Henry Pearce, the Champion of England, who was known as the 'game chicken'. Later on, Gully became Champion of England himself. When he retired from the ring he became the landlord of *The Plough* in Carey Street. He subsequently became a bookmaker, known as 'Honest John Gully'. Lord George Bentinck is reputed to have said of him: 'Gully might knock you down but he would never do you down.' Presumably Bentinck revised his opinion after the 1844 Derby.

Gully himself did manage to win the Derby. In fact, he won it three times with his horses, St Giles, Pyrrhus the First, and Andover.

In 1832 Gully became Member of Parliament for Pontefract. Later on he became a successful colliery owner and he died in his eighties, having achieved a high degree of respectability.

By the middle of the nineteenth century there were hundreds of 'legs' operating all over the country. Few of these, however, were 'safe', the majority being 'welshers', who could not be relied upon to pay up when required to do so. Today 'welshers' on racecourses are extremely rare, thanks to organisations such as the Bookmakers' Protection Association. At one time 'welshers' were quite common, both on and off the racecourse, although it could be extremely dangerous. Many a dishonest bookie attempting to decamp with the takings has been savagely beaten by dissatisfied customers.

However, not all the early 'legs' were dishonest, and two of the best examples of these are Leviathan Davis and Fred Swindell.

Davis began life as an artisan and is said to have become interested in betting when he was working at the Jockey Club Rooms at Newmarket carrying out some repairs. Davis started in a small way, taking bets from his fellow workers. He then began to compile his own lists of prices for big races, which he displayed at the *Durham Arms* in the Strand. Later he extended his business to other premises, and by the time the Act for the suppression of betting houses was introduced in the 1850s, he had become a rich man. He then transferred his business to the racecourses and remained a prominent figure in the betting ring until his death in 1857.

Fred Swindell (what an unlikely name for an honest bookmaker!) began life as a labourer in Derbyshire. He later became a commission agent and bookmaker. He was said to have been an intelligent and honest man. One contemporary wrote of him: 'Speaking from much experience, I can say unhesitatingly that he was as true as steel to those who trusted him with their racing transactions.'

It was Swindell who is supposed to have coined the phrase: 'There's a mug born every minute.' The story is also told of how he rented the house in Berkeley Square next door to Admiral Rous, the famous Dictator of the Turf and Jockey Club handicapper. The reason why he was supposed to have done this was that he wished to see who called on the Admiral prior to the announcement of the weights for an important handicap race. Swindell was also a horse owner, and won the Cambridgeshire with his mare, Weatherbound, which he had backed down from odds of 100–1.

In 1818 Tattersalls had opened their new Subscription Rooms, which became the centre of the betting ring. Here, bets were struck during the week and settled on the following Monday. By 1840 off-course betting had come into its own. Lists of runners were posted in public house windows all over the country. However, the off-course punters must have had a very hard time of it as there was very little racing information available and the news of results travelled slowly. Today, with regular racing information concerning runners, riders, prices, up-to-date form, etc., appearing daily in the sporting and national newspapers, and with instant communication by telephone, the 'blower', and radio and television, it is very hard to imagine how the early betting public managed. For the most part, they must have been betting 'blind', and were very much at the mercy of the bookmakers.

From the beginning of the nineteenth century, the general public had begun to bet in earnest; the rise in the popularity of betting created numerous problems for the Jockey Club, which was frequently asked to arbitrate in betting disputes. Eventually, in 1843, the Jockey Club announced that it would no longer be responsible for the settling of disputes connected with betting. They stated that, in future, such disputes were to be settled by the Committees of the Newmarket and the London Tattersalls' Subscription Rooms. Today, some 130 years later, Tattersalls' Committee is still the recognised arbiter in all matters relating to disputes connected with betting.

In 1849 bookmakers and their lists were banned from public houses. Immediately, hundreds of ready money betting houses opened, many of which were somewhat shady, to say the least. In 1853 these betting houses were suppressed by Act of Parliament although, no doubt, betting was carried on just as vigorously on the streets and elsewhere.

There were at that time no betting rings or enclosures on racecourses and in the early days of racing bookmakers used to gather around a 'betting post'. Later, betting rooms began to appear at racecourses up and down the country. Then, at Doncaster in 1849, bookmakers were transferred from the betting rooms to the outside betting ring, very much in the modern manner. The 1853 Act, which banned the lists, made it quite clear that no action was to be taken against on-course bookmakers. However, in 1897 a body called the Anti-Gambling League almost succeeded in putting a stop to on-course bookies altogether. The League brought a prosecution against a bookmaker for betting at Hurst Park racecourse, and a court ruled that the enclosure was a place prohibited for betting purposes under the Act. What a tremendous sigh of relief must have gone up from the bookmakers when this decision was later reversed by a majority decision in the Court of Appeal.

In 1899 the legality of on-course betting was confirmed in the House of Lords, and the 1928 Racecourse Betting Act made it a statutory requirement that a place should be reserved for bookmakers on racecourses.

Off-course cash betting continued to be illegal right up until the betting offices were legalised in 1961 – not that everyone bothered to take any notice of the law in respect of off-course betting. The English will bet, and no amount of legislation will stop them. It has, therefore, always been possible to place a bet in pubs and elsewhere, despite the law. Although cash betting was illegal, credit betting was quite permissible and by the late 1870s numerous legal credit betting houses had sprung up. For the most part, they dealt with postal bets.

By the latter end of the nineteenth century, the professional bookmaker was firmly established. 1860 saw the opening of the Victoria Sporting Club, originally at Blackfriars and later in the Strand. This Club gradually superseded Tattersalls' Rooms as the headquarters of betting and settling.

By the end of the century, on-course bookmakers had multiplied so rapidly that they vied for customers by wearing all manner of outlandish costumes. They adopted a variety of gimmicks to attract attention – one even sported the costume of an African explorer. Others dressed as sailors, and even went so far as to take a lifeboat to Epsom Races. Perhaps it was this period of the outlandish costume which established the image of the bookie as a loud-mouthed, vulgarly-dressed individual, sporting a large cigar, so beloved of dramatists and novelists.

ON-COURSE BOOKMAKERS

Five minutes before the 'off' at any race meeting, the scene is always the same. As the horses go down to the start, on the course and in the betting rings, long lines of arm-waving bookmakers, each with the names of the runners and the appropriate odds or prices chalked up beside them, loudly and literally shout the odds: 'Five to two the favourite'; 'Who wants a bet?'; 'Here you are, 5 to 2.' On the rails and in the stands, a white-gloved tic-tac man, using a form of hand semaphore, frantically signals the changes in the betting from one ring to another. On the rails, between Tattersalls' enclosure and the Members' enclosure (bookmakers are not allowed to operate in the Members' enclosure) the rails bookmakers conduct their business, usually on credit. Rails bookmakers do not display prices or lists of runners.

The punters (anyone who bets is a punter) pack round the bookies' stands, eagerly watching several boards at once, or else they hurry along the lines of bookies, carefully studying the fluctuations in the betting market, in the hope of beating the book, i.e., getting odds for their money which are better than the eventual returned starting price.

Before each race the prices on the runners fluctuate according to the amounts of money being staked on each horse. Thus, a horse may open in the betting at 2 to 1 and drift out to 5 to 2, 3 to 1, or even higher. Conversely, on a well-fancied, well-backed horse, the price could come in from 2 to 1, 6 to 4, even money, or odds on. The art of beating the book, therefore, consists of getting the best possible odds for one's stake money . . . before the start of the race. As soon as the race starts the odds cease to fluctuate and all prices are then at S.P. (starting price).

This starting price is decided by two independent S.P. reporters from the *Sporting Life* and the *Sporting Chronicle*, by their expert study of the pre-race changes in the betting market. Within minutes of the finish of a race the starting prices are transmitted to every one of the 12,500 or so betting shops in the country.

To the newcomer to racing, or to the overseas visitor going racing in Britain for the first time, this pre-race betting market, with its hurried changes of odds, bookies shouting and conversing with one another in their own jargon, punters hurrying back and forth, can be somewhat bewildering. It is really quite simple.

The on-course bookmakers are very much an integral part of the British racing scene – a tough, no-nonsense breed, they stand out in all weathers, offering odds on the runners in each race. On-course bookmakers 'make a book'. Quite simply, this book consists of all the odds on offer for a particular race. In theory, the bookmaker tries to make a 'round' book. That is, he adjusts the prices in such a way that, whichever of the fancied horses wins, he will show a profit on turnover.

According to the National Association of Bookmakers, however, this is not possible today, and the 'round' book, with a built-in profit for the bookmaker for every race, is a thing of the past. However, the bookies should win in the long run, because they can adjust the odds in their own favour.

Sometimes a bookmaker will form a strong opinion as to the chances of a particular horse in a race, and lay it to lose more than the book will stand. He may lengthen the price, in order to attract more bets, or alternatively shorten the price in order to deter punters. In this case, the bookmaker's own shrewdness and judgement will determine whether he has a winning or a losing race, as far as his profit is concerned.

Should a bookmaker find himself with particularly heavy commitments for one horse in a race, he normally 'hedges' – laying off part or all of the risk with one of the larger bookmakers. They will pay if the bet wins, and if it loses the original bookmaker collects a commission on the transaction.

Betting with an on-course bookmaker is very easy; all you have to do is to give him the amount you wish to stake (course bookmakers seldom deal in less than 50 pence or one pound stakes), state whether you want a winning or an each-way bet, and tell him the name of the horse you wish to back, and the price on offer, if you wish to take it – i.e., 'Two pounds to win on Jollylegs at 15 to 2'. The bookmaker will then give you a numbered ticket and at the same time he will call out the details of the bet to his clerk, who enters it in a ledger (the book). i.e., 'Jollylegs, £15 to £2, 486' (this last figure is the number of the ticket handed to you as a receipt). It is a good idea for the newcomer to make a note of the bet on the back of his ticket and also to listen carefully to what the bookie tells his clerk. This can sometimes help to clarify the situation if a mistake should occur. Bookmakers, despite rumours to the contrary are, after all, only human.

If you are lucky or clever enough to pick a winner, it is also worthwhile working out just how much money you have to collect. Some bookmakers will just say 'How much?' when you hand in a winning ticket. When estimating your returns (winnings plus original stake money) it must be remembered that all returns on the course are subject to a four per cent Betting Tax deduction.

If you find yourself in open disagreement with a bookmaker over a bet (and they can sometimes be pretty terrifying and extremely vocal in their wrath) there are forces which you can summon to your aid. On every racecourse, an officially appointed Ring Inspector is in attendance after each race, to assist the public if any dispute should arise. These Ring Inspectors are both helpful and knowledgeable and they will ensure that you are not cheated in any way.

Most bookmakers are, of course, honest. They have to be since their living depends on reputation. They are also licensed by the Bookmakers' Protection Association which has its own strict code of conduct, and which will investigate any complaint concerning any of its members. Nevertheless, it is just possible that there might be the odd one or two bookies who would try to 'come it' over an obvious newcomer to the game, so always check that your stake money is returned with any winnings.

On the other hand, and in fairness to the bookmakers, a great many of the disputes which do arise may be the result of ignorance or of sheer bloody-mindedness on the part of disgruntled punters who have either lost their money, failed to make their bet properly, or perhaps have spent too long in the bar. And, of course, every race crowd contains one or two 'wide boys' although, by and large, these are few and far between nowadays.

However, it is perhaps better not to play cards with genial strangers on race trains, wave large amounts of money about, or endeavour to 'find the lady', when invited to do so. It is difficult to believe, in this computer age, that there are still those who regularly fall for the three-card trick. But, apart from these minor hazards, the fact that racing in Britain today is among the safest and cleanest of the spectator sports is in no small way due to the bookmakers themselves.

Following the First World War, racing attracted a large public and the crooks moved in. Bookmakers were induced by threats to buy chalk and sponges from these villains at extortionate rates, and fights and beatings became regular occurrences. Rival gangs fought for control of the distribution of bookmakers' pitches at race meetings, and they fought quite literally, for there was open gang warfare on the racecourses. This tended to drive the public away (as does today's football hooliganism) and the reputable bookmakers, seeing that their living was at stake, joined together to protect themselves. In August 1921 they formed the Bookmakers' and Backers' Protection Association, comprised of the leading bookmakers of the day, plus members of the public who wished to see the end of the racecourse gangs. Eventually the Association became stronger than the gangs, and the trouble was stamped out. Also, in 1923, the Jockey Club appointed its own officials to supervise security arrangements on racecourses and these, working with the police and the bookmakers, ensured that the courses were kept free from trouble.

Today, the B.P.A. consists of bookmakers only, and its function is to protect the interests of reputable bookmakers and the public in its dealings with bookmakers. The B.P.A. is affiliated to the National Association of Bookmakers, which was formed in 1935. (The N.A.B. has upwards of 4,000 members, and there are approximately 12,500 betting offices in Great Britain and some 897 on-course bookmakers). The N.A.B. is responsible, through its affiliated associations, for the administration of bookmakers' pitches throughout the country, with the backing of the Jockey Club and the Racecourse Association.

From time to time claims are put forward concerning the sad plight of the modern bookmaker. Often, following a notable betting coup, heart-rending letters have been seen in the sporting papers. As regards the big off-course bookmakers, most punters tend to take such pathetic claims with a large pinch of salt. But there is no doubt that for some of the smaller on-course bookmakers, times have become very hard indeed. There are several reasons for this, the main one being smaller attendances at race meetings. Another reason is that licensed betting offices were legalised in 1961, and this was followed by a tax on betting.

As regards falling attendances on the courses, television has often been blamed for this. It is true that there seems little point in going to a race meeting on a cold, wet day when you can stay at home and see a variety of well-presented races from your own armchair. However, one thing that television cannot provide is the marvellous atmosphere of a good race meeting – an atmosphere which, by the way, is often greatly enhanced by the activities of the on-course bookmakers themselves. But there is now some evidence to suggest that people are going to the races again in slightly larger numbers.

If television has kept some people away from racing, it has also brought the excitement of racing into millions of homes for the first time, so that there must eventually be a 'feedback' when those viewers who have hitherto only experienced racing on television decide to take the plunge and enjoy a visit to a live race meeting.

The fact remains, however, that at present certain on-course bookmakers – the one or two-man businesses with second-rate pitches – are finding it difficult to make a living. Costs are continually increasing for wages, fares, printing, racecourse badges, etc., and the on-course men are also subject to a small Betting Levy contribution. The Betting Tax of 4 per cent on all stakes, which is passed on to the punters themselves, who pay tax on winning returns (i.e., on winnings and stake money) has driven away many of the really big backers and professional punters, who tended to favour short-priced horses. Now, they not only have to beat the bookmakers' profit margin but also the taxman as well, so much of the really big money has gone underground to illegal books. Few people connected with racing would dispute the fact that the removal of the on-course betting tax would encourage more people to go racing.

Another development which must take a certain amount of money out of the bookies' satchels is the increase in on-course betting shops. Although these shops, whether operated by the Tote or the B.P.A., are strictly controlled to ensure that they do no serious harm to the on-course bookmaker, there is no doubt that for the average racegoer who bets in small amounts, they must, on occasions, provide an attractive alternative to the on-course bookmaker. However, not all on-course bookmakers are one or two-man businesses; many are representatives from the larger bookmaking concerns, and others combine on-course work with either owning or having shares in off-course betting shops.

One example of a bookmaker, who combines on- and off-course work successfully is John White:

> Lingfield racecourse on a very hot August afternoon. A race has just ended in a photo-finish and the bookmakers are offering odds on the distance by which the race was won. 'A dead heat'; 'A neck'; 'A short head', etc. 'Never mind who won – just the distance. Who wants a bet?' Around one stand, some thirty punters are gathered, good-humouredly studying the changes in the prices on offer, and listening to bookmaker John White as he encourages them to bet. 'It's a neck. I really do believe it's a neck.' Suddenly the crowd goes quiet, as the official result comes over the public address system. The distance when it is announced is 'A neck.' John White laughs. 'There you are. I told you.' The crowd

laugh. The winners collect their money, and the losers and interested onlookers drift away. Five minutes later John White and the punters are hard at work studying the fluctuations of the market for the next race.

John White is a good example of an on-course bookmaker who has survived, in spite of dwindling racecourse crowds and taxation. A neatly dressed, good-humoured, resourceful man, he has been an on-course bookmaker for some forty years and his family connections with bookmaking go back a hundred years. John White now owns three betting shops and is a respected member and a director of the Southern Area Bookmakers' Protection Association. He admits that it is harder for the on-course bookmaker to make a living today and even though he doesn't have to rely on his course work, he still attends most meetings. 'It's a way of life. The people, the colour, the atmosphere – I enjoy it.'

As a director of the B.P.A., John White is very much concerned with the image of the on-course bookmaker, and he is quick to counter any suggestion of uncouth behaviour or of dishonesty. 'For the on-course bookmaker, integrity is everything. We want you to come back again. Remember, bookmakers are vetted and licensed by the B.P.A., and anyone breaking the rules has to face a committee made up of his fellow bookmakers. The old days of the villainy and the welshers are gone.'

John White also resents any suggestion that many people, especially women racegoers, are wary of betting with on-course bookmakers because of their brusque manners and language. John White junior, who works with his father, thinks that on occasion some on-course bookies can be rather more brusque than they need be. 'But you can understand it sometimes, especially with some women who tend to dither. They're not quite sure which horse they want to do or how much they want to bet, and while you're messing about, waiting for them to make up their minds, you're losing money.'

John White senior does not entirely agree. 'Look, we don't take bets of less than a pound; it's not really worth the trouble. But if a young lady wants to have a small bet, I'm happy to take it. Or she can always bet on the Tote. We don't mind Tote competition, and it's a good thing for the public to have two systems of betting.'

There is no doubt that many people, faced with a line of on-course bookmakers in full cry just before the start of a race, can find them rather formidable but, as John White says: 'They are part of the racing scene. You go racing abroad where they don't have on-course bookmakers and it's not the same at all. The on-course bookmaker is part of the atmosphere and the colour of racing, and he's only trying to make a living like everyone else. It'll be a sad day if they ever disappear.'

Indeed it will. But, according to the Whites, father and son, the younger element is not so interested in taking up on-course bookmaking. True, John has followed his father into the business but, as regards his own son's future, he is not so sure. 'We'll have to wait and see.'

From time to time it is suggested that eventually the on-course bookmaker will disappear altogether but this hardly seems likely. After all, they have been operating since about 1790 and they have managed to survive all manner of social, political and economic changes, and they do play a most important part in the structure of the betting industry. As the N.A.B. puts it: 'On the strength of the betting market formed on the racecourse depends the entire bookmaking industry, which provides not only the Treasury with the great bulk of its Betting Tax, but also furnishes the Horserace Betting Levy Board with practically all its income. It follows that the collapse of the racecourse betting market, through the decline of the on-course bookmaker, would be calamitous in its effect.'

So it seems a reasonably safe assumption that, for many years to come, barring the unlikely introduction of a Tote monopoly, there will still be a variety of Honest Joes, Freds and Morries 'shouting the odds' on British racecourses.

OFF-COURSE BOOKMAKERS AND BETTING SHOPS

Prior to the Betting and Gaming Act of 1960, illegal off-course betting took place on such a scale that it brought the then existing laws into contempt. Street bookmakers abounded and almost every pub was a collection and distribution centre for street bookies. Illegal betting in clubs, offices and factories was widespread. Then, in the late 1950s, the Government announced its intention of legalising off-course betting, in order to control it. The Betting and Gaming Act became law in 1960 and since then betting has become an industry with a £2,000 million turnover. It has also achieved a degree of respectability which the old street bookmakers would have found unbelievable thirty years ago.

Today there is still illegal off-course betting being carried on by people without bookmakers' permits, particularly in clubs and factories. And the Betting Tax, which was first introduced in 1966, may even have encouraged large sums of money to go 'underground'. (The Tax rate stands at 4 per cent on stakes on-course and at $7\frac{1}{2}$ per cent off-course – although some bookmakers charge 8 per cent or even more). But, compared with the amount of illegal betting which went on before the 1960 Act, illegal betting today is minimal.

At present, there are some 12,500 licensed betting shops in Great Britain, the majority of which are still controlled by small and medium-sized firms. In all, there are over 8,000 holders of bookmakers' permits. Contrary to popular belief, however, bookmaking is not a sure fire way to make money, especially for the bookmaker with limited capital. Whereas it is virtually impossible for a bookmaker to lose over the long term, short-term losses and set-backs have to be weathered and the business of getting one's mathematics right requires shrewd judgement and skill.

In theory, making a book is extremely simple. The principle is that whichever horse wins the race, the pay out should not exceed the total amount staked. In practice, however, this is not always so easy. The off-course bookmaker does not set his own prices or odds, but reflects those being offered on the racecourse. He can off-load money back to the course in order to adjust the odds but this requires a great deal of skill.

Again, if the weight of money on, for instance, a ten-horse race is only going on to four of the runners, it may be impossible for the bookmaker to adjust his book so that the oods are in his favour whatever the outcome of the race. It then becomes a matter of him having to back his own judgement. A bookmaker can lose a lot of money if a heavily-backed favourite wins but, overall, and always providing his capital lasts, it is invariably the bookie who wins over a long period.

As the betting industry has developed and betting has become 'respectable', there has come about the rise of the multiple betting chains, with hundreds of betting shops all over the country. Chains such as the Joe Coral Group, which now has over 500 betting shops, not to mention gaming, property, finance and other interests. The Coral Group is now a £30 million company, as the result of a merger which took place in 1971 between Corals and the late Mark Lane. It had its beginnings many years ago in the days of the street bookmaker.

Joe Coral was born in Poland and came to England at the age of eight in 1912. By 1923 he was collecting bets from his fellow workers in order to place them with a street bookmaker. Eventually he decided to take the bets himself and to become a bookmaker. By 1930 he had become a full-time bookmaker, with an office in Stoke Newington. Later he opened a trade bookmaker's office in the West End. He promptly lost his capital (something in the region of £30,000) and returned once more to street bookmaking. By 1960 Joe Coral, assisted by his two sons, Bernard and Nicholas, had built up a large credit betting concern. (It is curious, and surely ridiculous, that prior to 1960 credit betting was legal whereas cash betting was illegal).

Before the legalisation of betting shops the Corals were shrewd enough to realise what was about to happen and they obtained some splendid sites in prominent positions in a bid to remove the old backstreet image of bookmaking. In 1964 Joe Coral went public and was fifty-one times over-subscribed. By 1970 the Coral Company profits were in the region of £685,741.

Mark Lane, the other half, as it were, of the present-day organisation, started his bookmaking business in 1946. He was an ex-serviceman, with a capital of £200, taking two-shilling bets. He travelled round on a bicycle collecting the bets in Dagenham, Essex, and later started operating from private houses and street pitches – always subject to harassment by the police.

By the late 1950s, in anticipation of the 1960 Betting and Gaming Act, Mark Lane began to acquire the leases of premises suitable for betting shops. When the Act became law he was ready to start operations immediately with seventeen offices. The company went public, and pre-tax profits rose from £41,000 in 1962 to £888,000 in 1970.

In 1971 Corals and Mark Lane merged, and in 1972 the company had a turnover of £82,320 million and an after-tax profit of £2,567,786. Today Coral's bookmaking company is run from a central office in Regent Street. Security and administration are carried out at Mark Lane House, Dagenham. Here the activities of 550 or so betting shops are co-ordinated and scrutinised.

Corals carry out a massive security operation – every winning bet from the betting shops is returned to Dagenham and samples of the incoming slips are taken constantly. Bets of more than £10 are singled out, as, too, are bets which have been altered in any way. Samples of these are screened and re-calculated electronically, and the time recorded on the betting slip is also checked against the official time given for the start of the race.

Specialised staff are available to investigate any discrepancies, as well as to examine the findings of a team of travelling auditors, who carry out spot-checks of cash and bets in the Company's betting shops. They also investigate cases of suspected dishonesty. Coral's employees are not allowed to bet at any of the Company's betting shops or to hold an account with any of the Company's credit offices.

With so much money being handled daily by the Coral Group's betting offices, security and attention to detail are essential. It would be a foolhardy man, indeed, who tried to beat Coral's security system.

As regards staffing their shops, the Company is meticulous, and the rules laid down for shop manager and cashier procedure are rigid and comprehensive. The Company has even gone so far as to set up a Staff School with full-time training officers. Prospective shop managers are given an eight-week course in the basic techniques of settling bets, and this means learning what the odds really mean and working out the most complicated types of bets. They are also instructed in methods of shop procedure, and at the end of each course written and practical examinations have to be taken. A complete dossier on each trainee is compiled and sent to the appropriate area manager. A far-cry, indeed, from the methods of the old street bookies.

The Coral Group of Companies is rapidly expanding. One aspect of the Company's gaming interests provides an interesting link with the past, for Corals have recently acquired Crockford's Gaming Club, which they have restored – at a cost of £1 million. William Crockford, the poor fishmonger's son from the Borough, would have laughed had he known that his world-famous gaming club, which he opened in 1828, would end up as the property of two fellow bookmakers. Like him, they started from small beginnings and, like William Crockford, they have made large fortunes out of betting and gaming.

BETTING SHOPS

Betting shops tend to be rather dreary places for the most part. By law, the owners are not allowed to advertise individual shops, nor are they allowed to encourage people to remain on the premises once they have made their bets; even so, they are invariably crowded with punters. The glossy, gleaming pictures of betting shop interiors (issued by public relations organisations) which sometimes appear in trade journals, bear little resemblance to the smoky, litter-strewn reality. (Incidentally, this tends to be rather more the fault of the customers than the bookmaking concerns). Betting shops sell gambling: horse racing, tennis, beauty contests, football matches, golf matches, greyhound racing, even general elections, are all grist to the off-course bookmakers' mill.

By and large, the betting shops are not so much to do with racing as betting. Indeed, one is sometimes tempted to wonder whether the great percentage of the habitués have ever seen a horse, never mind a horse-race. Nevertheless, the off-course betting shops do offer good facilities for betting and there are any number of different types of bet available for the small punter in horse racing who wishes to try his luck.

In addition to the straight win or each-way bets, there are doubles, trebles, yankees, super yankees, round robins, accumulators, etc. (see details of popular wagers at the end of this chapter). There are enticing Jackpot bets and also the I.T.V. Seven, which is linked with televised racing. All of these offer the small stakes gambler the opportunity to make considerable amounts of money – if they win. But, as most hardened punters will tell you – the hardest thing in racing is to find one good priced winner.

Placing a bet in a betting shop is simplicity itself. All you have to do is to write the name of the horse you wish to back together with the amount of the stake on a betting slip and give details of the time of the race and the location of the meeting – i.e. 'Ascot 3.00 £1 win Jollylegs.'

The slip should then be handed to a cashier who will take the stake money and record the bet on a till. A copy of the betting slip or a receipt will then be handed to you. (In some betting shops – Corals, for example – the bets are also automatically photographed).

Almost every betting shop has a racecourse commentary link (the bookmakers pay the racecourses three-quarters of a million pounds each year for the right to broadcast commentaries). So, not only is it possible to hear the pre-race fluctuations in the betting market as they are relayed from the course, but it is also possible to hear a commentary on the race itself. If there are a number of meetings on the same day, when two or more races are being run at the same time, then the principal race is usually the one to be broadcast. The results of the other races are then announced by the commentator.

Off-course betting shops are a splendid hunting ground for the sociologist being the meeting places for men of all sorts and conditions. Betting shops are a great haunt for old age pensioners (no doubt trying to supplement their pension with a winner or two), the unemployed, the sick, the lame and the lazy, and all the other varied types who make up a betting or a racing crowd. It is the easiest thing in the world to get talking to someone in a betting shop (one often wishes this were not the case) and there is a great 'freemasonry' to be found amongst the regular customers in local betting shops. The regulars band together to exchange scraps of racing information (often nonsense) and commiserate with one another over bets which have not been successful.

In fact, one of the great hazards of the betting shop is the 'betting shop bore', the born loser who will regale you by the hour with stories of trebles, accumulators and so on which nearly made his fortune. These people are better avoided, as too are the regular borrowers of small amounts ('Lend me five pence; I want to make up a yankee'), and the well-meaning punters with 'systems'. Most of these people would 'talk the hind leg off a donkey'.

One serious word of warning, however; if you are lucky enough to have a really big win, it is advisable not to tell everyone about it, especially in big city betting shops. If the shop is really crowded it is better to wait until the crowd has gone before collecting your money. After all, you never know who is likely to be hanging about in a betting shop and it is amazing how quickly the word spreads when some lucky punter does hit the jackpot.

Many punters feel that there is a danger of the majority of betting shops ending up in the hands of one or two big combines, who will then be able to amend the rules to make things really difficult for the punter. Others feel that there are too many rules and regulations being introduced which deprive them of the chance to get big returns for small stakes. However, it should be remembered that the bigger the concern, the less likely that there will be limits imposed on the winnings paid on multiple bets (trebles, accumulators, etc., and bets made across the card).

It seems unlikely at present that the bulk of the betting shops will end up in the hands of one or two gigantic concerns. The majority of the 15,000 licensed betting offices in the country are in the hands of small and medium-sized firms, and the big combines – Ladbrokes, Corals, Sears and Windsor, Grand Metropolitan – control only some 2,500 shops at present. According to the National Association of Bookmakers, the punter in Great Britain has a betting service unequalled anywhere else in the world, and undoubtedly the main reason for this is the competition that exists between bookmakers.

BOARD PRICES

All betting shops display lists of the runners in each race, together with the prices on offer prior to the start of each race. It is possible to ask for the 'board price' when placing a bet. This means that the price written against a particular horse's name at the time of placing the bet will be the price paid to the punter (in the event of the bet being a successful one). Most regular punters ask for the 'board price' and it is fascinating to watch the fluctuations of the betting market and to try to obtain the best possible value for one's stake money.

For example, a horse could open in the betting at 4 to 1. If it is not a well-fancied runner its price could then drift out to 5 to 1, 6 to 1, or even higher. If it is well-fancied, however, and well-backed, it could move in to 3 to 1, 2 to 1, or even money.

Incidentally, settlement of the great bulk of bets in betting shops and credit offices off the course is ruled by the 'starting prices'. These are the average of the prices offered and laid on the course at the time when the race starts and they reflect the weight of money wagered on the course. If you ask for a 'board price', the cashier will immediately write on your betting slip details of the price you have asked for. Thereafter, whether the price drifts in or out, your odds for that bet will remain static.

BETTING TAX

The standard rate of betting tax off-course is $7\frac{1}{2}$ per cent. First introduced in 1967 at $2\frac{1}{2}$ per cent, it has gradually increased to the present rate, although some bookmakers charge 8 per cent or even more. With most leading bookmaking firms, it is possible to pay the tax in advance when making a bet. This means that the bet will cost that much more if it should prove to be a losing one, but, in the event of a win, no further deductions are made. Otherwise, tax is deducted at whichever rate your particular bookmaker charges on the total returns (that is, on winnings plus stake money).

It is worth remembering that, whereas on-course bookmakers charge only 4 per cent betting tax, on-course betting shops deduct 6 per cent from returns.

SOME POPULAR BETS

YANKEE Four selections, comprising 11 bets: 6 doubles, 4 trebles, and 1 fourfold accumulator.

SUPER YANKEE Five selections, comprising 26 bets: 10 doubles, 10 trebles, 5 fourfold accumulators, and 1 fivefold accumulator.

HEINZ Six selections, comprising 57 bets: 15 doubles, 20 trebles, 15 fourfold accumulators, 6 fivefold accumulators, and 1 sixfold accumulator.

PATENT/TWIST Three selections, comprising 7 bets: 3 singles, 3 doubles, and 1 treble.

ROUNDER Three selections, comprising 3 bets: single on the first selection (any to come), a double at the same stakes on the other two selections; the same bet commencing with the second selection and, finally, the same bet commencing with the third selection.

ROUNDABOUT Three selections, comprising 3 bets: single on the first selection (any to come), a double at twice the original stake on the other two, and then continuing as described above for a Rounder.

SINGLE STAKES ABOUT (S.S.A.) Two selections, comprising 2 bets: single on the first selection (any to come), same stake on the other, and vice-versa. If one or more crosses are written between the selections this will be taken to indicate S.S.A.

DOUBLE STAKES ABOUT (D.S.A.) Two selections, comprising 2 bets: single on the first selection (any to come), double stake on the second selection, and vice-versa. The double stakes must be clearly indicated, otherwise the bet will be executed as Single Stakes About.

ROUND ROBIN Three selections, comprising 10 bets; 3 pairs Single Stakes About bets, plus 3 doubles, and 1 treble.

DOUBLES, TREBLES, ACCUMULATORS

No. of Horses	Doubles	Trebles	4-horse Accumulators
3	3	1	0
4	6	4	1
5	10	10	5
6	15	20	15
7	21	35	35
8	28	56	70

9	36	84	126
10	45	120	210
11	55	165	330
12	66	220	495

BOOKMAKERS' RULES

It is as well to remember that bookmakers' rules do vary in respect of certain bets and it is always advisable to study a particular bookmaker's rules before placing a bet. All reputable bookmakers have their own sets of rules, a copy of which should be available upon request. Before betting with a bookmaker or bookmaking organisation, it is in your own interest to study the rules carefully.

The following rules have been included for general guidance only. They are the rules of one bookmaking organisation and are in no way definitive. Different bookmakers have different rulings regarding certain bets, and one should *always* study the rules of a particular bookmaker before placing a bet with him.

RULES FOR LICENSED BETTING OFFICES
(compiled 14th October 1975)

The following rules, which cancel all previous rules, are framed to meet the generally accepted conditions of betting and they will govern all future transactions between us. If any variance exists, the provisions of these rules take precedence over any rules or limits printed on our Ante-Post or Speciality betting slips.

Commissions may be placed with us simply by writing your bet on an investment form and then handing in the bet, together with your stake, to one of our staff who will, for your protection, photograph your original bet and give you a numbered and dated receipt for the amount of your investment. Unless a bet is dealt with in this way and a proper receipt issued the Company will accept no liability.

Upon production of your official receipt you will be paid your winnings in respect of fully settled slips; if you should lose your receipt we shall be pleased to make payment as soon as we are satisfied the claim is genuine. Subject to the Manager's discretion, even though the weigh-in has not been announced, amounts up to £100 can be paid out immediately unless an enquiry or objection has been indicated. No refund will be claimed in respect of an altered result.

Notices indicating the deductions made in respect of betting duty will be displayed in each branch.

Coral's 'Nationwide' service enables clients on production of their receipts to collect winnings from any office in the Joe Coral Group.

From time to time special bets will be introduced and these will be settled in accordance with the rules issued for such bets.

GENERAL RULES

1. *Conditions of Acceptance*

Subject to these rules we accept commissions for all meetings held under the rules of the Jockey Club (incorporating the National Hunt Committee) or the Irish Turf Club or the National Greyhound Racing Club provided in each case the programmes and results are published in *The Sporting Life*, with the additional proviso for Irish race meetings that race by race results should be announced by Exchange Telegraph. In addition any instructions issued by means of a press announcement or by way of a notice displayed in our betting offices are to be read as being part of these rules.

We reserve the right to refuse the whole or part of any commission offered to us, and to declare void any betting slip with whose bona-fides we are not satisfied. In addition we reserve the right to refuse payment on any lost or stolen bet that cannot be substantiated by reference to our photographic records or on any bet for which no claim has been received within two months of the date of the event.

2. *Maximum Payments*

Bets excluding any investment on a single selection for which there is NO LIMIT to the amount which can be won, are subject to a maximum payment to any one client in respect of any one day's betting.

Accumulative Ante-Post bets and Coral Speciality Bets are subject to the maximum payments given in the appropriate sections of these rules; other bets are subject to a maximum payment of £50,000 unless the bet contains a selection either engaged at a meeting where race by race results are not announced by Exchange Telegraph or engaged in a race whose advertised time is later than 6.30 p.m., in which cases the maximum payment will be £10,000.

3. *Settlement of Bets*

The advertised times of races, the runners, the returns and the results as published in *The Sporting Life* will govern the settlement of all bets, palpable errors excepted. 'Through the card' type instructions will be determined by reference to the race programme as published in *The Sporting Life*, as will instructions 'first race', 'last race', etc. In the event of no starting prices being returned, bets for horse racing will be settled at Tote returns and vice versa, but bets for greyhound racing will be declared void.

Each-way doubles, trebles and accumulators are settled win to win and place to place; if the instruction 'each-way all each-way' is clearly specified on the betting slip by the client, then the bet, unless it is one of our Speciality bets, will be settled by this method.

Commissions for a horse or greyhound that runs in a race at a meeting not precluded by our rules will be executed for that race unless the selection is specifically timed by the client or by our Rule 8 for another race for which it holds an engagement.

Where there is evidence of 'price rigging' of horserace Tote returns or starting prices we reserve the right to settle a Tote bet at starting price or vice-versa, or in the case of a horserace Tote forecast bet to settle it according to the appropriate National Sporting League Forecast Chart or vice-versa.

4. Time of Acceptance

In the case of races covered by Exchange Telegraph, for which an 'off' signal should be given, we officially cease to take bets after we have processed and photographed an 'off-slip'; for other races or events bets are only accepted up to the advertised time of starting. Should a client, subsequent to the result of a race having been determined or after we have officially ceased to take bets on a race, include in his instructions a selection for that race it will be treated as a non-runner.

5. Incorrect Stakes or Instructions

Incorrect number of bets or selections

Where an incorrect number of doubles is stated to cover the selections given, the total amount staked on the doubles will be divided and invested equally among the correct number of doubles. A similar rule will apply to singles, trebles, fourfolds, etc.; however, where a double, treble, fourfold, etc., is specified and it is clearly indicated that only one accumulative bet is required, it will be settled as an accumulative bet covering the number of selections given.

Where an incorrect number of selections is given in a 'yankee' or similar full cover 'named' bet, whether the instructions are specified by name or written out in full at *Equal* stakes, the total stake will be divided and invested equally on the full number of doubles, trebles, fourfolds, etc., as determined by the number of selections given.

Incorrect stakes

Unless covered by preceding section, where the amount of stake money received is more than that required to execute a wager in full the excess stake money will be refunded; where it is less the whole of the wager will be executed in proportion. Where understaking occurs with a bet on which the Betting Duty has been paid the bet will be settled with no tax deduction in the proportion of the actual amount paid to the stake plus Betting Duty required.

Ambiguous instructions

Should the name of a selection be incorrectly written or should an un-named selection be untimed or incorrectly timed or should a client's instructions be loosely worded the bet will be executed provided we are satisfied by reference to our security time stamp or 'off-slip' procedure or otherwise as to the client's intentions; if not, any selections so involved will be treated as non-runners as will any selections for races precluded by our rules. If no selection is given but a time and meeting are stated the favourite in that race will be taken as the client's selection.

If two selections which run in the same race are included in a double, treble or accumulator, or if the same selection is repeated in such a bet, both win and place stakes will be equally divided between the two; a double will become two singles, a treble will become two doubles and so on. If, however, either of the selections should be doubly engaged settlement will be determined by application of Rule 8.

6. *Board Prices*

At all horse or greyhound meetings where we are receiving a 'Course Betting Service' we will lay the current quoted price of the selection at the time the bet is accepted. Where a board price is laid this will apply to the selection throughout that slip. Should there be an official correction of a price which had earlier been wrongly transmitted all wagers struck at that price will be settled, whether to the client's advantage or not at the corrected price or starting price, whichever is the greater. A similar correction will be made, where due to a mistake by a member of our staff a price has been incorrectly quoted.

Clients wishing to bet at board prices must stipulate this when handing in the bet and ensure that the quoted price is marked on the betting slip by our staff, or countersigned by them, otherwise the bet will be settled at starting price. A similar rule will apply where prices are advertised on the day of an event.

7. *Favourites*

In any race the favourite is the horse quoted in the official starting price return at the shortest odds; the second favourite is the horse quoted at the next shortest odds and so on. If two horses should be quoted at the same odds and if these odds should be shorter than those quoted against any other horse then these two horses are the joint first and second favourites.

Where a client uses the word favourite, second favourite or third favourite to indicate his selection his stake will be invested on the horse defined in the preceding paragraph; if two or more horses are thus selected his stake will be divided and invested equally amongst each of the selected horses. However, if such joint favourites are returned at a price whereby irrespective of result no profit before deduction of tax could accrue to a backer of the favourite the un-named favourite will be treated as a non-runner. This paragraph and the one preceding apply equally to greyhound racing.

Commissions for un-named favourites, or in the case of horse-racing for un-named second or third favourites will be accepted to *Win Only*. The Place part of any such commission, if taken, will be declared void, as will any commission for un-named second or third favourites at greyhounds.

Should a favourite commission be timed for one of the races on the day's programme but no meeting be specified it will be executed as for the principal meeting unless the bet is clearly timed for another particular meeting. In this latter case if the time stated relates to several possible meetings, only one of which is covered by Exchange Telegraph, the commission will be executed as for that particular meeting. The principal meeting is that so designated by the Editor of *The Sporting Life*.

8. *Doubly Engaged*

An untimed single bet for a selection which is doubly engaged will be timed for the first race in which it runs excepting that where an 'if absent' selection is given this will be taken as timing the bet for the race in which both selections are engaged; if, however, an untimed bet for a horse engaged in a flat race and a hurdle race or steeplechase is taken it will be timed for the flat race.

If two selections, one of which is doubly engaged, are included in a double, treble, or accumulator but run in the same race, the selection which is doubly engaged will be automatically timed for the race in which the entries do not clash. If both are doubly engaged the selection written first in the client's instructions will be timed for the race in which it runs, the second selection being automatically timed for the race in which the entries do not clash. Should this paragraph apply to any part of a combination bet it will continue to apply to the whole of that combination except that single commissions will be treated as entirely separate bets.

9. *Place Betting at Starting Price or Board Price*
Horses

(a) If in a field of six or seven runners the horse selected runs first or second we pay one-fourth of the win odds.

(b) If in a field of eight or more runners the horse selected runs first, second or third we pay one-fifth of the win odds, except that

(c) In handicap races we pay in fields of:
12–15 runners, one-fourth the win odds, 1st, 2nd and 3rd places.
16–21 runners, one-fifth the win odds, 1st, 2nd, 3rd and 4th places.

22 or more runners, one-fourth the win odds, 1st, 2nd, 3rd and 4th places.

Where there are less than six runners the place money goes on the horse to win.

These place odds will be paid in full even when the favourite starts at odds-on, unless special place betting odds are returned by *The Sporting Life*, in which case, those odds will be paid.

'Pair' betting is also accepted in Handicap races of 8 or more runners and we pay in fields of:

8–15 runners, two-fifths the win odds, 1st and 2nd places.

16 runners and over, one-half the win odds, 1st and 2nd places.

In 'Pair' betting or where special place betting odds apply place only bets will be accepted based on S.P. returns, otherwise where a place investment is in excess of the amount staked on the horse to win, the difference will be settled at Totalisator returns.

10. *Conditional Bets*

When settling conditional bets the instructions 'if lose' will be read as 'if lose or non-runner' and the instructions 'if win' will be read as 'if win or non-runner'.

Subject to the selections being in different races 'stop at a winner' commissions will be accepted win or each-way and will be settled in the order written; a non-runner will not be counted as a winner and the bet will continue until one of the selections either occupies or dead-heats for first place.

11. *'Any-to-Come' or 'If Cash' Bets*

In deciding from which part of the bet the 'any-to-come' is to be taken or to which part the 'any-to-come' is to be applied a drawn line will be read as indicating the end of one bet and the start of another.

The conditional part of an 'any-to-come' bet will be executed on the understanding that the total cash-in-hand at any stage will be applied to the settlement in order as written of the remaining instructions, with the proviso that returns from a selection in a race cannot go on to a selection in the same race.

Should at any stage there be insufficient cash-in-hand to execute in full the next part of the 'any-to-come' instruction it will be settled in the proportion of the balance of cash-in-hand to the full stake required by that part of the instruction.

In the conditional part of an 'any-to-come' bet if the stake should be omitted the amount staked on the preceding selection will be invested.

12. *Jockey's Mounts, Owner's and Trainer's Selected*

Such commissions are accepted at starting price or Tote returns. In

Jockey's mounts if the actual races or the number of singles, doubles, trebles, etc., are specified and the Jockey rides less than the requisite number of mounts the missing mounts will be treated as non-runners; if the number is not specified or the Jockey rides more than the requisite number of mounts the number of singles, doubles, trebles, etc., will be determined by the actual number of mounts the Jockey rides and the amount staked will be divided and invested accordingly. Where a Jockey rides at two meetings on the same day, commissions for his mounts will be executed for the first meeting at which he rides unless the particular meeting or races are specified.

The Owner's or Trainer's selected will be the runner selected by the Owner or Trainer in a race, or if two or more are selected it will be the one starting at the shortest price; if two or more selections start at the same price the stake will be divided. Where Owner's and Trainer's selected are backed in singles, doubles, trebles, etc., the bets will be settled in the same manner as Jockey's mounts.

13. Dead Heats

In the event of a dead heat for first place the stake money on a winning selection will be divided by the number of winners in the dead-heat and the full odds will be paid to the divided stake with the remainder of the stake money being lost. A similar rule applies to place betting where, as the result of a dead-heat, more than the required number of horses are placed.

14. Late Withdrawals, Disqualifications and Re-Run Races
Horses

Where a horse is withdrawn before coming under starter's orders or in the event of a disqualification wagers will be settled in accordance with Tattersalls' rules.

In the event of a horserace being re-run all commissions will stand for the re-run race with bets being settled at the prices quoted or returned for the original race. Horses which came under starter's orders in the original race will be considered losers if not taking part in the re-run race.

15. Walk-Overs and Cancelled Races

Walk-overs, void and cancelled races count as races. Unless otherwise provided for in Rule 18 concerning Ante-Post betting, any selection so involved, or any selection engaged in a race that is postponed or abandoned will be treated as a non-runner. Whilst neither 'The Whip' nor 'A Match' shall constitute a race, wagers involving a selection in such an event will be settled in accordance with our rules provided starting prices or Tote returns are declared.

16. *Horserace Totalisator Board*

If a client does not specify Tote returns his bet will be settled at starting price unless our rules state otherwise. If there are insufficient runners for a place dividend the place part of any commission at Tote returns will go on the selection to win at Tote returns.

Horserace Totalisator Board Jackpot bets are not accepted; if any are taken they will be settled as accumulators at starting price.

Daily Tote Doubles or Trebles

Commissions will be accepted for named horses only and should be clearly marked 'Daily Tote Double' (D.T.D.) or 'Daily Tote Treble' (D.T.T.). If a client nominates a non-runner in any one of the designated races comprising the Daily Tote Double or Treble the horse which is returned favourite in that race will be substituted for his original selection; should the favourite be withdrawn without coming under orders too late for the market to be reformed the next shortest priced horse will be substituted; in all cases if two or more horses are thus selected the horse to be substituted will be the one with the lowest race card number. When the dividend is declared on fewer than the stipulated number of winners it will be paid to clients successfully nominating these fewer winners provided their subsequent selections are entered in the designated races.

If no dividend is declared or if the client nominates a horse not entered for one of the designated races or if the word 'Daily' or abbreviation 'D' is omitted from the instruction, the wager will be settled as a double or treble at Tote returns; wagers containing selections for fewer than the stipulated number of races or containing un-named favourites will be dealt with similarly.

If an each-way Daily Tote Double or Treble is specified the place part of the bet will be settled as a place double or treble at Tote returns.

17. *Forecasts*

Forecasts are accepted in singles, doubles, trebles or accumulators. If the forecast should contain a non-runner, if the same selection should be repeated, or if the selections should run in different races the forecast will be declared void and treated as a non-runner for the purposes of settling wagers.

Horses

Where a client nominates a dual forecast in a race for which a straight forecast dividend is declared the stake will be divided and invested as two straight forecasts; conversely if a forecast or straight forecast is nominated in a race for which a dual forecast dividend is declared the stake will be invested on a dual forecast.

Forecasts will be settled according to the officially declared Totalisator dividends except that in races of 11 or more runners or in races of 6 to 10 runners where, for any reason no dividend should be declared, forecasts will be settled by reference to the N.S.L. Dual Forecast Chart displays in this office and in accordance with the rules printed thereon; in races of less than 6 runners if no dividend should be declared the forecast will be void.

1-2-3 Forecasts

On certain races as indicated by us, we accept forecasts to place the first three horses in correct order, the returns being calculated by multiplying the starting prices together. If any of the selections do not run we will pay full multiplied odds the double or full odds to the single providing the runners are correctly placed as forecast.

18. Ante-Post

Subject to the bet as accepted being written on one of four special ante-post investment forms, with the quoted prices being marked on the form by one of our staff, the maximum payment will be £100,000; otherwise the maximum payment will be £10,000.

We lay CUMULATIVE ODDS for win and place doubles, trebles etc; for place bets the fractional odds and number of places relating to each event will be those pertaining on the date of acceptance.

Ante-post bets are bets made at a quoted price with the additional proviso for horse and greyhound racing that the bet must be made before the day on which the race is run. A horserace bet laid at a quoted price on the morning of the race will not count as an ante-post bet and in the event of any withdrawals such horse(s) will count as non-runners and bets for other horses will be subject to a deduction equivalent to that of Tattersalls' Rule 4(c), the rate depending upon our advertised price(s) of the withdrawn horse(s). Unless otherwise provided for, the following rules apply:—

(a) Where an event is postponed, ante-post bets will stand until the event is decided or abandoned.

(b) If the race is abandoned, declared void, or if the conditions of the race are altered after bets are made or if the horse selected is balloted out under the Jockey Club rule limiting the number of runners in the race, single ante-post bets will be void. Accumulative or combination ante-post bets will stand and will be settled at the ante-post price(s) laid on the remaining selection(s), with the void selection counting as a non-runner throughout the bet.

(c) Subject to (b) above, selection scratched from or not taking part in an ante-post event will be a losing one if at the time the bet was made there was a possibility to win.

19. *Disputes*

In the event of a bet giving rise to a dispute it is agreed that the matter will be submitted to the Editor of *The Sporting Life* or to the Directors of the National Sporting League or Bookmakers' Protection Association or to Tattersalls' Committee and the decision given by the appropriate body shall be final and binding upon both parties.

The Company's current rules of racing will apply to all circumstances not covered by these rules.

BETTING READY RECKONER

1. Original stake money is included in the returns – but tax has not been deducted.

2. *Betting Tax*

When assessing betting returns, it should be remembered that all winning bets are subject to Betting Tax, at the rate of 4 per cent for on-course bets and $7\frac{1}{2}$ per cent for off-course bets. However, it is now possible to pay Betting Tax on the original amount staked at most leading off-course betting shops, when placing a bet. If such a bet proves to be a winning one, no further tax deductions are made. If tax is not paid in advance, the same winning bet will be taxed at the current rate of $7\frac{1}{2}$ per cent, or even higher. (Some bookmakers charge $8\frac{1}{2}$ pence in the £1). This tax applies to all winnings, and includes the original stake money which is returnable on winning bets (something not always realised by newcomers to betting).

3. *Place Betting*

Most leading bookmakers pay a quarter of the win-odds for the 1st and 2nd horses in races of six or seven runners, and one-fifth of the odds for the 1st, 2nd and 3rd horse in races of eight or more runners in all non-handicap races. In handicap races, the odds are the same, up to and including eleven runners, but for races with 12 to 15 runners, a quarter of the odds is paid for the 1st, 2nd and 3rd horse; in races with 16 to 21 runners, one-fifth of the odds is paid for the 1st, 2nd, 3rd and 4th horse; in races with 22 or more runners, a quarter of the odds is paid for the 1st, 2nd, 3rd and 4th horse.

READY RECKONER

1–4

STAKE £.p	WIN £.p	$\frac{1}{5}$ ODDS £.p	$\frac{1}{4}$ ODDS £.p	STAKE £.p	WIN £.p	$\frac{1}{5}$ ODDS £.p	$\frac{1}{4}$ ODDS £.p
.01	.01	.01	.01	.30	.37½	.31½	.32
.02	.02½	.02	.02	.40	.50	.42	.42½
.02½	.03	.02½	.02½	.50	.62½	.52½	.53
.03	.03½	.03	.03	.60	.75	.63	.63½
.04	.05	.04	.04	.70	.87½	.73½	.74½
.05	.06	.05	.05½	.80	1.00	.84	.85
.06	.07½	.06½	.06½	.90	1.12½	.94½	.95½
.07	.08½	.07½	.07½	1.00	1.25	1.05	1.06
.08	.10	.08½	.08½	2.00	2.50	2.10	2.12½
.09	.11	.09½	.09½	3.00	3.75	3.15	3.18½
.10	.12½	.10½	.10½	4.00	5.00	4.20	4.25
.15	.18½	.15½	.16	5.00	6.25	5.25	5.31
.20	.25	.21	.21	10.00	12.50	10.50	10.62½
.25	.31	.26	.26½				

2–7

STAKE £.p	WIN £.p	$\frac{1}{5}$ ODDS £.p	$\frac{1}{4}$ ODDS £.p	STAKE £.p	WIN £.p	$\frac{1}{5}$ ODDS £.p	$\frac{1}{4}$ ODDS £.p
.01	.01½	.01	.01	.30	.38½	.31½	.32
.02	.02½	.02	.02	.40	.51½	.42½	.43
.02½	.03½	.02½	.02½	.50	.64½	.53	.53½
.03	.04	.03	.03	.60	.77	.63½	.64½
.04	.05	.04	.04½	.70	.90	.74	.75
.05	.06½	.05½	.05½	.80	1.03	.84½	.85½
.06	.07½	.06½	.06½	.90	1.15½	.95	.96½
.07	.09	.07½	.07½	1.00	1.28½	1.05½	1.07
.08	.10½	.08½	.08½	2.00	2.57	2.11½	2.14½
.09	.11½	.09½	.09½	3.00	3.85½	3.17	3.21½
.10	.13	.10½	.10½	4.00	5.14½	4.23	4.28½
.15	.19½	.16	.16	5.00	6.43	5.28½	5.35½
.20	.25½	.21	.21½	10.00	12.85½	10.57	10.71½
.25	.32	.26½	.27				

30–100

STAKE £.p	WIN £.p	$\frac{1}{5}$ ODDS £.p	$\frac{1}{4}$ ODDS £.p	STAKE £.p	WIN £.p	$\frac{1}{5}$ ODDS £.p	$\frac{1}{4}$ ODDS £.p
.01	$.01\frac{1}{2}$	.01	.01	.30	.39	.32	.32
.02	$.02\frac{1}{2}$	.02	.02	.40	.52	$.42\frac{1}{2}$	.43
$.02\frac{1}{2}$	.03	$.02\frac{1}{2}$	$.02\frac{1}{2}$	.50	.65	.53	$.53\frac{1}{2}$
.03	.04	.03	.03	.60	.78	$.63\frac{1}{2}$	$.64\frac{1}{2}$
.04	.05	.04	$.04\frac{1}{2}$	.70	.91	.74	.75
.05	$.06\frac{1}{2}$	$.05\frac{1}{2}$	$.05\frac{1}{2}$	.80	1.04	.85	.86
.06	.08	$.06\frac{1}{2}$	$.06\frac{1}{2}$	.90	1.17	$.95\frac{1}{2}$	$.96\frac{1}{2}$
.07	.09	$.07\frac{1}{2}$	$.07\frac{1}{2}$	1.00	1.30	1.06	$1.07\frac{1}{2}$
.08	$.10\frac{1}{2}$	$.08\frac{1}{2}$	$.08\frac{1}{2}$	2.00	2.60	2.12	2.15
.09	$.11\frac{1}{2}$	$.09\frac{1}{2}$	$.09\frac{1}{2}$	3.00	3.90	3.18	$3.22\frac{1}{2}$
.10	.13	$.10\frac{1}{2}$	$.10\frac{1}{2}$	4.00	5.20	4.24	4.30
.15	$.19\frac{1}{2}$	.16	.16	5.00	6.50	5.30	$5.37\frac{1}{2}$
.20	.26	.21	$.21\frac{1}{2}$	10.00	13.00	10.60	10.75
.25	$.32\frac{1}{2}$	$.26\frac{1}{2}$	.27				

1–3

STAKE £.p	WIN £.p	$\frac{1}{5}$ ODDS £.p	$\frac{1}{4}$ ODDS £.p	STAKE £.p	WIN £.p	$\frac{1}{5}$ ODDS £.p	$\frac{1}{4}$ ODDS £.p
.01	$.01\frac{1}{2}$	.01	.01	.30	.40	.32	$.32\frac{1}{2}$
.02	$.02\frac{1}{2}$	.02	.02	.40	$.53\frac{1}{2}$	$.42\frac{1}{2}$	$.43\frac{1}{2}$
$.02\frac{1}{2}$	$.03\frac{1}{2}$	$.02\frac{1}{2}$	$.02\frac{1}{2}$	.50	$.66\frac{1}{2}$	$.53\frac{1}{2}$	.54
.03	.04	.03	.03	.60	.80	.64	.65
.04	$.05\frac{1}{2}$	$.04\frac{1}{2}$	$.04\frac{1}{2}$	.70	$.93\frac{1}{2}$	$.74\frac{1}{2}$	.76
.05	$.06\frac{1}{2}$	$.05\frac{1}{2}$	$.05\frac{1}{2}$	.80	$1.06\frac{1}{2}$	$.85\frac{1}{2}$	$.86\frac{1}{2}$
.06	.08	$.06\frac{1}{2}$	$.06\frac{1}{2}$	.90	1.20	.96	$.97\frac{1}{2}$
.07	$.09\frac{1}{2}$	$.07\frac{1}{2}$	$.07\frac{1}{2}$	1.00	$1.33\frac{1}{2}$	$1.06\frac{1}{2}$	$1.08\frac{1}{2}$
.08	$.10\frac{1}{2}$	$.08\frac{1}{2}$	$.08\frac{1}{2}$	2.00	$2.66\frac{1}{2}$	$2.13\frac{1}{2}$	$2.16\frac{1}{2}$
.09	.12	$.09\frac{1}{2}$	$.09\frac{1}{2}$	3.00	4.00	3.20	3.25
.10	$.13\frac{1}{2}$	$.10\frac{1}{2}$	.11	4.00	$5.33\frac{1}{2}$	$4.26\frac{1}{2}$	$4.33\frac{1}{2}$
.15	.20	.16	.16	5.00	$6.66\frac{1}{2}$	$5.33\frac{1}{2}$	$5.41\frac{1}{2}$
.20	$.26\frac{1}{2}$	$.21\frac{1}{2}$	$.21\frac{1}{2}$	10.00	$13.33\frac{1}{2}$	$10.66\frac{1}{2}$	$10.83\frac{1}{2}$
.25	$.33\frac{1}{2}$	$.26\frac{1}{2}$	.27				

4–11

STAKE £.p	WIN £.p	⅕ ODDS £.p	¼ ODDS £.p	STAKE £.p	WIN £.p	⅕ ODDS £.p	¼ ODDS £.p
.01	.01½	.01	.01	.30	.41	.32	.32½
.02	.02½	.02	.02	.40	.54½	.43	.43½
.02½	.03½	.02½	.02½	.50	.68	.53½	.54½
.03	.04	.03	.03½	.60	.82	.64½	.65½
.04	.05½	.04½	.04½	.70	.95½	.75	.76½
.05	.07	.05½	.05½	.80	1.09	.86	.87½
.06	.08	.06½	.06½	.90	1.22½	.96½	.98
.07	.09½	.07½	.07½	1.00	1.36½	1.07½	1.09
.08	.11	.08½	.08½	2.00	2.72½	2.14½	2.18
.09	.12½	.09½	.10	3.00	4.09	3.22	3.27½
.10	.13½	.10½	.11	4.00	5.45½	4.29	4.36½
.15	.20½	.16	.16½	5.00	6.82	5.36½	5.45½
.20	.27½	.21½	.22	10.00	13.63½	10.72½	10.91
.25	.34	.27	.27½				

2–5

STAKE £.p	WIN £.p	⅕ ODDS £.p	¼ ODDS £.p	STAKE £.p	WIN £.p	⅕ ODDS £.p	¼ ODDS £.p
.01	.01½	.01	.01	.30	.42	.32½	.33
.02	.03	.02	.02	.40	.56	.45	.44
.02½	.03½	.02½	.02½	.50	.70	.54	.55
.03	.04	.03	.03½	.60	.84	.65	.66
.04	.05½	.04½	.04½	.70	.98	.75½	.77
.05	.07	.05½	.05½	.80	1.12	.86½	.88
.06	.08½	.06½	.06½	.90	1.28	.97	.99
.07	.10	.07½	.07½	1.00	1.40	1.08	1.10
.08	.11	.08½	.09	2.00	2.80	2.16	2.20
.09	.12½	.09½	.10	3.00	4.20	3.24	3.30
.10	.14	.11	.11	4.00	5.60	4.32	4.40
.15	.21	.16	.16½	5.00	7.00	5.40	5.50
.20	.28	.21½	.22	10.00	14.00	10.80	11.00
.25	.35	.27	.27½				

4–9

STAKE £.p	WIN £.p	⅕ ODDS £.p	¼ ODDS £.p	STAKE £.p	WIN £.p	⅕ ODDS £.p	¼ ODDS £.p
.01	.01½	.01	.01	.30	.43½	.32½	.33½
.02	.03	.02	.02	.40	.58	.43½	.44½
.02½	.03½	.02½	.03	.50	.72	.54½	.55½
.03	.04½	.03½	.03½	.60	.86½	.65½	.66½
.04	.06	.04½	.04½	.70	1.01	.76	.78
.05	.07	.05½	.05½	.80	1.15½	.87	.89
.06	.08½	.06½	.06½	.90	1.30	.98	1.00
.07	.10	.07½	.08	1.00	1.44½	1.09	1.11
.08	.11½	.08½	.09	2.00	2.89	2.18	2.22
.09	.13	.10	.10	3.00	4.33½	3.26½	3.33½
.10	.14½	.11	.11	4.00	5.78	4.35½	4.44½
.15	.21½	.16½	.16½	5.00	7.22	5.44½	5.55½
.20	.29	.22	.22	10.00	14.44½	10.89	11.11
.25	.36	.27	.28				

40–85

STAKE £.p	WIN £.p	⅕ ODDS £.p	¼ ODDS £.p	STAKE £.p	WIN £.p	⅕ ODDS £.p	¼ ODDS £.p
.01	.01½	.01	.01	.30	.44	.33	.33½
.02	.03	.02	.02	.40	.59	.44	.44½
.02½	.03½	.02½	.03	.50	.73½	.54½	.56
.03	.04½	.03½	.03½	.60	.88	.65½	.67
.04	.06	.04½	.04½	.70	1.03	.76½	.78
.05	.07½	.05½	.05½	.80	1.17½	.87½	.89½
.06	.09	.06½	.06½	.90	1.32½	.98½	1.00½
.07	.10½	.07½	.08	1.00	1.47	1.09½	1.12
.08	.12	.09	.09	2.00	2.94	2.19 ·	2.23½
.09	.13	.10	.10	3.00	4.41	3.28	3.35½
.10	.14½	.11	.11	4.00	5.88	4.37½	4.47
.15	.22	.16½	.17	5.00	7.35½	5.47	5.59
.20	.29½	.22	.22½	10.00	14.70½	‚10.94	11.17½
.25	.37	.27½	.28				

1–2

STAKE £.p	WIN £.p	$\frac{1}{5}$ ODDS £.p	$\frac{1}{4}$ ODDS £.p	STAKE £.p	WIN £.p	$\frac{1}{5}$ ODDS £.p	$\frac{1}{4}$ ODDS £.p
.01	.01½	.01	.01	.30	.45	.33	.33½
.02	.03	.02	.02	.40	.60	.44	.45
.02½	.03½	.02½	.03	.50	.75	.55	.56
.03	.04½	.03½	.03½	.60	.90	.66	.67½
.04	.06	.04½	.04½	.70	1.05	.77	.78½
.05	.07½	.05½	.05½	.80	1.20	.88	.90
.06	.09	.06½	.06½	.90	1.35	.99	1.01
.07	.10½	.07½	.08	1.00	1.50	1.10	1.12½
.08	.12	.09	.09	2.00	3.00	2.20	2.25
.09	.13½	.10	.10	3.00	4.50	3.30	3.37½
.10	.15	.11	.11	4.00	6.00	4.40	4.50
.15	.22½	.16½	.17	5.00	7.50	5.50	5.62½
.20	.30	.22	.22½	10.00	15.00	11.00	11.25
.25	.37½	.27½	.28				

8–15

STAKE £.p	WIN £.p	$\frac{1}{5}$ ODDS £.p	$\frac{1}{4}$ ODDS £.p	STAKE £.p	WIN £.p	$\frac{1}{5}$ ODDS £.p	$\frac{1}{4}$ ODDS £.p
.01	.01½	.01	.01	.30	.46	.33	.34
.02	.03	.02	.02½	.40	.61½	.44½	.45½
.02½	.04	.03	.03	.50	.76½	.55½	.56½
.03	.04½	.03½	.03½	.60	.92	.66½	.68
.04	.06	.04½	.04½	.70	1.07½	.77½	.79½
.05	.07½	.05½	.05½	.80	1.22½	.88½	.90½
.06	.09	.06½	.07	.90	1.38	.99½	1.02
.07	.10½	.07½	.08	1.00	1.53½	1.10½	1.13½
.08	.12½	.09	.09	2.00	3.06½	2.21½	2.26½
.09	.14	.10	.10	3.00	4.60	3.32	3.40
.10	.15½	.11	.11½	4.00	6.13½	4.42½	4.53½
.15	.23	.16½	.17	5.00	7.66½	5.53½	5.66½
.20	.30½	.22	.22½	10.00	15.33½	11.06½	11.33½
.25	.38½	.27½	.28½				

4–7

STAKE £.p	WIN £.p	$\frac{1}{5}$ ODDS £.p	$\frac{1}{4}$ ODDS £.p	STAKE £.p	WIN £.p	$\frac{1}{5}$ ODDS £.p	$\frac{1}{4}$ ODDS £.p
.01	.01½	.01	.01	.30	.47	.33½	.34½
.02	.03	.02	.02½	.40	.63	.44½	.45½
.02½	.04	.03	.03	.50	.78½	.55½	.57
.03	.04½	.03½	.03½	.60	.94½	.67	.68½
.04	.06½	.04½	.04½	.70	1.10	.78	.80
.05	.08	.05½	.05½	.80	1.25½	.89	.91½
.06	.09½	.06½	.07	.90	1.41½	1.00½	1.03
.07	.11	.08	.08	1.00	1.57	1.11½	1.14½
.08	.12½	.09	.09	2.00	3.14½	2.23	2.28½
.09	.14	.10	.10½	3.00	4.71½	3.34½	3.43
.10	.15½	.11	.11½	4.00	6.28½	4.45½	4.57
.15	.23½	.16½	.17	5.00	7.85½	5.57	5.71½
.20	.31½	.22½	.23	10.00	15.71½	11.14½	11.43
.25	.39½	.28	.28½				

8–13

STAKE £.p	WIN £.p	$\frac{1}{5}$ ODDS £.p	$\frac{1}{4}$ ODDS £.p	STAKE £.p	WIN £.p	$\frac{1}{5}$ ODDS £.p	$\frac{1}{4}$ ODDS £.p
.01	.01½	.01	.01	.30	.48½	.33½	.34½
.02	.03	.02	.02½	.40	.64½	.45	.46
.02½	.04	.03	.03	.50	.81	.56	.57½
.03	.05	.03½	.03½	.60	.97	.67½	.69
.04	.06½	.04½	.04½	.70	1.13	.78½	.81
.05	.08	.05½	.06	.80	1.29	.90	.92½
.06	.09½	.06½	.07	.90	1.45½	1.01	1.04
.07	.11½	.08	.08	1.00	1.61½	1.12½	1.15½
.08	.13	.09	.09	2.00	3.23	2.24½	2.31
.09	.14½	.10	.10½	3.00	4.84½	3.37	3.46
.10	.16	.11	.11½	4.00	6.46	4.49	4.61½
.15	.24	.17	.17½	5.00	8.07½	5.61½	5.77
.20	.32½	.22½	.23	10.00	16.15½	11.23	11.54
.25	.40½	.28	.29				

4–6

STAKE £.p	WIN £.p	$\frac{1}{5}$ ODDS £.p	$\frac{1}{4}$ ODDS £.p	STAKE £.p	WIN £.p	$\frac{1}{5}$ ODDS £.p	$\frac{1}{4}$ ODDS £.p
.01	.01½	.01	.01	.30	.50	.34	.35
.02	.03½	.02½	.02½	.40	.66½	.45½	.46½
.02½	.04	.03	.03	.50	.83½	.56½	.58½
.03	.05	.03½	.03½	.60	1.00	.68	.70
.04	.06½	.04½	.04½	.70	1.16½	.79½	.81½
.05	.08½	.05½	.06	.80	1.33½	.90½	.93½
.06	.10	.07	.07	.90	1.50	1.02	1.05
.07	.11½	.08	.08	1.00	1.66½	1.13½	1.16½
.08	.13½	.09	.09½	2.00	3.33½	2.26½	2.33½
.09	.15	.10	.10½	3.00	5.00	3.40	3.50
.10	.16½	.11½	.11½	4.00	6.66½	4.53½	4.66½
.15	.25	.17	.17½	5.00	8.33½	5.66½	5.83½
.20	.33½	.22½	.23½	10.00	16.66½	11.33½	11.66½
.25	.41½	.28½	.29				

8–11

STAKE £.p	WIN £.p	$\frac{1}{5}$ ODDS £.p	$\frac{1}{4}$ ODDS £.p	STAKE £.p	WIN £.p	$\frac{1}{5}$ ODDS £.p	$\frac{1}{4}$ ODDS £.p
.01	.01½	.01	.01	.30	.52	.34½	.35½
.02	.03½	.02½	.02½	.40	.69	.46	.47½
.02½	.04½	.03	.03	.50	.86½	.57½	.59
.03	.05	.03½	.03½	.60	1.03½	.68½	.71
.04	.07	.04½	.04½	.70	1.21	.80	.82½
.05	.08½	.05½	.06	.80	1.38	.91½	.94½
.06	.10½	.07	.07	.90	1.55½	1.03	1.06½
.07	.12	.08	.08½	1.00	1.72½	1.14½	1.18
.08	.14	.09	.09½	2.00	3.45½	2.29	2.36½
.09	.15½	.10½	.10½	3.00	5.18	3.43½	3.54½
.10	.17½	.11½	.12	4.00	6.91	4.58	4.72½
.15	.26	.17	.17½	5.00	8.63½	5.72½	5.91
.20	.34½	.23	.23½	10.00	17.27½	11.45½	11.82
.25	.43	.28½	.29½				

4–5

STAKE £.p	WIN £.p	$\frac{1}{5}$ ODDS £.p	$\frac{1}{4}$ ODDS £.p	STAKE £.p	WIN £.p	$\frac{1}{5}$ ODDS £.p	$\frac{1}{4}$ ODDS £.p
.01	.02	.01	.01	.30	.54	.35	.36
.02	.03$\frac{1}{2}$	.02$\frac{1}{2}$	.02$\frac{1}{2}$	.40	.72	.46$\frac{1}{2}$	.48
.02$\frac{1}{2}$	.04$\frac{1}{2}$	.03	.03	.50	.90	.58	.60
.03	.05$\frac{1}{2}$	.03$\frac{1}{2}$	.03$\frac{1}{2}$	.60	1.08	.69$\frac{1}{2}$	.72
.04	.07	.04$\frac{1}{2}$	.05	.70	1.26	.81	.84
.05	.09	.06	.06	.80	1.44	.93	.96
.06	.11	.07	.07	.90	1.62	1.04$\frac{1}{2}$	1.08
.07	.12$\frac{1}{2}$	.08	.08$\frac{1}{2}$	1.00	1.80	1.16	1.20
.08	.14$\frac{1}{2}$	.09$\frac{1}{2}$	.09$\frac{1}{2}$	2.00	3.60	2.32	2.40
.09	.16	.10$\frac{1}{2}$	.11	3.00	5.40	3.48	3.60
.10	.18	.11$\frac{1}{2}$	.12	4.00	7.20	4.64	4.80
.15	.27	.17$\frac{1}{2}$	.18	5.00	9.00	5.80	6.00
.20	.36	.23	.24	10.00	18.00	11.60	12.00
.25	.45	.29	.30				

5–6

STAKE £.p	WIN £.p	$\frac{1}{5}$ ODDS £.p	$\frac{1}{4}$ ODDS £.p	STAKE £.p	WIN £.p	$\frac{1}{5}$ ODDS £.p	$\frac{1}{4}$ ODDS £.p
.01	.02	.01	.01	.30	.55	.35	.36
.02	.03$\frac{1}{2}$	.02$\frac{1}{2}$	.02$\frac{1}{2}$	.40	.73$\frac{1}{2}$	.46$\frac{1}{2}$	.48$\frac{1}{2}$
.02$\frac{1}{2}$	.04$\frac{1}{2}$	.03	.03	.50	.91$\frac{1}{2}$	.58	.60$\frac{1}{2}$
.03	.05$\frac{1}{2}$	.03$\frac{1}{2}$	.03$\frac{1}{2}$	.60	1.10	.70	.72$\frac{1}{2}$
.04	.07$\frac{1}{2}$	.04$\frac{1}{2}$	.05	.70	1.28$\frac{1}{2}$	.81$\frac{1}{2}$	.84$\frac{1}{2}$
.05	.09	.06	.06	.80	1.46$\frac{1}{2}$	.93$\frac{1}{2}$	.96$\frac{1}{2}$
.06	.11	.07	.07	.90	1.65	1.05	1.08$\frac{1}{2}$
.07	.13	.08	.08$\frac{1}{2}$	1.00	1.83$\frac{1}{2}$	1.16$\frac{1}{2}$	1.21
.08	.14$\frac{1}{2}$	.09$\frac{1}{2}$	.09$\frac{1}{2}$	2.00	3.66$\frac{1}{2}$	2.33$\frac{1}{2}$	2.41$\frac{1}{2}$
.09	.16$\frac{1}{2}$	.10$\frac{1}{2}$	.11	3.00	5.50	3.50	3.62$\frac{1}{2}$
.10	.18$\frac{1}{2}$	.11$\frac{1}{2}$	.12	4.00	7.33$\frac{1}{2}$	4.66$\frac{1}{2}$	4.83$\frac{1}{2}$
.15	.27$\frac{1}{2}$	.17$\frac{1}{2}$	.18	5.00	9.16$\frac{1}{2}$	5.83$\frac{1}{2}$	6.04
.20	.36$\frac{1}{2}$	.23$\frac{1}{2}$	.24	10.00	18.33$\frac{1}{2}$	11.66$\frac{1}{2}$	12.08$\frac{1}{2}$
.25	.46	.29	.30				

10–11

STAKE £.p	WIN £.p	$\frac{1}{5}$ ODDS £.p	$\frac{1}{4}$ ODDS £.p	STAKE £.p	WIN £.p	$\frac{1}{5}$ ODDS £.p	$\frac{1}{4}$ ODDS £.p
.01	.02	.01	.01	.30	$.57\frac{1}{2}$	$.35\frac{1}{2}$	.37
.02	.04	$.02\frac{1}{2}$	$.02\frac{1}{2}$	.40	$.76\frac{1}{2}$	$.47\frac{1}{2}$	.49
$.02\frac{1}{2}$	.05	.03	.03	.50	.95	.59	$.61\frac{1}{2}$
.03	$.05\frac{1}{2}$	$.03\frac{1}{2}$	$.03\frac{1}{2}$	.60	$1.14\frac{1}{2}$	.71	$.73\frac{1}{2}$
.04	$.07\frac{1}{2}$	$.04\frac{1}{2}$	.05	.70	$1.33\frac{1}{2}$	$.82\frac{1}{2}$	.86
.05	$.09\frac{1}{2}$	.06	.06	.80	$1.52\frac{1}{2}$	$.94\frac{1}{2}$	.98
.06	$.11\frac{1}{2}$	.07	$.07\frac{1}{2}$	.90	1.72	$1.06\frac{1}{2}$	$1.10\frac{1}{2}$
.07	$.13\frac{1}{2}$	$.08\frac{1}{2}$	$.08\frac{1}{2}$	1.00	1.91	1.18	$1.22\frac{1}{2}$
.08	$.15\frac{1}{2}$	$.09\frac{1}{2}$	.10	2.00	3.82	$2.36\frac{1}{2}$	$2.45\frac{1}{2}$
.09	.17	$.10\frac{1}{2}$	.11	3.00	$5.72\frac{1}{2}$	$3.54\frac{1}{2}$	3.68
.10	.19	.12	$.12\frac{1}{2}$	4.00	$7.63\frac{1}{2}$	$4.72\frac{1}{2}$	4.91
.15	$.28\frac{1}{2}$	$.17\frac{1}{2}$	$.18\frac{1}{2}$	5.00	$9.54\frac{1}{2}$	5.91	$6.13\frac{1}{2}$
.20	.38	$.23\frac{1}{2}$	$.24\frac{1}{2}$	10.00	19.09	11.82	$12.27\frac{1}{2}$
.25	$.47\frac{1}{2}$	$.29\frac{1}{2}$	$.30\frac{1}{2}$				

20–21

STAKE £.p	WIN £.p	$\frac{1}{5}$ ODDS £.p	$\frac{1}{4}$ ODDS £.p	STAKE £.p	WIN £.p	$\frac{1}{5}$ ODDS £.p	$\frac{1}{4}$ ODDS £.p
.01	.02	.01	.01	.30	$.58\frac{1}{2}$	$.35\frac{1}{2}$	.37
.02	.04	$.02\frac{1}{2}$	$.02\frac{1}{2}$	.40	.78	$.47\frac{1}{2}$	$.49\frac{1}{2}$
$.02\frac{1}{2}$	.05	.03	.03	.50	$.97\frac{1}{2}$	$.59\frac{1}{2}$	.62
.03	.06	$.03\frac{1}{2}$	$.03\frac{1}{2}$	.60	1.17	$.71\frac{1}{2}$	$.74\frac{1}{2}$
.04	.08	.05	.05	.70	$1.36\frac{1}{2}$	$.83\frac{1}{2}$	$.86\frac{1}{2}$
.05	.10	.06	.06	.80	1.56	.95	.99
.06	$.11\frac{1}{2}$	.07	$.07\frac{1}{2}$	.90	$1.75\frac{1}{2}$	1.07	$1.11\frac{1}{2}$
.07	$.13\frac{1}{2}$	$.08\frac{1}{2}$	$.08\frac{1}{2}$	1.00	1.95	1.19	1.24
.08	$.15\frac{1}{2}$	$.09\frac{1}{2}$	.10	2.00	$3.90\frac{1}{2}$	2.38	$2.47\frac{1}{2}$
.09	$.17\frac{1}{2}$	$.10\frac{1}{2}$	.11	3.00	$5.85\frac{1}{2}$	3.57	$3.71\frac{1}{2}$
.10	$.19\frac{1}{2}$	.12	$.12\frac{1}{2}$	4.00	7.81	4.76	4.95
.15	$.29\frac{1}{2}$	.18	$.18\frac{1}{2}$	5.00	9.76	5.95	6.19
.20	.39	.24	.25	10.00	$19.52\frac{1}{2}$	$11.90\frac{1}{2}$	12.38
.25	.49	.30	.31				

EVENS

STAKE £.p	WIN £.p	$\frac{1}{5}$ ODDS £.p	$\frac{1}{4}$ ODDS £.p	STAKE £.p	WIN £.p	$\frac{1}{5}$ ODDS £.p	$\frac{1}{4}$ ODDS £.p
.01	.02	.01	.01	.30	.60	.36	.37½
.02	.04	.02½	.02½	.40	.80	.48	.50
.02½	.05	.03	.03	.50	1.00	.60	.62½
.03	.06	.03½	.03½	.60	1.20	.72	.75
.04	.08	.05	.05	.70	1.40	.84	.87½
.05	.10	.06	.06	.80	1.60	.96	1.00
.06	.12	.07	.07½	.90	1.80	1.08	1.12½
.07	.14	.08½	.08½	1.00	2.00	1.20	1.25
.08	.16	.09½	.10	2.00	4.00	2.40	2.50
.09	.18	.11	.11	3.00	6.00	3.60	3.75
.10	.20	.12	.12½	4.00	8.00	4.80	5.00
.15	.30	.18	.18½	5.00	10.00	6.00	6.25
.20	.40	.24	.25	10.00	20.00	12.00	12.50
.25	.50	.30	.31				

21–20

STAKE £.p	WIN £.p	$\frac{1}{5}$ ODDS £.p	$\frac{1}{4}$ ODDS £.p	STAKE £.p	WIN £.p	$\frac{1}{5}$ ODDS £.p	$\frac{1}{4}$ ODDS £.p
.01	.02	.01	.01½	.30	.61½	.36½	.38
.02	.04	.02½	.02½	.40	.82	.48½	.50½
.02½	.05	.03	.03	.50	1.02½	.60½	.63
.03	.06	.03½	.04	.60	1.23	.72½	.75½
.04	.08	.05	.05	.70	1.43½	.84½	.88½
.05	.10	.06	.06½	.80	1.64	.97	1.01
.06	.12½	.07½	.07½	.90	1.84½	1.09	1.13½
.07	.14½	.08½	.09	1.00	2.05	1.21	1.26
.08	.16½	.09½	.10	2.00	4.10	2.42	2.52½
.09	.18½	.11	.11½	3.00	6.15	3.63	3.78½
.10	.20½	.12	.12½	4.00	8.20	4.84	5.05
.15	.30½	.18	.19	5.00	10.25	6.05	6.31
.20	.41	.24	.25	10.00	20.50	12.10	12.62½
.25	.51	.30	.31½				

11–10

STAKE £.p	WIN £.p	$\frac{1}{5}$ ODDS £.p	$\frac{1}{4}$ ODDS £.p	STAKE £.p	WIN £.p	$\frac{1}{5}$ ODDS £.p	$\frac{1}{4}$ ODDS £.p
.01	.02	.01	.01½	.30	.63	.36½	.38
.02	.04	.02½	.02½	.40	.84	.49	.51
.02½	.05	.03	.03	.50	1.05	.61	.63½
.03	.06½	.03½	.04	.60	1.26	.73	.76½
.04	.08½	.05	.05	.70	1.47	.85½	.89
.05	.10½	.06	.06½	.80	1.68	.97½	1.02
.06	.12½	.07½	.07½	.90	1.89	1.10	1.14½
.07	.14½	.08½	.09	1.00	2.10	1.22	1.27½
.08	.17	.10	.10	2.00	4.20	2.44	2.55
.09	.19	.11	.11½	3.00	6.30	3.66	3.82½
.10	.21	.12	.12½	4.00	8.40	4.88	5.10
.15	.31½	.18½	.19	5.00	10.50	6.10	6.37½
.20	.42	.24½	.25½	10.00	21.00	12.20	12.75
.25	.52½	.30½	.32				

6–5

STAKE £.p	WIN £.p	$\frac{1}{5}$ ODDS £.p	$\frac{1}{4}$ ODDS £.p	STAKE £.p	WIN £.p	$\frac{1}{5}$ ODDS £.p	$\frac{1}{4}$ ODDS £.p
.01	.02	.01	.01½	.30	.66	.37	.39
.02	.04½	.02½	.02½	.40	.88	.49½	.52
.02½	.05½	.03	.03	.50	1.10	.62	.65
.03	.06½	.03½	.04	.60	1.32	.74½	.78
.04	.09	.05	.05	.70	1.54	.87	.91
.05	.11	.06	.06½	.80	1.76	.99	1.04
.06	.13	.07½	.08	.90	1.98	1.11½	1.17
.07	.15½	.08½	.09	1.00	2.20	1.24	1.30
.08	.17½	.10	.10½	2.00	4.40	2.48	2.60
.09	.20	.11	.11½	3.00	6.60	3.72	3.90
.10	.22	.12½	.13	4.00	8.80	4.96	5.20
.15	.33	.18½	.19½	5.00	11.00	6.20	6.50
.20	.44	.25	.26	10.00	22.00	12.40	13.00
.25	.55	.31	.32½				

5–4

STAKE £.p	WIN £.p	$\frac{1}{5}$ ODDS £.p	$\frac{1}{4}$ ODDS £.p
.01	.02	.01	.01½
.02	.04½	.02½	.02½
.02½	.05½	.03	.03½
.03	.06½	.03½	.04
.04	.09	.05	.05
.05	.11	.06	.06½
.06	.13½	.07½	.08
.07	.15½	.08½	.09
.08	.18	.10	.10½
.09	.20	.11	.12
.10	.22½	.12½	.13
.15	.33½	.18½	.19½
.20	.45	.25	.26
.25	.56	.31	.33
.30	.67½	.37½	.39½
.40	.90	.50	.52½
.50	1.12½	.62½	.65½
.60	1.35	.75	.78½
.70	1.57½	.87½	.92
.80	1.80	1.00	1.05
.90	2.02½	1.12½	1.18
1.00	2.25	1.25	1.31
2.00	4.50	2.50	2.62½
3.00	6.75	3.75	3.93½
4.00	9.00	5.00	5.25
5.00	11.25	6.25	6.56
10.00	22.50	12.50	13.12½

11–8

STAKE £.p	WIN £.p	$\frac{1}{5}$ ODDS £.p	$\frac{1}{4}$ ODDS £.p
.01	.02½	.01½	.01½
.02	.04½	.02½	.02½
.02½	.06	.03	.03½
.03	.07	.04	.04
.04	.09½	.05	.05½
.05	.12	.06½	.06½
.06	.14	.07½	.08
.07	.16½	.09	.09½
.08	.19	.10	.10½
.09	.21½	.11½	.12
.10	.23½	.12½	.13½
.15	.35½	.19	.20
.20	.47½	.25½	.27
.25	.59½	.32	.33½
.30	.71	.38	.40½
.40	.95	.51	.53½
.50	1.18½	.63½	.67
.60	1.42½	.76½	.80½
.70	1.66	.89	.94
.80	1.90	1.02	1.07½
.90	2.13½	1.14½	1.21
1.00	2.37½	1.27½	1.34½
2.00	4.75	2.55	2.68½
3.00	7.12½	3.82½	4.03
4.00	9.50	5.10	5.37½
5.00	11.87½	6.37½	6.72
10.00	23.75	12.75	13.43½

6–4

STAKE £.p	WIN £.p	$\frac{1}{5}$ ODDS £.p	$\frac{1}{4}$ ODDS £.p	STAKE £.p	WIN £.p	$\frac{1}{5}$ ODDS £.p	$\frac{1}{4}$ ODDS £.p
.01	.02½	.01½	.01½	.30	.75	.39	.41
.02	.05	.02½	.02½	.40	1.00	.52	.55
.02½	.06	.03	.03½	.50	1.25	.65	.68½
.03	.07½	.04	.04	.60	1.50	.78	.82½
.04	.10	.05	.05½	.70	1.75	.91	.96
.05	.12½	.06½	.07	.80	2.00	1.04	1.10
.06	.15	.08	.08	.90	2.25	1.17	1.23½
.07	.17½	.09	.09½	1.00	2.50	1.30	1.37½
.08	.20	.10½	.11	2.00	5.00	2.60	2.75
.09	.22½	.11½	.12½	3.00	7.50	3.90	4.12½
.10	.25	.13	.13½	4.00	10.00	5.20	5.50
.15	.37½	.19½	.20½	5.00	12.50	6.50	6.87½
.20	.50	.26	.27½	10.00	25.00	13.00	13.75
.25	.62½	.32½	.34½				

13–8

STAKE £.p	WIN £.p	$\frac{1}{5}$ ODDS £.p	$\frac{1}{4}$ ODDS £.p	STAKE £.p	WIN £.p	$\frac{1}{5}$ ODDS £.p	$\frac{1}{4}$ ODDS £.p
.01	.02½	.01½	.01½	.30	.78½	.39½	.42
.02	.05	.02½	.03	.40	1.05	.53	.56
.02½	.06½	.03½	.03½	.50	1.31	.66	.70½
.03	.08	.04	.04	.60	1.57½	.79½	.84½
.04	.10½	.05½	.05½	.70	1.83½	.92½	.98½
.05	.13	.06½	.07	.80	2.10	1.06	1.12½
.06	.15½	.08	.08½	.90	2.36	1.19	1.26½
.07	.18½	.09½	.10	1.00	2.62½	1.32½	1.40½
.08	.21	.10½	.11	2.00	5.25	2.65	2.81
.09	.23½	.12	.12½	3.00	7.87½	3.97½	4.22
.10	.26	.13	.14	4.00	10.50	5.30	5.62½
.15	.39½	.20	.21	5.00	13.12½	6.62½	7.03
.20	.52½	.26½	.28	10.00	26.25	13.25	14.06
.25	.65½	.33	.35				

7–4

STAKE £.p	WIN £.p	⅕ ODDS £.p	¼ ODDS £.p	STAKE £.p	WIN £.p	⅕ ODDS £.p	¼ ODDS £.p
.01	.02½	.01½	.01½	.30	.82½	.40½	.43
.02	.05½	.02½	.03	.40	1.10	.54	.57½
.02½	.07	.03½	.03½	.50	1.37½	.67½	.72
.03	.08	.04	.04½	.60	1.65	.81	.86
.04	.11	.05½	.05½	.70	1.92½	.94½	1.00½
.05	.13½	.06½	.07	.80	2.20	1.08	1.15
.06	.16½	.08	.08½	.90	2.47½	1.21½	1.29½
.07	.19	.09½	.10	1.00	2.75	1.35	1.43½
.08	.22	.11	.11½	2.00	5.50	2.70	2.87½
.09	.24½	.12	.13	3.00	8.25	4.05	4.31
.10	.27½	.13½	.14½	4.00	11.00	5.40	5.75
.15	.41	.20	.21½	5.00	13.75	6.75	7.18½
.20	.55	.27	.28½	10.00	27.50	13.50	14.37½
.25	.68½	.33½	.36				

15–8

STAKE £.p	WIN £.p	⅕ ODDS £.p	¼ ODDS £.p	STAKE £.p	WIN £.p	⅕ ODDS £.p	¼ ODDS £.p
.01	.03	.01½	.01½	.30	.86	.41	.44
.02	.05½	.02½	.03	.40	1.15	.55	.58½
.02½	.07	.03½	.03½	.50	1.43½	.68½	.73½
.03	.08½	.04	.04½	.60	1.72½	.82½	.88
.04	.11½	.05½	.06	.70	2.01	.96	1.03
.05	.14½	.07	.07½	.80	2.30	1.10	1.17½
.06	.17	.08	.09	.90	2.58½	1.23½	1.32
.07	.20	.09½	.10½	1.00	2.87½	1.37½	1.47
.08	.23	.11	.11½	2.00	5.75	2.75	2.93½
.09	.26	.12½	.13	3.00	8.62½	4.12½	4.40½
.10	.28½	.13½	.14½	4.00	11.50	5.50	5.87½
.15	.43	.20½	.22	5.00	14.37½	6.87½	7.34½
.20	.57½	.27½	.29½	10.00	28.75	13.75	14.68½
.25	.72	.34½	.36½				

2–1

STAKE £.p	WIN £.p	⅕ ODDS £.p	¼ ODDS £.p	STAKE £.p	WIN £.p	⅕ ODDS £.p	¼ ODDS £.p
.01	.03	.01½	.01½	.30	.90	.42	.45
.02	.06	.03	.03	.40	1.20	.56	.60
.02½	.07½	.03½	.03½	.50	1.50	.70	.75
.03	.09	.04	.04½	.60	1.80	.84	.90
.04	.12	.05½	.06	.70	2.10	.98	1.05
.05	.15	.07	.07½	.80	2.40	1.12	1.20
.06	.18	.08½	.09	.90	2.70	1.26	1.35
.07	.21	.10	.10½	1.00	3.00	1.40	1.50
.08	.24	.11	.12	2.00	6.00	2.80	3.00
.09	.27	.12½	.13½	3.00	9.00	4.20	4.50
.10	.30	.14	.15	4.00	12.00	5.60	6.00
.15	.45	.21	.22½	5.00	15.00	7.00	7.50
.20	.60	.28	.30	10.00	30.00	14.00	15.00
.25	.75	.35	.37½				

85–40

STAKE £.p	WIN £.p	⅕ ODDS £.p	¼ ODDS £.p	STAKE £.p	WIN £.p	⅕ ODDS £.p	¼ ODDS £.p
.01	.03	.01½	.01½	.30	.93½	.42½	.46
.02	.06	.03	.03	.40	1.25	.57	.61
.02½	.08	.03½	.04	.50	1.56	.71	.76½
.03	.09½	.04½	.04½	.60	1.87½	.85½	.92
.04	.12½	.05½	.06	.70	2.18½	.99½	1.07
.05	.15½	.07	.07½	.80	2.50	1.14	1.22½
.06	.18½	.08½	.09	.90	2.81	1.28	1.38
.07	.22	.10	.10½	1.00	3.12½	1.42½	1.53
.08	.25	.11½	.12	2.00	6.25	2.85	3.06
.09	.28	.13	.14	3.00	9.37½	4.27½	4.59½
.10	.31	.14	.15½	4.00	12.50	5.70	6.12½
.15	.47	.21½	.23	5.00	15.62½	7.12½	7.65½
.20	.62½	.28½	.30½	10.00	31.25	14.25	15.31
.25	.78	.35½	.38½				

9–4

STAKE £.p	WIN £.p	$\frac{1}{5}$ ODDS £.p	$\frac{1}{4}$ ODDS £.p	STAKE £.p	WIN £.p	$\frac{1}{5}$ ODDS £.p	$\frac{1}{4}$ ODDS £.p
.01	.03	.01½	.01½	.30	.97½	.43½	.47
.02	.06½	.03	.03	.40	1.30	.58	.62½
.02½	.08	.03½	.04	.50	1.62½	.72½	.78
.03	.09½	.04½	.04½	.60	1.95	.87	.93½
.04	.13	.06	.06	.70	2.27½	1.01½	1.09½
.05	.16	.07	.08	.80	2.60	1.16	1.25
.06	.19½	.08½	.09½	.90	2.92½	1.30½	1.40½
.07	.22½	.10	.11	1.00	3.25	1.45	1.56
.08	.26	.11½	.12½	2.00	6.50	2.90	3.12½
.09	.29	.13	.14	3.00	9.75	4.35	4.68½
.10	.32½	.14½	.15½	4.00	13.00	5.80	6.25
.15	.48½	.21½	.23½	5.00	16.25	7.25	7.81
.20	.65	.29	.31	10.00	32.50	14.50	15.62½
.25	.81	.36	.39				

5–2

STAKE £.p	WIN £.p	$\frac{1}{5}$ ODDS £.p	$\frac{1}{4}$ ODDS £.p	STAKE £.p	WIN £.p	$\frac{1}{5}$ ODDS £.p	$\frac{1}{4}$ ODDS £.p
.01	.03½	.01½	.01½	.30	1.05	.45	.48½
.02	.07	.03	.03	.40	1.40	.60	.65
.02½	.08½	.03½	.04	.50	1.75	.75	.81
.03	.10½	.04½	.05	.60	2.10	.90	.97½
.04	.14	.06	.06½	.70	2.45	1.05	1.13½
.05	.17½	.07½	.08	.80	2.80	1.20	1.30
.06	.21	.09	.09½	.90	3.15	1.35	1.46
.07	.24½	.10½	.11½	1.00	3.50	1.50	1.62½
.08	.28	.12	.13	2.00	7.00	3.00	3.25
.09	.31½	.13½	.14½	3.00	10.50	4.50	4.87½
.10	.35	.15	.16	4.00	14.00	6.00	6.50
.15	.52½	.22½	.24½	5.00	17.50	7.50	8.12½
.20	.70	.30	.32½	10.00	35.00	15.00	16.25
.25	.87½	.37½	.40½				

11–4

STAKE £.p	WIN £.p	$\frac{1}{5}$ ODDS £.p	$\frac{1}{4}$ ODDS £.p	STAKE £.p	WIN £.p	$\frac{1}{5}$ ODDS £.p	$\frac{1}{4}$ ODDS £.p
.01	.03½	.01½	.01½	.30	1.12½	.46½	.50½
.02	.07½	.03	.03½	.40	1.50	.62	.67½
.02½	.09½	.04	.04	.50	1.87½	.77½	.84½
.03	.11	.04½	.05	.60	2.25	.93	1.01
.04	.15	.06	.06½	.70	2.62½	1.08½	1.18
.05	.18½	.07½	.08½	.80	3.00	1.24	1.35
.06	.22½	.09½	.10	.90	3.37½	1.39½	1.52
.07	.26	.11	.12	1.00	3.75	1.55	1.68½
.08	.30	.12½	.13½	2.00	7.50	3.10	3.37½
.09	.33½	.14	.15	3.00	11.25	4.65	5.06
.10	.37½	.15½	.17	4.00	15.00	6.20	6.75
.15	.56	.23	.25½	5.00	18.75	7.75	8.43½
.20	.75	.31	.33½	10.00	37.50	15.50	16.87½
.25	.93½	.38½	.42				

3–1

STAKE £.p	WIN £.p	$\frac{1}{5}$ ODDS £.p	$\frac{1}{4}$ ODDS £.p	STAKE £.p	WIN £.p	$\frac{1}{5}$ ODDS £.p	$\frac{1}{4}$ ODDS £.p
.01	.04	.01½	.01½	.30	1.20	.48	.52½
.02	.08	.03	.03½	.40	1.60	.64	.70
.02½	.10	.04	.04½	.50	2.00	.80	.87½
.03	.12	.05	.05	.60	2.40	.96	1.05
.04	.16	.06½	.07	.70	2.80	1.12	1.22½
.05	.20	.08	.08½	.80	3.20	1.28	1.40
.06	.24	.09½	.10½	.90	3.60	1.44	1.57½
.07	.28	.11	.12	1.00	4.00	1.60	1.75
.08	.32	.13	.14	2.00	8.00	3.20	3.50
.09	.36	.14½	.15½	3.00	12.00	4.80	5.25
.10	.40	.16	.17½	4.00	16.00	6.40	7.00
.15	.60	.24	.26	5.00	20.00	8.00	8.75
.20	.80	.32	.35	10.00	40.00	16.00	17.50
.25	1.00	.40	.43½				

100–30

STAKE £.p	WIN £.p	⅕ ODDS £.p	¼ ODDS £.p	STAKE £.p	WIN £.p	⅕ ODDS £.p	¼ ODDS £.p
.01	.04½	.01½	.02	.30	1.30	.50	.55
.02	.08½	.03½	.03½	.40	1.73½	.66½	.73½
.02½	.11	.04	.04½	.50	2.16½	.83½	.91½
.03	.13	.05	.05½	.60	2.60	1.00	1.10
.04	.17½	.06½	.07½	.70	3.03½	1.16½	1.28½
.05	.21½	.08½	.09	.80	3.46½	1.33½	1.46½
.06	.26	.10	.11	.90	3.90	1.50	1.65
.07	.30½	.11½	.13	1.00	4.33½	1.66½	1.83½
.08	.34½	.13½	.14½	2.00	8.66½	3.33½	3.66½
.09	.39	.15	.16½	3.00	13.00	5.00	5.50
.10	.43½	.16½	.18½	4.00	17.33½	6.66½	7.33½
.15	.65	.25	.27½	5.00	21.66½	8.33½	9.16½
.20	.86½	.33½	.36½	10.00	43.33½	16.66½	18.33½
.25	1.08½	.41½	.46				

7–2

STAKE £.p	WIN £.p	⅕ ODDS £.p	¼ ODDS £.p	STAKE £.p	WIN £.p	⅕ ODDS £.p	¼ ODDS £.p
.01	.04½	.01½	.02	.30	1.35	.51	.56
.02	.09	.03½	.03½	.40	1.80	.68	.75
.02½	.11	.04	.04½	.50	2.25	.85	.93½
.03	.13½	.05	.05½	.60	2.70	1.02	1.12½
.04	.18	.07	.07½	.70	3.15	1.19	1.31
.05	.22½	.08½	.09½	.80	3.60	1.36	1.50
.06	.27	.10	.11	.90	4.05	1.53	1.68½
.07	.31½	.12	.13	1.00	4.50	1.70	1.87½
.08	.36	.13½	.15	2.00	9.00	3.40	3.75
.09	.40½	.15½	.17	3.00	13.50	5.10	5.62
.10	.45	.17	.18½	4.00	18.00	6.80	7.50
.15	.67½	.25½	.28	5.00	22.50	8.50	9.37½
.20	.90	.34	.37½	10.00	45.00	17.00	18.75
.25	1.12½	.42½	.47				

4−1

STAKE £.p	WIN £.p	$\frac{1}{5}$ ODDS £.p	$\frac{1}{4}$ ODDS £.p	STAKE £.p	WIN £.p	$\frac{1}{5}$ ODDS £.p	$\frac{1}{4}$ ODDS £.p
.01	.05	.02	.02	.30	1.50	.54	.60
.02	.10	.03$\frac{1}{2}$	.04	.40	2.00	.72	.80
.02$\frac{1}{2}$	.12$\frac{1}{2}$	.04$\frac{1}{2}$	.05	.50	2.50	.90	1.00
.03	.15	.05$\frac{1}{2}$	.06	.60	3.00	1.08	1.20
.04	.20	.07	.08	.70	3.50	1.26	1.40
.05	.25	.09	.10	.80	4.00	1.44	1.60
.06	.30	.11	.12	.90	4.50	1.62	1.80
.07	.35	.12$\frac{1}{2}$	.14	1.00	5.00	1.80	2.00
.08	.40	.14$\frac{1}{2}$	.16	2.00	10.00	3.60	4.00
.09	.45	.16	.18	3.00	15.00	5.40	6.00
.10	.50	.18	.20	4.00	20.00	7.20	8.00
.15	.75	.27	.30	5.00	25.00	9.00	10.00
.20	1.00	.36	.40	10.00	50.00	18.00	20.00
.25	1.25	.45	.50				

9−2

STAKE £.p	WIN £.p	$\frac{1}{5}$ ODDS £.p	$\frac{1}{4}$ ODDS £.p	STAKE £.p	WIN £.p	$\frac{1}{5}$ ODDS £.p	$\frac{1}{4}$ ODDS £.p
.01	.05$\frac{1}{2}$	.02	.01	.30	1.65	.57	.63$\frac{1}{2}$
.02	.11	.04	.04	.40	2.20	.76	.85
.02$\frac{1}{2}$	.13$\frac{1}{2}$	.04$\frac{1}{2}$	.05$\frac{1}{2}$	.50	2.75	.95	1.06
.03	.16$\frac{1}{2}$	.05$\frac{1}{2}$	.06$\frac{1}{2}$	.60	3.30	1.14	1.27$\frac{1}{2}$
.04	.22	.07$\frac{1}{2}$	.08$\frac{1}{2}$	.70	3.85	1.33	1.48$\frac{1}{2}$
.05	.27$\frac{1}{2}$	.09$\frac{1}{2}$	.10$\frac{1}{2}$	.80	4.40	1.52	1.70
.06	.33	.11$\frac{1}{2}$	.12$\frac{1}{2}$	.90	4.95	1.71	1.91
.07	.38$\frac{1}{2}$	.13$\frac{1}{2}$	.15	1.00	5.50	1.90	2.12$\frac{1}{2}$
.08	.44	.15	.17	2.00	11.00	3.80	4.25
.09	.49$\frac{1}{2}$	.17	.19	3.00	16.50	5.70	6.37$\frac{1}{2}$
.10	.55	.19	.21	4.00	22.00	7.60	8.50
.15	.82$\frac{1}{2}$	.28$\frac{1}{2}$	.32	5.00	27.50	9.50	10.62$\frac{1}{2}$
.20	1.10	.38	.42$\frac{1}{2}$	10.00	55.00	19.00	21.25
.25	1.37$\frac{1}{2}$	.47$\frac{1}{2}$	.53				

5–1

STAKE £.p	WIN £.p	$\frac{1}{5}$ ODDS £.p	$\frac{1}{4}$ ODDS £.p	STAKE £.p	WIN £.p	$\frac{1}{5}$ ODDS £.p	$\frac{1}{4}$ ODDS £.p
.01	.06	.02	.02	.30	1.80	.60	.67$\frac{1}{2}$
.02	.12	.04	.04$\frac{1}{2}$	.40	2.40	.80	.90
.02$\frac{1}{2}$	.15	.05	.05$\frac{1}{2}$	.50	3.00	1.00	1.12$\frac{1}{2}$
.03	.18	.06	.06$\frac{1}{2}$	.60	3.60	1.20	1.35
.04	.24	.08	.09	.70	4.20	1.40	1.57$\frac{1}{2}$
.05	.30	.10	.11	.80	4.80	1.60	1.80
.06	.36	.12	.13$\frac{1}{2}$	.90	5.40	1.80	2.02$\frac{1}{2}$
.07	.42	.14	.15$\frac{1}{2}$	1.00	6.00	2.00	2.25
.08	.48	.16	.18	2.00	12.00	4.00	4.50
.09	.54	.18	.20	3.00	18.00	6.00	6.75
.10	.60	.20	.22$\frac{1}{2}$	4.00	24.00	8.00	9.00
.15	.90	.30	.33$\frac{1}{2}$	5.00	30.00	10.00	11.25
.20	1.20	.40	.45	10.00	60.00	20.00	22.50
.25	1.50	.50	.56				

11–2

STAKE £.p	WIN £.p	$\frac{1}{5}$ ODDS £.p	$\frac{1}{4}$ ODDS £.p	STAKE £.p	WIN £.p	$\frac{1}{5}$ ODDS £.p	$\frac{1}{4}$ ODDS £.p
.01	.06$\frac{1}{2}$	.02	.02$\frac{1}{2}$	.30	1.95	.63	.71
.02	.13	.04	.04$\frac{1}{2}$	.40	2.60	.84	.95
.02$\frac{1}{2}$	.16	.05	.06	.50	3.25	1.05	1.18$\frac{1}{2}$
.03	.19$\frac{1}{2}$	.06$\frac{1}{2}$	.07	.60	3.90	1.26	1.42$\frac{1}{2}$
.04	.26	.08$\frac{1}{2}$	.09$\frac{1}{2}$	.70	4.55	1.47	1.66
.05	.32$\frac{1}{2}$	.10$\frac{1}{2}$	.12	.80	5.20	1.68	1.90
.06	.39	.12$\frac{1}{2}$	.14	.90	5.85	1.89	2.13$\frac{1}{2}$
.07	.45$\frac{1}{2}$	.15	.16$\frac{1}{2}$	1.00	6.50	2.10	2.37$\frac{1}{2}$
.08	.52	.17	.19	2.00	13.00	4.20	4.75
.09	.58$\frac{1}{2}$	.19	.21$\frac{1}{2}$	3.00	19.50	6.30	7.12$\frac{1}{2}$
.10	.65	.21	.23$\frac{1}{2}$	4.00	26.00	8.40	9.50
.15	.97$\frac{1}{2}$	.31$\frac{1}{2}$	.35$\frac{1}{2}$	5.00	32.50	10.50	11.87$\frac{1}{2}$
.20	1.30	.42	.47$\frac{1}{2}$	10.00	65.00	21.00	23.75
.25	1.62$\frac{1}{2}$	.52$\frac{1}{2}$	.59$\frac{1}{2}$				

6−1

STAKE £.p	WIN £.p	$\frac{1}{5}$ ODDS £.p	$\frac{1}{4}$ ODDS £.p	STAKE £.p	WIN £.p	$\frac{1}{5}$ ODDS £.p	$\frac{1}{4}$ ODDS £.p
.01	.07	.02	$.02\frac{1}{2}$	.30	2.10	.66	.75
.02	.14	$.04\frac{1}{2}$	.05	.40	2.80	.88	1.00
$.02\frac{1}{2}$	$.17\frac{1}{2}$	$.05\frac{1}{2}$	.06	.50	3.50	1.10	1.25
.03	.21	$.06\frac{1}{2}$	$.07\frac{1}{2}$	.60	4.20	1.32	1.50
.04	.28	.09	.10	.70	4.90	1.54	1.75
.05	.35	.11	$.12\frac{1}{2}$	.80	5.60	1.76	2.00
.06	.42	.13	.15	.90	6.30	1.98	2.25
.07	.49	$.15\frac{1}{2}$	$.17\frac{1}{2}$	1.00	7.00	2.20	2.50
.08	.56	$.17\frac{1}{2}$	.20	2.00	14.00	4.40	5.00
.09	.63	.20	$.22\frac{1}{2}$	3.00	21.00	6.60	7.50
.10	.70	.22	.25	4.00	28.00	8.80	10.00
.15	1.05	.33	$.37\frac{1}{2}$	5.00	35.00	11.00	12.50
.20	1.40	.44	.50	10.00	70.00	22.00	25.00
.25	1.75	.55	$.62\frac{1}{2}$				

13−2

STAKE £.p	WIN £.p	$\frac{1}{5}$ ODDS £.p	$\frac{1}{4}$ ODDS £.p	STAKE £.p	WIN £.p	$\frac{1}{5}$ ODDS £.p	$\frac{1}{4}$ ODDS £.p
.01	$.07\frac{1}{2}$	$.02\frac{1}{2}$	$.02\frac{1}{2}$	.30	2.25	.69	$.78\frac{1}{2}$
.02	.15	$.04\frac{1}{2}$	.05	.40	3.00	.92	1.05
$.02\frac{1}{2}$	$.18\frac{1}{2}$	$.05\frac{1}{2}$	$.06\frac{1}{2}$	.50	3.75	1.15	1.31
.03	$.22\frac{1}{2}$	.07	.08	.60	4.50	1.38	$1.57\frac{1}{2}$
.04	.30	.09	$.10\frac{1}{2}$	.70	5.25	1.61	$1.83\frac{1}{2}$
.05	$.37\frac{1}{2}$	$.11\frac{1}{2}$	.13	.80	6.00	1.84	2.10
.06	.45	.14	$.15\frac{1}{2}$	.90	6.75	2.07	2.36
.07	$.52\frac{1}{2}$	.16	$.18\frac{1}{2}$	1.00	7.50	2.30	$2.62\frac{1}{2}$
.08	.60	$.18\frac{1}{2}$	.21	2.00	15.00	4.60	5.25
.09	$.67\frac{1}{2}$	$.20\frac{1}{2}$	$.23\frac{1}{2}$	3.00	22.50	6.90	$7.87\frac{1}{2}$
.10	.75	.23	.26	4.00	30.00	9.20	10.50
.15	$1.12\frac{1}{2}$	$.34\frac{1}{2}$	$.39\frac{1}{2}$	5.00	37.50	11.50	$13.12\frac{1}{2}$
.20	1.50	.46	$.52\frac{1}{2}$	10.00	75.00	23.00	26.25
.25	$1.87\frac{1}{2}$	$.57\frac{1}{2}$	$.65\frac{1}{2}$				

HORSE RACING IN BRITAIN

7–1

STAKE £.p	WIN £.p	$\frac{1}{5}$ ODDS £.p	$\frac{1}{4}$ ODDS £.p	STAKE £.p	WIN £.p	$\frac{1}{5}$ ODDS £.p	$\frac{1}{4}$ ODDS £.p
.01	.08	.02½	.02½	.30	2.40	.72	.82½
.02	.16	.05	.05½	.40	3.20	.96	1.10
.02½	.20	.06	.07	.50	4.00	1.20	1.37½
.03	.24	.07	.08	.60	4.80	1.44	1.65
.04	.32	.09½	.11	.70	5.60	1.68	1.92½
.05	.40	.12	.13½	.80	6.40	1.92	2.20
.06	.48	.14½	.16½	.90	7.20	2.16	2.47½
.07	.56	.17	.19	1.00	8.00	2.40	2.75
.08	.64	.19	.22	2.00	16.00	4.80	5.50
.09	.72	.21½	.24½	3.00	24.00	7.20	8.25
.10	.80	.24	.27½	4.00	32.00	9.60	11.00
.15	1.20	.36	.41	5.00	40.00	12.00	13.75
.20	1.60	.48	.55	10.00	80.00	24.00	27.50
.25	2.00	.60	.68½				

15–2

STAKE £.p	WIN £.p	$\frac{1}{5}$ ODDS £.p	$\frac{1}{4}$ ODDS £.p	STAKE £.p	WIN £.p	$\frac{1}{5}$ ODDS £.p	$\frac{1}{4}$ ODDS £.p
.01	.08½	.02½	.03	.30	2.55	.75	.86
.02	.17	.05	.05½	.40	3.40	1.00	1.15
.02½	.21	.06	.07	.50	4.25	1.25	1.43½
.03	.25½	.07½	.08½	.60	5.10	1.50	1.72½
.04	.34	.10	.11½	.70	5.95	1.75	2.01
.05	.42½	.12½	.14½	.80	6.80	2.00	2.30
.06	.51	.15	.17	.90	7.65	2.25	2.58½
.07	.59½	.17½	.20	1.00	8.50	2.50	2.87½
.08	.68	.20	.23	2.00	17.00	5.00	5.75
.09	.76½	.22½	.26	3.00	25.50	7.50	8.62½
.10	.85	.25	.28½	4.00	34.00	10.00	11.50
.15	1.27½	.37½	.43	5.00	42.50	12.50	14.37½
.20	1.70	.50	.57½	10.00	85.00	25.00	28.75
.25	2.12½	.62½	.72				

8–1

STAKE £.p	WIN £.p	⅕ ODDS £.p	¼ ODDS £.p	STAKE £.p	WIN £.p	⅕ ODDS £.p	¼ ODDS £.p
.01	.09	.02½	.03	.30	2.70	.78	.90
.02	.18	.05	.06	.40	3.60	1.04	1.20
.02½	.22½	.06½	.07½	.50	4.50	1.30	1.50
.03	.27	.08	.09	.60	5.40	1.56	1.80
.04	.36	.10½	.12	.70	6.30	1.82	2.10
.05	.45	.13	.15	.80	7.20	2.08	2.40
.06	.54	.15½	.18	.90	8.10	2.34	2.70
.07	.63	.18	.21	1.00	9.00	2.60	3.00
.08	.72	.21	.24	2.00	18.00	5.20	6.00
.09	.81	.23½	.27	3.00	27.00	7.80	9.00
.10	.90	.26	.30	4.00	36.00	10.40	12.00
.15	1.35	.39	.45	5.00	45.00	13.00	15.00
.20	1.80	.52	.60	10.00	90.00	26.00	30.00
.25	2.25	.65	.75				

17–2

STAKE £.p	WIN £.p	⅕ ODDS £.p	¼ ODDS £.p	STAKE £.p	WIN £.p	⅕ ODDS £.p	¼ ODDS £.p
.01	.09½	.02½	.03	.30	2.85	.81	.93½
.02	.19	.05½	.06	.40	3.80	1.08	1.25
.02½	.23½	.06½	.08	.50	4.75	1.35	1.56
.03	.28½	.08	.09½	.60	5.70	1.62	1.87½
.04	.38	.11	.12½	.70	6.65	1.89	2.18½
.05	.47½	.13½	.15½	.80	7.60	2.16	2.50
.06	.57	.16	.18½	.90	8.55	2.43	2.81
.07	.66½	.19	.22	1.00	9.50	2.70	3.12½
.08	.76	.21½	.25	2.00	19.00	5.40	6.25
.09	.85½	.24½	.28	3.00	28.50	8.10	9.37½
.10	.95	.27	.31	4.00	38.00	10.80	12.50
.15	1.42½	.40½	.47	5.00	47.50	13.50	15.62½
.20	1.90	.54	.62½	10.00	95.00	27.00	31.25
.25	2.37½	.67½	.78				

9–1

STAKE £.p	WIN £.p	$\frac{1}{5}$ ODDS £.p	$\frac{1}{4}$ ODDS £.p	STAKE £.p	WIN £.p	$\frac{1}{5}$ ODDS £.p	$\frac{1}{4}$ ODDS £.p
.01	.10	.03	.03	.30	3.00	.84	.97$\frac{1}{2}$
.02	.20	.05$\frac{1}{2}$	.06$\frac{1}{2}$	.40	4.00	1.12	1.30
.02$\frac{1}{2}$	.25	.07	.08	.50	5.00	1.40	1.62$\frac{1}{2}$
.03	.30	.08$\frac{1}{2}$	.09$\frac{1}{2}$	.60	6.00	1.68	1.95
.04	.40	.11	.13	.70	7.00	1.96	2.27$\frac{1}{2}$
.05	.50	.14	.16	.80	8.00	2.24	2.60
.06	.60	.17	.19$\frac{1}{2}$	.90	9.00	2.52	2.92$\frac{1}{2}$
.07	.70	.19$\frac{1}{2}$	.22$\frac{1}{2}$	1.00	10.00	2.80	3.25
.08	.80	.22$\frac{1}{2}$	.26	2.00	20.00	5.60	6.50
.09	.90	.25	.29	3.00	30.00	8.40	9.75
.10	1.00	.28	.32$\frac{1}{2}$	4.00	40.00	11.20	13.00
.15	1.50	.42	.48$\frac{1}{2}$	5.00	50.00	14.00	16.25
.20	2.00	.56	.65	10.00	100.00	28.00	32.50
.25	2.50	.70	.81				

10–1

STAKE £.p	WIN £.p	$\frac{1}{5}$ ODDS £.p	$\frac{1}{4}$ ODDS £.p	STAKE £.p	WIN £.p	$\frac{1}{5}$ ODDS £.p	$\frac{1}{4}$ ODDS £.p
.01	.11	.03	.03$\frac{1}{2}$	.30	3.30	.90	1.05
.02	.22	.06	.07	.40	4.40	1.20	1.40
.02$\frac{1}{2}$	.27$\frac{1}{2}$	.07$\frac{1}{2}$	.08$\frac{1}{2}$	.50	5.50	1.50	1.75
.03	.33	.09	.10$\frac{1}{2}$	.60	6.60	1.80	2.10
.04	.44	.12	.14	.70	7.70	2.10	2.45
.05	.55	.15	.17$\frac{1}{2}$	.80	8.80	2.40	2.80
.06	.66	.18	.21	.90	9.90	2.70	3.15
.07	.77	.21	.24$\frac{1}{2}$	1.00	11.00	3.00	3.50
.08	.88	.24	.28	2.00	22.00	6.00	7.00
.09	.99	.27	.31$\frac{1}{2}$	3.00	33.00	9.00	10.50
.10	1.10	.30	.35	4.00	44.00	12.00	14.00
.15	1.65	.45	.52$\frac{1}{2}$	5.00	55.00	15.00	17.50
.20	2.20	.60	.70	10.00	110.00	30.00	35.00
.25	2.75	.75	.87$\frac{1}{2}$				

11–1

STAKE £.p	WIN £.p	$\frac{1}{5}$ ODDS £.p	$\frac{1}{4}$ ODDS £.p	STAKE £.p	WIN £.p	$\frac{1}{5}$ ODDS £.p	$\frac{1}{4}$ ODDS £.p
.01	.12	.03	.03$\frac{1}{2}$	.30	3.60	.96	1.12$\frac{1}{2}$
.02	.24	.06$\frac{1}{2}$	.07$\frac{1}{2}$	.40	4.80	1.28	1.50
.02$\frac{1}{2}$	.30	.08	.09$\frac{1}{2}$	.50	6.00	1.60	1.87$\frac{1}{2}$
.03	.36	.09$\frac{1}{2}$	.11	.60	7.20	1.92	2.25
.04	.48	.13	.15	.70	8.40	2.24	2.62$\frac{1}{2}$
.05	.60	.16	.18$\frac{1}{2}$	.80	9.60	2.56	3.00
.06	.72	.19	.22$\frac{1}{2}$	.90	10.80	2.88	3.37$\frac{1}{2}$
.07	.84	.22$\frac{1}{2}$	.26	1.00	12.00	3.20	3.75
.08	.96	.25$\frac{1}{2}$	.30	2.00	24.00	6.40	7.50
.09	1.08	.29	.33$\frac{1}{2}$	3.00	36.00	9.60	11.25
.10	1.20	.32	.37$\frac{1}{2}$	4.00	48.00	12.80	15.00
.15	1.80	.48	.56	5.00	60.00	16.00	18.75
.20	2.40	.64	.75	10.00	120.00	32.00	37.50
.25	3.00	.80	.93$\frac{1}{2}$				

12–1

STAKE £.p	WIN £.p	$\frac{1}{5}$ ODDS £.p	$\frac{1}{4}$ ODDS £.p	STAKE £.p	WIN £.p	$\frac{1}{5}$ ODDS £.p	$\frac{1}{4}$ ODDS £.p
.01	.13	.03$\frac{1}{2}$	.04	.30	3.90	1.02	1.20
.02	.26	.07	.08	.40	5.20	1.36	1.60
.02$\frac{1}{2}$	.32$\frac{1}{2}$	.08$\frac{1}{2}$	.10	.50	6.50	1.70	2.00
.03	.39	.10	.12	.60	7.80	2.04	2.40
.04	.52	.13$\frac{1}{2}$	.16	.70	9.10	2.38	2.80
.05	.65	.17	.20	.80	10.40	2.72	3.20
.06	.78	.20$\frac{1}{2}$	.24	.90	11.70	3.06	3.60
.07	.91	.24	.28	1.00	13.00	3.40	4.00
.08	1.04	.27	.32	2.00	26.00	6.80	8.00
.09	1.17	.30$\frac{1}{2}$	.36	3.00	39.00	10.20	12.00
.10	1.30	.34	.40	4.00	52.00	13.60	16.00
.15	1.95	.51	.60	5.00	65.00	17.00	20.00
.20	2.60	.68	.80	10.00	130.00	34.00	40.00
.25	3.25	.85	1.00				

13–1

STAKE £.p	WIN £.p	$\frac{1}{5}$ ODDS £.p	$\frac{1}{4}$ ODDS £.p	STAKE £.p	WIN £.p	$\frac{1}{5}$ ODDS £.p	$\frac{1}{4}$ ODDS £.p
.01	.14	.03½	.04	.30	4.20	1.08	1.27½
.02	.28	.07	.08½	.40	5.60	1.44	1.70
.02½	.35	.09	.10½	.50	7.00	1.80	2.12½
.03	.42	.11	.12½	.60	8.40	2.16	2.55
.04	.56	.14½	.17	.70	9.80	2.52	2.97½
.05	.70	.18	.21	.80	11.20	2.88	3.40
.06	.84	.21½	.25½	.90	12.60	3.24	3.82½
.07	.98	.25	.29½	1.00	14.00	3.60	4.25
.08	1:12	.29	.34	2.00	28.00	7.20	8.50
.09	1.26	.32	.38	3.00	42.00	10.80	12.75
.10	1.40	.36	.42½	4.00	56.00	14.40	17.00
.15	2.10	.54	.63½	5.00	70.00	18.00	21.25
.20	2.80	.72	.85	10.00	140.00	36.00	42.50
.25	3.50	.90	1.06				

14–1

STAKE £.p	WIN £.p	$\frac{1}{5}$ ODDS £.p	$\frac{1}{4}$ ODDS £.p	STAKE £.p	WIN £.p	$\frac{1}{5}$ ODDS £.p	$\frac{1}{4}$ ODDS £.p
.01	.15	.04	.04½	.30	4.50	1.14	1.35
.02	.30	.07½	.09	.40	6.00	1.52	1.80
.02½	.37½	.09½	.11	.50	7.50	1.90	2.25
.03	.45	.11½	.13½	.60	9.00	2.28	2.70
.04	.60	.15	.18	.70	10.50	2.66	3.15
.05	.75	.19	.22½	.80	12.00	3.04	3.60
.06	.90	.23	.27	.90	13.50	3.42	4.05
.07	1.05	.26½	.31½	1.00	15.00	3.80	4.50
.08	1.20	.30½	.36	2.00	30.00	7.60	9.00
.09	1.35	.34	.40½	3.00	45.00	11.40	13.50
.10	1.50	.38	.45	4.00	60.00	15.20	18.00
.15	2.25	.57	.67½	5.00	75.00	19.00	22.50
.20	3.00	.76	.90	10.00	150.00	38.00	45.00
.25	3.75	.95	1.12½				

15–1

STAKE £.p	WIN £.p	$\frac{1}{5}$ ODDS £.p	$\frac{1}{4}$ ODDS £.p	STAKE £.p	WIN £.p	$\frac{1}{5}$ ODDS £.p	$\frac{1}{4}$ ODDS £.p
.01	.16	.04	.04½	.30	4.80	1.20	1.42½
.02	.32	.08	.09½	.40	6.40	1.60	1.90
.02½	.40	.10	.12	.50	8.00	2.00	2.37½
.03	.48	.12	.14	.60	9.60	2.40	2.85
.04	.64	.16	.19	.70	11.20	2.80	3.32½
.05	.80	.20	.23½	.80	12.80	3.20	3.80
.06	.96	.24	.28½	.90	14.40	3.60	4.27½
.07	1.12	.28	.33	1.00	16.00	4.00	4.75
.08	1.28	.32	.38	2.00	32.00	8.00	9.50
.09	1.44	.36	.42½	3.00	48.00	12.00	14.25
.10	1.60	.40	.47½	4.00	64.00	16.00	19.00
.15	2.40	.60	.71	5.00	80.00	20.00	23.75
.20	3.20	.80	.95	10.00	160.00	40.00	47.50
.25	4.00	1.00	1.18½				

16–1

STAKE £.p	WIN £.p	$\frac{1}{5}$ ODDS £.p	$\frac{1}{4}$ ODDS £.p	STAKE £.p	WIN £.p	$\frac{1}{5}$ ODDS £.p	$\frac{1}{4}$ ODDS £.p
.01	.17	.04	.05	.30	5.10	1.26	1.50
.02	.34	.08½	.10	.40	6.80	1.68	2.00
.02½	.42½	.10½	.12½	.50	8.50	2.10	2.50
.03	.51	.12½	.15	.60	10.20	2.52	3.00
.04	.68	.17	.20	.70	11.90	2.94	3.50
.05	.85	.21	.25	.80	13.60	3.36	4.00
.06	1.02	.25	.30	.90	15.30	3.78	4.50
.07	1.19	.29½	.35	1.00	17.00	4.20	5.00
.08	1.36	.33½	.40	2.00	34.00	8.40	10.00
.09	1.53	.38	.45	3.00	51.00	12.60	15.00
.10	1.70	.42	.50	4.00	68.00	16.80	20.00
.15	2.55	.63	.75	5.00	85.00	21.00	25.00
.20	3.40	.84	1.00	10.00	170.00	42.00	50.00
.25	4.25	1.05	1.25				

18–1

STAKE £.p	WIN £.p	$\frac{1}{5}$ ODDS £.p	$\frac{1}{4}$ ODDS £.p	STAKE £.p	WIN £.p	$\frac{1}{5}$ ODDS £.p	$\frac{1}{4}$ ODDS £.p
.01	.19	.04½	.05½	.30	5.70	1.38	1.65
.02	.38	.09	.11	.40	7.60	1.84	2.20
.02½	.47½	.11½	.13½	.50	9.50	2.30	2.75
.03	.57	.14	.16½	.60	11.40	2.76	3.30
.04	.76	.18½	.22	.70	13.30	3.22	3.85
.05	.95	.23	.27½	.80	15.20	3.68	4.40
.06	1.14	.27½	.33	.90	17.10	4.14	4.95
.07	1.33	.32	.38½	1.00	19.00	4.60	5.50
.08	1.52	.37	.44	2.00	38.00	9.20	11.00
.09	1.71	.41½	.49½	3.00	57.00	13.80	16.50
.10	1.90	.46	.55	4.00	76.00	18.40	22.00
.15	2.85	.69	.82½	5.00	95.00	23.00	27.50
.20	3.80	.92	1.10	10.00	190.00	46.00	55.00
.25	4.75	1.15	1.37½				

20–1

STAKE £.p	WIN £.p	$\frac{1}{5}$ ODDS £.p	$\frac{1}{4}$ ODDS £.p	STAKE £.p	WIN £.p	$\frac{1}{5}$ ODDS £.p	$\frac{1}{4}$ ODDS £.p
.01	.21	.05	.06	.30	6.30	1.50	1.80
.02	.42	.10	.12	.40	8.40	2.00	2.40
.02½	.52½	.12½	.15	.50	10.50	2.50	3.00
.03	.63	.15	.18	.60	12.60	3.00	3.60
.04	.84	.20	.24	.70	14.70	3.50	4.20
.05	1.05	.25	.30	.80	16.80	4.00	4.80
.06	1.26	.30	.36	.90	18.90	4.50	5.40
.07	1.47	.35	.42	1.00	21.00	5.00	6.00
.08	1.68	.40	.48	2.00	42.00	10.00	12.00
.09	1.89	.45	.54	3.00	63.00	15.00	18.00
.10	2.10	.50	.60	4.00	84.00	20.00	24.00
.15	3.15	.75	.90	5.00	105.00	25.00	30.00
.20	4.20	1.00	1.20	10.00	210.00	50.00	60.00
.25	5.25	1.25	1.50				

25–1

STAKE £.p	WIN £.p	$\frac{1}{5}$ ODDS £.p	$\frac{1}{4}$ ODDS £.p	STAKE £.p	WIN £.p	$\frac{1}{5}$ ODDS £.p	$\frac{1}{4}$ ODDS £.p
.01	.26	.06	.07	.30	7.80	1.80	2.17½
.02	.52	.12	.14½	.40	10.40	2.40	2.90
.02½	.65	.15	.18	.50	13.00	3.00	3.62½
.03	.78	.18	.21½	.60	15.60	3.60	4.35
.04	1.04	.24	.29	.70	18.20	4.20	5.07½
.05	1.30	.30	.36	.80	20.80	4.80	5.80
.06	1.56	.36	.43½	.90	23.40	5.40	6.52½
.07	1.82	.42	.50½	1.00	26.00	6.00	7.25
.08	2.08	.48	.58	2.00	52.00	12.00	14.50
.09	2.34	.54	.65	3.00	78.00	18.00	21.75
.10	2.60	.60	.72½	4.00	104.00	24.00	29.00
.15	3.90	.90	1.08½	5.00	130.00	30.00	36.25
.20	5.20	1.20	1.45	10.00	260.00	60.00	72.50
.25	6.50	1.50	1.81				

28–1

STAKE £.p	WIN £.p	$\frac{1}{5}$ ODDS £.p	$\frac{1}{4}$ ODDS £.p	STAKE £.p	WIN £.p	$\frac{1}{5}$ ODDS £.p	$\frac{1}{4}$ ODDS £.p
.01	.29	.06½	.08	.30	8.70	1.98	2.40
.02	.58	.13	.16	.40	11.60	2.64	3.20
.02½	.72½	.16½	.20	.50	14.50	3.30	4.00
.03	.87	.20	.24	.60	17.40	3.96	4.80
.04	1.16	.26½	.32	.70	20.30	4.62	5.60
.05	1.45	.33	.40	.80	23.20	5.28	6.40
.06	1.74	.39½	.48	.90	26.10	5.94	7.20
.07	2.03	.46	.56	1.00	29.00	6.60	8.00
.08	2.32	.53	.64	2.00	58.00	13.20	16.00
.09	2.61	.59½	.72	3.00	87.00	19.80	24.00
.10	2.90	.66	.80	4.00	116.00	26.40	32.00
.15	4.35	.99	1.20	5.00	145.00	33.00	40.00
.20	5.80	1.32	1.60	10.00	290.00	66.00	80.00
.25	7.25	1.65	2.00				

33–1

STAKE £.p	WIN £.p	$\frac{1}{5}$ ODDS £.p	$\frac{1}{4}$ ODDS £.p	STAKE £.p	WIN £.p	$\frac{1}{5}$ ODDS £.p	$\frac{1}{4}$ ODDS £.p
.01	.34	.07½	.09	.30	10.20	2.28	2.77½
.02	.68	.15	.18½	.40	13.60	3.04	3.70
.02½	.85	.19	.23	.50	17.00	3.80	4.62½
.03	1.02	.23	.27½	.60	20.40	4.56	5.55
.04	1.36	.30½	.37	.70	23.80	5.32	6.47½
.05	1.70	.38	.46	.80	27.20	6.08	7.40
.06	2.04	.45½	.55½	.90	30.60	6.84	8.32½
.07	2.38	.53	.64½	1.00	34.00	7.60	9.25
.08	2.72	.61	.74	2.00	68.00	15.20	18.50
.09	3.06	.68½	.83	3.00	102.00	22.80	27.75
.10	3.40	.76	.92½	4.00	136.00	30.40	37.00
.15	5.10	1.14	1.38½	5.00	170.00	38.00	46.25
.20	6.80	1.52	1.85	10.00	340.00	76.00	92.50
.25	8.50	1.90	2.31				

40–1

STAKE £.p	WIN £.p	$\frac{1}{5}$ ODDS £.p	$\frac{1}{4}$ ODDS £.p	STAKE £.p	WIN £.p	$\frac{1}{5}$ ODDS £.p	$\frac{1}{4}$ ODDS £.p
.01	.41	.09	.11	.30	12.30	2.70	3.30
.02	.82	.18	.22	.40	16.40	3.60	4.40
.02½	1.02½	.22½	.27½	.50	20.50	4.50	5.50
.03	1.23	.27	.33	.60	24.60	5.40	6.60
.04	1.64	.36	.44	.70	28.70	6.30	7.70
.05	2.05	.45	.55	.80	32.80	7.20	8.80
.06	2.46	.54	.66	.90	36.90	8.10	9.90
.07	2.87	.63	.77	1.00	41.00	9.00	11.00
.08	3.28	.72	.88	2.00	82.00	18.00	22.00
.09	3.69	.81	.99	3.00	123.00	27.00	33.00
.10	4.10	.90	1.10	4.00	164.00	36.00	44.00
.15	6.15	1.35	1.65	5.00	205.00	45.00	55.00
.20	8.20	1.80	2.20	10.00	410.00	90.00	110.00
.25	10.25	2.25	2.75				

50 – 1

STAKE £.p	WIN £.p	⅕ ODDS £.p	¼ ODDS £.p	STAKE £.p	WIN £.p	⅕ ODDS £.p	¼ ODDS £.p
.01	.51	.11	.13½	.30	15.30	3.30	4.05
.02	1.02	.22	.27	.40	20.40	4.40	5.40
.02½	1.27½	.27½	.33½	.50	25.50	5.50	6.75
.03	1.53	.33	.40½	.60	30.60	6.60	8.10
.04	2.04	.44	.54	.70	35.70	7.70	9.45
.05	2.55	.55	.67½	.80	40.80	8.80	10.80
.06	3.06	.66	.81	.90	45.90	9.90	12.15
.07	3.57	.77	.94½	1.00	51.00	11.00	13.50
.08	4.08	.88	1.08	2.00	102.00	22.00	27.00
.09	4.59	.99	1.21½	3.00	153.00	33.00	40.50
.10	5.10	1.10	1.35	4.00	204.00	44.00	54.00
.15	7.65	1.65	2.02½	5.00	255.00	55.00	67.50
.20	10.20	2.20	2.70	10.00	510.00	110.00	135.00
.25	12.75	2.75	3.37½				

66 – 1

STAKE £.p	WIN £.p	⅕ ODDS £.p	¼ ODDS £.p	STAKE £.p	WIN £.p	⅕ ODDS £.p	¼ ODDS £.p
.01	.67	.14	.17½	.30	20.10	4.26	5.25
.02	1.34	.28½	.35	.40	26.80	5.68	7.00
.02½	1.67½	.35½	.43½	.50	33.50	7.10	8.75
.03	2.01	.42½	.52½	.60	40.20	8.52	10.50
.04	2.68	.57	.70	.70	46.90	9.94	12.25
.05	3.35	.71	.87½	.80	53.60	11.36	14.00
.06	4.02	.85	1.05	.90	60.30	12.78	15.75
.07	4.69	.99½	1.22½	1.00	67.00	14.20	17.50
.08	5.36	1.13½	1.40	2.00	134.00	28.40	35.00
.09	6.03	1.28	1.57½	3.00	201.00	42.60	52.50
.10	6.70	1.42	1.75	4.00	268.00	56.80	70.00
.15	10.05	2.13	2.62½	5.00	335.00	71.00	87.50
.20	13.40	2.84	3.50	10.00	670.00	142.00	175.00
.25	16.75	3.55	4.37½				

CHAPTER TEN

The Tote

'There is a glamour, there is a charm about the Turf, quite apart from the sordid aspects of gain or loss.'

(*The Earl of Durham*)

In 1919 the Jockey Club appointed a committee to enquire into the future of racing in Britain, and it was the Chairman of this Committee, Lord Hamilton of Dalzell – described by a contemporary as 'the ablest Steward of the Jockey Club' – who was responsible for the instigation of one of the most important innovations in the history of racing – the setting-up of the Totalisator.

It was Lord Hamilton's contention that betting should contribute to racing and that at least some of the enormous profits being made out of racing through the medium of betting should be ploughed back into the sport. He was the prime mover in the Jockey Club's decision to advocate the introduction of the Totalisator on racecourses.

In 1926, Mr Winston Churchill, then Chancellor of the Exchequer, introduced his ill-fated betting duty – ill-fated because it was based on bookmakers' profits rather than turnover. Following its introduction, bookmakers' profits slumped so alarmingly that eventually the tax cost more to collect than it brought in. (Today, both tax and levy are based on turnover). However, Mr Churchill's tax did one good thing, in that it officially recognised the existence of betting and provided Lord Hamilton with the opportunity of putting his plans into effect.

A joint meeting of the Jockey Club and the National Hunt Committee reported in favour of betting being made to contribute to the maintenance of racing. As a result of this, an approach was made to the Chancellor, who promised that facilities would be given to a Private Member's Bill legalising the Tote, providing that the Bill obtained a second reading. The Bill was subsequently introduced by Sir Ralph Glynn. After a very stormy passage through the House of Commons, with opposition coming from the anti-gambling factions as well as the bookmakers' lobby, the Bill was eventually passed and became law in August 1928.

From the very beginning, the Government's attitude towards the Tote was based on the same sort of double-think which today insists that there should be 'health warnings' printed on cigarette packets (the Government meanwhile collecting millions of pounds in tobacco tax). The original Bill, as presented to Parliament, would have left control of the Tote in the hands of the Jockey Club. However, the final version of the Bill, as passed by Parliament, called for the setting-up of a somewhat cumbersome organisation, known as the Racecourse Betting Control Board, which was responsible to Parliament.

The Board was made up as follows:

A Chairman and one member appointed by the Home Secretary;
Three members from the Jockey Club;
Two members from the National Hunt Committee;
One member appointed by the Chancellor of the Exchequer;
One member appointed by the Secretary for Scotland;
One member appointed by the Minister of Agriculture;
One member appointed by the Racecourse Association and
One member appointed by Tattersalls' Committee.

It has been said that a camel is a horse designed by a Committee. Given the above set-up, the Tote was well on the way to becoming a dromedary. Also, and much more important, Parliament, having given its consent to the setting-up of the Tote, had no intention of giving any financial support to the enterprise. It was decided that, although the Tote would have to borrow in order to commence its operations, all profits should be placed into a fund. After taxes and expenses had been met (the Government had no objection to taking money through the medium of gambling) and contributions had been made to a variety of charitable organisations – these to be decided upon by the Board – the remainder of the funds might then be distributed each year for the benefit of breeding and the sport of racing. The Tote, not unreasonably, claimed that since it was required to disburse most, if not all, of its profit, it should be treated as a charity and be exempt from profits tax. This claim failed on an appeal to the House of Lords.

The first Tote offices made their appearance on the racecourse on July

2nd, 1929, at Newmarket and Carlisle. At that time they operated in marquees. As there was still a certain amount of race gang activity going on, special look-outs had to be posted to prevent the guy-ropes from being cut or the canvas being slit. However, on the very first day at Newmarket, some bright spark cut the Tote's telephone wires.

Since its inception, the Tote has had a somewhat chequered career. Indeed, that it has managed to survive at all is quite remarkable as it has always been hampered by being unable to compete with the bookmakers on equal terms and has also been increasingly beset by financial difficulties. Mr Pat Reekie, the Tote Public Relations Officer, recently pointed out in a magazine article: 'In 1961 the Horserace Betting Levy Board was set up to raise money for racing. It took over the distributive functions of the Tote and immediately became entitled to the £626,440 the Tote had at the time in its profits kitty. That £626,440 was the whole of the Levy Board's income for the first six months of its existence. In the following twelve months the Tote paid to the Levy Board, as its contribution to the first annual levy, £927,993. For the same twelve months the levy contribution from the whole of the bookmaking profession, who do 95 per cent of the total business of betting on horseracing, amounted to only £892,617.'

The bookmakers' levy, at that stage, was based on profit – the Tote's on turnover. Today, both levy and betting duty for bookmakers and the Tote are based on turnover, and the bookmakers are obliged to make a much more realistic contribution to the Levy Board.

It was in 1961 also that betting shops became legal, and this innovation greatly affected the Tote's credit betting market (half the Tote's turnover comes from its credit betting offices). In 1966 betting duty was imposed, causing the Tote to increase its rates of deduction to provide for tax. The larger bookmaking concerns absorbed the tax (then $2\frac{1}{2}$ per cent on turnover) on credit betting while, at the same time, charging tax in the betting shops and reducing their place betting terms. At that time, the Tote was operating fifty betting shops, but these could only offer bets at Tote prices, and then only on horses racing in Great Britain. The bookmakers, on the other hand, were entitled to offer a much more comprehensive service, with bets at starting prices, at board prices, and even at Tote returns (although for this they did have to pay an authorisation fee).

The bookmakers also offered a much wider range of events, including Irish racing, football, golf, greyhound racing, and even political elections and beauty contests. In 1967/68, when all racing was temporarily abandoned, because of a foot-and-mouth disease epidemic, the Tote betting shops were forced to close down, while the bookmakers were still able to operate their shops, by virtue of their much wider

17. The Jockey Club or Newmarket Meeting, 1790, by Thomas Rowlandson.

18. The Jockey Club Rooms in Newmarket High Street. Beneath the archway is the original Coffee House.

19. A Horse Auction at Tattersalls', Hyde Park Corner, 1800, by Thomas Rowlandson.

20. The Houghton Yearling Sales at Newmarket in 1973.

21. John White and Son –
on-course bookmaker.

22. The interior of a
betting shop.

23. A smiling Lester Piggott presents the Apprentice Trophy. On the right is Anthony Fairbairn of the Racegoers' Club and Racing Information Bureau.

24. H.M. the Queen, with Lord Porchester, at Royal Ascot.

range of betting facilities. From 1966 racecourse attendances began to decline and the Tote's on-course turnover was affected. Happily, during the past few years, there are signs that this decline has ceased, although the present economic recession is causing very serious problems for the racing industry generally.

In 1969 the Rateable Value Tax was introduced and the Tote was in serious financial difficulty. The Rateable Value Tax, which only lasted for one year, took the form of a special tax of three times the rateable value of premises used for off-course betting. This tax almost completely ruined the Tote's betting shop business as the Tote, with its limitations of betting, was required to pay the same amount of tax as the bookmakers, whilst only enjoying a fraction of the off-course betting turnover. In order to ensure itself an income for the future, the Tote hived off its betting shops into a separate organisation run by City Tote Offices Ltd. This organisation operated 100 betting shops, offering a full bookmaker service, and the Tote received a special authorisation fee based on turnover.

By the 1970s it had become obvious that if the Tote were to survive at all it had to be able to compete on equal terms with the bookmakers. This came about in 1972, when the Horserace Totalisator and Levy Boards Act extended the Tote's power to include betting on all sporting events. The Tote can now offer both Tote returns and starting price bets (including board prices and ante-post). It can also offer betting on horseracing anywhere in the world, as well as on greyhound racing, football, boxing and other events. There is no doubt that the Tote is going to take full advantage of its new-found freedom.

To date, the Tote is operating thirty-five credit offices all over the country, taking bets at Tote Odds and S.P., and offering a comprehensive credit betting service. It is planned to increase the number of credit offices as soon as possible. The Tote has also taken over the 100 betting shops formerly run by City Tote Offices Ltd, and is now operating 116 betting shops, all of which offer a full bookmaker service.

Another innovation, and a most useful one, as far as the small stakes punter is concerned, has been the setting-up of some nineteen course S.P. Tote cash betting offices at seventeen courses, where every type of bet may be made, both on the actual course where racing is taking place and at away meetings on other courses.

The Tote's new image and, in particular, the new cash offices, must come as a relief to many of the racegoing public for, although the Tote had previously had offices on every racecourse in the country, the general effect has been institutional, to say the least. The standard Tote office is invariably painted in drab colours and the pokey little betting windows are neither inviting nor efficient. One has to queue up in order to place a bet, and queue up again to collect any winnings – the whole process being vaguely reminiscent of a war-time British restaurant. The new offices, with large open windows, are a great improvement and it is to be hoped that the existing Tote buildings will be up-dated and brought into line with the new cash offices.

To provide an adequate service on racecourses spread all over the country (with some 900 race meetings taking place each year) is no mean feat. The Tote has, therefore, organised forty-five teams of part-time workers centered upon main towns, and these workers are called upon, as and when required. The Tote's busiest day is Easter Monday, when Tote services are in operation at every one of the day's sixteen or so race meetings, as well as at a number of point-to-point meetings. The total staff employed on that day is in the region of 2,700, backed up by another 2,000 off the course, and in cash and credit offices throughout the country – a tremendous organisational feat, to say the least.

At long last the Tote's old institutional image is beginning to disappear. Modern marketing methods are being brought into use, improved technical facilities are being investigated, and modern publicity techniques are being brought into play. There is no doubt that these new methods are beginning to pay off. In 1974/75, for example, the Tote's betting turnover was over £44 million; it is estimated at £48 million for 1975/76.

When Lord Hamilton of Dalzell and his colleagues pressed for the introduction of the Tote, they foresaw inestimable benefits for the racing industry. Legislation strangled their brainchild and, alas, these benefits were never to be wholly realised. Let us hope that the 1972 Act, by setting the Tote free to compete with the bookmakers on equal terms, will now enable the Tote to be the medium through which the millions of punters and racegoers who derive enjoyment from racing will be able to support, to a much greater degree, the sport which has given them so much entertainment for so little return.

The Tote today offers the punter a fully comprehensive betting service and, in so doing, provides a service to racing. From 1928 until 1972 the Tote was effectively hamstrung as it was unable to compete with the bookmakers. Now that it is able to do so, the bookmakers may find that they have a real fight on their hands.

BETTING WITH THE TOTE

On every racecourse in Britain there are Tote buildings in each enclosure where you may make your bets.

Tote betting is pool betting. The money invested goes into a pool and after making a deduction for betting duty and operating expenses, the whole pool is shared among the winners.

The minimum stake for win, place and forecast bets is 30p. Dividends in these pools are declared to 10p. This means that winners in these pools get back three times the declared dividends if they bet 30p, five times if they bet 50p, and ten times the declared dividend if their winning stake was £1, and so on.

Betting tax has already been deducted, so winnings are paid in full, with no further deductions.

Tote buildings on most courses are divided into four sections – some windows for 30p bets, some for 50p bets, some for £1 bets and others for £5 – all are marked accordingly. There are signs, however, that in the near future the 30p windows will disappear altogether.

WIN AND PLACE

When you approach the window give the racecard number of the horse you wish to back and state win, or place, or win and place, as the case may be.

The place pool is separate from the win pool, and on the Tote you may back a horse for a place only. Place pools operate on every race where there are six or more runners. If there are six or seven runners your place bet wins if your horse finishes first or second. If there are eight runners or more your place bet wins if your horse finishes first, second or third. You can even get fourth place if there are sixteen runners or more and the race is a handicap race, as shown on the racecard in the title of the race.

FORECAST BETTING

In fields of up to and including ten runners you may have a forecast bet, selecting the first two horses to finish. In races where there are three to six runners your two selections must finish in the order in which you nominate them. This is known as a straight forecast. In fields of seven, eight, nine or ten runners (dual forecast) you win if the two horses you select finish first and second in either order.

DAILY DOUBLE

For the Tote Daily Double you are required to select the winners of two separate races – the third and fifth races on the card. The stake is 50p. Before the third race go to the window marked 'Daily Double' and take a ticket on the horse you select for that race. If it wins return to the Daily Double window before the fifth race and exchange your winning ticket for one bearing the number of your selection for the fifth race.

DAILY TREBLE

The Tote Daily Treble operates in much the same way as the Daily Double, but here you are required to select the winners of three races – the second, fourth and sixth races on the card. The unit stake is 25p. Exchange any ticket you have on the winner of the second race (the first leg), for a ticket on the fourth race (second leg) and any winning ticket(s) you still have after that race for a ticket on the sixth race (third leg).

It happens quite often in the course of a season that no punter manages to select all three winners consecutively, and the pool is paid out on the first two legs (or even first leg) only. So do not throw away any ticket on the second or third legs until after the result of the pool has been announced. The same remarks apply to a ticket exchanged for a winner on the first leg in the Daily Double.

THE JACKPOT

A Jackpot pool is run at selected meetings throughout the year. The stake is 25p, and you are required to select the winners of each of the first six races at the Jackpot meeting.

There are special windows for the sale of Jackpot tickets. When you have decided on the amount of your investment, go to the Jackpot window and purchase a Jackpot entry form – it can be for a single bet, or a combination of bets – and fill in the numbers of the horses you select. Use the three-figure numbers printed in the racecard.

Post your Jackpot entry form in any of the special Jackpot boxes you will find on the course and retain your copy. You must post your tickets before the time of the first race. Keep your copy until a dividend has been announced.

On days when the Jackpot is not won outright, 20 per cent of that day's pool is reserved for payment of the Consolation Dividend to those clients who have nominated, in consecutive racecard order commencing with the first Jackpot race, the *highest* number of winners with a minimum of four.

If the Jackpot pool is not won outright and no Consolation Dividend is paid, the gross pool, including the Consolation Dividend reserve, will be carried forward and added to the gross pool for the next Jackpot day.

CREDIT BETTING

The Tote also operates a credit betting service, so that you may bet by telephone or on credit whilst on the course. There are some thirty-five Tote Credit Offices in Great Britain, some of which also offer bets at starting price as well as Tote returns. Details may be obtained from Tote Credit Information, 8–12, New Bridge Street, London, E.C.4.

ON-COURSE BETTING OFFICES

Since April 7th, 1973 the Tote has operated a number of cash betting offices on certain racecourses (there are now nineteen such offices in operation) where racegoers may bet exactly as they would do in an off-course betting shop. Bets are taken for both Tote and Starting Price, and, in addition to win bets, place and each-way bets, doubles, trebles, accumulators, forecasts, etc., are all accepted.

This is an extremely useful innovation, especially for the punter who wishes to confine himself or herself to small stakes. It is not necessary to bet in large sums in order to enjoy a day's racing, but certain on-course bookmakers have been known to refuse bets of less than one pound. The taking of so many small bets must involve the Tote in a great deal of extra work, but the cash betting offices are very much a service. It is hoped that this service will eventually be extended to every racecourse in the country.

BRANCH OFFICE TELEPHONE NUMBERS

Branch	Tel. No.	Branch	Tel. No.
*Aldershot	22581	Luton	26551
*Birmingham	236-3311	*Maidstone	61141
*Blackburn	49223	*Manchester	834-3404
*Bournemouth	25601	Middlesbrough	45651
Bradford	33377	*Newcastle	29051
*Brighton	29721	Newmarket	4801
*Bristol	290531	*Northampton	30531
*Canterbury	66194	*Norwich	29891
*Cardiff	42561	*Nottingham	56262
Cheltenham	55232	Oxford	49951
*Coventry	27691	*Plymouth	66231
Doncaster	66821	Portsmouth	25251
Exeter	34444	*Reading	55713
*Glasgow	332-2966	Salisbury	27261
Grimsby	55035	*Sheffield	78691
*Hull	23751	Southampton	24911
*Ipswich	57291	*Stoke-on-Trent	86391
*Leeds	35311	*Swansea	51591
*Leicester	23861	*Taunton	82141
*Lincoln	23481	*Torquay	25171
*Liverpool	236-9981	*Worcester	23484
*London	(01)353-7411	*York	58751

(Offices marked * accept bets at both Tote Returns *and* Starting Price)

CHAPTER ELEVEN

The Racegoers' Club

'I would go to the Turf to get friends.'

(*Harriet, Lady Ashburton*)

I n May 1968 a new and enterprising organisation appeared on the British racing scene. This was the Racegoers' Club, a non-profit-making concern, inaugurated by the Racing Information Bureau and intended, in the words of the Club's Chairman, Anthony Fairbairn, 'to encourage more people to go racing more often'. The idea of a nationwide club, designed to give support to all aspects of British racing, proved immediately attractive to those many thousands of racegoers who wished to participate more actively in their favourite sport, and applications for membership poured into the Club's headquarters in Great Marlborough Street, London W.1. Within a year the Club's membership stood at between six and seven thousand.

Under the leadership of an energetic and imaginative Committee, and welcomed by the Turf authorities, the Racegoers' Club developed quickly and today, with a membership of around eight thousand, the Club is an established part of British racing.

Initially, Club membership cost £1.00 a year, but at the beginning of 1972 this was raised to £2.00 a year and to £3.50 in 1977 in order to meet increased costs. For this small outlay members receive extremely good value for money and the benefits, activities and events arranged by the Club's organisers are many and varied. They include: regular Club news bulletins, a 'concession' scheme, whereby each year members receive a

book of vouchers which enables them, on certain specified 'concession days', to obtain considerable reductions in the prices of admission to Tattersalls' and, in some cases, to Members' enclosures at fifty-four of the sixty-one racecourses in Great Britain.

In addition to encouraging members to participate in racing, the Racegoers' Club also offers them the opportunity and encourages them to learn more about the sport. One of the most popular activities organised by the Club is that of small group visits to racing training stables, designed to give members an insight into the training and preparation of horses for racing. Nowadays these visits are invariably over-subscribed and preference is given to members who have not previously taken part in such a visit. The fact that such a scheme could be successfully implemented says much for the Club's organisation and public relations, not to mention its members' obvious keen interest in racing. Most leading trainers are extremely busy people and must have viewed the prospect of regular visits by groups of 'enthusiasts' with some apprehension. However, whatever doubts may have existed on the part of the trainers, or, indeed of the Club's Committee, these were quickly dispelled by the success of the very first stable visit to Staff Ingham's stables at Epsom in August 1968. The visit not only over-ran its scheduled time by several hours, but ended with a group of very happy Club members being entertained by Staff Ingham to drinks on the lawn.

Since then stable visits have become a regular feature of the Club's programme; to date over four thousand Racegoers' Club members have not only enjoyed the privilege of seeing many of their favourite racehorses 'at home', but they have also taken the opportunity of increasing their knowledge of racing by being able to question and discuss various aspects of the sport with leading trainers and their staff.

The cost of such visits is nominal, averaging 75 pence per member, and visits are usually arranged to coincide with a nearby race meeting, so that members can make a day of it.

In addition to stable visits, the Club also makes regular visits to the National Stud and the Jockey Club Rooms at Newmarket. For the more ambitious and intrepid racegoer, the Club arranges charter flights to some of the more important overseas race meetings, in order to see races of the calibre of the Washington D.C. International or the Prix de l'Arc de Triomphe. These charter trips which, incidentally, involve a tremendous amount of pre-planning, have become an important feature in the Club's annual programme and are always very well supported. Parties of Club members have already visited the racecourses at Longchamps, Chantilly, Auteuil, Laurel, Camden, Ovrevoll and the Curragh. (Since 1968 the Club has organised twenty-five overseas visits).

In addition to being able to watch important races overseas and, incidentally, to cheer on any British entries, Club members also have the advantage of being conducted around racing stables in other countries and of being able to meet, and take part in discussions with, trainers and racing personalities from these countries. There is no doubt that these Club trips abroad do much to promote friendship and interest between British and overseas racegoers. The Racegoers' Club is especially interested in forming ties with overseas racing clubs. To this effect, it is planning to stage an international weekend at the Ascot July meeting in 1977. Racing enthusiasts are expected from America, Italy, Scandinavia and Germany.

Another innovation introduced by the Racegoers' Club as part of its policy to educate (in the best sense of the word) its members is the 'Race In'. Held annually, this takes the form of an eight-hour event, devoted to discussions, film shows, lectures and talks, culminating in a prolonged 'question and answers' session, at which a panel of racing experts answer questions connected with their particular branch of racing. Past panellists have included Major-General Sir Randle Feilden (a former Senior Steward of the Jockey Club), trainer Ian Balding, Brigadier Sam Waller of the Racecourse Association, Lord Willoughby de Broke, and Brough Scott, ex-National Hunt jockey and now a well-known television racing commentator.

Members of the Racegoers' Club who wish to learn more about the intricacies of racehorse ownership are encouraged to do so in two ways: by associating themselves with the Club's general ownership, or by joining an owning syndicate. Since it was first formed, the Club has owned seven horses – Durability, Concession Day, Hardessence, Special Event, Violinist, Lough Neagh and Madman. The Racegoers' Club was the first club to be permitted by the Jockey Club to run horses in its own name and first did so in May 1969, when Durability ran in a hurdle race at Taunton. Since then Racegoers' Club horses have run regularly in the Club's colours (silver with black-striped sleeves and gold cap) – with varying degrees of success.

The idea of syndicating racehorses, both Flat and National Hunt, within the Club was introduced late in 1971 and almost immediately the Club Secretary was inundated with requests for information by members who were interested in joint ownership. The Club bought three yearlings at the Autumn sales and these were offered in ten shares, each averaging £150, plus a further £100 per share to cover the first season's expenses. These horses were later named Me Tarzan, Sally Viking and Opening Gambit, and they were trained by Tommy Gosling, Sam Hall and Doug Marks, respectively.

Several more syndicates have been formed within the Club and there is every indication that the demand for further syndicated shares amongst members will continue. Beholden, Grist Mill, Park Paddocks, Sailing Fair and Voucher Book have all been successful.

In addition to those activities already mentioned, the Club has also successfully sponsored a number of races, including an Apprentice Jockeys' Championship. This consisted of a series of races, run over a mile and a quarter, for three-year old horses. A points system was operated throughout the series and a final (open only to apprentice jockeys who had ridden in one or more of the qualifying races) was run at Newmarket on Cambridgeshire day.

A 'Racecourse of the Year' competition has been instituted, based upon letters and votes of Club members. The writer of the most interesting letter receives a year's membership to the winning racecourse.

At the suggestion of a number of its members, the Club launched and administered the Arkle Memorial Fund which resulted in a statue of Arkle (sculpted by Miss Doris Lindner) being erected at Cheltenham Racecourse, to commemorate this most popular of all modern steeplechasers.

The Club has also sponsored closed-circuit television in the bars and restaurants of the Cheltenham Racecourse.

Many of the Club's activities are run in conjunction with the Jockeys' Association and several jockeys have given talks to members and shown them over racecourses such as the Aintree Grand National course. (The proceeds from these joint ventures, incidentally, go to the Injured Jockeys' Fund).

There is no doubt that the Racegoers' Club is now an established fact in the British racing world. It has been successfully launched by people with a flair for organisation and publicity and, more important perhaps, by people whose love of racing has enabled them to establish strong ties with those most concerned with racing in Britain. The Racegoers' Club has become much more than a mere fan club; rather it has become a part of the sport which it encourages and supports so enthusiastically.

A TYPICAL RACEGOERS' CLUB EVENTS SHEET

THE RACEGOERS CLUB

Special Events – April–June 1976

DATE	EVENT	DETAILS
Thursday–Saturday April 1–3	Special arrangements for the Ladbroke Grand National Meeting	For details see Newsletter and booking form
Saturday April 3	Visit to Ken Oliver's stable at Hassendean Bank, Hawick, Roxburghshire. (Concession day at Kelso)	Time: 10.00 Cost: 75p Booking: March 22–29
Saturday April 10	Visit to Gavin Hunter's stable at Kennet House, East Ilsley, Berks. (Concession day at Newbury)	Time: 10.00 Cost: 75p Booking: March 29 – April 5
Saturday April 24	Visit to Neil Adam's stable at Racecourse Farm, Bescaby, Melton Mowbray, Leics. (Racing at Leicester)	Time: 09.30 Cost: 75p Booking: April 12–19
	Visit to Steve Nesbitt's stable at Newby Hall Stables, Ripon, Yorks. (Concession day at Thirsk)	Time: 10.00 Cost: 75p Booking: April 12–19
Saturday May 8	Visit to Nigel Angus' stable at Cree Lodge, Craigie Road, Ayr. (Racing at Ayr)	Time: 10.15 Cost: 75p Booking: April 26–May 3

DATE	EVENT	DETAILS
Saturday May 15	Visit to Dick Hern's stable at West Ilsley Stables, West Ilsley, Berks. (Racing at Newbury)	Time: 10.00 Cost: 75p Booking: May 3–10
Wednesday May 19	Racegoers Club Special Day at Goodwood.	For details see Newsletter and booking form.
Friday– Monday May 21–24	Racegoers Club visit to Baden-Baden	For details see Newsletter and booking form.
Saturday May 22	Visit to Harry Wragg's stable at Abington Place, Bury Road, Newmarket. (Concession day at Newmarket)	Time: 10.00 Cost: 75p Booking: May 10–17
Tuesday June 1	'Racehorse of the Year' Dinner at the Savoy Hotel, London.	For details see Newsletter and booking form.
Sunday June 20	Visit to Guy Harwood's stable at Coombelands Racing Stables, Pulborough, Sussex.	Time: 11.00 Cost: 75p Booking: June 7–14

THE RACEGOERS' CLUB

1976

Patrons
The Viscount Leverhulme, T.D.
J. M. Tilling, Esq.
The Marquess of Abergavenny, O.B.E.
T. F. Blackwell, Esq.
Major-General Sir Randle Feilden, K.C.V.O., C.B., C.B.E.
S. H. Hyde, Esq., J.P.
Lord Willoughby de Broke, M.C.
Lt.-Col. Sir Martin Gilliat, K.C.V.O., M.B.E., D.L.
Captain H. M. Gosling
Gay Kindersley, Esq.
The Earl of March

THE RACEGOERS' CLUB

1976

Committee

A. M. Fairbairn, Esq. (*Chairman*)
(Director, The Racing Information Bureau)

A. C. Newton, Esq.
(Managing Director, Newcastle)

Air Cmdr. W. T. Brooks
(Managing Director, United Racecourses Ltd.)

O. W. Fletcher, Esq.
(Editor, *The Sporting Life*)

Jimmy Hill, Esq.

Miss Louise Gold (Secretary)

G. T. Webster, Esq.

Phil Bull, Esq.

CHAPTER TWELVE

The Sporting Life

'The Sporting Life of England,
The Charter of the Isle.'

(Old song)

In 1859 Charles Darwin published his *Origin of Species*, Mr Charles Dickens was editor of a new magazine called *All the Year Round* and a Mr Charles Maddick introduced *Bell's Life and Sporting News*. Just how many of today's racing enthusiasts have actually read *The Origin of Species* is a matter of some doubt . . . how many have even heard of *All the Year Round* is even more doubtful. But one thing is certain – every day some 91,000 people read and study avidly *The Sporting Life*, which is the direct successor of Charles Maddick's 1859 publication.

It seems a far cry from the Downs at Epsom or the green hills of Cheltenham to Fetter Lane in the City of London, but here every day a team of racing and statistical experts (the *Life* has an editorial staff of seventy-two), under the guidance of the Editor, Mr O. W. Fletcher, produces the newspaper which has become the racing man's 'bible'. Runners and riders, up-to-date form, possible starting prices, racing results, racing commentaries, informed articles on racing topics, a punters' advisory service – are all to be found in *The Sporting Life*, six days a week, fifty-two weeks a year.

In 1959, in order to celebrate its one hundredth anniversary, a special edition of *The Sporting Life* was produced, and in addition to carrying a special message of congratulation from Her Majesty Queen Elizabeth II, this edition also contained many fascinating extracts taken from earlier editions of the paper and *Bell's Life*, some of which throw an interesting light on the sporting interests and attitudes of our racing forebears. The advertisements, in particular, are fascinating:

> March 24th, 1859. Wanted a person who would engage to extirpate rats off a sugar plantation in the West Indian Islands. Testimonials required.

> March 31st, 1860. Spanish Fly is the acting ingredient in Alex Ross's Cantharides Oil which produces whiskers and thickens hair.

One advertisement provides food for thought in our modern society when racing is available to all:

> August 8th, 1818. Racing for the Workers on Saturday afternoons. Petition forms for signatures can be obtained free.

In addition to a variety of often outlandish advertisements, the early editions of *The Sporting Life* carried many interesting letters from its correspondents:

> January 22nd, 1858. Sir, The fact is that nowadays, owners, trainers, and parties immediately connected with the horses conspire to deceive the public.

It would seem that, whatever the age, hell hath no fury like an irate punter, or, indeed, an angry tipster:

> Sir, I protest against your correspondent's assertion that all tipsters are vermin, pickpockets, etc. . .

And, finally, just to prove that those punters who will bet on anything have always been with us:

> Only a week ago I called attention to a bottle-washing competition, a mussel-opening match, and a flying haircutting tourney. Haddock splitting has gone out of season. . .

Today, the letters and advertisements in *The Sporting Life* tend to be of a much more serious nature, although perhaps in a hundred years' time our ancestors will find them just as quaint as we do those of earlier times. Modern advertisements tend to deal with bookmakers' staff requirements, stable staff and horse sales or syndication. The letters, on the whole, tend to be rather more technical and somewhat dull to the general reader but these are, after all, incidental and nobody buys a newspaper solely for its letters or advertisements. What they do buy *The Sporting Life* for are the 'form' pages, which appear daily, and it is the 'form' which undoubtedly sells the *Life*. What is form?

Julian Simcocks, Editor of *Ruff's Guide to the Turf* has defined it in a *Sporting Life* handbook as, 'All the data concerning the past racing performances of a horse. The courses and distance over which it ran, types of races, the jockeys, weights carried, finishing positions, condition of the turf on which it galloped (known as the state of the going), number of runners in each race, the winner's time, the distance by which it was beaten (if in the first six to finish), and brief comments by race readers on its actual performances.' At first sight this seems a lot of information to take in, but as Mr Simcocks points out, 'At least 90 per cent of the winning horses in Britain each year achieve success because they have the right form background'. So it is all very well for the occasional punter who has a mild flutter on the Derby or the National to pick a winner with a pin or because his girl friend's name is Gladys, but for those who wish to take a serious interest in backing horses a study of form is essential.

Every day *The Sporting Life* publishes lists of runners, riders and possible starting prices for all the race meetings taking place that day. For example:—

Alfriston Stakes, run at Brighton, August 7th 1973

2.00 – ALFRISTON STAKES, six furlongs, £600 added to stakes, for two-year-old maiden fillies which, before July 8, have not been placed second or third in any race; £1 to enter, £3 ex. if dec to run; 2nd £120, 3rd £60; weights: 8 st 11 lb each (175 cent. ft dec for 150) – Closed July 11. Value to the winner £666; 2nd £116, 3rd £56.

103	0	AUTUMN BALLAD (Col Sir D. Clague) C. Benstead	8–11 . . .W. Williamson	3
104		CALL ME MADAM (Miss I. Ritchie) P. Haslam	8–11 . . . J. Hayward	4
105	000	CHARLMORIN (K. Maharaj) Ryan Price	8–11 . . . A. Murray	1
109	0	INDIAN TIGRESS (H. Joel) N. Murless	8–11 . . . G. Lewis	8
110	0	MINOR CHORD (R. Bulfield) D. Whelan	8–11 . . .E. Eldin	7
114		RIVOLI BAR (Lady T. Agnew) H. Smyth	8–11 . . . P. Proc (7)	6
119	0	SELLA BELLA (D. Prenn) J. Winter	8–11 . . . B. Taylor	5
121	0032	SOUTHWARK STAR (Mrs J. Bamberg) G. Peter-Hoblyn	8–11 . . . P. Cook	2

WITHDRAWN OVERNIGHT: Nos. 1, 2, 6, 7, 8, 11, 12, 13, 15, 16, 17, 18, 20, 22, 23, 24, 25. Eight Runners. DUAL FORECAST

FORECAST: 2 Southwark Star, 5–2 Indian Tigress, 7–2 Minor Chord, 11–2 Charlmorin, 7 Sella Bella, 8 Autumn Ballad, 16 others

Last year. – IBIS, 8–11, B. Taylor, 9/4 fav (J. Winter). 12 ran.

In addition to the above information, *The Sporting Life* also gives the form for every horse in the race.

HOW TO READ THE FORM

2.0 – ALFRISTON STAKES (2-y-o), 6f (£666).

6 AUTUMN BALLAD (Mar 20) (8–00), b f, Tudor Melody-Soft Fall, by Chamossaire.

> July 26, Kempton, 5f (2-y-o) (stalls), good, £731:
> 1 Royal Track (0-0); 2 Santa's Sister (8–10); 3 Dame Fortune (8–10); 6 Autumn Ballad (8–6, P. Tulk, 4), progress last furlong and a half, going on at finish (33 to 1). 16 ran. 2L, 2L, 2L, ¾L, 1m 1.99s (a 2.59s).

CALL ME MADAM (Apr 21) (8–11), b f, First Base-Smock Alley, by Grandmaster.

655 CHARLMORIN (Apr 9) (8–11), ch f, Charlottown–Miss Maverick, by Vilmorin.

> July 12, Brighton, 7f (2-y-o) (stalls), good to firm, £836:
> 1 Starboard Belle (8–13); 2 Manipulation (8–13); 3 Ma Reine (8–8); 5 Charlmorin (8–8, A. Murray, 1), every chance two out, never nearer (15 to 2 from 8 to 1). 13 ran. ¾L, 1½L, 1L, ¾L, 1L. 1m 25.74s (a 3.34s).
> May 30, Brighton, 5f (stalls), good, £536:
> 1 Alinda (8–8); 2 Atout (8–8); 3 Dinah Do (8–8); 5 Charlmorin (8–8, G. Kyle, 10), never nearer (10 to 1). 10 ran. ¾L, ½L, 3L, 5L, ½L. 1m 5.67s (a 4.27s).
> May 19, Kempton, 5f (stalls), good to firm, £673.
> 1 Streak of Honour (9–3); 2 Centime (8–8); 3 Generous Thought (8–1 7*) 6 Charlmorin (8–8, G. Kyle, 1), never nearer (20 to 1). 11 ran. ¾L, hd, 1½L, 4L, 1L. 60.90s (a 1.50s).

0 INDIAN TIGRESS (May 6), ch f, Charlottown-Indian Game, by Big Game.

> July 4, Newmarket, 6f (2–y–o), mdn (stalls), good, £690:
> 1 Polygamy (8–11); 2 Highclere (8–11); 3 Northern Gem (8–11); 0 Indian Tigress (8–11, G. Lewis, 18), (16 to 1, from 20 to 1). 28 ran, 3L, sht. hd., ¾L, 2.L, 2L. 1m 15.19s (a 1.79s).

0 MINOR CHORD (Feb 21), (8–11), b f, Major Portion-Ali Drake, by Dicta Drake.

> June 27, Salisbury, 5f (2–y–o), (stalls), good, £435:
> 1 Red Berry (8–11); 2 Dancing Girl (8–11); 3 Crucial Gift (8–11); 7 Minor Chord (8–11, B. Rouse, 18), (25 to 1). 22 ran. 5L, nk, ¾L, 2½L, 1L. 1m 3.8s (a 2.8s).

RIVOLI BAR (Mar 11), (8–11), b f, Darling Boy-Ritz Bar, by Royal Palm.
5 SELLA BELLA (Feb 10) (8–11), ch f, Ballyciptic-Selaginella, by Mossborough.

> June 27, Yarmouth, 6f (2–y–o) (stalls), good to firm, £414:
> 1 Caught In the Rye (9–4); 2 Floral (8–8); 3 Open Air (8–8); 5 Sella Bella (8–8, B. Taylor, 3), ran on well final two furlongs without being near enough to challenge (16 to 1 op 8 to 1), 16 ran. 2L, 1½L, 1½L, 6L, nk. 1m 11.6s (a 0.4s).

5032 SOUTHWARK STAR (March 7) (8–11), b f, Midsummer Night II–True Course II, by Sea Charger.

> July 19, Nottingham, 6f (2–y–o) mdn (stalls), soft, £276:
> 1 Dancing Girl (8–11); 2 Southwark Star (8–11, P. Cook, 7), headway final two furlongs, ran on, no chance with winner (7 to 2 from 3 to 1); 3 Calkin (8–11). 14 ran. 5L, ½L, 2½L, 2½L, 2.L. 1m 18.6s (a 7.6s).

> July 13, Newbury, 6f (2–y–o) (stalls), good, £1,465:
> 1 Red Berry (8–9); 2 Generous Thought (8–4); 3 Southwark Star (8–4, Ron Hutchinson, 11), progress inside last quarter mile, ran on final furlong (33 to 1). 11 ran. ¾L, 1½L, 1½L, 3L, ½L, 1m 17.41s (a 4.01s).

> June 23, Warwick, 5f (2–y–o) mdn (stalls), good to firm, £432:
> 1 Kissing (9–0); 2 Hally High (9–0); 3 Blessings (9–0); 8 Southwark Star (8–7, A. Bond, 7 *, 3) (20 to 1), 21 ran. 2L, ½L, 3L, 1½L, ¾L. 1m 1.6s (a 2.6s).

The figures before the horse's name indicate its placings on this season's outings, the most recent being on the right. Where a hyphen appears, form figures to the left of it are figures from last season. Where a diagonal stroke appears, form figures on the left are from previous seasons.

Figures in brackets after the name indicate the horse's age and weight in stones and pounds that it is set to carry. The weight only is given where a race is for horses all of the same age. For two-year-olds only, the foaling date is shown in parentheses immediately following the name.

The letters that come next indicate the horse's colour and sex (example: 'b c' = bay colt) and the names that follow are those of its sire, dam and grandsire. Next in black type is the horse's winning record – year, distance, state of the going and course. For horses aged below nine, the total win prize money is then given, with this season's winnings in parentheses, for all except two-year-olds. For the horse's most recent outings the nature of the information given is largely self evident.

The monetary figure is the value of the race to the winner. The letters 'bl' after the jockey's name indicate that the horse wore blinkers or a hood. A figure with an asterisk (e.g. 5 *) after the name indicates that the jockey was a claiming rider and the figure denotes how many pounds he claimed. In all cases the weight the horse is shown as having carried is the actual weight carried after deduction of any allowance, but including any overweight put up. The figure appearing after the jockey's name and immediately before the bracket indicates the horse's draw position. For all placed horses, penalties and overweight are indicated by 'ex' and 'ow'.

N.B. National Hunt form includes symbols, as follows:

> b. brought down;
> f. fell;
> r. refused;
> p. pulled up (and Flat racing)
> u. unseated rider (and Flat racing)
> s. slipped up (and Flat racing)

For those without either the time or the inclination to study form the *Life* also gives a list of selections as forecast by the leading daily newspapers, as well as selections by its own tipsters. Concerning the Alfriston Stakes, *The Sporting Life* 'Man On the Spot' wrote:

2.0 – Alfriston Stakes (2–y–o fillies) (6f).
The two most recent efforts of
    SOUTHWARK STAR
clearly show there is a race waiting for her. She was going about her work in good style nearing the finish when third to Red Berry at Newbury last month and again at Nottingham, where she chased home Dancing Girl.

Indian Tigress, a half-sister to several winners, including Oaks second Maina, finished out of the first ten in the 28-runner Newmarket maiden won by Polygamy last month.

The Murless filly was not given a hard race once it became clear she was not going well enough to win, but she was not discredited.

Indian Tigress, a daughter of Charlottown, will probably do better when tackling longer distances, but still looks the one my fancy has to fear.

The following day *The Sporting Life* gives not only the results and starting prices for each race, but also gives a close-up of the running of the race:

2.0 ALFRISTON STAKES of £666; 2nd £116, 3rd £56; two-year-old maiden fillies. Six furlongs.
SOUTHWARK STAR, b f, by Midsummer Night II–True Course II, by Sea
    Charger (Mrs J. Bamberg), 8–11 . . . P. Cook 1 (2)

AUTUMN BALLAD, b f by Tudor Melody–Soft Fall (Col Sir D. Clague), 8–11
. . . W. Williamson 2 (3)
CHARLMORIN, ch f by Charlottown – Miss Maverick (K. Maharaj), 8–11
. . . A. Murray 3 (1)
     Indian Tigress, 8–11 . . . G. Lewis 4 (8)
     Minor Chord, 8–11 . . . E. Eldin 5 (7)
     Sella Bella, 8–11 . . . B. Taylor 6 (5)
     Rivoli Bar, 8–4 (7 *) . . . P. Proc 7 (6)
     Call Me Madam, 8–11 . . . J. Hayward 8 (4)
   Winner bred by the Derisley Wood Stud Ltd., trained by G. Peter-
Hoblyn, at East Ilsley, Berks. (off 2.3).
Betting: Southwark Star and Indian Tigress each touched 7–2 from a
    point or so less, before ending together at 3–1, despite hefty
    support for Autumn Ballad from 5–1 to 7–2. Sella Bella was easy at
    4–1 and 5–1, and not much else was seen.
Sporting Life Official S.P.: 3 Indian Tigress, SOUTHWARK STAR, 7–2
Autumn Ballad, 5 Sella Bella, 12 Charlmorin, Minor Chord, 20 others.
TOTE: 37p; pl 14p, 13p, 21p. Dual Forecast: 67p.

CLOSE-UP

1. Southwark Star, soon well placed, led below distance, came clear.
2. Autumn Ballad, led for more than three furlongs, kept on same pace
   final furlong.
3. Charlmorin, always in touch, led approaching last quarter-mile until
   below distance, no extra.
4. Indian Tigress, soon in touch, no headway last two furlongs.
5. Minor Chord, well placed to half-way.
6. Sella Bella, prominent three furlongs.

Rivoli Bar and Call Me Madam, started slowly, always behind.

Distances: 5L, ¾L, ¾L, 5L, ¾L. Official time: 1m 15.86s (a 6.46s).

   In this case, it will be seen that the form worked out and that Southwark
Star, the form horse and one-time joint favourite of two, won the race.
Incidentally, the form horse does not always start favourite, and of course,
the form horse does not always win – how boring racing would be if it were
so predictable and how quickly the bookmakers would shut up shop. But
there is no doubt that, for those wishing to back horses over a long period
of time, a serious study of form is essential.
   The most difficult races to assess are handicaps. These are races where
each horse is judged to have an equal chance of winning by virtue of
weight allowances and adjustments. The Jockey Club has seven
handicappers and they assess all the entries for every handicap race by

allotting different weights to each horse according to its ability. At first sight, the importance of the weight carried by a particular horse might not seem to be of major importance, but most experienced backers bear in mind the general rule that one length equals three pounds.

Of course, weight alone is not the sole deciding factor, but it is important, and must be considered (as must form) against all the other considerations which affect the outcome of a race: i.e., distance, state of the going, jockey, trainer, state of the betting market, time, etc. The best advice for those wishing to bet on handicaps is 'Don't'. Indeed, one famous racing expert once expressed the opinion that the golden rule for backers of horses was never to bet on the result of a handicap.

For those who are prepared to disregard this advice, *The Sporting Life* offers assistance in the form of Mr Dick Whitford, an accomplished journalist and mathematician, who has been compiling his universal handicaps for over thirty years. Throughout the flat racing season *The Sporting Life* publishes daily up-to-date Whitford Ratings and these ratings can be very helpful indeed when attempting to assess the merits of various horses running in handicap races. They are, also, incidentally, published in book form each year and are well worth the money.

GREEN SEAL SERVICE

Finally, for those punters who find themselves in disagreement with bookmakers and others concerning the results of wagers, *The Sporting Life* has instituted a 'Green Seal Service'. Disgruntled or puzzled punters have only to cut out the green seal, which appears at the top of the front page of the *Life*, attach it to their letters of complaint or enquiry and they will receive expert opinion and advice from *The Sporting Life* staff. Every day *The Sporting Life* offices receive between thirty and forty such letters. The following are a few of the answers, taken at random, from *The Sporting Life* and they will give some indication of the type and range of queries dealt with:

LEGAL

J.A.B. (Aberdeen). – The bookmaker is correct. There is no legal compulsion for the shop to be kept open until 6.30.

TURF

Mrs E.R. (London, S.W.6.) – Please ask the bookmaker to write giving us his version of the matter. The Green Seal Service does not calculate bets. W.S. (Emsworth). – There is no reason why bets on the 3.15 at Ripon on August 16 should be void. Backers of the favourite would have won their bets if the horse had won the race.

'Red' (Darlington). – We cannot agree that the clerk was entitled to alter the time of the race, and in our opinion the duplicated selection should be deleted, reducing the bet to six doubles with the overstaked cash returned.

'Stanley' (Hull). – We agree with your ruling. As there was no 2.45 at York the bet on the favourite was void and should be treated as a non-runner in calculating the doubles.

E.R.F. (Rainham). – Please ask the bookmaker to write giving his version of the matter.

N.A. (Twickenham). – Unless the bookmaker can produce a set of rules current at the time you made your bet showing limits he is not entitled to apply any.

D.M.H. (Portsea). – We regret the nature of the dispute makes it one in which we cannot intervene.

G.P. and K.M. (Llanelli). – We agree with the bookmaker's decision.

H.W.M. (Chertsey). – The bookmaker's application of the limit is correct. An across-the-card limit applies to complete bets, not just to the races which actually come within the interval laid down.

W.S.O. (Romford). – There is no indication on the slip you sent as to who marked the odds. Unless they were added by or initialled by the bookmaker you are not entitled to them and the bet would normally be regarded as an SP bet.

A.R.H. (Maldon). – Without the receipt there is nothing you can do.

F.D. (Loughborough). – Obviously you have not read the bookmaker's rules, which state that forecasts are laid at Tote odds unless otherwise requested. You did not request chart or SP so the bet has been settled correctly at the dividend declared for a dual forecast.

G.R. (Neath). – Gardenia foaled a bay filly named Sheik's Delight by Gulf Pearl on Feb 7 1963. She slipped her foal by Falcon in 1974.

Readers wishing to take advantage of this 'Replies to Correspondents' service should address their letters to Green Seal Service, *The Sporting Life*, 9 New Fetter Lane, London, EC4A 1AR, and always enclose with their query a tear-off of the green seal appearing daily at the top of Page One of *The Sporting Life*.

Letters not accompanied by the green seal will not be answered and enclosures will not be returned unless a stamped addressed envelope is enclosed.

Whilst every care is taken, no legal responsibility can be accepted for the accuracy of answers.

There is no doubt that *The Sporting Life* is very much a part of the British racing scene. The *Life* is often advertised as 'the paper the professionals use', but for the non-professional and the newcomer to racing, it is every bit as useful and there is no better way to obtain an insight or an introduction to British racing than by a study of this most informative sporting daily paper.

CHAPTER 13

Racecourses in Great Britain

L ike most costs these days, racecourse admission prices are subject to fluctuation. On the advice of the Racing Information Bureau, therefore, racecourse admission charges have been excluded from the following details. As a general guide, however, it is possible on most courses to go racing for as little as 50 pence. Tattersalls' enclosure prices vary between £1.50 and £2.50, depending on the course and whether or not it is a special race meeting, and Members' enclosure prices vary from £2 to £4, again depending on the course and the class of meeting.

AINTREE (*Flat* * *and National Hunt meetings*)

Clerk of the Course: Mr John Hughes.
Enquiries to: The Secretary, Racecourse Offices, Aintree, Liverpool 9.
Principal Races: Grand National, Topham Trophy, Littlewoods Spring Cup *.
Effect of Draw: 6 furlongs and 1 mile races – low numbers favoured. High numbers favoured in races of 5 furlongs.
Travel Information: Special trains from London and other places on Grand National Day. Distances by road: Warrington 17 miles; Chester 18 miles; Manchester 35 miles.
Party Rates: Available upon application to the Secretary.

Children: Admission at half price through the turnstiles. Also reduced
   charge for entry to the County Stand.
Car Parks: Available at reasonable costs. Weekly tickets for reserved
   spaces are bookable in advance.

The opening of a flat race course at Aintree by Mr Lynn in 1827 was met
with immediate approval. Prior to this date, the only racing which could
be seen around this area took place either on the sands of the Mersey or
at Ormskirk, which was 15 miles away. Flat racing took place there until
1836, when a steeplechase course was built. This was largely a natural
course which crossed brooks and hedges. The first steeplechase race was
the 'Grand Liverpool Steeplechase', a sweepstakes for gentleman riders
carrying 12 stone. The first winner was The Duke, ridden by Captain
Becher. A syndicate took over Aintree racecourse in 1839, among the
members of which were Lord George Bentinck and Lord Derby, who did
much to encourage racing at this famous course. Unique in the history of
horseracing is the fact that the Topham family was connected with the
organisation and staging of racing at Aintree for well over a century.

   Among the many great horses which have won the Grand National are
Peter Simple, Abd-el-Kadar, The Colonel, The Lamb, Manifesto,
Poethlyn, Golden Miller, Reynoldstown and Red Rum.

   Aintree boasts the first tipster to operate in public on a racecourse – a
man called 'Liverpool Charlie', who stood outside the Sefton Arms at
Aintree selling sealed envelopes for threepence each.

   In 1973 Mrs Mirabel Topham sold the Aintree racecourse to a
property tycoon, Mr William Davies, for three million pounds. Since
then the whole future of Aintree, and especially of the Grand National,
has been the subject of a great deal of doubt and speculation. Each year,
following the running of the race, journalists have written articles under
headlines such as, 'Is this the last National?' However, the 1974 and 1975
Grand Nationals were both run, although in each case there was a
hullabaloo prior to the running.

   In 1974 a row over television fees threatened to black out television
coverage of the race, and in 1975 Mr Davies came into conflict with the
racing authorities. As late as December 1975 the future of the 1976 Grand
National was again in jeopardy, with the Jockey Club even going as far
as nominating Doncaster as an alternative course for the running of the
race. However, Mr Cyril Stein of Ladbrokes then concluded a £1,600,000
deal with Mr Davies, with the result that Ladbrokes agreed to take over
the management of the course for seven years. In December 1975 also,
Mr John Hughes was appointed Clerk of the Course, and so the 136th
running of this world-famous race was assured.

   Ladbrokes, together with John Hughes, have brought to the whole

RACECOURSES

Flat only .. .. ○
National Hunt only .. .. ●
Flat and National Hunt .. .. ◉

affair an expertise and a flair which must surely be envied by others in the racing world. So successful was their organisation that not only did the prize money for the three-day Aintree Meeting exceed £100,000 but on the day of the Grand National over 50,000 flocked to Aintree to watch the thirty-two magnificent steeplechasers racing over 4½ miles and thirty fences, and saw the thrilling spectacle of Mr Raymond's horse, Rag Trade, win by 2 lengths from the great horse, Red Rum, who was trying to win his third National. There is no doubt that Ladbrokes did racing a great service by saving the National.

There are those, however, who are concerned by the increasing involvement in racing of the larger bookmaking concerns. Ladbrokes, for example (a £50 million concern, with interests in property, holiday camps, hotels, casinos, etc.) already own Lingfield racecourse, and there is some speculation as to whether in the future it will be the bookmakers who will eventually control racing. That remains to be seen but, at the moment, given the successful methods employed by Ladbrokes, it certainly seems that for the next seven years at least the greatest of all chases is here to stay.

ASCOT (*Flat and National Hunt meetings*)

Clerk of the Course and Secretary: Captain the Hon. E. N. C. Beaumont, Royal Enclosure, Ascot, Berkshire. Telephone: Ascot 22211; Home: Ascot 23127.

Enquiries to: The Secretary, Box SMG, Ascot Racecourse, Ascot, Berkshire. Telephone: Ascot 22211.

Principal Races: *Flat:* Ascot 2,000 Guineas Trial Stakes, Ascot 1,000 Guineas Trial Stakes, Top Rank Victoria Cup, St James's Palace Stakes, Royal Hunt Cup, Gold Cup, Hardwicke Stakes, Churchill Stakes, Hyperion Stakes, King George VI and Queen Elizabeth Diamond Stakes, Cumberland Lodge Stakes, Queen Elizabeth II Stakes, Cornwallis Stakes.
National Hunt: Whitbread Trial Stakes, Heinz Chase, Kirk and Kirk Steeplechase, Black & White Whisky Gold Cup, S.G.B. Chase, Blue Circle Chase, W.D. & H.O. Wills Premier Chase Qualifier.

Effect of Draw: No marked advantage.

Travel Information: Ascot Station is a quarter of a mile from the course. Half-hourly train service from Waterloo. Distances by road: Reading 14 miles; Guildford 16 miles; Basingstoke 24 miles; London 26 miles; Oxford 42 miles. Readily accessible from M.3 and M.4 motorways. Helicopter pad available.

Party Rates: Groups of 40 or more, booking in advance, may gain admission to the Grand Stand, Tattersalls' and Paddock Enclosure and enjoy a three-course meal before or after racing. These facilities are available at all the Ascot fixtures, with the exception of the Royal Meeting. A special booking form, giving details of party rates, menus, etc., is available from The Secretary.

Royal Enclosure: Application for vouchers to the Royal Ascot Enclosure should be made to Her Majesty's Representative, Ascot Office, St James's Palace, London, S.W.1., during March and April. First-time applicants are required to complete a form, to be signed by a sponsor. Visitors from abroad make applications through their Ambassadors, High Commissioners, or through the Commonwealth Office in London.

Children: Under 16 years of age are entitled to free admission to the Grand Stand, Silver Ring and all enclosures, if accompanied by an adult. There are two playgrounds: that in the Silver Ring is used in the summer and is open to children from any enclosure; supervision is by trained nurses. In bad weather, the Silver Ring playroom is open. During the winter an indoor playroom in Tattersalls is available.

Car Parks: Available at reasonable costs. Three of the car parks are reserved during the Royal Meeting for those who book for the four days. There are also four car parks which may be booked on a daily basis. Applications to the Secretary for reserved berths may be made at the beginning of the year for any meeting during the 12 months.

Other Facilities: Dinners, dances, receptions, auctions, exhibitions, horticultural shows, dog shows, fairs, etc.

It was Queen Anne who decided in 1711 that Ascot Common was the perfect site upon which to organise race meetings. But it was not until 1745 that the Duke of Cumberland, then Ranger of Windsor Forest Park, managed to create some general interest in the idea. By 1791 encouraged, no doubt, by the Prince of Wales's enthusiasm for racing, a crowd of some 40,000 people turned up to see the colt, Baronet, win a £3,000 race in the Royal colours.

In 1820 the Prince succeeded to the throne and, as King George IV, instituted the first Royal Procession from Windsor Castle to the course, a tradition which continues to this day during Ascot week.

The Gold Cup race was instituted in 1807 and was to become the most important event of the meeting; it is regarded as the supreme test of stamina for the thoroughbred horse. Winners include such great names as Persimmon, The Flying Dutchman, Gladiateur and St Simon.

The Royal Hunt Cup, which was first run in 1843, has also gained a great reputation and is one of the many attractions in Ascot's programme of events.

In 1945, the late Duke of Norfolk was appointed His Majesty's Representative, and under his direction many improvements were made to the course. Before the last war the Ascot programme consisted of four days of the Royal meeting, but in 1946 King George VI approved three extra meetings and today Ascot offers racing throughout the year.

In 1951 the King George VI and Queen Elizabeth Festival of Britain Stakes was run; the race is now known as the King George VI and Queen Elizabeth Diamond Stakes and is the most important weight-for-age race in England.

The Royal Ascot Meeting is famous both as a high-class social gathering and also as a fashion spectacle. It is, in fact, one of the few places, in these days of denim austerity, where really well-dressed women may be seen. There are, of course, many eccentric and publicity-seeking women who vie with one another in the matter of dress and hats. However, they are only of interest to women journalists and to television commentators filling in the time between races.

AYR (Flat* and National Hunt meetings)

Clerks of the Course: Mr W. W. McHarg and Mr C. D. Patterson.

Enquiries to: The Secretary, Ayr Racecourse, 2 Whitletts Road, Ayr. Telephone: Ayr 64179; Telegrams: 'Western, Ayr'.

Principal Races: Scottish Grand National, Scottish Champion Hurdle, London & Northern Securities Future Champions Chase*, William Hill Handicap*, Tennent Trophy*, Burmah-Castrol Ayr Gold Cup*.

Effect of Draw: 5 furlongs and 6 furlongs – high numbers favoured. 7 furlongs and up – low numbers favoured.

Travel Information: By rail from Euston to Ayr. (Station half a mile from course). Trains from Glasgow every half hour. One hour by car from Glasgow Airport, and by bus or taxi. Prestwick (International) Airport is only 3 miles away. Distances by road: Kilmarnock 12 miles; Cumnock 16 miles; Glasgow 33 miles; London 390 miles.

Party Rates: There is a 10% reduction on normal admission rates into the Eglinton and Carrick/Craigie Stands for parties of 20 or more, if booked and paid for in advance.

Children: Under 15 admitted free to all enclosures, if accompanied by an adult, and there is a well-equipped playground in the Carrick/Craigie Stand.

Car Parks: Free

Other facilities: Aircraft landing facilities: there is a grass strip in the centre of the course for helicopters.

BANGOR-ON-DEE (National Hunt racing only)

Clerk of the Course: Major J. Moon.

Enquiries to: The Secretary: Norman Johnson, Esq., Bangor-on-Dee Steeplechases Ltd, 29 Eastgate Road North, Chester. Telephone: Chester 28301.

Travel Information: Nearest Station: Wrexham 5½ miles. Leave London from Paddington. Distances by road: Whitchurch 12 miles; Chester 16 miles; Shrewsbury 22 miles.

Car Parks: Free.

BATH (Flat racing only)

Clerk of the Course: Captain C. Toller.

Enquiries to: Captain C. Toller, Greenfields, Little Rissington, Cheltenham, Gloucestershire. Telephone: Bourton-on-the-Water 517.

Effect of the Draw: Low numbers have the advantage from 5 furlongs to 1 mile.

Travel Information: Bath Station. Bristol 13 miles; London 105 miles.

Party Rates: 25% reduction on admission charges to Tattersalls or the Silver Ring for parties of more than 20. Bookings should be made at least seven days in advance.

Children: Under 16 admitted free to all enclosures, except the Club, where a charge is made.

Car Park: Free.

BEVERLEY (Flat racing only)

Clerk of the Course: J. G. Cleverly, Esq.

Enquiries to: The Secretary, 9 North Bar Without, Beverley, Yorkshire. Tel: Beverley 882587.

Principal Races: Hilary Needler Trophy, William Hill Vase, The Welbred Sweepstakes, The R. B. Massey Trophy, The Hoveringham Handicap, The Richard Hodgson Stakes, The Watt Memorial Handicap.

Effect of the Draw: Advantage to high numbers from 5 furlongs to 1 mile.

Travel Information: By rail from King's Cross to Beverley, via Hull. (Buses from Hull, Ferensway Coach Station, 31 minutes journey to Beverley). By road: Hull 8 miles; York 29 miles; Scarborough 34 miles; Doncaster 44 miles; London 204 miles.

Party Rates: Available for groups of 20 or more to Tattersalls, Silver
    Ring and No 3 Ring. A complimentary pass is given to the organiser.
Children: Under 15 admitted free, if accompanied by an adult.
Car Parks: Free.
Other Facilities: Aircraft landing facilities by arrangement with R.A.F.
    Leconfield.

BRIGHTON (Flat racing only)

Clerk of the Course: Mr D. Hubbard.
Enquiries to: The Hon Secretary, Brighton Race Ground Lessees,
    Town Hall, Brighton, Sussex. Tel: Brighton 29801.
Principal Races: Brighton Mile, Brighton Cup, Brighton Sprint.
Effect of the Draw: 5 furlongs, 7 furlongs, 8 furlongs: low numbers
    favoured.
Travel Information: Brighton Station from Victoria, London Bridge or
    Portsmouth. (Buses to course). Distances by road: Worthing 11 miles;
    Eastbourne 22 miles; Horsham 23 miles; Chichester 31 miles; London
    53 miles.
Party Rates: For more than 20 admission tickets booked in advance,
    three complimentary tickets are given to the party organiser. Coach
    drivers are admitted free.
Children: Under 16 admitted free, if accompanied by an adult, except
    in the Club, where there is a small charge.
Car Parks: Available at reasonable costs. Coaches free.
Other Facilities: There is a picnic car park in the Silver Ring on the
    west side of the course; also in the East Enclosure.

CARLISLE (Flat and National Hunt meetings)

Clerk of the Course: Mr C. D. Patterson.
Enquiries to: The Secretary, Carlisle Racecourse Co., 4 Gilesgate Bank,
    Hexham, Northumberland. Tel: Hexham 3320.
Effects of the Draw: 5 furlong, 6 furlong and 8 furlong races: high
    numbers favoured.
Travel Information: By rail from Euston to Carlisle. By road: Penrith
    18 miles; Cockermouth 26 miles; Dumfries 33 miles; Hexham 38
    miles; London 300 miles. The course is 1½ miles south-west of Carlisle
    city, with an intersection off the M.6. (Carlisle by-pass intersection
    No. 42 is 1½ miles from the course.) Airport: Carlisle.
Party Rates: For parties of 30 or more, prices are reduced for advance

bookings. Coach parking is free and the coach driver is also admitted free of charge to the course.

Children: Under 15 admitted free, if accompanied by an adult.

Car Parks: Free.

CARTMEL (National Hunt racing only)

Clerk of the Course: Capt. T. J. C. Mordaunt

Enquiries to: Mr James Harrison, Cark Manor, Cark-in-Cartmel, Cumbria. Tel: Flookburgh 214.

Travel Information: By road on the B.5271 – Kendal 15 miles; Barrow-in-Furness 15 miles; London 260 miles.

Children: There is a nominal charge for children on the course.

Car Park: Free parking on the course.

Other Facilities: There is a Fair in the centre of the course on race days.

CATTERICK (Flat and National Hunt meetings)

Clerks of the Course: *Flat racing:* Mr J. F. Sanderson
National Hunt: Mr C. D. Patterson.

Enquiries to: Catterick Racecourse Co. Ltd., Liverton Lodge, Loftus, Saltburn, Cleveland. Tel: Loftus 40318.

Effect of the Draw: Low numbers best for races over 5 furlongs and 7 furlongs. Fast start essential.

Travel Information: Darlington Station, and then by bus. By road adjacent to A.1: Richmond 5 miles; Darlington 13 miles; London 229 miles.

Party Rates: Reductions for parties of 30 or more.

Children: Under 16 admitted free to all enclosures.

Car Park: Free.

CHELTENHAM (National Hunt racing only)

Clerk of the Course: Capt. C. B. Toller.

Enquiries to: Pratt & Co., 59–63 South Road, Haywards Heath, Sussex. Tel: 0444 50989/51597.

Principal Races: Sun Alliance Champion Chase, Champion Hurdle, Piper-Champagne Gold Cup, Mackeson Gold Cup, Massey-Ferguson Gold Cup, *Daily Express* Triumph Hurdle.

Travel Information: Cheltenham Lansdowne Station. By road: Gloucester 9 miles; Broadway 16 miles; Cirencester 16 miles; Evesham 16 miles; Bristol 44 miles; London 98 miles

Party Rates: For parties of 30 or more, reductions are available, upon
   application.
Car Parks: Free except Festival meeting. Free coach park.
Other Facilities: Caravan site open from the end of May until mid-
   September. Reasonable overnight charges.

Cheltenham's National Hunt Meeting in March each year is the climax of
the jumping season. The three-day meeting is dominated by the
Champion Hurdle and the Cheltenham Gold Cup, both of which were
founded in the 1920s.

   Flat racing at Cheltenham started in about 1815. This was very
successful, despite the efforts of the Reverend Mr Close (later Dean of
Carlisle) who tried to stop racing by preaching and publishing
pamphlets on its evils.

   The Cheltenham Grand Annual Steeplechase was founded in 1834.
This race was won in 1837 by Captain Becher riding Vivian. It was won
in 1839 and 1840 by Jem Mason on Lottery.

   In 1861 a new race was brought to Cheltenham. This was Fothergill
Rowland's Grand National Hunt Steeplechase, run for hunting men
riding hunters, over a distance of 4 miles. Before the 1920s, this was the
only important conditions race at Cheltenham.

   In 1924 the Cheltenham Gold Cup was instituted. This race has been
won by many famous steeplechasers, including Easter Hero, Golden
Miller, Cottage Rake and Arkle. Golden Miller won the race five years in
succession and Arkle won it three times.

   The Champion Hurdle was first run in 1927 and the race was won in
1928 by the famous horse, Brown Jack. Since then the winners have
included Hatton's Grace, Sir Ken and Persian War, all of whom have won
the race three times.

CHEPSTOW (Flat and National Hunt meetings)

Clerk of the Course: J. P. V. Hughes Esq, High Warren, The Warren,
   Ashtead, Surrey. Tel: Ashtead 75393.
Enquiries to: The Secretary, Chepstow Racecourse Co. Ltd., 17 Welsh
   Street, Chepstow, Monmouthshire. Tel: Chepstow 2237.
Principal Races: Welsh Grand National, Welsh Champion Novices
   Chase, Welsh Champion Hurdle, Chepstow Cup, Free Handicap
   Hurdle. No major flat races.
Effect of the Draw: High numbers slightly favoured on straight course
   (5 furlongs to 1 mile).

Travel Information: By rail from Paddington. Chepstow Station is a mile from the course. Buses. By road: Bristol 14 miles; Monmouth 16 miles; Newport 16 miles; Gloucester 28 miles; Cardiff 30 miles, London 135. The M.4 is very close.

Party Rates: For parties of 25 or more, Tattersalls tickets may be bought at a 25% reduction. Applications, with remittance, must be made at least seven days in advance.

Children: Under 14 admitted free of charge. There is a childrens' sandpit in the public enclosure.

Car Parks: Available at reasonable costs.

Other Facilities: The stands are available for hire for dances and other private functions. Dog shows may also be staged on the course, and the centre area is suitable for caravan rallies and camping. Caravan sites are available in the summer on days when racing is not taking place.

CHESTER (Flat racing only)

Clerk of the Course: Capt. C. B. Toller.

Enquiries to: Warmsley, Henshall & Co., 29 Eastgate Row North, Chester. Tel: Chester 28301.

Principal Races: Chester Cup, Chester Vase, Ormonde Stakes, Dee Stakes, Cheshire Oaks.

Effect of the Draw: Over all distances, low numbers favoured. Speed from gate a vital asset in sprints.

Travel Information: Chester General Station from Euston. By road: Liverpool 18 miles; Manchester 39 miles; London 180 miles.

Party Rates: 20% discount for parties visiting Tattersalls and Dee Stand in July and September.

Children: Full price except for Junior badges.

Car Parks: Available at reasonable costs.

Other Facilities: Stands are available for hire for exhibitions, weddings, private dinners, parties and conferences. Private land available for caravans.

DEVON AND EXETER (National Hunt racing only)

Clerk of the Course: Commander E. W. Sykes, DSC, RN (Rtd.)

Enquiries to: The Secretary, Newton Abbot Racecourse, Newton Abbot, Devonshire. Tel: Newton Abbot 3235.

Travel Information: Frequent bus services from Exeter to Haldon. By road: Exeter 5 miles; Newton Abbot 8 miles; Torbay 15 miles; London 175 miles.

Party Rates: On application to Secretary.

Children: Under 16 admitted free, if accompanied by an adult.

Car Park: Available at reasonable costs. There is also a picnic car park on the rails.

DONCASTER (Flat* and National Hunt meetings)

Clerk of the Course: Major G. G. R. Boon, MBE.

Enquiries to: The Racecourse Manager, D. Cox, Grand Stand, St Leger Way, Doncaster, Yorkshire. Tel: Doncaster 62706.

Principal Races: John Smith's Great Yorkshire Chase; Princess Royal Hurdle; Irish Sweeps Lincoln Handicap*, Zetland Handicap*, Champagne Stakes*, Park Hill Stakes*, Doncaster Cup*, Portland Handicap*, St Leger*, Flying Childers Stakes*, William Hill Futurity Stakes*, Manchester Handicap*.

Effect of the Draw: High numbers favoured on straight course; low numbers best on round course.

Travel Information: Doncaster Station one mile from course. By road: Rotherham 12 miles; Barnsley 15 miles; Sheffield 18 miles; Leeds 28 miles; York 34 miles; London 162 miles. The M.1 is very close.

Party Rates: There is a 20% reduction for parties of 30 or more, with a free Tattersalls ticket for the coach driver and free coach label.

Children: Free admission to all enclosures for accompanied children under 16. However, children under 10 are not admitted to the Club Stand at the St Leger meeting, and there is a small charge for those between 10 and 16.

Car Parks: Available at reasonable costs.

Other Facilities: The grandstand may be hired for dinners, dances, shows and wrestling. There is a golf course in the centre of the course, and accommodation for up to 60 caravans for overnight stops.

EDINBURGH (Flat racing only)

Clerk of the Course: Mr W. W. McHarg.

Enquiries to: The Secretary, 2 Whitletts Road, Ayr. Tel: Ayr 64179.

Principal Race: The Ladbroke Musselburgh Handicap.

Effect of the Draw: High numbers best over 5 furlongs, 7 furlongs and 8 furlongs.

Travel Information: Edinburgh Station. (From London, use King's Cross.) Buses to the course. By road on the A.1 at Musselburgh, 6 miles east of Edinburgh. Dunfermline 16 miles; Linlithgow 18 miles; Glasgow 44 miles; London 373 miles.

Party Rates: Reduction of 10% on normal rates of admission for parties of 20 or more, booked in advance. Coach parking is free, and a complimentary ticket is given to the organiser and to the driver.

Children: Under 15 admitted free to all enclosures.

Car Parks: Available at reasonable costs.

EPSOM (Flat racing only)

Clerk of the Course: Major P. M. Beckwith-Smith, The Racecourse Paddock, Epsom, Surrey. Tel: Epsom 26311 (3 lines).

Enquiries to: General Manager and Secretary, Epsom Grandstand Association, The Racecourse Paddock, Epsom, Surrey. Tel: Epsom 26311.

Principal Races: The Derby, The Oaks, Coronation Cup, Great Metropolitan Handicap, City and Suburban Handicap, Moet & Chandon Silver Magnum.

Effect of Draw: Low numbers favoured in races of up to $1\frac{1}{4}$ miles. Speed from starting gate all important in sprints.

Travel Information: By rail from Charing Cross, Waterloo and Victoria to Tattenham Corner, Epsom Downs or Epsom Town Stations. Underground trains to Morden and then by bus to the course. By road: London 15 miles; Guildford 17 miles; Newmarket 77 miles.

Party Rates: Available upon application to the Secretary.

Children: Under 16 years of age admitted free, if accompanied by an adult.

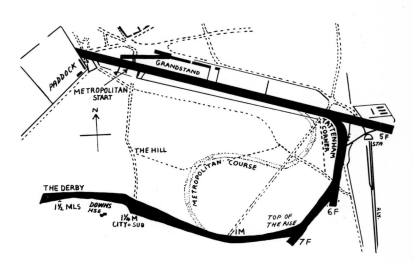

Car Parks: More than 20,000 vehicles can be accommodated in the car parks, which are supervised by National Car Parks. (Special rates apply on Derby Day). Full details of parks and seating may be found in the brochure published by United Racecourses, and which may be obtained from the Secretary.

Racing has taken place at Epsom for at least three hundred years. Samuel Pepys, the diarist, recorded a visit in 1667, when he stayed at the old *King's Head* in Epsom, and then watched Charles II and his court at the races. In 1730 racing at Epsom became an annual event for the first time. By 1743 many good horses were run there for substantial prizes and by the year 1776 Epsom had become one of the major race courses, holding two meetings a year.

The two principal races at Epsom are the Derby and the Oaks. The Oaks was originated by Lord Derby for 3-year-old fillies, and was first run in 1779. The Derby was first run in 1780, being a sweepstakes for 3-year-old colts and fillies. This race was originally run over 1 mile, but in 1784 the distance was changed to $1\frac{1}{2}$ miles.

As Epsom continued to flourish, two more important races were founded: the Great Metropolitan Handicap in 1846 and the City and Suburban five years later. The prize money for these races was provided by publicans, who thus became the first sponsors of racing.

Derby Day is the day which sets Epsom apart from any other course. The downs are crowded with thousands of people, enjoying the racing as well as the fairground atmosphere. But it is the course itself which provides the unique test for a thoroughbred. The horses run anti-clockwise with a long uphill start, a sharpish descent to Tattenham Corner and an undulating run-in.

Lester Piggott, who has mastered the course's trickiness better than anyone living, considers the Derby is the finest Classic test. The only jockey this century to have almost matched Piggott's success in the Derby was Steve Donoghue, who won it six times.

FAKENHAM (National Hunt racing only)

Clerk of the Course: Mr P. B. Firth.

Enquiries to: Clerk of the Course, Fakenham Racecourse Ltd., 6 Church Road, Moulton, Newmarket, Suffolk. Tel: Newmarket 750010.

Travel Information: By train to Norwich Station, then by bus. (London Station: Liverpool St.) By road: King's Lynn 21 miles; Cromer 22 miles; Norwich 26 miles; London 120 miles.

Party Rates: 33% discount in all enclosures for parties of 10 or more, booked in advance.

Children: Under 15 admitted free, if accompanied by an adult.

Car Parks: Members and course enclosure car parks (both suitable for picnics). Other parking also available at reasonable costs.

Other Facilities: Rooms may be hired, by arrangement with the Clerk to the North Norfolk District Council, Baron's Hall, Fakenham, Norfolk. There are also indoor bowling rinks and a golf course. Overnight accommodation is available for caravans, from end of June until beginning of September.

FOLKESTONE (Flat* and National Hunt meetings)

Clerk of the Course: Major D. Cameron.

Enquiries to: Pratt & Co., 59–63 South Road, Haywards Heath, Sussex. Tel: 0444 50989/51597.

Principal Races: Privy Councillor Stakes*, Metropole Challenge Cup*, Friends of Folkestone Amateur Riders Handicap Stakes*.

Effect of the Draw: Low numbers slightly favoured in sprints.

Travel Information: By rail: from Charing Cross to Westenhanger Station, which adjoins the course. By road: Dover 7 miles; Folkestone 8 miles; Ashford 12 miles; Maidstone 35 miles; London 70 miles.

Party Rates: There is a 20% reduction for parties of 20 or more, if booked in advance.

Children: Under 16 admitted free to all enclosures, except the Club. There is an excellent children's playground adjacent to Members' car park, with swings, etc., supervised by the St John's Ambulance Brigade.

Car Parks: Public car park free. Coaches free. Charges are made for course and enclosure car parks.

Other Facilities: Picnic areas. Caravans may make overnight stops and use course facilities from May 26th until September 24th. Reasonable overnight charges.

FONTWELL PARK (National Hunt racing only)

Clerk of the Course: Mr D. Hubbard.

Enquiries to: Pratt & Co., 59–63 South Road, Haywards Heath, Sussex. Tel: 0444 50989/51597.

Travel Information: By rail to Barnham Station, then by bus. (London station: Victoria or London Bridge.) By road: Arundel 5 miles; Bognor 6 miles; London 59 miles.

Party Rates: Reduction of 20% for parties of 20 or more, booked in advance.

Children: Under 16 admitted free (except to the Club) if accompanied by an adult.

Car Park: The public car park, which is close to the Enclosure, is free. Members' car park and picnic car park in the course enclosure available at reasonable costs.

Other Facilities: The car park may be hired for shows, rallies, etc., and the Club luncheon room is available for social functions.

GOODWOOD (Flat racing only)

Clerk of the Course: Mr R. A. Hubbard.

Enquiries to: The General Manager, Goodwood Racecourse Ltd., Chichester, Sussex. Tel: Chichester 527107.

Principal Races: Spillers' Stewards Cup, Sussex Stakes, Goodwood Cup, Extel Stakes, P.T.S. Laurels Stakes, Bentinck Stakes, March Stakes, Royal Sussex Stakes.

Effect of Draw: High numbers favoured in sprint races, but a quick start is essential.

Travel Information: Chichester Station, and then by bus to the course. (London station: Victoria or London Bridge.) By road: Chichester 5 miles; Brighton 32 miles; London 58 miles.

Party Rates: 20% reduction for parties of 30 or more.

Children: Under 17 years of age, if accompanied by adults, are admitted free of charge to the Richmond Stand at the May, August and September meetings, and to all other enclosures at all meetings. There is a children's playground open for all meetings, which is available for children up to the age of 12, and which is supervised by trained staff and St John's Ambulance personnel. The playground is provided with a drinking-water fountain, suitable lavatories and hospital facilities, etc.

Car Park: Free parking near the course, area close to stands restricted, reservations for this area must be made to Goodwood Racecourse Ltd.

Other Facilities: All the car parks at Goodwood are suitable for picnic parties, particularly Number 2 car park, opposite the stands.

In addition to the race meetings, the Goodwood Estate offers several other attractions. Opposite the course is the new Country Park (with a warden and information centre). Within its 60 acres there are lovely walks, picnic areas and ample car parking. The racecourse restaurant is open and so, too, is the children's playground.

Goodwood House is open to the public from May until September, and visits may be arranged to include luncheon and tea in the State Apartments. The Ballroom Suite is also available for those who desire a superb setting for social or business functions. The Nassau Suite, on the racecourse, is let on non-racing days.

All enquiries regarding visits to Goodwood House and hirings should be made to The House Manager, Goodwood House, Chichester, Sussex.

Other leisure attractions include an attractive 18-hole golf course and the Flying School and Club at Goodwood airfield.

Racing has taken place at 'glorious Goodwood' for over 170 years. The original course was laid out by the 3rd Duke of Richmond on Charlton Downs, part of his private estate in Sussex. Initially, races were held for hunters ridden, for the most part, by members of the Duke's Hunt and the local military.

The first recorded meeting to be held at Goodwood took place in 1801. In 1812 a Gold Cup replaced a race called the Silver Cup, the trophy for which had been won outright by a horse called Bucephalus. It is the race for this Gold Cup which is the event we know today as the Goodwood Cup, the oldest surviving race at the meeting.

Under the guidance of the 5th Duke of Richmond and his friend, Lord George Bentinck, the reputation of Goodwood continued to grow. In 1823 the Goodwood Stakes was instituted, and in 1834 a cup was presented by one of the Stewards for a 6 furlong handicap – the race which has become famous as the Stewards Cup. It was Lord George Bentinck's imaginative management of the course which really established Goodwood as one of the foremost racecourses in the country.

To commemorate Lord George Bentinck's association with Goodwood, there is a course named the Bentinck Course, of 1 mile 6 furlongs.

Like Ascot, Goodwood existed for many years on one meeting alone. Since the last war, however, the economics of racing have changed; it was not possible to justify the installation of modern technical equipment on a course which staged four days racing a year. The number of meetings was, therefore, increased.

GREAT YARMOUTH (Flat racing only)

Clerk of the Course: Mr D. W. Bushby.

Enquiries to: The Treasurer, Yarmouth Races, Town Hall, Yarmouth. Tel: Yarmouth 3233.

Travel Information: Yarmouth Vauxhall Station; buses to course. (London station: Liverpool Street.) By road: Norwich 20 miles; Newmarket 71 miles; London 126 miles.

Party Rates: Over 30 booked in advance may gain admission to Tattersalls at a reduced rate.

Children: Under 16 admitted free, if accompanied by an adult. There is a childrens' playground in the East enclosure.

Car Parks: Available at reasonable costs.

HAMILTON PARK (Flat racing only)

Clerk of the Course: Mr C. D. Patterson.

Enquiries to: The Secretary: Miss J. I. C. Grant, Penrose Hill, Moffat, Dumfriesshire. Tel: Moffat 20131.

Effect of the Draw: Middle to high numbers best.

Travel Information: By rail to Hamilton West Station. (London station: Euston.) By road: Glasgow 11 miles; Edinburgh 37 miles; London 383 miles.

Party Rates: 10% reduction in Tattersalls' enclosure for parties of 20 or more, paid for in advance.

Children: Under 12 admitted free, if with an adult, except in the Club, where a charge is made.

Car Park: Free.

HAYDOCK PARK (Flat* and National Hunt meetings)

Clerk of the Course: Mr P. Firth.

Enquiries to: The Secretary, Haydock Park Racecourse, Newton-le-Willows, Merseyside. Tel: Ashton-in-Makerfield 77345.

Principal Races: Tote Northern Chase, W.D. & H.O. Wills Premier Chase Final; Wills Hurdle, Victor Ludorum Hurdle, Greenall Whitley Chase, Lancashire Oaks*, Old Newton Cup*, Vernons Sprint Cup*.

Effect of the Draw: Low numbers favoured, from 6 furlongs to one mile.

Travel Information: By rail to Newton-le-Willows, then a 2-mile bus ride. (London station: Euston.) M.6 motorway exit is 100 yards from course. Manchester 19 miles; Birmingham 91 miles; London 200 miles.

Party Rates: Available for coach parties of over 30, booked in advance. Free coach parking and free admission to the Newton Stand for the driver.

Children: Reduced rates for juniors.

Car Parks: Ample public car parks available.

Other Facilities: Special facilities are available for party catering through the Secretary.

HEREFORD (National Hunt racing only)

Clerk of the Course: Mr J. H. Meredith.

Enquiries to: Secretary, Hereford Racecourse Co. Ltd; 8 King Street, Hereford. Tel: Hereford 2330.

Travel Information: Hereford Station, one mile from course. (London station: Paddington). Buses. By road: Monmouth 18 miles; Ludlow 24 miles; Worcester 26 miles; Gloucester 28 miles; London 133 miles;

Party Rates: Available upon application to Secretary.

Children: Admitted free, if accompanied by an adult.

Car Park: Available at reasonable costs.

Other Facilities: Stands are available for hire for dinners, dances, receptions, etc. Details of the caravan site available upon application.

HEXHAM (National Hunt racing only)

Clerk of the Course: Mr C. D. Patterson.

Enquiries to: The Secretary, Hexham Racecourse, 4 Gilesgate Bank, Hexham, Northumberland.

Travel Information: Hexham Station, then by bus. (London station: King's Cross). By road: Newcastle 20 miles; Durham 30 miles; Carlisle 38 miles; London 282;

Party Rates: Parties of 30 or more may gain admission into Tattersalls at reduced rates, if bookings are made in advance.

Children: Under 16 admitted free, if with an adult.

Car Parks: Free.

HUNTINGDON (National Hunt racing only)

Clerk of the Course: Mr H. Bevan.

Enquiries to: The Secretary, 4b Market Hill, Huntingdon. Tel: Huntingdon 53373.

Travel Information: Huntingdon Station. (London station: King's Cross). By road: Cambridge 16 miles; Peterborough 19 miles, Bedford 21 miles; London 62 miles.

Party Rates: 20% reduction for organised parties of 20 or more.

Children: Under 14 admitted free, if with an adult.

Car Park: Free – but there is a picnic park alongside the road, for which a small charge is made.

KELSO (National Hunt racing only)

Clerk of the Course: Mr W. W. McHarg.

Enquiries to: The Secretary, Kelso Races, Kelso, Roxburgh. Tel: Kelso 2311.

Travel Information: Berwick-on-Tweed Station is 24 miles from the course. (London station: King's Cross). Buses run from Newcastle and Carlisle. By road: Edinburgh 43 miles; Carlisle 65 miles; Newcastle 68 miles; Glasgow 87 miles; London 336 miles;

Party Rates: By arrangement with the Secretary.

Children: Under 15 admitted freee, if with an adult.

Car Parks: Available at reasonable costs. Coaches free.

KEMPTON PARK (Flat * and National Hunt meetings)

Clerk of the Course: Major G. G. R. Boon, MBE.

Enquiries to: The Racecourse Manager, Kempton Park Racecourse, Sunbury-on-Thames, Middlesex. Tel: Sunbury-on-Thames 82292.

Principal Races: *Yellow Pages* Hurdle; Rosebery Stakes*, Queen's Prize*, Jubilee Stakes*, King George VI Chase, Christmas Hurdle.

Effect of the Draw: High numbers on the round course; otherwise no advantage.

Travel Information: From Waterloo to Sunbury Station (500 yards from course) or Kempton Park Racecourse Station (alongside the course). By road: Kingston 5 miles; Staines 6 miles; London 14 miles; Reading 27 miles; Basingstoke 30 miles.

Party Rates: 25% discount for parties of 25 or more in the Grandstand and Silver Ring. Free parking and ticket for driver. Bookings must be made in advance.

Children: Accompanied children under 16 admitted free to all enclosures.

Car Parks: Available at reasonable costs. Coaches admitted free of charge, plus free admission for drivers.

Other Facilities: Kempton Manor restaurant is available for wedding receptions, etc. An extensive range of menus is available, and facilities include dance floor, air-conditioning, public address system and unlimited car parking. Bookings may be arranged through Trust House Forte Manager, at Kempton Manor, Kempton Park, Sunbury-on-Thames, Middlesex. Tel: Sunbury-on-Thames 86199.

LANARK (Flat racing only)

Clerk of the Course: Mr C. D. Patterson.

Enquiries to: The Secretary: Miss J. I. C. Grant, Penrose Hill, Moffat, Dumfriesshire. Tel: Moffat 20131.

Effect of the Draw: Low numbers favoured in races over 5 furlongs; high numbers favoured over 7 furlongs and 8 furlongs.

Travel Information: Lanark Station. (London station: Euston.) Buses. By road: Glasgow 25 miles; Edinburgh 33 miles; Ayr 44 miles; London 375;

Party Rates: 10% reduction in Tattersalls' enclosure for parties of 20 or more, paid in advance.

Children: Under 12 admitted free, if accompanied by an adult, except in the Club, where a charge is made.

Car Parks: Free.

LEICESTER (Flat and National Hunt meetings)

Clerk of the Course: Captain N. E. S. Lees.

Enquiries to: The Secretary, Leicester Racecourse, Oadby, Leicestershire. Tel: Leicester 716515 and 712367.

Effect of the Draw: 5 furlongs and 6 furlongs: low numbers favoured.

Travel Information: 2 miles from Leicester Station. (London station: St Pancras.) Buses. By road: Coventry 24 miles; Nottingham 25 miles; Northampton 32 miles; Birmingham 39 miles; London 98 miles;

Party Rates: 10% reduction for parties of 30 or more, booked in advance.

Children: Under 15 admitted free, if with an adult.

Car Parks: Available at reasonable prices. There is a picnic park in the Silver Ring, for which an overall charge is made for a car and four occupants.

LINGFIELD PARK (Flat and National Hunt meetings)

Clerk of the Course: Mr J. Hughes.

Enquiries to: The Secretary, Lingfield Park Racecourse, Lingfield, Surrey. Tel: Lingfield 832009.

Principal Races: Ladbroke Derby Trial, Oaks Trial, both Flat.

Effect of the Draw: High numbers have advantage in distances of up to 1 mile, except in heavy going.

Travel Information: By rail from Victoria and London Bridge to Lingfield Station (400 yard covered walk to the course). By road: East Grinstead 4 miles, London 27 miles; Brighton 30 miles.

Party Rates: Special rates. Applications should be made not less than 7 days before the day of racing.

Children: Under 16 admitted free of charge, if accompanied.

Car Park: Available at reasonable cost. Coaches free.

LUDLOW (National Hunt racing only)

Clerk of the Course: Major J. G. Moon.

Enquiries to: The Secretary, Ludlow Racecourse, Bradburn House, Darlington Street, Wolverhampton. Tel: Wolverhampton 29811.

Travel Information: Ludlow Station; buses to course. (London station: Paddington or Euston.) By road: Shrewsbury 28 miles; Birmingham 40 miles; London 143 miles;

Party Rates: By arrangement with the Secretary.

Children: Under 16 admitted free of charge.

Car Parks: Available at reasonable costs in centre of course.

MARKET RASEN (National Hunt racing only)

Clerk of the Course: Mr J. Lucas.

Enquiries to: The Secretary, Market Rasen Racecourse, Market Rasen, Lincolnshire. Tel: Market Rasen 3434.

Travel Information: Market Rasen Station. (London station: King's Cross.) By road: Lincoln 16 miles; Grimsby 16 miles; London 148 miles;

Party Rates: Parties of 20 or more get special rates.

Children: Under 15 admitted free of charge, if accompanied. There is a children's playground in the Silver Ring, under the supervision of the St John's Ambulance Brigade.

Car Parks: Free. In addition, there is a picnic park, for which a charge is made.

Other Facilities: There is a rugby pitch in the middle of the course, and the grandstand may be hired for dinners, dances, etc. Space is also available for caravan rallies. Racecards are issued free of charge.

NEWBURY (Flat* and National Hunt meetings)

Clerk of the Course: Captain C. B. Toller.

Enquiries to: The Manager, Newbury Racecourse, Newbury, Berkshire. Tel: Newbury 40015.

Principal Races: Schweppes Gold Trophy*, John Porter Stakes*, Lockinge Stakes*, Newbury Summer Cup*, Morland Brewery Stakes *, Joe Coral Newbury Autumn Cup *, St Simon Stakes *, Hennessy Cognac Gold Cup, Metrostore Mandarin Chase.

Effect of the Draw: No significant effect.

Travel Information: From Paddington to Newbury Racecourse Station. By road: Reading 17 miles; Oxford 27 miles; London 56 miles. The M.4 is fairly close.

Party Rates: 20% discount for parties of 20 or more, except for the Club, provided bookings are made at least a week in advance. Payment should be made at least 3 days before the meeting.

Children: Under 17 admitted free of charge, if accompanied by an adult, except for the Club, where a charge is made. There is a well-equipped and supervised children's playground behind the Geoffrey Freer Stand, which is open to children from other enclosures.

Car Parks: Free.

Other Facilities: Catering: Menus for luncheon and high teas from Ring and Brymer Ltd, Catering Office, Sandown Park Racecourse, Portsmouth Road, Esher, Surrey. Tel: Esher 65308.

NEWCASTLE (Flat* and National Hunt meetings)

Clerk of the Course: A. C. Newton, Esq.

Enquiries to: The Secretary, Gosforth Park Co. Ltd., Newcastle-upon-Tyne. Tel: Wideopen 2020.

Principal Races: Eider Chase; Northern Free Handicap*, Top Rank Club Handicap*, Beeswing Stakes*, Virginia Fillies Stakes*, Gosforth Park Cup*, Joe Coral Northumberland Plate*, Harry Peacock Challenge Cup*, Northumberland Sprint Trophy*, Seaton Delaval Stakes*, Northern Goldsmiths Handicap*, Ladbroke Trophy Steeplechase, Fighting Fifth Hurdle

Effect of the Draw: No advantage.

Travel Information: By rail from King's Cross to Newcastle-on-Tyne Station; buses to the course. By road: South Shields 11 miles; Sunderland 11 miles; York 81 miles; Manchester 129 miles; London 274 miles.

Party Rates: A 25% reduction is available to parties of 25 or more for Tattersalls' enclosure, except in June. There is a free pass into Tattersalls for each driver of a coach party. Applications should be made at least a week in advance, and payment made not later than 3 days before the meeting.

Children: Free to all enclosures, if accompanied by adults. The Gosforth Park Executive pride themselves on having the most unusual and modern equipment for their children's playground.

Car Parks: Free to cars and coaches.

Other Facilities: There is a championship golf course in the centre of the racecourse, also a golf driving range, with a nine-hole course, soccer and rugby pitches, an archery club, a squash club and a bird sanctuary. There are caravan and camping facilities. The racecourse also provides a permanent base for the Northumberland Boy Scouts. The stands are used for exhibitions and trade shows.

NEWMARKET (Flat racing only)

Clerk of the Course: Captain N. E. S. Lees.

Enquiries to: Clerk of the Course & Manager, Jockey Club Office, 101 High Street, Newmarket, Suffolk. Tel: Newmarket 4151.

Principal Races: 2,000 Guineas, 1,000 Guineas, Champion Stakes, Irish Sweeps Cambridgeshire, S.K.F. Cesarewitch, William Hill Middle Park Stakes, William Hill Cheveley Park Stakes, William Hill Dewhurst Stakes, July Cup, Jockey Club Cup, Totalisator Free Handicap.

Effect of Draw: No advantage.

Travel Information: By rail from Liverpool Street to Cambridge Station, and then by bus. By road: Cambridge 13 miles; Norwich 49 miles; London 62 miles;

Party Rates: 20% discount for all enclosures when parties of 10 or more book in advance.

Children: Under 15 years of age admitted free of charge, if accompanied by an adult. There is a staffed playground in both enclosures.

Car Parks: All public car parks are free.

Other Facilities: The Members' Stand on the Rowley Mile is available for dances, trade exhibitions, etc., and the Paddock area is available for dog shows and other open air events. The July course car parks are available for caravan rallies. Overnight accommodation for caravans is provided on the Rowley Mile, from June until September.

Newmarket is the heart of the British racing, with an influence which is felt throughout the world. Its two racecourses offer many of the season's most important events, while the town is also the home of the Jockey Club, about forty training yards, numerous studs, Tattersalls' Sales Paddocks, the National Stud and the Equine Research Station.

Newmarket Heath has been important in British racing since Charles II established regular racing there more than three hundred years ago. He rode his own hack Old Rowley (part of the principal course is now called the Rowley Mile) and also competed in several races. He founded the Newmarket Town Place which, until recently, was the only Flat race in Britain open to women riders.

The Jockey Club moved to Newmarket in 1752 and today its bow-fronted premises dominate the High Street, surrounded by saddlers, bootmakers, corn and feed merchants and souvenir shops.

Many of the earlier top-class jockeys learned their trade at Newmarket; for example, Sam Chifney Senior and Frank Buckle. By the end of the eighteenth century, Newmarket offered more racing than any other course in Britain.

In 1809 a sweepstakes for 3-year-old horses was inaugurated; this had 23 starters at 100 guineas each. The race was, therefore, somewhat illogically called the 2,000 Guineas. This race was run over the Rowley Mile and now forms the first Classic of the year. The fillies' race was started in 1814. There were 10 horses at 100 guineas each; the race was, therefore, called the 1,000 Guineas.

Apart from these Classic races, other important races are the July Stakes (first run in 1786) and the July Cup (first run in 1876), the Cambridgeshire, the Cesarewitch and the Champion Stakes.

NEWTON ABBOT (National Hunt racing only)

Clerk of the Course: Mr C. C. Whitley.

Enquiries to: The Secretary, Newton Abbot Racecourse, Newton Abbot, Devon. Tel: Newton Abbot 3235.

Travel Information: Newton Abbot Station. (London station: Paddington.) By road: Torquay 6 miles; Exeter 17 miles; London 184 miles;

Party Rates: Details obtainable upon application to the Secretary.

Children: Under 16 admitted free, if with an adult.

Car Parks: Available at reasonable costs. There is also a picnic car park on the rails.

Other Facilities: The main restaurant in the stand is available for dances and other functions, and the car park may be used for summer fêtes. Rugby and soccer pitches may also be hired. Stock car racing takes place every Wednesday evening during the summer. There is a golf driving range open daily, between 10.00 a.m. and 10.00 p.m., and clay pigeon shooting is available on Sunday mornings.

NOTTINGHAM (Flat and National Hunt meetings)

Clerk of the Course: Mr D. Heyman.

Enquiries to: The Secretary, Nottingham Racecourse, Bradburn House, Darlington Street, Wolverhampton. Tel: Wolverhampton 29811.

Effect of the Draw: Low numbers have a slight advantage on the round course. High numbers favoured in sprints.

Travel Information: Nottingham Station is a mile and a half from the course; bus services. (London station: St Pancras.) By road: Derby 16 miles; Leicester 25 miles; Birmingham 50 miles; London 123 miles.

Party Rates: Rates may be obtained by arrangement with the Secretary.

Children: Under 16 admitted free of charge.

Car Parks: Available at reasonable costs.

PERTH (National Hunt racing only)

Clerk of the Course: Mr W. W. McHarg.

Enquiries to: The Secretary, The Perth Hunt, 17 York Place, Perth. Tel: Perth 23471.

Travel Information: Perth Station, then by bus. (London station: Euston.) By road: Edinburgh 44 miles; Glasgow 61 miles; London 415 miles;

Party Rates: Details available upon application to the Secretary.

Car Parks: Available at reasonable cost. Coaches may be parked free of charge.

PLUMPTON (National Hunt racing only)

Clerk of the Course: Mr B. E. Robinson.

Enquiries to: Pratt & Co., 59–63, South Road, Haywards Heath, Sussex. Tel: Haywards Heath 50989 and 51597.

Travel Information: Plumpton Station adjoins the course. (London station: Victoria or London Bridge.) By road: Lewes 3 miles; Brighton 11 miles; London 49 miles.

Party Rates: 20% discount for parties of 20 or more.

Children: Under 16 admitted free, if with an adult (except in Regency Stand).

Car Parks: Available at reasonable costs.

Other Facilities: The Regency Stand offers facilities for receptions, dinners, etc. The centre of the course is available for shows and other open air events.

PONTEFRACT (Flat racing only)

Clerk of the Course: Colonel C. Egerton.

Enquiries to: The Secretary, Pontefract Racecourse Ltd., 33 Ropergate, Pontefract, Yorks. Tel: Pontefract 3224.

Principal Races: Websters Brewery Handicap, Darley Brewery Handicap.

Effect of the Draw: Low numbers have slight advantage in sprints.

Travel Information: Pontefract Baghill and Pontefract Monkhill Stations. (London station: St Pancras.) By road: Leeds 13 miles; Barnsley 14 miles; Doncaster 15 miles; London 177 miles;

Party Rates: For 20 or more, reduced prices are available.

Children: Admitted free, if accompanied by an adult.

Car Parks: Free.

REDCAR (Flat racing only)

Clerk of the Course: Mr J. F. Sanderson.

Enquiries to: The Secretary, Redcar Races Co. Ltd., Liverton Lodge, Loftus, Saltburn, Cleveland. Tel: Loftus 40318.

Principal Races: Zetland Gold Cup, Vaux Gold Tankard, Andy Capp Handicap, William Hill Gold Cup.

Effect of the Draw: No effect.

Travel Information: Redcar Station, then by bus. (London station: King's Cross.) By road: Saltburn 5 miles; Middlesbrough 9 miles; London 252 miles;

Party Rates: Available for parties of 30 or more.

Children: Under 16 admitted free of charge. Children's playground accessible from all enclosures.

Car Parks: Free.

RIPON (Flat racing only)

Clerk of the Course: Mr A. C. Newton.

Enquiries to: Mr C. B. Hutchinson, P.O. Box 1, Ripon, Yorkshire. Tel: Ripon 2156.

Principal Races: R. W. Armstrong Cup, Hornblower Stakes, Great St Wilfrid Handicap, Ripon Rowels Stakes, Champion Two-Year-Old Stakes.

Effect of Draw: Low numbers best on straight course; high numbers best on round course.

Travel Information: Harrogate or York Stations, then by bus. (London station: King's Cross.) By road: Harrogate 11 miles, York 24 miles; Leeds 27 miles; London 213 miles.

Party Rates: One free admission is allowed per 10 people paid for in advance. Special concession charge into Tattersalls for parties of 30 or more, paid in advance.

Children: Under 15 admitted free of charge. There are two play-
grounds.
Car Parks: Free.
Other Facilities: For hire, by arrangement.

SALISBURY (Flat racing only)

Clerk of the Course: Major H. W. Hibbert.
Enquiries to: The Secretary, The Racecourse, Salisbury, Wiltshire.
Tel: Salisbury 4854.
Principal Races: Bibury Cup, Gwen Blagrave Memorial Handicap,
Champagne Stakes.
Effect of the Draw: High numbers are favoured in straight races. Slight
advantage for low numbers in races of more than one mile.
Travel Information: Salisbury Station, and then by special buses to
course. (London station: Waterloo.) By road: Southampton 23 miles;
Marlborough 28 miles; London 84 miles.
Party Rates: Details available upon application to the Secretary.
Children: Admitted free, if with an adult. Children's playground in
course enclosure.
Car Parks: Free.
Other Facilities: The Bibury Suite is available for dinners, dances,
receptions, etc. Details of the caravan site are available upon
application to the Secretary.

SANDOWN PARK (Flat* and National Hunt meetings)

Clerk of the Course: Major P. M. Beckwith-Smith.
Enquiries to: The Racecourse Manager, Sandown Park, Esher, Surrey.
Tel: Esher 63072.
Principal Races: Eclipse Stakes*, National Stakes*, Esher Cup*, Henry
II Stakes*, Solario Stakes*, Whitbread Gold Cup, William Hill
Imperial Cup*.
Effect of the Draw: Low numbers are slightly favoured in sprint races.
High numbers are best on the round course.
Travel Information: From Waterloo to Esher Station. By road, via A.3:
Kingston 5 miles; Epsom 7 miles; Guildford 14 miles; London 14
miles;
Party Rates: 25% discount for parties of 25 or more booked in
advance. Free parking and ticket for coach driver. A leaflet giving
details is available from the racecourse.
Children: Under 16 years of age admitted free of charge, if with an
adult. There is a playground in the centre of the course.

Car Parks: Available at reasonable costs. Free coach park.

Other Facilities: There is a golf driving range and a nine-hole par three course. There is also an artificial ski-slope. For banqueting facilities, *see* Kempton.

Sandown Park racecourse was built in 1875. It was one of five courses built at around that period on similar plans. Of these, only Sandown Park, Kempton Park and Lingfield Park still exist. Sandown was the first enclosed or park course to be built near London – it was fenced in and everyone had to pay to get onto the course. The first meeting was a mixed affair – Flat racing and steeplechasing. King Edward VII, the then Prince of Wales, was an early supporter and won his first race on the Flat at Sandown.

Sandown was the first racecourse to develop a private 'Club' system – a Members' Enclosure, where only people who had been proposed and seconded were allowed entry. This made Sandown one of the most fashionable courses during the late nineteenth century.

In 1886 the first ever race with a prize of £10,000 was run at Sandown – the Eclipse Stakes. The race was won by Bendigo, who beat the Derby winner, St Gatien. King Edward VII twice won the Eclipse Stakes with his horses, Persimmon and Diamond Jubilee. This is now one of the most important races in England, apart from the Classics. Previous winners include St Paddy, Ragusa, Mill Reef and Brigadier Gerard.

Another race which is a feature in the Sandown Park calendar is the Imperial Cup. At one time this race was considered to be the most important race for hurdlers and it still attracts many of the best competitors.

The Whitbread Gold Cup was first held in 1957; this was one of the first great sponsored steeplechase races (the other being the Hennessy Cognac Gold Cup at Newbury). Previous winners of the Whitbread Gold Cup include Taxidermist, Arkle and Mill House.

SEDGEFIELD (National Hunt racing only)

Clerk of the Course: Col. C. D. Egerton.

Enquiries to: The Secretary, Sedgefield Racecourse, Russell House, Russell St., Stockton-on-Tees, Cleveland. Tel: Stockton-on-Tees 67154.

Travel Information: Stockton or Durham Stations, then by bus to the course. (London station: King's Cross.) By road: Stockton 9 miles; Durham 11 miles; London 252 miles.

Party Rates: Available for parties of 30 or more in Tattersalls, provided bookings are made in advance.

Children: Under 16 admitted free of charge, if with an adult.

Car Parks: Available at reasonable costs. Coaches admitted free of charge.
Other Facilities: Picnic park in main enclosure.

SOUTHWELL (National Hunt racing only)

Clerk of the Course: Mr Keith S. Ford.
Enquiries to: The Secretary, 6 Castle Gate, Newark, Nottinghamshire. Tel: Newark 5624.
Principal Races: Colonel R. Thompson Memorial Chase, James Seeley Memorial Hunters Chase.
Travel Information: Rolleston Junction Station adjoins the course. (London station: St Pancras). By road: Southwell 3 miles; Newark 5 miles; Nottingham 14 miles; London 132 miles;
Party Rates: 20% discount for parties of 30 or more, with 2 free tickets for organiser.
Children: Admitted free of charge, if with an adult. Children's playground in course enclosure.
Car Park: Free.
Other Facilities: Club bar available for dances. Course enclosure available for sports, galas, etc.

STRATFORD (National Hunt racing only)

Clerk of the Course: Cmdr. John Ford.
Enquiries to: J. H. Kenny Esq., 76 High Street, Uttoxeter, Staffordshire. Tel. Uttoxeter 2530.
Principal Races: Horse and Hound Champion Hunters Chase, Roddy Baker Gold Cup, Oslo Trophy Hurdle, Ladbroke Handicap Hurdle, John Corbet Cup.
Travel Information: Stratford-on-Avon Racecourse Station. (London station: Paddington). By road: Birmingham 26 miles; Cheltenham 31 miles; London 91 miles.
Party Rates: 20% discount for parties of 20 or more, paid in advance.
Children: Under 16 admitted free of charge.
Car Parks: Available at reasonable costs.
Other Facilities: The stands are available for hire for dinners, dances, exhibitions, etc. The car parks are available for caravan rallies and Pony Club camps.

TAUNTON (National Hunt racing only)

Clerk of the Course: Cmdr. E. W. Sykes.

Enquiries to: The Secretary, Taunton Racecourse Co. Ltd., The Old Vicarage, Elm Grove, Taunton, Somerset. Tel: Taunton 2858.

Travel Information: Taunton Station, and then by bus to course. (London station: Paddington.) By road: Exeter 32 miles; Bristol 40 miles; London 145 miles;

Party Rates: Available upon application to the Secretary.

Children: Under 16 admitted free of charge. Juniors, between the ages of 16 and 22, may get an annual Club badge at a reduced rate.

Car Parks: Charged by entrance to the course. Other parking free of charge.

TEESSIDE PARK (Flat* and National Hunt meetings)

Clerk of the Course: Mr John Chapman.

Enquiries to: Denis Riley, Esq., Russell House, Russell Street, Stockton-on-Tees. Tel: Stockton 67154.

Principal Race: Rosebery Handicap*.

Travel Information: Thornaby Station. (London station: King's Cross.) By road: Darlington 11; Newcastle 34 miles; London 243 miles.

Party Rates: 50% discount for parties of 40 or more. 25% discount for parties of 20 or more.

Children: Under 16 admitted free of charge. Children's playground in the Silver Ring, attended by St John's Ambulance Brigade.

Car Park: Free.

Other Facilities: The stands are available for hire for exhibitions. The car park is available for fairs, circuses and exhibitions. There is a golf course on the site.

THIRSK (Flat racing only)

Clerk of the Course: Major D. W. A. Swannell, MBE.

Enquiries to: Thirsk Racecourse Co. Ltd., Racecourse, Station Road, Thirsk. Tel: Thirsk 22276.

Principal Races: Thirsk Hunt Cup, Bass Rose Bowl, Hambleton Cup.

Effect of the Draw: High numbers best in sprints; low numbers favoured for races of 7 furlongs and upwards.

Travel Information: Thirsk Station is one mile from the course. (London station: King's Cross.) By road: Ripon 12 miles; York 24 miles; London 218 miles.

Party Rates: Reductions available for parties of 20 or more. The organiser and coach driver each get a free pass.
Children: Under 16 admitted free of charge, if with an adult.
Car Parks: Free.

TOWCESTER (National Hunt racing only)

Clerk of the Course: Mr D. W. Bushby.
Enquiries to: The Secretary, Mill House, Towcester, Northants. Tel: Towcester 50424.
Travel Information: Northampton Station, then by bus to the course. (London station: Euston.) By road: Northampton 9 miles; Buckingham 11 miles; London 60 miles. The course is on the A.5, and within 6 miles of Exit No. 15 on the M.1.
Party Rates: $33\frac{1}{3}\%$ discount for parties of 30 or more in the Tattersalls and course enclosures.
Children: Under 12 free.
Car Park: Available at reasonable costs.
Other Facilities: On non-racing days, the refreshment rooms and stables may be hired.

UTTOXETER (National Hunt racing only)

Clerk of the Course: Cmdr. John Ford.
Enquiries to: The Racecourse Manager, Uttoxeter, Staffordshire. Tel: Uttoxeter 2561.
Travel Information: Uttoxeter Station adjoins the course. (London station: St Pancras.) By road: Stoke 16 miles; Derby 18 miles; London 148 miles.
Party Rates: Reduction for admission into all enclosures for party bookings made in advance.
Children: Under 16 admitted free of charge.
Car Park: Available at reasonable costs.
Other Facilities: There is a sports ground in the centre of the course, which is let to local organisations. There are also ballroom and dining facilities, with excellent car parking available.

WARWICK (Flat and National Hunt meetings)

Clerk of the Course: Mr D. Heyman.
Enquiries to: The Secretary, Warwick Racecourse Co. Ltd., Bradburn House, Darlington Street, Wolverhampton. Tel: Wolverhampton 24481/772038.

Effect of the Draw: Low numbers best.

Travel Information: Leamington Spa Station, then by bus to the course. (London station: Paddington.) By road: Stratford-on-Avon 8 miles; Rugby 17 miles; Birmingham 21 miles; Gloucester 47 miles; London 91 miles.

Children: Under 16 admitted free of charge. There is a children's playground in the course enclosure.

Car Parks: Available at reasonable costs.

WETHERBY (National Hunt racing only)

Clerk of the Course: Major J. Moon.

Enquiries to: The Secretary, The Racecourse, Wetherby, Yorkshire. Tel: Wetherby 2035.

Principal Races: Rowland Meyrick Chase, Wetherby Pattern Chase, Wetherby Handicap Chase.

Travel Information: Leeds Station. (London station: King's Cross.) Frequent buses from Vicar Lane (about 40 minutes to course). By road: Leeds 13 miles; York 14 miles; Doncaster 32 miles; London 194 miles.

Party Rates: Special rates available for coach parties, with a free ticket for the driver.

Children: Free, if with an adult. There is a children's playground situated on the course.

Car Parks: Free.

Other Facilities: Horse sales take place throughout the year, and a caravan site is available during the summer.

WINCANTON (National Hunt racing only)

Clerk of the Course: Major W. Hibbert.

Enquiries to: Major W. Hibbert, Netton House, Salisbury, Wiltshire. Tel: Middle Woodford 377.

Principal Races: Badger Beer Handicap Chase, Lord Stalbridge Memorial Gold Cup, Kingwell Pattern Hurdle.

Travel Information: Gillingham Station, then by bus. (London station: Waterloo.) By road: Yeovil 15 miles; Bristol 34 miles; London 111 miles.

Party Rates: Available upon application to the Secretary.

Children: Under 16 admitted free, if with an adult.

Car Parks: Free.

Other Facilities: The Tattersalls' Stand is available for hire for dances, dinners, receptions, etc. There is also a caravan site available.

WINDSOR (Flat and National Hunt meetings)

Clerk of the Course: D. W. Bushby, Esq.

Enquiries to: The Secretary, Royal Windsor Races, Windsor, Berkshire. Tel: Windsor 65234/64726.

Effect of the Draw: High numbers have an advantage.

Travel Information: Windsor & Eton Central Station from Paddington. Windsor Riverside Station from Waterloo. By road: on M.4 approximately 20 miles from London; Guildford 22 miles; Oxford 39 miles.

Party Rates: There is a discount for advance bookings for parties of 20 or more to Tattersalls and Silver Ring. Organised parties get free coach parking and free admission to the Silver Ring for the coach driver.

Children: Under 16 admitted free of charge to all enclosures.

Car Parks: Available at reasonable costs for cars and coaches.

WOLVERHAMPTON (Flat* and National Hunt meetings)

Clerk of the Course: Lt. Commander J. W. Ford.

Enquiries to: The Secretary, Wolverhampton Racecourse Co., Bradburn House, Darlington Street, Wolverhampton. Tel: Wolverhampton 24481/772038.

Principal Races: Nuneaton Hurdle, *Yellow Pages* Long Distance Handicap Hurdle, Champion Hurdle Trial, Mitchell & Butlers Hunters Chase, Midlands Cesarewitch*, Midlands Cambridgeshire*.

Effect of the Draw: High numbers favoured in races of 5 furlongs.

Travel Information: Wolverhampton High Level Station, then by bus. (London station: Euston.) By road: Walsall 6 miles; Birmingham 13 miles; Stafford 17 miles; London 124 miles. (The racecourse is 8 miles from the M.6, using exit 14.)

Party Rates: Rates are available upon application to the Secretary.

Children: Under 16 admitted free of charge. Children's playground in the Dunstall Enclosure.

Car Parks: Available at reasonable costs.

WORCESTER (National Hunt racing only)

Clerk of the Course: Mr H. Bevan.

Enquiries to: Racecourse Manager, Pitchcroft, Worcester. Tel: 0905-25364 or Guildhall, Worcester. Tel: 0905-23471, Ext. 37.

Principal Races: Worcester Royal Porcelain Chase, Sir Ken Pattern Hurdle, Harold Rushton Hunters Chase.

Travel Information: Worcester (Shrub Hill) and Worcester (Foregate Street) Stations. (London station: Paddington.) By road on A.44 and via M.5: Cheltenham 25 miles; Birmingham 27 miles; Gloucester 27 miles; Warwick 33 miles; London 113 miles.

Party Rates: Reductions available for parties of 15 or more in Tattersalls enclosure. Special rates available for coach parties.

Children: Under 14 admitted free of charge.

Car Parks: Available at reasonable costs.

Other Facilities: Pitchcroft is situated close to the centre of Worcester, and catering for parties is available on the racecourse, or may be arranged at nearby hotels and restaurants. The centre course enclosure of 100 acres provides ideal picnic facilities and, on non-racing days, it is used extensively for other sports.

WYE

Wye Racecourse recently closed down, ostensibly because of lack of support from the Levy Board in the matter of a few thousand pounds, which were required in order to improve the very sharp bends and to make various other improvements required by the Jockey Club.

Wye was a pleasant country meeting, and while it is true that the course lacked certain facilities, it did have a charm of its own, and gave pleasure to thousands of Kentish racegoers.

Recently there has been much speculation in the Press as to whether or not racing can survive unless the number of racecourses is drastically reduced. It has been suggested that the answer is to have fewer and more centralized and more modern racecourses. However, National Hunt racing originated through the small country meetings such as Wye, and it does seem a great pity that the course should be closed down for want of such a small amount of money. After all, escalators and smart bars are not the be all and end all of racing, and it would be a dreadful state of affairs if we were to end up with half a dozen or so racing 'supermarkets' and at the same time lose the flavour of racing altogether.

YORK (Flat racing only)

Clerk of the Course: Mr J. F. Sanderson.

Enquiries to: York Race Committee, The Racecourse, York. Tel: York 22260.

Principal Races: Dante Stakes, Yorkshire Cup, John Smith's Magnet Cup, Benson & Hedges Gold Cup, Yorkshire Oaks, Tote Ebor Handicap, Gimcrack Stakes, William Hill Sprint Championship.

Travel Information: York Station, then by bus to course. (London station: King's Cross.) By road: Leeds 24 miles; Doncaster 34 miles; Hull 38 miles; Scarborough 41 miles; London 196 miles.

Party Rates: Special rates available for parties of 30 or more using Tattersalls' enclosure, except for the Tote Ebor fixture in August.

Children: Under 16 admitted free, if with an adult, except to the Club at the May and August meetings, when only children between 12 and 15 years are admitted free. Children's playground in course enclosure open to children from all enclosures.

Car Parks: Free, but reserved places available if booked in advance at a small cost.

Other Facilities: The racecourse may also be hired for a wide range of functions, from dinners and dances in the stands, to agricultural shows, etc., in the centre of the course.

Appendices

GLOSSARY

Most trades and professions have their own technical and/or slang terms and in this respect racing is no exception. For the newcomer to racing, many of these terms can lead to confusion and, indeed, to a feeling of complete bewilderment. Writers of racing fiction have perpetuated the mystique of a colourful slang by liberally sprinkling their novels with such terms as 'monkeys' (£500) and 'ponys' (£25), thus helping to create the image of a close-knit racing fraternity. While this image attracted some people, it gave many others the feeling that they were encountering a new religion and made them feel that they were 'outsiders'.

Many of the slang terms used in racing originated in the early days of the sport when racecourses were not the well-run, well-ordered, well-policed places that they are today. Consequently, the on-course bookmakers felt it necessary to keep much of their business private, and to this end they evolved a language of their own. Also, no doubt, some of the 'sharper' characters were able to impose upon a gullible public by the use of this Turf argot, which was often a mixture of cockney rhyming slang, backslang, technical racing terms and God knows what else. With the introduction of the off-course betting shops and the new 'respectability' of betting, much of the old slang is disappearing, although it is still in use amongst members of the on-course bookmaking fraternity.

For instance, 'Neves on your bladder' = Seven on your card (Horse number 7 on your racing card). The word 'neves' is 'seven' spelt backwards; 'bladder' is the rhyming slang word for 'card' (bladder of lard = card).

This sort of thing is, however, best left to the bookmakers. It need not concern the ordinary racegoer or the small punter. Indeed, no bookmaker is going to refuse to take your money merely because you don't happen to know what he is talking about. The fact that one is not familiar either with betting slang or with racing terminology need not spoil the enjoyment of a day's racing in any way.

The following is a selection of racing and betting terms which might prove useful to those unfamiliar with racing:

BETTING

Ante-post prices: bookmaker's prices on offer in advance of the day of a particular (usually big) race. Bets on eventual non-runners are forfeited.

A.T.C./A.B./I.C.: any to come, any back, if cash.

Bar: Prices in betting shows of all horses not previously quoted.

Blower: A private telephone service subscribed to by the bookmakers, to keep them in direct and immediate contact with the racecourse.

Board Prices: Making a bet with a bookmaker by taking the price that he is showing on his board. One takes the board price in the hope of obtaining better odds than the eventual starting price.

Call-Over: A bookmaking procedure which determines ante-post prices for big races.

Each Way: Bet to win or be placed. The return for the win is as normal. For the place part of the bet, bookmakers pay a quarter the odds for 1 and 2 in races of six or seven runners and one-fifth the odds 1, 2 and 3 in races of eight or more runners, in all non-handicaps. In handicaps the odds are the same up to and including eleven runners, twelve to fifteen runners a quarter the odds 1, 2 and 3, sixteen to twenty-one runners one-fifth the odds 1, 2, 3 and 4, twenty-two or more runners a quarter the odds 1, 2, 3 and 4.

Even Money: Betting odds one to one.

'Extel' (Exchange Telegraph Service) a service which provides racing information and relays racecourse commentaries to off-course bookmakers and other subscribers.

Favourite: In any race the horse (or horses) quoted at the shortest odds.

Hedging: Bookmakers' practice of reducing their liability on a runner or runners by laying off a certain amount of money with another bookmaker.

Monkey: £500.

Nap: A racing tipster's 'confident' selection.

Nobble: To lame, dope, or otherwise interfere with a fancied racehorse.

Odds: The prices offered by bookmakers against any horse winning a race.

Odds Against: A price which is greater than 'even money'.

Odds On: A price which is less than 'even money'.

Patent: A bet involving three selected horses and comprising seven bets: 3 singles, 3 doubles and 1 treble (win *or* each way).

Tattersalls: The famous firm of bloodstock auctioneers. Also, the enclosure on a race course, between the Silver Ring and Members' Enclosure, where the main volume of betting takes place.

Tattersalls' Committee: A committee authorised by the Jockey Club to arbitrate in all matters and disputes connected with betting (*see* Tattersalls' Rules of Betting).

Tic-Tac: A form of hand signalling used by on-course bookmakers and professional tic-tac men to relay changes in the betting market from one betting ring to another.

Tote: Horserace Totalisator Board, a statutory body answerable to Parliament, which runs its own betting on all races. No prices are quoted, but dividends are returned according to the number of winning units in the pool.

Yankee: A bet involving four selected horses, comprising eleven bets: 6 doubles, 4 trebles, 1 four-horse accumulator (win *or* each way).

RACING

Acceptors: Horses left in a race after a specified date.

Allowance: Weight concession given to riders or horses of limited experience.

Apprentice: Young rider who has signed indentures with a licensed trainer.

Blinkers: A hood with stiffened eyeshields, designed to keep a horse looking straight ahead during a race.

Calendar: Issued every Thursday – the *Racing Calendar* is the official publication of the Jockey Club.

Classics: The One Thousand Guineas, the Two Thousand Guineas, the Derby, the Oaks and the St Leger.

Colt: Male thoroughbred up to and including four years of age.

Distance: 240 yards from the winning post.

Enquiry: The Stewards of a racing meeting have the power to enquire into any aspect of the running of any race.

Filly: Female thoroughbred up to four years of age.

Form: All data concerning a horse's past racing performances.

Gelding: Castrated horse.

Handicap: A race in which every horse taking part is given an equal chance of winning, by virtue of weight allotment, calculated by the Jockey Club handicappers, and based mainly on each horse's previous form. Principal handicap races include: the City and Suburban Handicap, at Epsom; the Chester Cup, the Ascot Stakes, the Royal Hunt Cup, at Ascot; the Stewards' Cup, at Goodwood; the Ebor Handicap, at York; the Cesarewitch and the Cambridgeshire, at Newmarket.

Hanging: Used to describe a horse (usually a tired one) which does not run straight but veers either to the left or right.

Horse: An entire male thoroughbred, aged five and upwards.

Maiden: A horse of either sex which has not won a race.

Match: A race between horses, the property of two different owners, on terms agreed by them, and to which no money or other prize is added.

Nursery: A handicap race for two-year-olds.

Objection: Owner, trainer, rider, official or Stewards may object to a horse if it is thought to have infringed the Rules of Racing during the running of a race. A red flag (in respect of the leading horse) or a red and white flag (in respect of a placed horse) is raised when an objection is lodged. It is advisable to keep all betting tickets until after the result of any objection or enquiry has been announced.

Seller: A race in which the conditions require that the winner shall be offered for sale by auction immediately after the race.

Triple Crown: Winner of the Two Thousand Guineas, the Derby and the St Leger.

Under Orders: A few moments before the start of a horse race a white flag is raised, and at this point the runners are deemed to be 'under Orders', i.e., ready to run. (All bets stand.)

Weighed in: Immediately following each race, every jockey must present himself to be weighed in by the Clerk of the Scales. Bookmakers are not obliged to settle winning bets until after the 'weigh in' has been announced.

Weight for Age Races: Races in which 3-year-olds, 4-year-olds and older horses may compete against each other on weight for age terms. The younger and less mature horses carry less weight than the more fully developed horses, according to the weight for age scale first drawn up by Admiral Rous in 1855 and subsequently modified by the Jockey Club. Principal weight for age races include: the Jockey Club Cup, at Newmarket; the Coronation Cup, at Epsom; the Ascot Gold Cup, at Ascot; the Eclipse Stakes, at Sandown Park; the King George VI and Queen Elizabeth Stakes, at Ascot; the Goodwood Cup, at Goodwood; the Jockey Club Stakes, at Newmarket.

SCALE OF WEIGHT FOR AGE FOR FLAT RACES

NOTE. – Attention is drawn to the provisions of Rule 91 (vi).

The scale of weight for age is published by authority of the Stewards of the Jockey Club as a guide to Clerks of Courses in the framing of races. It is founded on the scale published by Admiral Rous and revised by him in 1873. It has been modified in accordance with suggestions from the principal trainers and practical authorities; it has been further revised since and republished in 1976 in its present form.

ALLOWANCE, ASSESSED IN LBS, WHICH 3 YRS OLD WILL RECEIVE FROM 4 YRS OLD, AND 2 YRS OLD WILL RECEIVE FROM 3 YRS OLD

Distance	Age	MARCH APRIL		MAY		JUNE		JULY		AUG		SEPT		OCT		NOV
		March & 1-15	16-30	1-15	16-31	1-15	16-30	1-15	16-31	1-15	16-31	1-15	16-30	1-15	16-31	
5 Furlongs	2	32	31	29	27	26	25	25	23	21	20	19	18	17	16	15
	3	13	12	11	10	9	8	7	6	5	4	3	2	1	—	—
6 Furlongs	2	—	—	30	29	29	28	27	26	26	24	22	21	21	20	18
	3	15	14	13	12	11	10	9	8	7	6	5	4	3	2	1
7 Furlongs	2	—	—	—	—	—	—	—	—	—	—	24	23	23	22	21
	3	16	15	14	13	12	11	10	9	8	7	6	5	4	3	2
1 Mile	2	—	—	—	—	—	—	—	—	—	—	27	27	26	25	24
	3	18	17	16	15	14	13	12	11	10	9	8	7	6	5	4

ALLOWANCE, ASSESSED IN LBS, WHICH 3 YRS OLD WILL RECEIVE FROM 4 YRS OLD.

		MARCH APRIL		MAY		JUNE		JULY		AUG		SEPT		OCT		NOV
		March & 1–15	16–30	1–15	16–31	1–15	16–30	1–15	16–31	1–15	16–31	1–15	16–30	1–15	16–31	
9 Furlongs	3	18	17	16	15	14	13	12	11	10	9	8	7	6	5	4
1¼ Miles	3	19	18	17	16	15	14	13	12	11	10	9	8	7	6	5
11 Furlongs	3	20	19	18	17	16	15	14	13	12	11	10	9	8	7	6
1½ Miles	3	20	19	18	17	16	15	14	13	12	11	10	9	8	7	6
13 Furlongs	3	21	20	19	18	17	16	15	14	13	12	11	10	9	8	7
1¾ Miles	3	21	20	19	18	17	16	15	14	13	12	11	10	9	8	7
15 Furlongs	3	22	21	20	19	18	17	16	15	14	13	12	11	10	9	8
2 Miles	3	22	21	20	19	18	17	16	15	14	13	12	11	10	9	8
2¼ Miles	3	23	22	21	20	19	18	17	16	15	14	13	12	11	10	9
2½ Miles	3	25	24	23	22	21	20	19	18	17	16	15	14	13	12	11

SCALE OF WEIGHT-FOR-AGE FOR STEEPLE CHASES AND HURDLE RACES

The Stewards of the Jockey Club recommend the following revised Scale of Weight-for-Age:—

(Weights are given as st. lb. — stone and pounds.)

Steeple Chases

Distance	Age	Jan.	Feb.	Mar.	April	May	June	July	Aug.	Sept.	Oct.	Nov.	Dec.
2 miles	4 YRS							11 2	11 2	11 3	11 4	11 5	11 6
	5 YRS	11 7	11 8	11 9	11 10	11 11	11 11	12 0	12 0	12 1	12 2	12 3	12 3
	6 YRS	12 3	12 3	12 3	12 3	12 3	12 3	12 3	12 3	12 3	12 3	12 3	12 3
2½ miles	4 YRS							11 1	11 1	11 2	11 3	11 4	11 5
	5 YRS	11 6	11 7	11 8	11 9	11 10	11 10	11 13	11 13	12 0	12 1	12 2	12 3
	6 YRS	12 3	12 3	12 3	12 3	12 3	12 3	12 3	12 3	12 3	12 3	12 3	12 3
3 miles	4 YRS							11 0	11 0	11 1	11 2	11 3	11 4
	5 YRS	11 5	11 6	11 7	11 8	11 9	11 9	11 12	11 12	11 13	12 0	12 1	12 2
	6 YRS	12 3	12 3	12 3	12 3	12 3	12 3	12 3	12 3	12 3	12 3	12 3	12 3

Hurdle Races

Distance	Age	Jan.	Feb.	Mar.	April	May	June	July	Aug.	Sept.	Oct.	Nov.	Dec.
2 miles	3 YRS							10 7	10 7	10 8	10 9	10 10	10 12
	4 YRS	11 0	11 2	11 4	11 6	11 7	11 7	11 10	11 10	11 11	11 12	11 13	12 0
	5 YRS	12 1	12 3	12 3	12 3	12 3	12 3	12 3	12 3	12 3	12 3	12 3	12 3
	6 YRS	12 3	12 3	12 3	12 3	12 3	12 3	12 3	12 3	12 3	12 3	12 3	12 3
2½ miles	3 YRS							10 6	10 6	10 7	10 8	10 9	10 11
	4 YRS	10 13	11 1	11 3	11 5	11 6	11 6	11 9	11 9	11 10	11 11	11 12	11 13
	5 YRS	12 0	12 3	12 3	12 3	12 3	12 3	12 3	12 3	12 3	12 3	12 3	12 3
	6 YRS	12 3	12 3	12 3	12 3	12 3	12 3	12 3	12 3	12 3	12 3	12 3	12 3
3 miles	3 YRS							10 5	10 5	10 6	10 7	10 8	10 10
	4 YRS	10 12	11 0	11 2	11 4	11 5	11 5	11 8	11 8	11 9	11 10	11 11	11 12
	5 YRS	11 13	12 3	12 3	12 3	12 3	12 3	12 3	12 3	12 3	12 3	12 3	12 3
	6 YRS	12 3	12 3	12 3	12 3	12 3	12 3	12 3	12 3	12 3	12 3	12 3	12 3

METRIC COMPARISON TABLE

As yet, no firm date has been fixed for racing to go metric, although metric distances were added to race conditions in 1975. The following, in anticipation of the sad day when the Derby is run over a distance of 2,400 metres, are lists of metric comparisons:

Distances

200 metres = 1 furlong
1,000 metres = 5 furlongs
1,200 metres = 6 furlongs
1,400 metres = 7 furlongs
1,600 metres = 1 mile
1,700 metres = 1 mile, ½ furlong
1,800 metres = 1 mile, 1 furlong
2,000 metres = 1¼ miles

Distances

2,200 metres = 1 mile, 3 furlongs
2,400 metres = 1½ miles
2,600 metres = 1 mile, 5 furlongs
3,000 metres = 1 mile, 7 furlongs
3,200 metres = 2 miles
3,600 metres = 2¼ miles
4,000 metres = 2½ miles
4,800 metres = 3 miles

(In assessing the distances of races in kilometres, 200 metres shall be taken to equal one furlong. Rule 101.)

Kilogrammes
(The English weights are given to the nearest half-lb.)

kg.	st.	lb.	kg.	st.	lb.	kg.	st.	lb.
44½	7	0	51	8	0½	57½	9	1
45	7	1	51½	8	1½	58	9	2
45½	7	2	52	8	3	58½	9	3
46	7	3	52½	8	4	59	9	4
46½	7	4½	53	8	5	59½	9	5
47	7	6	53½	8	6	60	9	6
47½	7	7	54	8	7	60½	9	7
48	7	8	54½	8	8	61	9	8½
48½	7	9	55	8	9	61½	9	10
49	7	10	55½	8	10	62	9	11
49½	7	11	56	8	11½	62½	9	12
50	7	12	56½	8	13	63	9	13
50½	7	13	57	9	0	63½	10	0

RACING ADDRESSES

The Bookmakers' Protection Association, Sabian House, 26/27 Cowcross Street, London E.C.1. (Tel: 01-230 0044)
The Horserace Betting Levy Board, 17/23 Southampton Row, London W.C.1. (Tel: 01-405 5346)

Horserace Totalisator Board, Tote House, 8/12 New Bridge Street, London E.C.4. (Tel: 01-353 1066)

The Injured Jockeys' Fund, 5 New Square, Lincoln's Inn, London W.C.2.

The International Racing Bureau, 16 Grosvenor Place, London S.W.1. (Tel: 01-235 0995)

Jockeys' Association, 16 The Broadway, Newbury, Berks. (Tel: Newbury (0635) 4102)

The Jockey Club, 42 Portman Square, London W.1. (Tel: 01-486 4921)

The Racecourse Association, 42 Portman Square, London W.1. (Tel: 01-486 3082)

The Racegoers' Club, 42 Portman Square, London W.1. (Tel: 01-486 4571)

The Racing Information Bureau, 42 Portman Square, London W.1. (Tel: 01-486 4571)

The Racehorse Owners' Association, 42 Portman Square, London W.1. (Tel: 01-486 6977)

Racecourse Security Services Ltd. 42 Portman Square, London, W.1. (Tel: 01-935 9251)

Racecourse Technical Services Ltd. 88 Bushey Road, Raynes Park, London S.W.20. (Tel: 01-947 3333)

Tattersalls' Committee, 7/9 Hatherley Road, Reading, Berkshire.

The Thoroughbred Breeders' Association, 42 Portman Square, London W.1. (Tel: 01-487 4586)

Weatherby & Sons, 42 Portman Square, London W.1. (Tel: 01-486 4921)

BIBLIOGRAPHY

REFERENCE

Encyclopaedia of Flat Racing by Roger Mortimer
Horse and Hound Yearbook
International Encyclopedia of the Horse, edited by Lt. Col. C. E. G. Hope
Raceform Annual
Ruff's Guide to the Turf and Sporting Life Annual
Training the Racehorse by Tim Fitzgeorge Parker

TURF HISTORY AND MEMOIRS

Bred For the Purple by Michael Seth-Smith
The Captain — A Biography of Captain Sir Cecil Boyd Rochfort by Bill Curling
Far From a Gentleman by John Hislop

Flat Race Jockeys – The Great Ones by Tim Fitzgeorge Parker
Fred Archer – His Life and Times by John Welcome
Great Racehorses of the World by Roger Mortimer and Peter Willett
Heard in the Paddock by Roderick Bloomfield
The History of the Derby Stakes by Roger Mortimer
Men and Horses I have Known by the Hon. George Lambton
Neck or Nothing by John Welcome
The Pocket Venus by Henry Blyth
The Racing Game by R. Rodrigo
Racing Reflections by John Hislop
Racehorse Trainers – The Great Ones by Tim Fitzgeorge Parker
Royal Newmarket by R. C. Lyle
Tattersalls, Two Hundred Years of Sporting History by Vincent Orchard

NATIONAL HUNT RACING
Arkle the Wonder Horse by John Richmond
Cheltenham Gold Cup by John Welcome
From Start to Finish by John Hislop
The Grand National by Clive Graham and Bill Curling
The History of Steeplechasing by Michael Seth-Smith, John Lawrence,
Peter Willet and Roger Mortimer
Mr Grand National by David Hedges
The Queen Mother's Horses by Ivor Herbert
The Sport of Queens by Dick Francis
Steeplechasing edited by Lord Willoughby de Broke

RACING FICTION
All the racing novels by Dick Francis
The Calendar by Edgar Wallace
Good Evans by Edgar Wallace
Grand National by John Welcome
The Last Furlong by Sir Mordaunt Milner, Bt.
Minstrel Boy by Vian Smith
The Racing Man's Bedside Book, an anthology by Dick Francis and John
Welcome

RACING PUBLICATIONS
The British Racehorse (quarterly)
Horse and Hound (weekly)
Pacemaker (monthly)
The Racehorse (weekly Fridays)
The Racing Calendar (weekly
   Thursdays)
The Sporting Chronicle (daily)
The Sporting Life (daily)
The Sporting Record (weekly
   Tuesdays)
Stud and Stable (monthly)
The Winner (weekly Wednesdays)

Index

Names of horses are in italics